Panzerkrieg

The Rise and Fall of
Hitler's Tank Divisions

Peter McCarthy & Mike Syron

CARROLL & GRAF PUBLISHERS
New York

Carroll & Graf Publishers
An imprint of Avalon Publishing Group, Inc.
161 William Street
New York
NY 10038 2607
www.carrollandgraf.com

First published in the UK by Constable,
an imprint of Constable & Robinson Ltd 2002

First paperback edition published by Carroll & Graf 2003

ISBN 0-7867-1264-3

Printed and bound in the EU

Library of Congress Cataloging-in-Publication Data is available on file.

MIKE SYRON, an archaeologist, and PETER MCCARTHY, a journalist, met while attending University College Dublin in the mid-nineties and soon discovered that they shared a fascination with the history of the Second World War, in particular that of the German armoured forces.

For Avril, Scott and the memory of A.J.
Mike

To my family
Peter

Also to all the tankers of World War Two.

Panzerlied

(Tank Song)

I

Whether in storm or in snow
Whether the sun smiles on us
The day blazing hot
Or the night ice cold
Our faces are dusty
But our spirits are cheerful
Yes, our spirits are cheerful
Our tank roars
Into the windstorm.

II

With thundering engines
As fast as lightning
We engage the enemy
Safe in our tanks
Far ahead of our comrades
In battle we stand alone
Yes, stand alone
We strike deep
Into enemy territory.

III

If an enemy tank
Appears in our sight
We ram throttles full
And close with the foe!

We give our lives freely
For the army of our realm
Yes, the army of our realm
To die for Germany
Is our highest honour.

IV

With barriers and tanks
Our opponent tries to stop us
We laugh at his efforts
And travel around them.
And when guns threatingly
Hide in the yellow sand
Yes, in the yellow sand
We search for paths
No-one else has found.

V

And if some day
Faithless luck abandons us
And we can't return home
The deadly bullet strikes
And fate calls us,
Yes, fate calls us
Then our tank is
An honourable grave.

Written by Oberleutnant Wiehle in June 1933.

Contents

Illustrations

Between pages 128 and 129

A Stug struggles through swampy conditions on the Eastern Front

Pioniers (combat engineers) at work constructing a pontoon bridge as a tank crosses

A tank pulls a Stug from a snowdrift on the Eastern Front

A German Panzer III passing through a destroyed French village along the Aisne on 12 July 1940

All photographs listed are used with the kind permission of The Trustees of The Imperial War Museum, London, unless otherwise stated.

Maps

Introduction

THIS is the story of the Panzerwaffe, the German armoured divisions in the Second World War, the elite tank forces of the Wehrmacht. It is a dramatic story as befits a dramatic war, recounting great victories and crushing defeats, in battlefields ranging from the bocage country of France and the endless steppes of Russia to the deserts of North Africa.

At almost every decisive moment of the war, the panzers can be found. They were the instrument used to achieve the Anschluss in 1938 and to occupy Czechoslovakia a year later. When the Wehrmacht rumbled across the Polish frontier in September 1939, igniting the Second World War, it was the mobility and speed of the panzers that so captured the imagination of the world and created the myth of whole armies of tanks.

William L. Shirer, that self-appointed expert on all aspects of the Third Reich vividly, if somewhat inaccurately, described this new method of waging war:

> the sudden surprise attack; the fighter planes and bombers roaring overhead, reconnoitring, attacking, spreading flame and terror; the Stukas screaming as they dove; the tanks, whole divisions of them, breaking through and thrusting forward thirty or forty miles in a day; self-propelled, rapid-firing heavy guns rolling forty miles an hour down even the rutted Polish roads; the incredible speed of even the infantry, of the whole vast army of a million and a half men on motorised wheels, directed and co-ordinated through a maze of electronic communications

consisting of intricate radio, telephone and telegraphic networks. This was a monstrous mechanised juggernaut such as the earth had never seen.[1]

Had his book, *The Rise and Fall of the Third Reich,* only been as well researched as it was widely read, then perhaps the above popular misconception about the German war machine might never have got such firm hold. It is ironic that a man who took great pride in sorting the Nazi propaganda ministry's wheat from the chaff should succumb so readily to the carefully crafted newsreels supplied by Goebbels. Of the fifty or so German divisions which invaded Poland, only six were panzer divisions and the vast majority of the 1.5 million-strong army travelled on foot, with no better mobility than Napoleon's armies.

In fact at that time, the Panzerwaffe, the newest German arm, was still little more than an exercise unit for flag-trooping, sabre-rattling and parade ground displays. Their tanks were small, cheap and, in keeping with Hitler's megalomania, numerous, but of little practical value on the battlefield. Within a year however the Panzerwaffe would truly come of age, evolving into something greater than even its progenitors dared hope for, even if it never quite became the monstrous, mechanised juggernaut its opponents claimed it was.

In May 1940 came the panzer's greatest victory. Seven panzer divisions slashed their way through the Ardennes (terrain the Allies declared impassable for tanks) and raced for the English Channel. By so doing they trapped a million Allied soldiers, forcing the British to evacuate at Dunkirk and the French to surrender. It remains one of the most startling victories in modern warfare; the largest army in Europe, with tanks superior to the German's both in number and quality, was defeated in weeks by a new method of war: Blitzkrieg.

The unstoppable panzers became a convenient alibi for the Allies in defeat, yet what the Germans had done with their tanks was in fact not so radical or unexpected; it had been theorised about for the past twenty years, mainly by Englishmen. All they had done in reality was to take a twenty-year-old weapon, largely unproven in battle and downgraded between the wars to a mere infantry support weapon, and used it to its full potential. While other nations theorised and debated about the merits of the tank, the Germans acted, successfully turning the weapon against its own inventors.

A year later the panzers were taking on Russia, pitting themselves against the 20,000 tanks of the Red Army – they came within a hair's breadth of victory, halted at the gates of Moscow by winter and Siberian reinforcements. In 1942, they were again close to success when the Stalingrad disaster changed everything. In that same year in North Africa, the panzers were just miles from Alexandria when defeated at El Alamein by vastly superior forces.

From 1943 on, the Panzerwaffe was largely on the backfoot, fighting defensively to slow down the inexorable Allied advance and make them pay a high price for every yard gained. In this enforced role they pioneered new ways of fighting and new weapons which proved highly effective. In 1944, the Battle of the Bulge became their offensive swansong in the West, just as Kursk had the previous year in the East, yet they were still able to seize local victories from the jaws of defeat. Small numbers of German tanks often inflicted heavy losses when the Allies got careless, such as at Villers Bocage in June 1944.

Why then were the panzers so successful? And why did it take six years of war and the combined industrial and military resources of three great powers to defeat them? It must be borne in mind that even at their height, the Panzertruppen never constituted more than 10 per cent of the German Army's manpower. It wasn't because they had more tanks than everyone else; in fact they were outnumbered in the attacks on France and Russia and were to become increasingly so as the war continued. Germany built around 30,000 tanks during the war, a substantial figure, but not so impressive when one considers America turned out 49,000 Shermans and Russia 70,000 of the T-34 model alone. Nor were these products of German engineering automatically superior; the aforementioned T-34 outclassed every German tank except the late-war Tigers and Panthers. And in 1940 the two finest tanks in service, the gargantuan Char B1 and the Medium Somua, were both French.

The real superiority of the Panzerwaffe lay not in the quality of its machines, but in the quality of its officers and men. Allied commanders never became as adept at handling tanks as the Germans and even at the end of the war, individual British, American and Russian tank crews still hadn't attained the same level of skill as the panzer crews. Undoubtedly, on the strategic level the Panzerwaffe was squandered by Hitler and his lackeys in the OKW (German High Command) and many divisions were destroyed because of senseless orders prohibiting them to retreat from battles where their continued mobility might have brought victory.

But on the tactical and operational levels, the panzers remained unsurpassed right to the end. Without the negative interference of Hitler and the OKW on their operations, the Panzerwaffe could well have won the war or at least imposed a stalemate. Panzer officers were consummate professional soldiers who directed and led tank forces better than anyone else. Men like Guderian, the founder of the Panzerwaffe; Rommel, the famed Desert Fox; the excellent Oberst Balck, whose fire-brigade actions had shored up a crumbling front so many times; Panzer Baron von Manteuffel and Field Marshal Von Manstein, widely acknowledged as the most brilliant brain in the German Army – all these men set high standards for their opponents to imitate.

And imitate them they did, as soon as the Allies realised that to beat the Germans they had to adopt their methods. Then Blitzkrieg became the order of the day – for example Patton's eastward thrust in France in 1944 was like a carbon copy of Guderian's westward one in 1940. And the methods the Panzerwaffe used are as valid for any present-day war as they were then – first soften up the enemy by bombardment from the air, thus disrupting his communications, command and supplies and then send in the armour, heavy tanks first to smash through the enemy front, quickly followed up by lighter, faster tanks and motorised infantry.

The purpose of this book is to look at the dramatis personae of the Panzerwaffe and to examine their successes and failures, strengths and weaknesses. There are scores of books about German armoured fighting vehicles, but less about the men who actually crewed and led them. This book aims to go some way towards correcting that deficiency. We also hope to try to explode some of the many myths and fallacies that have grown up around this superlative fighting force.

CHAPTER ONE

The Indirect Approach

From a mockery the tanks have become a terrible weapon.
Armoured they come rolling on in long lines, and more
than anything else embody for us the horror of war.

Erich Maria Remarque,
All Quiet on the Western Front

THE tank, itself such a potent symbol of modern war, is really just the latest evolution of an ancient idea and the story of the tank goes back over 2,000 years, to when armies first experimented with fighting vehicles and armour. Generals have always searched for the new weapon or fighting method which would give them a competitive advantage over their enemy and history gives us many examples of stunning victories won because of these; in their day, the Roman phalanx, the Celtic iron sword, the English longbow, siege artillery and the breech-loading rifle were all battle-winning weapons. Of course the best weapon of all would be one that would allow the soldier to strike at his enemies while at the same time protecting him from their blows.

Armour offered this possibility. With advances in metallurgy, it became possible to build helmets and metal body plates to offer the soldier some protection against enemy blows. The Greeks and Romans were able to craft highly effective bronze armour and by the time of the Normans, iron chain-mail was both cheap and commonplace. However the battle for supremacy between missile and armour is never-ending and so the invention of gunpowder eventually more or less banished personal armour from the field, with the exception of the helmet.

But useful though armour was in protecting soldiers, it hampered their mobility and speed – only a powered vehicle could possess all of these desirable qualities. It soon became obvious that armour could as easily be applied to a horse as a man and so the creation of armoured cavalry was the next stage, which ruled the battlefield until Agincourt.

The real precursor of the modern battle tank was the horse-drawn war chariot. Its origins can be traced right back to the second millennium in the Middle East, where it was used by the warlike Hyksos tribe as they overran Upper Egypt in 1700 BC. The chariot's success, both as a means of transporting soldiers to the battle and as a fighting vehicle, meant it was adopted in turn by the Persians, the Israelites, the Hittites and the Assyrians.

It is recorded that in the sixth century BC, Cyrus, King of Persia, brought three types of chariot to bear on his foes: one type carried a battering ram on a tower, a second carried twenty fighting men and the third type was fast and light with a two-man crew. The horses themselves were protected by armour and long scythes protruded from the axles. The shock value of these war carts must have been nearly as great as their destructive power.

Alexander the Great used chariots against the Persians in 331 BC. The Romans too used chariots extensively and not just for races in the arena; Julius Caesar fully utilised them in his many campaigns against the barbarians. Chariots at that time were used in ways very similar to the ways tanks would be in the twentieth century: that is to break up and rout the enemy foot soldiers, while affording the occupants some protection and also to serve as mobile artillery platforms – the bowmen of those times can be seen as an early form of mobile light artillery.

According to Caesar, the Celts were said to be so agile that they could balance on the yoke poles of their chariots even while travelling at full speed. In Celtic society, chariots were a symbol of nobility and so were highly ornamented and often buried with their owners. The nobleman even had his own charioteer to drive him to the battle. Once battle was joined, the noble dismounted to fight, but the charioteer remained standing by, ready to whisk his master away to safety if the fight was going against him.

Finally and inevitably, armour and the chariot were combined to produce the first real armoured fighting vehicle (AFV). This kind of vehicle possessed great advantages – it was proof against most of the weapons of the time and yet still possessed greater mobility and speed than the foot soldiers it was to attack. In medieval times, carts reinforced with sheet steel carried large siege-crossbows as their main armament. By the fifteenth century some of these war carts even carried guns. The Middle Ages offered other prototype armoured fighting vehicles, such as wheeled siege towers or battering rams designed to protect their crews from burning pitch and arrows.

In 1420, John Zizka and the Hussites of Bohemia used 'wagon forts' in their battles against the Holy Roman Empire. These were heavy wagons fortified by sheet steel and pulled by horses while their crews fired crossbows and guns through holes in the sides. With their help, the 25,000 Hussites shattered an invasion force of 200,000 and went on to ravage Central Europe for over a decade. The AFV had proven its worth on the battlefield.

In 1482, Leonardo da Vinci drew up a design for what he called 'a secure and covered chariot'. Tent-shaped and wheeled, it was to be equipped with guns protruding from loopholes. Although it never actually left the drawing board, da Vinci's vehicle would have required an eight-man crew to fire the guns and to crank the gear-operated wheels. Over a century later, in 1596, an English mathematician, John Napier, proposed an armoured assault car, which he described as a 'moving mouth of metal', the motion of which 'serveth to break the array of the enemy'.

The steam engine accelerated development – now vehicles could be powered by something more effective than horsepower. In 1855, the British inventor, James Cowen, patented a turtle-shaped, armoured vehicle which was based on a steam tractor, equipped with a cover of hardened steel to shatter shells and armed with 14-pounder guns firing through loopholes. But the Prime Minister of the time, Lord Palmerston, declared the machine 'too brutal for human use'. Around the same time, the Crimean War (1853–56) saw another important innovation: for the first time steam tractors, rather than horses or men, were used to pull artillery pieces. In the Boer War (1899–1902), the British used armoured steam tractors to haul supplies across the veldt. The obvious next step was to produce a vehicle that was both armoured and armed.

This came in 1900 when the first modern armoured car, one of the final steps in the evolutionary ladder that eventually led to the tank, saw the light of day. It was named 'Pennington' after its inventor, had a quarter of an inch of armour and was crewed by two drivers and two machine-gunners. Two years later, Frederick Simms produced a similar car with a fringe of chain mail to protect the tyres, two Maxim machine-guns and a 'Pom-pom' automatic one-pounder cannon. A year later he had mounted the machine-guns in rotating turrets in a boat-shaped vehicle which was exhibited at the Crystal Palace.

As we have seen, the queen of the battlefield was not so much an outright invention as an evolution of an old idea and it was the First World War that gave this evolutionary process the final push. Once the Western Front had settled into static trench warfare, several Allied officers began to consider the possibility of adding armour to the American Holt steam tractors then in use as artillery prime movers. These far-sighted men saw the offensive opportunities offered in such a vehicle's ability to cross trenches, crush barbed wire, overrun machine-gun nests and carry infantry and artillery pieces across enemy lines. One of the foremost advocates of this idea was an Englishman, Lieutenant Colonel E.D. Swinton. Swinton's superiors however dismissed his suggestions on the grounds that such a vehicle would be very susceptible to enemy artillery fire.

The tank idea would probably have been stillborn in the British Army had not the First Lord of the Admiralty, Winston Churchill, interested himself in the concept. Churchill had been involved in the scheme to protect the air base at Dunkirk with 100 specially armed and armoured Rolls-Royce cars. Even though such vehicles had no cross-country capability and as such were useless in trench warfare conditions, the experiment had suggested to Churchill the potential of armoured vehicles. So he assumed full responsibility for the tank development project and conducted both the development and the subsequent trials without informing either the War Office or the Treasury.

The quaintly named 'Admiralty Landships Committee' was set up under Churchill's stewardship and rapid progress was made, the results of which were revealed in September 1915 when 'Little Willy', the world's first tank, churned up Lord Salisbury's golf course during its maiden trial. The vehicle was fully tracked and powered by an internal combustion engine. The Army immediately placed orders for one hundred more and for security reasons referred to them as 'water tanks'. The new weapon had gained not only tacit official acceptance, but also a name that stuck.

Due to the prototype's many deficiencies, an improved and larger version appeared a few months later. 'Big Willy' or the Mark I was rhomboid-shaped, weighed 30 tons, carried two 57 mm guns and four machine-guns and was crewed by eight men. This particular model was to bear the brunt of the tank fighting in the First World War and over 1,000 were eventually built. Crewing one wasn't a very pleasant experience as the noise, stench of cordite and engine fumes and the constant jolting left the men feeling bruised, exhausted and nauseous after a short time; there was also the alarming tendency of pieces of the armour plate to flake off and fly around the interior if the vehicle was hit.

The Mark I made its battlefield debut on 15 September 1916 in the first ever tank attack. It was an inauspicious start for a new weapon, thrown into the stalemated, $2^1/_2$ month-old Battle of the Somme in a desperate attempt to obtain a result. General Douglas Haig, Commander-in-Chief of the British Army in France, decided to disperse the tanks as infantry support, viewing them as little more than slightly mobile armoured pillboxes. Haig introduced only forty tanks into his meat grinder on the Somme, thus disregarding one of the tank men's pre-requisites for a successful attack – attack en masse. He also senselessly threw away the potential for surprise that all new weapons possess on their first employment.

On that historic September day, fifty Mark Is trundled off across the no man's land of the Somme. The attack was only a limited success. While small local gains were made and initial panic induced amongst the German front-line units, the small number of tanks used and their dispersed nature allowed the Germans to rapidly seal off and contain any breakthroughs. On top of this, the terrain, moon-cratered by continual artillery bombardment, proved largely impassable even to tracked vehicles.

Nevertheless, the attack encouraged the army to order 1,000 more tanks and to establish a tank unit – which quickly developed into the Royal Tank Corps – under the command of Lieutenant Colonel Hugh Elles and his chief of staff, J.F.C. 'Boney' Fuller, who was later to find fame as the interwar tank theorist. The opportunity was heartily seized to offload difficult and insubordinate officers and men onto this new formation, but given the nature of the British Army and its senior commanders at the time, the undesirable qualities of these men included imagination, an openness to fresh ideas and a willingness to improvise. Yet Swinton, the man who had done so much to get the British tank forces up and running, was now sidelined completely.

Elles and Fuller lost no time in creating a blueprint for the employment of the new weapon: surprise and concentration were their watchwords. Tanks would mass secretly for the attack during darkness. The attack would not be preceded by the usual heavy artillery bombardment as this would only churn up the ground and alert the enemy. As we will see, these sound concepts were to prove just as valid during the Second World War.

The most famous and significant tank battle of the First World War was the battle of Cambrai. After the lacklustre debut of the tank in the Somme debacle, 'Boney' Fuller conceived a plan to raid the headquarters of Crown Prince Rupprecht of Bavaria, located some distance behind enemy lines. He foresaw a fast foray behind the German front, disrupting communications and spreading panic before the tanks withdrew after a few hours. Fuller hoped that the repercussions would foster a fear of repeated surprise attacks amongst the German command, as well as garnering the tank corps some much-needed kudos with both the public and the high command.

Haig however wouldn't hear tell of the plan until he had slaughtered many thousands more of his soldiers in the quagmire of Passchendaele. Only when he had satisfied himself that the reclaimed marsh, heavily cratered after ten days of bombardment and stubbornly defended, was indeed impassable to infantry, did he consider Fuller's plan. Not content with the limited objective of the original plan, he expanded the scope to a full-scale offensive without any consideration for the follow-up and exploitation of any breakthrough that might occur. Having said that, it is hardly fair to expect Haig to have had any ideas on how to follow up a breakthrough, as his career as an offensive General had never yet produced one.

The attack was aimed at a 6-mile (10-km) section of the Hindenburg Line with the ultimate objective being the capture of Cambrai. Nineteen divisions were to take part, along with about 320 Mark IV tanks; these looked like the Mark Is of a year before, but with the addition of thicker armour and an unditching beam to help them cross trenches. The idea was that while one tank brought the troops in a trench under fire, another would clamber up and throw in a fascine (logs lashed together to form a bridge) over which the tanks could move to attack the next trench. The following infantry would hold the territory gained and the cavalry would come galloping up to exploit any opportunities thrown up by the tanks' advance.

Unlike the abortive Somme assault, the Cambrai attack actually fulfilled the three preconditions for a successful tank attack as laid down by the tank men: suitable terrain, employment en masse and surprise. The ground was good going for tanks because for once it had not been turned into a lunar landscape by a lengthy preliminary bombardment. As well as this, the British assembled all their available tanks secretly, attacked with them all in the one place and as a result, achieved complete surprise.

Beginning on 20 November 1917, the assault at Cambrai met with initial success when the tanks penetrated several miles behind the German lines and captured 7,500 prisoners at little cost to themselves. Interestingly, a notable American observer rode in one of the lead tanks, a brash redneck captain called George S. Patton. Yet despite the bells of England pealing in celebration of a great victory, it was nothing of the sort. By the 29th the offensive had broken down, by which time the tanks had advanced only 10 km (6 miles). The tanks had been let down by the inability of the cavalry to live up to their bold claims of being the only arm capable of exploiting the situation and consolidating the gains. Bad weather and the lack of infantry reinforcements also played a part in the attack's ultimate failure. At this point the Germans counter-attacked and by 5 December the British had been driven back to their original start-lines.

In April 1918 a historic event occurred at Villers-Bretonneux: the first tank versus tank battle when thirteen German tanks met ten British in an engagement that can be classified as a draw. The most notable tank battle in the last year of the war was that of Amiens in August 1918, the offensive which eventually forced the Germans to seek surrender terms. Six hundred British and French tanks were thrown into the fray. British 'Whippet' light tanks and armoured cars managed to penetrate the rear of the German lines, where they attacked artillery positions and various headquarters. Gains of up to 18 km were reported, but not held. By now German artillery had become quite proficient at knocking out tanks and the Tank Corps paid a heavy price, losing almost three-quarters of its vehicles in just four days fighting. Again, as at Cambrai, tanks brought no decisive result.

By the end of the war, the Germans were knocking out tanks faster than the British could build them. Travelling at little more than walking pace, tanks were very vulnerable to skilfully directed artillery fire – a fact which led many post-war commentators to completely devalue the potential of tanks, even though they had by then become much faster. Late in 1918, the effective strength of the Tank Corps was below ten machines, about half of tank losses being due to mechanical failure. Indeed, the last week of the war was fought without any tanks at all.

The French also made extensive use of tanks in the First World War. In fact, they were only narrowly beaten by the British to the laurels for the first tank, as the two countries were working on tank development simultaneously, but independently. The first French tank was called the 'Schneider' and was merely an armoured box on a tractor chassis, mounting a 75 mm gun; ironically all sides would revert to this kind of primitive combination as the Second World War dragged on. Its boat-shaped prow was prone to bogging down in soft terrain and the prototypes were scrapped. But before the war had ended the French had developed the excellent light tank, the Renault FT. Fast and lightly armed, it was essentially an infantry support tank and was still being used well into the 1930s and beyond. Renault also built the first tank with a rotating turret.

French tanks didn't see service until April 1917 and then only as infantry support. The French never developed the kind of doctrine that men like Fuller were advancing in the British Army and as a result, their use of tanks was never radical or adventurous. Rather they retained a belief in the primacy of the infantry and so the tank remained just a subordinate weapon used to bolster the foot soldier. This belief, which persisted throughout the inter-war period, proved disastrous in May 1940.

By the end of the war, Britain had produced 2,500 tanks, the French nearly 4,000 and the Germans a mere 20. Having wasted too much time and effort going up the blind alley of poison gas, the Germans had left it too late to develop proper tank forces of their own. In the autumn of 1916 they had set up the 'A7V Committee' to look into the subject and several Sturmpanzer Abteilungs (assault tank battalions) were formed. These battalions were to be equipped with the A7V, a huge and clumsy-looking landship with a crew of eighteen and the LK II, a copy of the British Whippet. However, the few tanks that were produced didn't see service until 1918 and then to no real effect. Some captured machines were also pushed into service, but it was a case of too little, too late. The war ended before the ambitious expansionary plans of the Imperial German Army's Tank Force could be fulfilled, but one Bavarian sergeant major of the force was to later make a name for himself in the Panzerwaffe: Joseph 'Sepp' Dietrich.

The roots of both Blitzkrieg and the Panzerwaffe can be seen in traditional German tactical thinking as exhibited in the First World War. The German Army had always engendered a tradition of initiative in its officers and soldiers. Staff training encouraged adaptability and flexibility at all levels and orders were not always sacrosanct – nor was constructive criticism necessarily seen as insubordinate. This belief in initiative found fulfilment in the doctrine of *Auftragstaktik*, which may be loosely translated as 'Mission Tactics.' The concept was simple. The high command formulated a strategic plan, laying out the key targets and objectives and the various military units from army level down to squad were allocated these objectives, but the nuts and bolts of their attainment was left to the commanders on the ground.

In this way German officers often disobeyed orders, but escaped punishment by dint of reading their superior's intent and achieving the desired result by other means. The realities of trench warfare didn't allow for the successful exercise of this technique, but the Ludendorff offensives of 1918 drew heavily upon it and it was this very tradition that was later to give the Panzerwaffe its tactical superiority over its opponents. Where opposing armoured forces were often hidebound by rigid orders, the panzer's 'saddle orders' allowed them to react quickly and effectively to events on the ground.

The Germans also had a tradition of independent, decisive operations in which ad hoc battle groups were given 'long-distance tickets' to carry out their objectives; a good example is Hauptmann Picht's motorised battalion which succeeded in seizing the Iron Gate into Romania by coup de main in 1916, thus opening the way into that country. Another German method which was to be used by panzers to such effect on the Ostfront was the practice of beating the enemy's forces in detail – a small force held the first enemy formation while the bulk went to deliver a decisive blow to the second, before returning to finish off the first. It was this method which allowed one German

Army to destroy two Russian armies in the battles of Tannenburg and the Masurian Lakes in August 1914. Although dependent on rail in the above example, the arrival of the internal combustion engine onto the battlefield was to make this technique an ever available option.

In the spring of 1918 the Germans unleashed their last attack of the war, the so-called Ludendorff offensive. After short, intense artillery bombardments, Stoss (assault) battalions – armed with light machine-pistols, flame-throwers, grenades and also hauling with them mortars and light artillery pieces – infiltrated the Allied defences, bypassing strongpoints and seeking out command posts and artillery positions as their objectives. Ground support aircraft flew in close support, straf-ing and bombing enemy positions. The goal of these attacks was maximum disruption to the chain of command and the prevention of withdrawal to new lines of defence. It was imperative if these tactics were to succeed that the front be pierced, not merely pushed back. This technique was revolutionary in concept, because rather than a trial of strength as warfare had become, it sought what Liddell Hart later termed the 'Indirect Approach'. Surprise, guile, speed and imagin-ation were as important a weapon as firepower. These kinds of infantry penetration tactics had worked to great effect on other fronts, routing the Russians, Serbians and Italians in various battles.

The Ludendorff offensive came close to success, but bogged down in the end because of the exhaustion of the assault troops and their lack of supplies. These tactics, though not widely heralded at the time, formed the later basis of what was to become Blitzkrieg – lightning war. A young Jäger (light) infantry officer named Heinz Guderian acted as a quartermaster to one of these Stoss units and drew on these experi-ences after the war in the formation of his theories on the employment of armour. He had realised that this kind of attack would be much more effective with tanks.

Fuller was also deeply impressed with the new German Storm tactics and their reliance on speed, manoeuvrability, adaptability and self-sufficiency in the attack. During the late spring of 1918 he formulated his ideas into a new proposal which was to become known as Plan 1919. It was a development of his Cambrai idea where units of fast-moving tanks would strike various German headquarters, thereby eliminating the enemy's 'brain'. He believed that newer, faster and better-engineered tanks could make a decisive difference. Whether his ideas would have borne fruit remains a mystery as the Germans asked for an armistice in November 1918.

During the war the Allied High Command sought to play down the significance of the new weapon and no great effort was made to progress its development. This didn't really change after the war and tanks remained a marginal weapon, a minority interest championed by a few. In Germany, the generals saw the tank as a convenient way of explaining their defeat and the ban on Germany possessing tanks laid down at Versailles also vested the weapon with a certain glamour. Ironically, the Germans' wartime failure to produce any more than a handful of tanks and prototypes, or to create independent tank units, allowed them to begin afresh after the war and to move ahead of their erstwhile foes.

In Britain the isolation of and lack of interest in the Tank Corps continued post-war and a period of uncertainty about the future of armour began. The tank hadn't been the decisive weapon that its supporters had promised it would be, prompting many commentators to write it off completely or belittle its future potential. However, more far-sighted people saw a time and a place when the tank would prove its true value in combat. The proposals put forward in the inter-war period vacillated between two extremes: all-tank armies or reintegration into the infantry. But men like Fuller and B.H. Liddell Hart put forward more realistic possibilities.

J.F.C. Fuller was born in 1878 and served as a staff officer both in the Boer War and the First World War. As we have seen, he was one of the driving forces behind the British Tank Corps and developed the innovative Plan 1919. After the war he embarked on a staff training and military advisory career. His writings from this period proved extremely influential, with both the German and Russian armies drawing inspiration from them, ironically much more so than did his own army. His ambitions to see the British Army fully motorised only met with a modicum of success and despite some promising experiments combining tanks with infantry conveyed in armoured vehicles, the army establishment was reluctant to follow through with his radical proposals.

He refined his ideas on armoured warfare through his writings and by the time he retired to devote himself entirely to them in the early 1930s, his theory was clearly defined. The progression from Cambrai is clear to see. Fast tanks and aircraft would attack the enemy's 'brain' (his chain of command and forward communications). This would create panic and quickly paralyse the enemy's control over a co-ordinated defence. The main assault, comprising heavy tanks accompanied by infantry and artillery, would swiftly follow to consolidate the gains. The objective was to force a breech that would allow fast armour, cavalry and motorised troops to pursue the by now disorganised enemy. Fuller predicted the elimination of conventional infantry from the offensive – they would serve in the rear echelons protecting lines of communication and holding captured ground. Only armoured infantry could accompany the attack. He also foresaw that artillery would have to be self-propelled if it were to accompany the assault successfully.

Captain Basil Henry Liddell Hart was born in 1895 and saw action in the First World War. After the war he wrote the official infantry training manual which stressed his ideas of an 'expanding torrent', a method developed from the German infiltration tactics. He envisaged the attackers piercing points of least resistance, bursting through the forward lines and striking deep into the enemy's rear, spreading disruption and chaos as they went. He also advocated what he termed an 'indirect approach', in which surprise and movement were the key concepts. Success was to be reinforced quickly and resistance bypassed wherever possible. Liddell Hart's writings also found favour in Germany, but not to the extent that his imprisoned German officer friends, grateful for his support after the war, liked to tell him.

How then did the two theories compare? Fuller was of the opinion that the issue would be decided at the front, namely in the defenders' forward defences. Even the rapid pursuit phase was to involve a dogleg after 35 km to roll up the enemy's defensive lines. Liddell Hart, on the other hand, advocated deep thrusts into enemy territory. Both men agreed that the paralysis of the enemy command structure had to be the ultimate aim, rather than the more traditional destruction of his army – this was a radical departure from the senseless battles of attrition, or 'ironmongery' as Fuller dubbed them, that had characterised the First World War. Instead of destroying the body of the enemy army in battle, limb by limb, they just wanted to put a bullet in its brain. They differed however on the role of infantry – Fuller saw them only in terms of consolidation and defence whereas Liddell Hart saw armoured infantry as an integral aspect of the offensive.

The British Army in the 1920s and 1930s embarked on a series of worthwhile experiments combining tanks, artillery, infantry and specialists in a variety of manners. Radio was experimented with as a method of command and control; the most notable result was the Salisbury Plain exercises during the summer of 1927 where a radio-controlled tank force got the better of a much larger non-mechanised opponent. But unfortunately for the British, due to the wide divergence of opinions, they never managed to attain as effective a combination as the German panzer division; ideas ranged from every man having a Bren-gun carrier tankette to motorised units in trucks to unsupported tanks. In the end, little of lasting value was achieved.

Meanwhile in France things were progressing differently. Their most notable tank proponent, Colonel Charles de Gaulle, had received an academic upbringing, but left this for the lure of a military career. He excelled at the military academy and a promising career seemed assured. He also had the good fortune to enlist in a regiment commanded by the future Marshal Pétain and his powerful benefactor ensured a relatively steady series of promotions in the inter-war years. During the First World War he was wounded several times and captured at Verdun after which he spent time as a POW. Even at this stage of his career, the reckless tenacity and stubbornness that so easily segued into arrogance was in evidence as he repeatedly attempted escape from his German captors and just as repeatedly failed.

The 1920s saw the fruits of his academic background emerge as he set about penning military works. His most notable piece was called *Vers Un Armée De Métier* – Towards a Professional Army – and was published in 1934. His thesis was simple – France needed a small and fully mechanised, well-armed, non-conscripted army. Although not widely read, the work aroused a fair amount of criticism in France. The officer corps interpreted his title as a smear on their professionalism rather than emphasising the elimination of conscripted recruits while socialists were terrified that such an army would be the ideal tool for staging a coup d'état.

From the perspective of tank theory this work was very different to the supposedly far-seeing and influential material that the post-war rewritten editions convey. It was bland and diffuse, written in an attempt to air his notions on how the Army in general, and not just a Tank Corps, should be operated. At best it was merely a shopping list for de Gaulle's new model army. Even though Hitler claimed to have read the book repeatedly, all the great theorists paid it scant attention – Liddell Hart was derisive of the book's contribution to armoured warfare and Guderian simply ignored it, much as he did de Gaulle's actual tank forces in May 1940.

In the aftermath of the First World War, France was left with a huge surplus of tanks, including several thousand of the light infantry support tank, the Renault FT. Conservative French generals, hankering after the proud arms of their youth, sought to divide this tank surplus into fast pursuit tanks for the cavalry and heavy breakthrough tanks for the infantry. Meanwhile officers like de Gaulle, Colonel Jean Baptiste Estienne, who had played an important part in developing France's tank forces in the First World War, and General Aimé Doumenc considered the possibilities of mechanised or armoured units.

The result was the creation of the world's first armoured division in 1934, the first Division Légère Mécanique (DLM); this was created by adding more tanks to an already mechanised cavalry division. By the time of the German attack in May 1940, the French had three of these and a fourth was almost complete. Their tasks echoed those of the cavalry – screening other units, reconnaissance and pursuit. Mainly equipped with the world's finest tank of the time, the Somua, as well as the Hotchkiss H35, each division had a full complement of around 200 medium tanks as well as light reconnaissance tanks.

September 1939 saw the creation of the first Division Cuirassée Rapide (DCR). This division and its sister formations were infantry support units equipped with the heavier tanks like the Char B1 and their role was to reinforce assaults. By May 1940, three were formed and a fourth was forming under the command of de Gaulle. Each of these divisions comprised about ninety medium Hotchkiss H35's and seventy Char B1s. Although these units had fewer tanks than a panzer division they comprehensively outgunned the Germans, while the larger number of medium tanks in the DLMs also lent them a strong paper advantage over their rivals.

Little real thought went into the development or deployment of these units and both types were unwieldy and badly led in combat. Staff and officer training was inflexible and theory hidebound and outdated. One major logistical flaw was that they carried their fuel in tankers and so were forced to withdraw from combat to replenish. Both types of armoured unit proved pretty useless in 1940, despite having some excellent tank models in their ranks.

Fuller and Liddell Hart were in broad agreement as to the role of aircraft. Their views were influenced to a certain extent, as were the views of many other theorists, by the somewhat fantastical theories of the Italian General Douhet. Douhet imagined great fleets of battle-planes – bombers armed for defence – shooting it out with enemy formations and the victor progressing to bomb the vanquished cities into submission. To be fair to his fertile imagination, he believed chemical weapons would be dropped on the civilian population ensuring a more rapid capitulation than conventional explosives could bring. Perhaps he was seeing a precursor of the Flying Fortresses and Liberators that appeared later, but more likely he was imagining a twentieth-century version of ships of the line, firing broadsides across the clouds.

Douhet also believed that victory was assured if the enemy's air-fleet was wiped out on the ground – this was indeed shown to be accurate by the early German victories in the Second World War. As it turned out, aircraft were to become the artillery of Blitzkrieg, but Douhet paid little attention to close co-operation with ground forces, a factor that both Fuller and Liddell Hart stressed as essential and which future events proved conclusively.

In Germany, one man in particular read the various and contradictory theories of tank warfare with enthusiastic interest. This man was Hauptmann Heinz Wilhelm Guderian, the officer whose name would become synonymous with the Panzerwaffe. Born in the Prussian town of Kulm, now in Poland, in 1888 to a family of Prussian landowners, it was almost inevitable that Heinz would follow the family tradition of military service – his father Friedrich had risen to the rank of Generalmajor in the Kaiser's army. The young Heinz attended a series of military schools, proving himself a serious-minded, if unremarkable, student. One indicator of what was to come was given on the occasion he was dropped from the cadet choir for singing different tunes to everyone else – the adult Guderian was rarely to sing from the same hymn sheet as his colleagues. In 1907 Guderian enlisted as a Fahnrich in the Jäger or light infantry battalion his father commanded and in 1908 was commissioned as a Leutnant.

There then followed the fairly uneventful life of a junior officer in peacetime. In 1912 the young officer decided to specialise in some

technical discipline, the available options being radio or machine-guns
– Guderian Senior could see no future in machine-guns, so his son
joined a radio company in a choice that was to prove fortuitous in the
years to come. Guderian also trained as a French interpreter and became
fluent in English. In 1913 he married Margarete Goerne and went to
attend the Kriegsakademie, becoming the youngest officer in his class.

However the three-year course was interrupted by the outbreak of
the First World War in August 1914. Because of his experience in
signals, Guderian was initially given charge of Heavy Wireless Station
No. 3 attached to a cavalry division which was part of I Cavalry Corps;
from this vantage point he witnessed the horsemen and infantry thread
their way through the Ardennes and cross the Meuse, just as he himself
would do with tanks in 1940. But the successful German advances of
the early weeks of the war soon fizzled out, partly due to the inability
of the cavalry to hold the gains, and trench warfare took permanent
hold.

For the rest of the war Guderian held a series of signals and staff
appointments and saw little actual combat himself. In early 1918 he
took a staff officers' course at Sedan, scene of Moltke's great breakthrough in 1870 and Guderian's own future one; no doubt he filed the
lay of the land away in his mind for future reference. Later that year
he served as a quartermaster to a corps in the Ludendorff offensive;
here he saw the new infiltration tactics of the storm troop battalions
first hand, an experience which was later to influence his views on
Blitzkrieg.

Almost all of Guderian's experiences in the war were to prove useful
to him in the years to come. He witnessed the utter failure of the cavalry
and the power of new defensive weapons; he saw first hand the early
tank attacks and experienced the bankruptcy and slaughter of static
warfare. His expertise as a radio specialist, the intellectual training he
received as a General Staff officer and his solid grounding in logistics
were all to serve him well in the future. He also became personally
familiar with the Ardennes and the terrain around the Meuse.

After the war, Guderian, by now a captain, was retained in the
100,000-man army laid down by the Treaty of Versailles. He served
for a time as a senior staff officer in the famous 'Iron Division' engaged
in frontier defence in the East, where the Poles were trying to seize
territory from a weakened Germany. Then in 1922, the Inspector of

Transport Troops asked for a General Staff-educated officer to assist in a study being made into the transport of troops by motor vehicle. Guderian was appointed and thus began his interest in tanks.

Guderian was first sent to a Bavarian motor transport battalion for three months training; the battalion's commander was Major Oswald Lutz, an officer who was to be a great help to him in pushing the panzer cause over the next decade and a half. Guderian soon discovered that if troops were to be transported into combat by motor vehicle, they needed better protection from the enemy than an ordinary truck could provide. The obvious answer was armoured vehicles. But Versailles had banned Germany from having tanks or tracked vehicles of any kind, along with many other modern weapons. Armoured troop carriers were permitted, mainly for putting down civil unrest, but these were only allowed to possess immovable turrets and very thin armour. These troop carriers were really no more than ordinary trucks with sheet steel bolted on and had no cross-country capability at all.

As a result, during the 1920s Guderian was unable to gain any practical experience of tanks, so instead he boned up on theory, avidly devouring all the foreign publications concerning tank theory and the current experiences of other nations. As he later wrote:

> In the country of the blind, the one-eyed man is king. Since nobody else busied himself with this material, I was soon by way of being an expert.[1]

Fluent in both English and French, Guderian translated these books for other officers to read, sometimes publishing them at his own expense. He also began to contribute articles to military journals such as the *Militar Wochenblatt*, where he laid out his theory of *Stosskraft* (dynamic punch), which in his opinion could only be delivered by tanks.

He was particularly influenced by the works of the Englishmen Liddell Hart, Martel and Fuller, who stressed the tank as a wholly independent and separate arm, unlike the French theorists who still saw it primarily as an infantry support weapon. In fact, at this time, Britain was leading the world in tank warfare developments, engaging in successful field exercises using radio-controlled tanks and experimenting in 1927 with a 'mechanised force' that contained tanks, artillery and motorised infantry, in essence a nascent panzer division. Unfortunately for the British, their senior officers were even more hostile to the tank than their German counterparts and as a result this early advantage was squandered.

In the end, Guderian chose the middle ground between the two great extremes of inter-war tank theory, namely that of the all-tank army versus the tank as mere infantry support. For financial reasons the Germans could only afford to choose one of these options anyway. Guderian realised that a compromise between the two extremes was the best option, because it became clear to him that, although a very potent weapon, the tank would simply be unable to win battles all on its own – it would need the support of the traditional arms, such as the infantry and artillery. But at the same time to make the tank subservient to these other arms was to nullify its true potential.

Guderian adapted Liddell Hart's theory of the long-range armoured thrust, the so-called 'expanding torrent' that would bypass points of enemy resistance in order to go straight for the jugular. As Guderian saw it, the tanks would assault the enemy's defence zone along a narrow frontage (maybe as little as a kilometre), break through and then accelerate as they headed for their strategic objective. The armoured cars of the reconnaissance units would go on ahead to probe points of resistance and once the tanks had broken through, the motorised infantry and then the ordinary infantry would follow in their wake. The whole operation would be supported from the air, in particular by the tank-busting Stukas. This theory was to be the essence of Blitzkrieg.

So what kind of a man was Heinz Guderian? In formal portraits he looks very much the stiff-necked Prussian officer in the Bismarck mould, all bristling moustache and serious mien, but less staged pictures show him laughing and bantering with his troops. Like Rommel, he made a poor subordinate, impatient with higher authority and eager to get his own way at all times. Also like Rommel, he cared deeply for the troops under his command and was extremely popular with them. His reputation as a hothead earned him the affectionate and well deserved nicknames 'Brausewetter' (Stormy Weather) and 'die Schnelle Heinz' (Hurrying Heinz).

General Hasso von Manteuffel, himself a top-notch panzer commander, said of Guderian after the war:

It was Guderian – and at first he alone – who introduced the tank to the army and its use as an operative weapon. In the best sense of the word, this new weapon bears the stamp of his personality. Its successes during the war are due to him. He was the creator and master-teacher of our armoured forces – and I lay particular stress on the word 'master'.[2]

General Hermann Balck, an old friend of Guderian and one of the best tank commanders of the war, said Hurrying Heinz was like a coiled spring and concluded that 'to understand Guderian, you have to understand Prussian discipline'.[3] Another panzer general, Geyr von Schweppenburg said:

> Sixty per cent of what the German Panzer forces became was due to him. Ambitious, brave, a heart for his soldiers, who liked and trusted him; rash as a man, quick in decisions, strict with officers, real personality, therefore many enemies. Blunt, even to Hitler. As a trainer – good; thorough, progressive. If you suggest revolutionary ideas, he will say in 95 per cent of cases: 'Yes', at once.'[4]

Guderian was indeed a proponent of revolutionary ideas, but a modernizer and technologist was not always the most welcome thing in a small, conservative army that still depended on the horse for transport. The two mechanisms he championed, the internal combustion engine and the tank, were still unproven in combat. In the First World War, trucks had been used to move men and supplies behind the static front lines, but never to move troops towards the enemy. The tank too had failed to prove its real value in battle, largely due to the way it was handled rather than because of the weapon itself, but some commentators were already declaring it obsolete, especially with the development of new anti-tank weapons.

In 1927 Guderian was promoted to major and sent to the transport department of the Truppenamt (Troop Office – a cover for the banned General Staff). By 1928 Guderian had made enough of a reputation for himself to be made a teacher of tank tactics and he lectured extensively on them. In 1929 he encountered real tanks for the first time when invited to visit a Swedish tank battalion. Here he saw the next best thing to a German tank: the Swedish M21, a derivative of the German LK II, which Bofors were allowed to build by arrangement with Krupps. That same year, he used cars in the place of tanks in divisional-sized summer exercises. Meanwhile the Treaty of Rapallo with Soviet Russia had allowed the Germans to test tanks and other tracked vehicles at a secret proving ground at Kazan in Russia since 1926, where they experimented with prototypes such as the Leichter Traktor and the Grosstraktor. Secret tank building cells were set up in Rheinmetall, Daimler-Benz and Krupps.

The early armoured manoeuvres carried out in Germany were fairly risible affairs, involving mere improvisations of tanks, such as canvas and sheet-steel mock-ups, dummy vehicles with wooden guns and broomsticks masquerading as anti-tank guns. The few armoured troop carriers they did possess didn't even take to the field for fear of wearing them out prematurely. Guderian recalled how children used to push pencils through the 'armour' of these so-called tanks to see what was inside.

In January 1930 Guderian was made commander of the 3rd Prussian Motorised Battalion. Although armed only with dummy tanks and guns, a few armoured cars and a motorcycle company, he manoeuvred them as if they were a fully equipped panzer division. It proved a useful opportunity to try out his ideas on the ground and Guderian practised attack, defence and retreat drills as well as co-operation with infantry, artillery, cavalry and aircraft. He proved a popular commander and succeeded in turning his troops into tank fanatics like himself. On one occasion they overtook him during ski training and Guderian gently rebuked them over drinks that night in his usual bantering style: 'In the tank force the commander leads from the front – not from behind!'[5] In April Guderian achieved the rank of Oberst.

In 1931 he was promoted to Chief of Staff of the Inspectorate of Motorised Troops and served again under Generalmajor Oswald Lutz who gave him every possible help in pushing forward the cause of tanks. Lutz's influence on the development of the Panzerwaffe has often tended to be overlooked in contrast to his more colourful junior, yet he possessed great technical know-how and lent Guderian his full support in his early battles. Lutz was the first general in the German Army to wholeheartedly embrace the new ideas and also the first to attain the rank of General der Panzertruppen. In the opinion of Walther Nehring, who was a staff officer at the Inspectorate, Lutz was the father of motorised army units, while Guderian was the creator of the Panzerforce.

In January 1933, a man became Chancellor of Germany who was to have as big an impact on the Panzerwaffe as Guderian, albeit in an ultimately destructive way: Adolf Hitler. Under his influence, the

Wehrmacht began to expand and rearm, and new weapons and methods were examined. Early in 1935, he visited the army ordnance testing ground at Kummersdorf, where he saw a platoon of Panzer I tanks in action. This precision display is said to have excited him so much that he declared; 'That's what I need! That's what I want to have!' From then on Hitler championed the panzers, seeing in them a potent political and military tool.

Inevitably, Guderian's message met resistance from many of the more conservative senior officers, particularly from cavalry officers who saw their traditional role and importance being undermined by the brash new tank forces. The artillery with their supreme confidence in heavy bombardment, and the traditional 'Queen of the Battlefield', the infantry, were equally unconvinced. But in Guderian's view they could offer no viable alternative to tanks. He didn't help the cause of friendly relations by contemptuously dismissing 'the Gentlemen of the Horse Artillery' as a spent force who travelled to the battlefield with their guns pointing backwards. Ironically nearly half of the Panzertruppe's officers were eventually to come from the cavalry, including many of the best commanders.

Even some of the incumbents in the office of Inspector of Transport Troops seemed as hostile to Guderian's ideas as his enemies – one declared that motorised units would never do more than carry flour, while another predicted that neither he nor Guderian would ever see German tanks in operation in their lifetime; this was in 1931.

Guderian believed that tank commanders should be up front with their troops, not stuck in a HQ miles behind the lines and that radio was the appropriate means of communication for this type of command. But the Chief of the General Staff, the conservative old artilleryman General Beck, couldn't accept this radical concept. He remarked, 'But you can't command without maps and telephones. Haven't you ever read Schlieffen?'[6] But Hitler's firm support for the panzers made up for the hostility they faced in some quarters of the Army; with his liking both for radical new ideas and the internal combustion engine, he favoured tank development over other arms of the military. So in the end Guderian's revolutionary views won the day. As he commented in his memoirs, 'Finally the creators of the fresh ideas won their battle against the reactionaries; the combustion engine defeated the horse; and the cannon, the lance.'[7]

By June 1934, German experiments with tanks had developed far enough to require a new command, Kommando der Panzertruppen, to be set up, of which Guderian was made Chief of Staff under his old supporter, Generalmajor Lutz. The first panzer battalion, made up of the lightweight Pz Is, was also formed that year. In 1935, Hitler repudiated the military clauses of the Versailles Treaty and Germany began to rearm in earnest. With the pace of development thus accelerated, the first improvised panzer division, cobbled together from the few units then available, was able to take to the field for manoeuvres at Munster-Lager in July 1935.

This exercise proved so successful that on 15 October of the same year, the first three panzer divisions, the 1st, 2nd and 3rd, were formally established from cavalry cadres, although as yet they had no tanks. Each division consisted of a panzer brigade with two tank regiments equipped with only light tanks and a motorised rifle brigade. The 2nd Panzer was placed under Guderian's command, even though he was still only an Oberst; this had the effect of sidelining him from the centre of action and his old job as Chief of Staff was taken by the weaker-willed Oberst Friedrich von Paulus, later of Stalingrad fame.

Without Guderian to aggressively fight its case, the inevitable result was an erosion of the Panzertruppe's influence and strength. The Army's Chief of Staff, Generaloberst Beck, refused to give the Panzer Command equal status with those of the artillery and infantry. Within the panzer divisions, reconnaissance units were handed over to the cavalry and motorised rifle units to the infantry until eventually the Panzertruppe was only responsible for the actual tank units. The equipping of the Leichte and motorised infantry divisions also reduced the number of vehicles available to the panzer divisions.

There was little Guderian could do about these developments so he threw himself wholeheartedly into technical matters. He worked closely with the Inspector of the Signal Corps to produce good tank radios and also sought half-tracked and four-wheel-drive vehicles to transport the divisions' supplies and infantry. After a disastrous demonstration of ineffectual two-wheel drive vehicles in 1937, Guderian marched up to the Army's Commander-in-Chief, Generaloberst Fritsch, and loudly announced, 'Had my advice been followed we would now have had a real armoured force!'[8] Guderian's misgivings about this kind of transport were to be proved all too correct during Barbarossa.

During the winter of 1936, Guderian had quickly written *Achtung Panzer*, a short polemical work describing First World War experiences with tanks and laying out his views on the future of armoured warfare. He took the opportunity to have another go at the reactionaries in the cavalry and elsewhere and their bankrupt methods of 'self-massacre'. It became a best-seller in Germany and the proceeds were enough for Guderian to buy his first car, allowing him to practice his mobility theories in person.

In Guderian's original conception, each panzer division was to be an army in miniature. A division would be a self-contained, all-arms unit – that is to say, it would contain tanks, infantry, artillery, engineers, reconnaissance, anti-tank and anti-aircraft units as well as supply services, all the units necessary to fight and survive in the field, independent of reinforcements and supplies for as long as possible. Each division was to carry enough fuel, ammunition and other supplies to be fully self-sufficient for at least five days. All of the division's components were to be fully mobile, preferably on fully tracked or half-tracked vehicles, but in reality more likely in trucks. Guderian realised that in order to be in a position to fully exploit a breakthrough, a division had to be made as independent and mobile as possible.

This had been the fatal flaw of tank operations in the First World War. After making a breakthrough in the enemy lines, the tanks had had no choice but to wait for the foot-slogging infantry and the horse-drawn artillery to catch up with them so as to exploit the breach. In the process valuable time was lost, during which the enemy could rebuild his defence lines. But as Guderian saw it, rather than slowing down the tanks so that the infantry and artillery could catch up, the infantry and artillery should be brought up to the speed of the tanks. For this to happen, they had to be put on wheels or tracks.

The artillery was pulled by tracked prime movers or eventually installed on tracked chassis which produced vehicles such as the Wespe self-propelled field howitzer. The bulk of the Panzergrenadiers (motorised infantry) continued to be truck-borne throughout the war, although trucks were unarmoured and had poor cross-country capability. The best solution was tracked, armoured troop-carriers. Two principal troop-carrying half-tracks saw service in a number of variants: the Leichter Schützenpanzerwagen SdKfz 250 and the Mittlerer Schützenpanzerwagen SdKfz 251. These were developed from the chassis of tractors used to pull guns and were a compromise between tracked vehicles and wheeled ones – driven by tracks, but steered by two front wheels.

The SdKfz 250 was a light half-track troop carrier based on a one-ton prime mover chassis. This 5-ton vehicle could transport half a platoon – up to eight men – and its standard armament was an MG-34. A total of 7,000 were built in a number of variants including command and anti-aircraft vehicles and ammunition carriers for the Stugs.

The SdKfz 251 was a medium half-track troop carrier based on a 3-ton prime-mover chassis. This 9-ton vehicle first issued to the panzer divisions in 1939 could carry twelve men and the standard type was armed with two machine-guns. The 251 played a variety of roles during the war, including as a special armoured command vehicle equipped with a range of radio sets, an Enigma machine and a large bedstead frame aerial. Other variants included an ambulance, a transport for Pioniers (combat engineers), a vehicle for laying telephone and telegraph cables, a flame-thrower, an artillery spotter, a mobile telephone exchange, a transporter for an 88 and its crew and when mounted with a 75 mm gun, a Panzerjäger. In total 15,000 of all types were built.

The 250 and 251 were such versatile vehicles that they were able to serve in an extraordinary variety of roles – unfortunately the many uses they were put to meant that there were never enough of the standard troop carriers available. Throughout the war never more than one third of Panzergrenadiers were transported by half-track.

The early panzer divisions each had a panzer brigade of two regiments and a motorised infantry brigade, the men of which were conveyed by truck or motorcycle. Along with a regiment of motorised artillery, there was a battalion each of anti-tank, reconnaissance and signal units, plus one company of engineers and a Luftwaffe flak detachment. These early divisions had an establishment strength of 560 tanks and 12,000 men, although by 1940 rapid expansion meant that each division had only an average of about 250 tanks. Deep, forward reconnaissance was vital to the panzer divisions and the reconnaissance battalion contained two armoured car squadrons.

The Panzerwaffe was to employ a series of four-, six- and eight-wheeled Panzerspahwagen (armoured reconnaissance vehicles) in its reconnaissance battalions during the war. Motorcyclists were also used initially, but were scrapped after 1941 because of their vulnerability.

Armoured cars were one of the few types of weapon not prohibited by the Versailles Treaty so Germany had been working on them since the 1920s. Among the specifications demanded was a second steering position in the rear of the vehicle so as to allow speedy movement in either direction.

From 1936 on the Germans were working a eight-wheeled armoured cars, the distinctive 'Achtrads' which served right through the war. The basic model was the insect-like SdKfz 231 – armed with a 20 mm cannon and an MG-34 mounted in a turret, it had a range of 300 km (185 miles) and a top speed of 50 m.p.h. It could change direction in under ten seconds and thanks to its all-wheel drive and all-wheel steering, had excellent off-road performance. The SdKfz 232 (8-rad) was identical except for mounting a large frame aerial for a powerful medium-range radio. The SdKfz 233 carried a short 75 mm howitzer for close support.

The fast and hard-hitting eight-wheeled 234 series appeared from 1943 onwards and incorporated lessons learnt in battle. They had a monocoque construction – the chassis and body were a single unit – and the frontal armour was increased. The sleek 234/2 Puma entered service in 1944 and mounted a long 50 mm gun in a turret developed for the proposed Leopard light tank. It had a top speed of 55 m.p.h. (85 km/h) and a range of 350 miles (550 km), but only 100 turretted Pumas were ever built. The 234/4 was armed with a long 75 mm gun in an open turret, making it suitable for an anti-tank role.

Guderian's advice to the panzer reconnaissance battalions was simple: 'See much, but don't be seen!' Their job was to observe the enemy positions and then quickly withdraw back to their own lines, avoiding a fight whenever possible. But as the war went on and the weapons mounted on armoured cars grew heavier, the crews were more likely to engage the enemy than run away. These wheeled vehicles had many disadvantages when compared to tanks – they were lightly gunned and armoured and their cross-country performance was relatively poor, but their speed and silence made up for these faults. All in all, the Panzerspahwagen gave sterling service as the eyes and ears of the panzer divisions.

Of course, Guderian's ambitious plans never came to full fruition. Originally he had wanted each panzer division to have 500 tanks as well as a host of other tracked and half-tracked vehicles. But with an entire army clambering for motor vehicles of their own and a German automotive industry simply incapable of meeting demand, he was never going to get all the vehicles he needed. But he was a pragmatist, making the best of what was available and improvising for the rest. As it was, for the entire duration of the war, never more than 10 per cent of the German Army was motorised and the trusty horse was never retired as a beast of burden.

Germany had produced only a few tanks in the First World War and then was banned from building or possessing them by the Versailles Treaty. So in the 1930s, the German Army and armaments industry had to start from scratch in designing and building tanks, without the years of experience of the British and French. In a way, this was an advantage, as it gave them the opportunity to build a thoroughly modern tank force, without the many outdated machines and equally outdated ideas still in service with the Allies. But inevitably it took some time for German industry to learn the new skills and techniques required and to develop the necessary plants. So it is understandable that the early panzers were simple affairs.

When Guderian became Chief of Staff to the Inspector of Motor Transport Troops in 1931, he envisaged two kinds of tanks being necessary to equip the panzer divisions: a light tank with an armour-piercing gun and a medium tank with a large-calibre gun (these tanks, once developed, became the Panzer III and Panzer IV respectively and formed the bulk of German tank forces throughout the war). However, these new tanks would take some years to be developed and in the meantime a light training tank was urgently required.

As a result, in 1932 the Army issued specifications to the main armaments manufacturers to produce a light tank of 5 tons, armed with two machine-guns mounted in a turret with all-round traverse. In addition, the armour should be thick enough to withstand small-arms fire. To maintain secrecy, the project was given the name of an agricultural tractor. The resulting vehicle was designated the Panzerkampfwagen (Battle Tank) I.

The basic design of the Pz I was heavily influenced by the British Carden Lloyd Mk IV. The Germans had tested these little tankettes in the Kazan testing ground in the late 1920s and early 1930s and had bought two of them from the Russians. After extensive testing of all the prototypes submitted by the manufacturers, the Daimler-Benz superstructure and turret mounted on the Krupps chassis was chosen for service.

Full-scale production began in 1934 and in April of that year, fifteen Pz Is were displayed to Hitler. The Pz I was a simple, primitive and flimsy machine and was never intended to be anything more than a training tank. Lightly armoured, fast and with a two-man crew, its only weapons were two 7.92 mm machine-guns (MG-34s) in the turret, a puny armament considering that many modern tanks were by now fielding 50 mm guns or larger. The armour of this glorified machine-gun carrier couldn't withstand anything heavier than small-arms fire itself.

Yet the little tank fulfilled two important purposes: firstly it was the vehicle that most panzermen were trained in for years to come and secondly, it looked impressive on the parade ground or on the exercise field, an important consideration for a regime that wished to impress both the domestic and foreign audience with propaganda about its military might. Although totally unfit for the modern battlefield, the cheapness and simplicity of the Pz I meant that over 1,500 were built between 1934 and 1939. Many were later converted into other vehicles such as the Panzerjäger I.

Because production of the two main battle tanks, the Pz III and the Pz IV, was much slower than expected, a second stop-gap training tank was built, the Pz II. Specifications were issued in July 1934 and MAN eventually chosen as the manufacturer. The Pz II weighed in at 7.5 tons, had a 3-man crew and carried a 20 mm gun, as well as a co-axial machine-gun. Overall, it was a small improvement on the Pz I, yet still inadequate by contemporary standards. Under-gunned and under-armoured, it was incapable of firing high-explosive (HE) shells, the type needed for soft targets such as infantry. It also proved very vulnerable to both modern anti-tank guns and heavier tanks.

Despite its obvious limitations, the High Command ordered large-scale production and by the time production ceased in 1942, 1,800 had been built. In the Spanish Civil War they proved no match for the heavier Soviet tanks. Despite these obvious shortcomings, the Pz II remained the main battle tank of the Panzerwaffe until 1941 and about 1,000 of them participated in the attacks both on France and Russia. After that, many were used as command tanks or transformed into tank destroyers like the Marder II.

In the final analysis, the Pz I and II represented a lot of machinery and manpower to bring some pretty ineffectual guns to bear, but they did teach the Germans many valuable lessons about tank building and filled out the panzer divisions' establishments when there was nothing else available.

So by the late 1930s Guderian had prevailed in establishing a professional and modern German tank force, a military formation which was at least the equal of any in the world. Most importantly, the Panzerwaffe's promise of short, sharp campaigns made war economically viable for Germany. Hitler now had in the Panzerwaffe and the doctrine of Blitzkrieg his battle-winning weapon and it wouldn't be very long before he used it. Soon the panzers would be in action and would remain so until the end of the war.

CHAPTER TWO

The Expanding Torrent

If the tanks succeed, then victory follows

Guderian, 1937

IN 1937 the Panzerwaffe made its battlefield debut when Hitler included tanks in the Kondor Legion sent to assist Franco's Nationalists in the Spanish Civil War. Just as this theatre allowed the Luftwaffe to try out its new weapons and tactics and to 'blood' its men in actual combat, so it gave the same opportunity on a more limited scale to the Panzerwaffe. In early 1937 a tank battalion, Panzer Abteilung 88, was shipped out to Spain. This was made up of Pz Is and Pz IIs and commanded by Oberst Wilhelm Ritter von Thoma, a tough tank man who later served under Rommel in North Africa where he was captured by the British at El Alamein. After Guderian, von Thoma was one of the earliest tank enthusiasts in the German Army and by the time of his capture in late 1942, had fought in 216 tank engagements, 192 of them in Spain. Liddell Hart described him as a kind of twentieth-century knight-errant who had exchanged his horse for a tank.

The German tank forces in Spain were never large – 600 men at most and about 200 tanks – the only tanks used being the lightweight Pz I and II training tanks, never the more modern Pz IIIs and IVs. Von Thoma's principal duty was to train Franco's men in the use of tanks, but being an old warhorse, he couldn't help joining in the fighting himself, despite the High Command's disapproval. By 1938 he had four tank battalions and thirty anti-tank companies under his command.

When Von Thoma returned to Germany in June 1939, he wrote a report on his experiences and the lessons learned. Spain offered no set-piece tank battles nor did it suggest any new tactical lessons about armour, but rather saw the tanks mainly confined to the conventional role of infantry support. As von Thoma said, 'General Franco wished to parcel out the tanks among the infantry – in the usual way of generals who belong to the old school.'[1] However the panzers did learn how to co-operate with ground-attack aircraft like the Stukas. It was also in Spain that the 88 mm Flak (Flieger Abwehr Kanone) first proved itself a formidable tank killer. This heavy artillery piece was first introduced in 1934 as an anti-aircraft gun, but its effectiveness against ground targets soon gave it a dual-purpose capability.

Co-operation between the panzers and the 88s in Spain led to the development of the Schild und Schwert (Shield and Sword) technique used to such effect in the years to come – by feigning retreat, the panzers drew the enemy armour onto anti-tank gun screens. Once the enemy tanks were safely held by the AT guns, the panzers would turn and drive into their flanks.

The Germans received a nasty shock when their panzers first came up against the Russian-built tanks of the Republicans. It soon became patently clear that the Pz I and II (which von Thoma contemptuously dubbed 'sardine tins') were no match for the more heavily armoured and better-armed Russian tanks, particularly the T-26, which fielded a 45 mm gun. Von Thoma had to resort to offering a reward of 500 pesetas for every T-26 captured so that they could be examined at close quarters and the Moors captured so many as a result that he was able to equip four whole companies with Russian tanks.

The Spanish experience pointed clearly to the inadequacy of the Pz I and Pz II. While they did prove suitable for reconnaissance and light infantry support, they were too under-gunned to take on modern tanks and too thinly armoured to withstand modern anti-tank guns. This discovery should have prompted the Germans to stop building these lightweight tanks altogether in favour of undiluted production of the Pz III and IV, yet it didn't. Spain should also have engendered a new respect for Soviet tanks, but it didn't have that effect either.

Meanwhile back in Germany, Guderian's two main battle tanks had gone into limited production. The Pz III and Pz IV were developed because Guderian wanted two different kinds of tank with which to equip his new panzer divisions and so in 1934 the Waffenamt (Ordnance Office) drew up specifications for these two tanks. The first would be a light tank with an effective armour-piercing gun for fighting other tanks. It would be the main battle tank of the panzer divisions and so would equip three of the four companies in every panzer battalion. This tank was the Panzer III.

The other kind of tank Guderian wanted was a medium tank with a high-calibre gun to support the Pz III and the infantry. The gun's low velocity wasn't seen as a problem initially as it wasn't anticipated that this tank would be fighting other tanks. This tank was the Panzer IV and would equip the fourth company of every Panzer battalion.

The first Pz III prototypes were built in 1935, with limited production by eight major companies beginning in 1936. Weaponry consisted of a 37mm main gun and two MG-34 machine guns, one in the hull and one in the turret. The Pz III was the first German tank to feature Dr Porsche's torsion bar suspension system and to be equipped with an intercom system for in-tank communications. It was also the first German tank with a five-man crew, a practice which became standard from then on.

Guderian had wanted the Pz III to mount a 50 mm gun in keeping with current developments in other countries, but the Ordnance Department, for ease of production and supply, wanted a 37 mm, the standard German anti-tank gun at the time. They got their way, but Guderian was subsequently proved right when combat in France showed that the 37 mm just wasn't powerful enough. Luckily, in keeping with Guderian's insistence on covering as many scenarios as possible, the original turret ring was big enough to mount a 50 mm gun.

In August 1940 Hitler ordered the 50 mm L/60 mounted in the Pz III, but the Ordnance Department, again thinking it knew better, installed the shorter-barrelled (and therefore less powerful) 50 mm L/42. Hitler was shown the newest Pz III variant on his birthday in April 1941 and was incensed when he saw it still carried the short gun. The longer L/60 was therefore quickly installed and by the end of 1942, most Pz IIIs had been refitted with the 50 mm L/60 gun. (The calibre or bore of a gun is a measurement of the internal diameter of the barrel. The length of the gun is then expressed as a multiple of this calibre, so in the case of the 50 mm L/60 gun, the gun's calibre was 50 mm and the barrel length was 60 times the calibre, i.e. 3 metres.)

The L/60 was an effective weapon and the British in North Africa dubbed panzers mounting it as 'Pz III Specials' because of their ability to knock out British tanks at long range. The Pz III was also fitted with thicker armour at various stages during the course of its life. The tank's greatest limitation was that the size of its turret ring meant it couldn't be equipped with a larger gun than 50 mm. By 1943 the Pz III was completely obsolete and began to be pulled out of front-line service, although some served on in quieter areas or as useful support tanks to the Tigers. By the time production ceased, 6,100 Pz IIIs had been built. Its chassis continued to be built as the basis for the highly effective Stug III.

Krupps started building the Pz IV in 1937 and the tank was to remain in production right up until March 1945, by which time 8,600 had been built, more than any other German tank. Because it was originally envisaged in only a limited support role, the Pz IV was initially built in small numbers by only one manufacturer, and until 1942 underwent no major design changes. It was armed with a low-velocity 75 mm gun, and two MG -34s. In shape and size, it looked very similar to the Pz III.

The Pz IV first saw combat in Poland; over 200 participated in this campaign and stood up well against the Polish 37 mm anti-tank guns, with only twenty destroyed. They also performed well in France, Greece and the Balkans, but the Pz III continued to bear the brunt of the tank battles in these theatres, the Pz IV only performing a supporting role.

The greatest weakness of the Pz IV was the low velocity of its 75 mm gun, which was one of the largest calibre guns mounted on a tank at that time, although its muzzle velocity was poor at only 1,263 feet per second. The resulting short range and poor penetrating power meant the Pz IV wasn't of much use in tank-to-tank combat unless the enemy tank was very close. Originally this wasn't seen as a problem as the Pz IV was designed to be a support tank with a gun to fire high-explosive (HE) shells at 'soft' targets such as infantry, soft-skinned vehicles and anti-tank batteries. By contrast, the Pz III's 37 mm gun had a muzzle velocity of 2,445 feet per second which made it suitable for tank-on-tank fighting, but not very effective for firing HE at soft targets.

For a tank to be able to destroy other tanks, it needs a gun with a flat trajectory and high muzzle velocity. To penetrate the armour of an enemy tank, a shell needs to be travelling at high speed and have plenty of kinetic energy when it hits its target. Velocity is a measure of the speed of the projectile when it leaves the barrel and the higher the velocity, the greater the range, accuracy and penetrating power of the gun. A low-velocity gun could fire a heavier calibre shell, but it wouldn't travel as far or have the same penetrating power. Len Deighton brilliantly compared this difference between a high- and low- velocity gun to the difference between a strong man throwing a stone (the Pz III) and a child throwing a brick (the Pz IV). Of course the ideal solution would have been a high-calibre, high-velocity gun like the Flak 88, but German turrets weren't able to incorporate guns that large when the Pz III and IV were being drawn up.

This deficiency did become a problem later. When it was decided that the Pz III would cease production in 1943, something had to take over the mantle of main battle tank until mass production of the Panther began. The Pz IV was the only contender. Fortunately its turret ring was big enough to take on the long-barrelled 75 mm gun. From March 1942 onwards the short 75 mm L/24 was replaced with either the long 75 mm L/43 or L/48. These guns, although of the same calibre as the L/24, had almost twice the muzzle velocity at 2,428 feet per second. As well as the new gun, the Pz IV's armour was thickened to 50 mm on the front and turret and 30mm on the sides and rear, and from July 1943 onwards, *Schurzen* were also added; these were sheets of armour hung from the tank's sides and rear to prematurely detonate hollow-charge projectiles.

Once up-gunned and up-armoured, the Pz IV was a match for the T-34 or the Sherman. The longer gun and extra armour pushed the tank's weight up from the original 18 tons to 25 tons and because the Pz IV had the more old-fashioned leaf-spring suspension system, unlike the Pz III, Tiger and Panther which had torsion bars, the additional weight left the front springs permanently bowed, causing the tank to yaw badly. The road wheels and tracks also had to be widened to distribute the extra weight more effectively. The Pz IV's chassis was the basis for several successful conversions, most notably the Stug IV and the Jagdpanzer IV tank destroyer.

Pz IIIs and IVs were sold in small numbers to Germany's allies, namely to the Romanians, Finns, Hungarians and Bulgarians. The Finns continued to use Pz IVs for training purposes until the 1960s. Pz IVs were even used by the Syrian Army in the 1967 Arab-Israeli War and the Israelis captured one of the war-weary old tanks dug in as a stationary fire-point on the Golan Heights.

Everyone has heard of the Tiger and the Panther, the glamorous stars of the German tank arm, and yet by the time those two legendary panzers joined the ranks, the war had already turned irretrievably against the Germans. Largely forgotten today are the two reliable and robust workhorses which won all the initial victories and staved off the inevitable defeat for so long, namely the Pz III and IV. These were the tanks which conquered Poland and France, came close in Russia and served right to the end of the war in various roles. They were far from perfect tanks, with relatively thin, unsloped armour and a high, boxy shape that produced many shot traps, but their greatest strength was that they had the capacity to be up-armoured and up-gunned as requirements changed. They were originally designed in the mid-1930s, when tank designers could only make an educated guess at what kind of tanks would be needed in a future war as no one at that time had any actual experience of tank-on-tank combat. That these two panzers were in effective service for so long says a lot for the strength of their original designs.

The Germans built around 50,000 AFVs during the war, a figure dwarfed by the tank production of both the USA and USSR – in the latter country, production of the T-34 alone was in excess of this number. There were a number of reasons for this disparity, one of the most important being that the Germans always aimed for a qualitative rather than a quantitative advantage – they wanted to build better tanks than their enemies, not more. This practice proved fruitful in the early years of the war when the superiority of German tank tactics and crews meant they could win victories over numerically superior foes. But as the war dragged on and became a series of massive battles of materiel, the Panzerwaffe became badly outnumbered and German industry was simply unable to supply enough tanks to equal the enemy.

The Germans never adopted the manufacturing practices that enabled the Allies to churn out so many tanks, in particular mass-production conveyor belts in operation twenty-four hours a day. For one thing German tanks were built by heavy manufacturing plants, not car manufacturers. These kinds of engineering firms normally built large single units like locomotives in small numbers and their output consisted of high-quality machines, hand built by skilled workers. They preferred to move the workers to the work, rather than vice versa. Understandably, speed was not a strong point and the concept of mass production was never embraced.

On top of the limitations imposed by production methods, Hitler resisted the idea of women working in armament factories as they did in the Allied countries; this large source of untapped labour would have released more men for the front, but Hitler wouldn't hear of *Mädchens* getting their hands dirty. The Germans did eventually introduce two 12-hour shifts per day, but the night shift was usually only half as productive as the day shift. While lip service was paid by Goebbels and others to the concept of 'Total War', in reality German war production in all weapon types was low until Albert Speer took over as Armaments Minister in 1944. By then it was too late with such severe reverses on all fronts and Allied bombing seriously hampering production and, even more disastrously, delivery of materiel to the front.

Building tanks the German way wasn't fast, even though the end products were superbly engineered vehicles – it took 150,000 man hours to produce a Panther, twice that to build a Tiger. During 1942 the average German tank production per month was only 500 units, while average Soviet tank production at the same time was 2,200 tanks per month, a figure Hitler refused to believe. At that rate every panzer would have to knock out four Russian tanks just to maintain levels as they were; that they came close to doing so is a fine testament to the panzers and their crews. The largest number of panzers ever produced in one month during the war was only 720.

Another factor which slowed output was the vast number of different models being built and the resources that were endlessly frittered away on pointless prototypes that never entered full-scale production. This was in contrast to the Soviets pre-war methods which resulted in countless prototypes having been produced, but the full-scale war production of only a handful of superb tanks and tank destroyers. When Guderian became General-Inspector of the Panzertruppen, he did his best to simplify production by reducing the number of models being made to a bare minimum.

Although major manufacturers such as Krupps, Daimler-Benz, MAN and Henschel built the panzers, the many components were manufactured in different firms all over Germany. In reality the building of a tank did not take place solely in any one location nor was any single manufacturer able to produce the entire tank. Separate firms and subcontractors specialised in building the armour, turret, engines, guns and all the other components of a tank, all of which only came together in the final assembly; for example Krupps built the main tank guns while Maybach Motorenbau built the engines.

First to be assembled was the hull and chassis. The hull was put together as an empty welded steel box with rough holes already bored in it for the various suspension arms. The hull went through various milling and lathing processes until the turret ring could be added and it then moved on to a final assembly line where the rest of the components were installed. The hulls moved nose to tail on the final assembly line and at each new station the workers added a few more components. At the same time as the hull was being put together, elsewhere in the factory workers would be milling the turret ring and producing the various other parts. The hull assembly lines usually adjoined large engineering bays and machine-tool shops where components such as road wheels, suspension arms and tracks were machined.

Eventually the engine was lowered by crane into its compartment at the rear of the hull and the transmission parts fitted. The tank was then placed over a pit so that the tracks could be attached; meanwhile the turret was assembled separately and then lowered onto the hull. Finally, the various internal fittings such as radios, optics and machine-guns were installed and the tank was painted.

Panzer interiors contained four main colours: red, green-grey, white and black. An anti-oxide red lead primer, brick-red in colour, was painted on all surfaces and the interior floor was then painted a grey-green. On the upper parts of the hull and turret an ivory-coloured paint called 'elfenbein' was applied – this bright colour had the advantage of increasing visibility in the dark interior. Finally all the mechanical and optical equipment used by the crew inside the tank was painted black, so as to highlight them against the white background and make them easy to find in the heat of battle.

The finished tank was then taken to the rail yard to be shipped by train to the front. In the later stages of the war, tanks were sometimes handed directly over to the crew at the factory gates and went straight into battle.

The year 1938 was an eventful one in Germany. Early that year, Hitler dismissed both the War Minister, General von Blomberg, and the Commander-In-Chief of the Army, General von Fritsch, on trumped-up charges and appointed himself as Commander-In-Chief of the Armed Forces. His chief lackey, General Wilhelm Keitel, was made head of the OKW (Oberkommando der Wehrmacht), an organisation which proved to be more of a military secretariat to Hitler than a powerful and independent decision-making body. There was now no one to challenge Hitler's control of the Army. Around the same time Guderian was promoted to Generalleutnant and given command of an army corps. The Panzerwaffe continued to expand with the 4th and 5th Panzer Divisions set up during the year. Also during 1938, the cavalry formed 4 Leichte (light) divisions – these contained 1 tank battalion and 4 motorised rifle battalions, yet another drain on slim tank resources.

In March 1938 Hitler decided to incorporate Austria into the Reich. The panzers were going to be among the first units into Austria and Guderian was told to take over command of the 2nd Panzer Division and the SS 'Liebstandarte Adolf Hitler' Motorised Division for the operation. Guderian ordered the tanks beflagged and covered in greenery and flowers to show their friendly intentions in this 'Blumenkrieg' (Flower war) and, placing himself at the head of the 2nd Panzer, set off on the long journey to Vienna.

The 2nd Panzer had to cover 675 km (420 miles) in just forty-eight hours and the LAH 1,000 km (600 miles). Not surprisingly many of the tanks broke down, perhaps as many as one-third. Churchill crowed about this high rate of breakdown in the nascent German tank arm in his memoirs of the Second World War, but as Guderian pointed out in his own memoirs, these same tanks were capable in 1940 of 'giving very short shrift indeed to the out-of-date armies of the Western Powers'.[2] This high breakdown rate was understandable in the light of the distances that had to be covered by the still largely untried tanks and the short time they'd had to prepare for the operation.

Guderian learned some important lessons from the panzers' involvement in the Anschluss and took steps to make sure the same problems never occurred again. He insisted that maintenance and repair facilities for the tanks were improved so that tanks that broke down on the march could be quickly repaired and set back on the road. Fuel supply had also been a problem and he took practical measures to ensure that in future both fuel and ammunition would be quickly supplied to the tanks in adequate quantities.

Hitler's next territorial aim was the Czech Sudetenland which he seized without bloodshed in October 1938 thanks to Chamberlain and the Munich agreement. The panzers were again at the forefront of the march and this time without the high level of breakdowns that occurred in the Anschluss. For this operation Guderian commanded an army corps containing the 1st Panzer Division and two motorised infantry divisions.

In November 1938, 'Schnelle Heinz', by now commanding the three panzer divisions of XVI Korps, was given the appropriately-titled new post of Chef der Schnellen Truppen (Chief of Fast Troops) which encompassed all panzer, motorised infantry and cavalry troops. He initially resisted, considering it a dummy appointment with no powers of command, but when Hitler promised that he would receive all the authority he needed, Guderian took the job and was promoted to the rank of General der Panzertruppen. He was now responsible for the training and tactics of all of Germany's armoured and motorised troops. He worked hard as usual and under his influence the first training manuals were drawn up for the panzer troops – up till then they'd used British training manuals. He also tried to reorganise the cavalry into a more modern form, but resistance within that arm prevented him from getting much of the work done before war broke out.

In March 1939, Hitler seized the rest of Czechoslovakia and so the second largest armaments industry in the world fell into Nazi hands – a real boon to the German war chest and in particular to the Panzerwaffe. Guderian went to examine the captured Czech tanks and declared them 'serviceable'. As a result two Czech tank models were pressed into German service, the Skoda LT35 and the CKD LT38. Both tanks mounted 37 mm guns as well as two machine-guns and were roughly comparable to the Pz III, although they only weighed half as much. Their greatest flaw was that their armour was riveted rather than welded and the rivets had an alarming tendency to fly off when hit. Both tanks carried crews of four.

The Czech tanks were primarily used to equip the new divisions formed when the four Leichte divisions were converted to full panzer status. Even though both of these tanks were clearly obsolete by 1939, they were superior to the Pz I and II and until such time as they had enough Pz IIIs and IVs, the Panzerwaffe had no choice but to use them. In fact it is unlikely that the Germans could have attacked France at all in 1940 except for them – excluding Pz Is, Czech tanks made up one third of the Panzer force deployed during the campaign.

The Germans redesignated the CKD LT38 as the Pz 38(t) and used it in large numbers in Poland, France, North Africa, the Balkans and during the first year of the Russian campaign. Half of the tanks in Rommel's famed 'Ghost Division', the 7th Panzer, were Pz 38(t)s. Under German licence the Skoda plant in Pilsen and the CKD plant in Prague continued to build them until 1942, by which time 1,400 had been built. The Germans added an extra ton of armour and ensured that it was welded rather than riveted. The chassis was reliable and durable and from 1943 on was used as the basis for the Hetzer, one of the best tank destroyers of the war. The Pz 38(t) itself remained in service until June 1942.

The Skoda LT35 was renamed the Pz 35(t) and used in much fewer numbers than the LT38; in total about 220 were pressed into service. Pz 35(t)s formed the bulk of the tanks in the 6th Panzer Division (formerly the 1st Leichte Division) and was used by that division in Poland, France and during Barbarossa. The few Pz 35(t)s that hadn't already been destroyed by late 1941 were transferred to second-line duties.

Before we look at the Polish campaign, it might be useful to look at some of the things that influenced the lives of the Panzermen themselves. Heer Panzer crews all wore the same standard-issue black uniform, the designers of which were heavily influenced by the uniform of the Death's Head Hussars, the elite cavalry regiments of the Imperial Reich. Indeed propagandists often referred to the Panzerwaffe as *Die neuen Schwarzen Husaren* – the new Black Hussars.

The Panzer uniform was the same for all ranks including generals and consisted of a hip length, double-breasted black tunic and full length black trousers. Unlike other arms of service which displayed rank insignia on both collar and shoulder, the Panzertruppen indicated rank on their shoulder straps only. The collar patches were used solely for decorative purposes – displaying the traditional Totenkopf (Death's Head) symbol. As a military insignia the Death's Head first appeared in the 18th century on the uniforms of elite Prussian units and during the First World War was adopted by German Storm Troop and tank battalions.

The tunic's collar patches were bordered by the *Waffenfarbe* (the colour coding used to identify each branch of the Heer and worn as piping around shoulder straps, collars and headgear – in the case of the Panzerwaffe, it was rose-pink). All awards and medals were worn on the left breast, the *Wehrmachtsadler* or Nazi eagle on the right (the eagle also featured on headgear). Rank chevrons were worn on the upper left sleeve. Cuff-titles and arm-shields were also worn depending on the Panzerman's division and the campaigns he had fought in.

The trousers featured buttoned-down side pockets, a built-in belt and drawstrings at the ankles and were worn over short black leather ankle boots. Unlike generals in other arms, Panzer generals didn't wear red stripes on their trousers. A standard army brown leather belt tied at the waist completed the ensemble. Panzermen were also equipped with the standard *'Feld-Grau'* (field-grey) army greatcoat and there were also black Panzer wraps in a similar style to the tunic.

The tankers wore the Panzer beret – the *Schutzmutze* (enlisted man's cap). This cumbersome-looking piece of headgear was composed of a crash liner casing covered by a cloth beret which could be folded down to provide winter protection. The liner was composed of felt padding lined with wool, cloth and a leather sweatband. This Panzermutze, which looked like a hybrid between a Russian fur hat and an English working man's cap, was large and heavy and protruded to the rear.

Because it was so unwieldy and unsuitable for wearing within the close confines of a tank interior, the Panzermutze was abandoned after the Polish campaign and replaced with a black cloth version of the Model 1938 *Feldmutze* (Field cap). This 'skullcap' or forage cap had no peak and was designed to fit snugly under the *Stalhelm* or coalscuttle helmet of the Wehrmacht. The cap proved popular and Manstein and Hoth even wore it in preference to the more usual officers' cap, the Schirmmutze.

The Feldmutze was widely issued within the army until it was replaced in 1943 by the M43 *Einheitsfeldmutze* (Replacement field cap). The M43 was intended to replace all other styles of field cap and was based on the Bergmutze (mountain cap) of the Gebirgsjäger (Mountain troops). This distinctive peaked field cap came in green, khaki, black and camouflage colours and served in all theatres until the war's end. The *Stahlhelm* was also issued to all Panzer crews and worn when the armoured vehicles were travelling over rough terrain.

This uniform was used both as a Service uniform and a Dress uniform and soon proved very popular with Panzermen. Its black colour was very effective at covering up dirt and oil stains and so continued to look smart even after days of fighting inside a tank. It was also important that the uniform have no features that might snag inside the vehicle if a Panzerman needed to make a speedy exit; for this reason there were few buttons, shoulder straps were usually sewn down and the jacket was buttoned from the inside. The Panzer parade uniform was the standard German 'Feld- grau' uniform with the addition of pink piping on shoulder straps and headgear, although the troops generally wore the black uniform on parade.

The Panzermen were also issued with a lightweight and durable reed-green two-piece denim suit for summer wear or to be worn over the standard uniform in winter. Cut identically to the black uniform, it had the usual insignia, shoulder straps and Totenkopf collar patches.

Like the rest of the Wehrmacht the Panzertruppen had various camouflage uniforms. During the winter of 1942–43, a reversible winter camouflage uniform was issued. This consisted of a well-padded jacket and trousers that could be worn over the standard uniform. It was reversible, white on one side and camouflage pattern on the other. From 1943 on, a one-piece camouflage Panzer overall was manufactured. It too was reversible with green spring colours on one side and brown autumn colours on the other. Early in 1944 a two-piece Panzer uniform of the same type as the black Panzer uniform was introduced with a green-brown camouflage scheme.

Waffen SS Panzer uniforms were broadly similar to the Heer version, except for the SS runes and rank markings worn on the collar. Of course the Waffen SS also used the Totenkopf symbol; this fact cost many Panzer troops their lives when taken prisoner because their black uniforms with the skull and crossbones symbol on the collar meant they were mistaken for the hated Waffen SS. The only difference between the two insignias was that the Panzerwaffe used the Prussian-style jawless Death's Head, whereas the Waffen SS version included a lower jaw.

The only real disadvantage to the black Panzer uniform was that its colour was unsuitable for camouflage and often prematurely alerted the enemy that Panzer units were in the area. With this factor in mind the crews of tank destroyers, Stugs and self-propelled guns wore a special field-grey uniform of the same cut and design as the black Panzer uniform.

Now that we know what they wore, what did the panzer crews actually do? The following account gives a general description of the working arrangement that applied to the Pz III, Pz IV, Panther, Tiger and King Tiger – these tanks all had five-man crews and each crewman had a specialised function to carry out. The tank was divided into four compartments; the two at the front housed the driver and the radio operator, separated by the massive gearbox that ran between them. The rear compartment contained the engine and the turret formed the fourth or fighting compartment. It wasn't a pleasant or easy working environment; the crew had to endure the din from the engine and gun, the stench of cordite and exhaust fumes and the constant jolting as the tank bumped its way over rough terrain. There was also the ever-present threat of being immolated in a steel box loaded with fuel and explosives. Because of the noise it was impossible for the crew to hear each other so each crewman wore a throat mike and headphones.

The driver sat on the left-hand side and controlled the tank using two steering levers or a wheel hydraulically connected to a differential steering unit. His principal method of seeing where he was going was through a visor set in the frontal armour plate – a thick, shell-proof glass block about the size of a letter box. An armoured shutter could be closed over the visor for extra protection and then the driver had to resort to a periscope to see his way. There was an escape hatch over the driver's head. On his instrument panel, he had a speedometer and a tachometer as well as gauges for fuel, oil pressure and engine temperature. The driver had a gear lever on his left and three pedals at his feet: accelerator, brake and clutch. At night he had a single headlight to show the way and often even this was partially blacked out as an anti-aircraft measure.

On the right-hand side sat the radio operator. His equipment was most likely a short-wave FuG5 (a receiver and 10-watt transmitter), the standard tank set with a range of 2 or 3 km – a commander's tank would have had a more powerful radio. The radios were clamped into place on a rack on the right-hand side of the tank's interior. There was also a telegraph key and a circuit box into which the jackplugs for the onboard intercom were plugged. The radio operator also manned the hull machine-gun and had a sighting optic for aiming mounted next to the breech. The standard German tank machine-gun throughout the war was the ball-mounted 7.92mm MG-34, the same superlative machine-gun used by the infantry. From the Pz III on, every panzer carried two MG-34s for close defence, one in the hull and one in the turret. The radio operator also had an escape hatch over his head.

Three men worked in the cramped turret: the loader, the gunner and the commander. The loader on the right-hand side of the gun had both the least specialised and physically hardest job – manhandling the tank shells from their storage bins into the gun's breech. He had a foldaway seat, but usually worked standing up in a crouch. The shells were stored in bins in the turret and hull and in the case of the 75 mm or 88 mm guns, each shell weighed 7.5 kg (15 lb) or more. The loader could fire the co-axial turret machine-gun using a trigger or else it could be fired by the gunner using a foot pedal. The loader had his own escape hatch overhead.

The gunner sat on the left-hand side of the gun. Like the commander, he sat in a seat that rotated with the gun and was the only member of the crew without his own escape hatch, having to clamber in and out through the commander's hatchway – no mean feat in a burning tank. He was equipped with a forward vision port, a periscope and a gunsight consisting of two plates – one for sighting and the other for range. Once a target was sighted, the gunner would rotate the turret until he'd brought the gun to bear in the general area of the enemy. In the earlier tanks, this traverse was manual, but from the Tiger on, turrets were so heavy, they had to be rotated by a hydraulic motor. Then while watching the target through a gunsight, the gunner would make the necessary fine adjustments of the gun using his hand traverse and elevation wheels. Once the target was properly in the sights and the gun was loaded, it was fired electrically by the gunner using a pedal or firing lever. There was a bag hanging from the breech to catch the spent shells and a fan in the turret roof to extract the fumes. The only illumination in the turret came from a few overhead lights.

The commander sat behind and above the gunner with his head stuck in the cupola that protruded from the turret roof. The inside of this cupola had a series of vision ports which gave the commander a panoramic view of the battlefield and allowed him to advise the gunner which targets to select. These vision ports, like the one the driver had, were laminated glass blocks built up of many layers. They were thick enough to be proof against bullets and shell splinters, but were also fitted with armoured shutters that could be closed from within the cupola. They allowed the commander a 360-degree field of vision of the outside world, but because the glass was so thick, everything looked slightly green.

The commander's cupola also contained a simple, but effective azimuth or turret direction indicator. The cupola itself was fixed to the hull and so didn't rotate with the turret. Within the cupola there was a toothed, white ring with black markings which did rotate. By comparing the markings on this ring indicator to the rest of the cupola, the commander could work out the orientation of the turret in relation to the hull and could then give the gunner directions on which way to turn the gun to bring it to bear on the target. The gunner did this by consulting his own azimuth indicator. The commander also had an auxiliary hand-traverse wheel in case the gunner needed help lining up the target.

Despite the claustrophobic confines of these steel vehicles, the Panzertruppen looked upon their tanks as home and these carefully crafted machines maintained their crews' confidence until the end.

Hitler was quite prepared to go to war with the Allies over his anticipated Polish invasion, if he had to, but the political magician in him couldn't resist one final trick. In August he concluded a non-aggression pact with Stalin, an unholy alliance which sent shock waves across the world. The trade aspects of this agreement allowed for the supply to Germany of vital raw materials, foodstuffs and oil in return for certain technologies and plans to key German military products including its tanks and battleships. The Germans benefited greatly over the two years of the agreement as it greatly enhanced their ability to conduct offensive operations in the West, courtesy of a secure rear and extra supplies for the munitions industries. In addition Hitler's aides created such a complex web of bureaucracy that few military secrets were handed over to the Soviets.

One other significant clause was kept secret. Poland was, for the fourth time in history, to be divided between Germany and Russia. The Russians agreed to attack the Poles from the rear after the Germans struck, thus guaranteeing the destruction of the Polish state. Under the deal, Stalin managed to extract not only half of Poland, but also added the Baltic states and a slice of Romania to his sphere of interest. Hitler smarted over these concessions and secretly vowed revenge.

Despite these new-found advantages, it was still essential that the Wehrmacht attain a rapid victory. The success of the German economy was the cornerstone of Hitler's popularity and he didn't want to endanger it by a protracted campaign in Poland. The condition of Germany's war supplies also had to be considered. Despite the spoils anticipated from the Russian agreement, oil was still a scarce commodity. As well as this, German heavy industry wasn't yet in a position to produce munitions in sufficient quantities.

Hitler believed a quick success would discourage the Western Allies from getting involved. If the Germans overran enough of the Polish supply depots, railheads and assembly areas, the calling up of Polish reserves would be greatly hindered. Additionally, the still largely unmotorised Wehrmacht needed to fight close to its own railheads in Silesia and Pomerania. In order to secure this lightning victory, Hitler turned to the Panzerwaffe. The traditional arms of service couldn't hope to attain the necessary pace, but discussions with Guderian and other tank enthusiasts over the preceding years convinced Hitler that he now possessed the ideal tool for short, sharp and successful offensives.

The Poles had concluded mutual assistance pacts with Britain and France and expected that German mobilisation would signal an imminent attack. However, throughout the latter part of August 1939, the German Army had been mobilising secretly and massing in East Prussia and along the western Polish border, thus denying the Poles any advance warning of their intentions. After several false alarms, border provocations and belated attempts to placate the Allies, Hitler finally gave the go-ahead for the attack. The SS created a so-called justification for the invasion by staging what looked like a Polish attack on a German radio station at Gleiwitz. Under this pretext of Polish aggression, the Germans attacked.

During the summer of 1939 the planners at the Oberkommando das Heer (OKH) – Army High Command – laboured at producing a plan for the invasion of Poland. The team with special responsibility for the general outline was Arbeitsstab Rundstedt, which was composed of only three men; Generaloberst Gerd von Rundstedt, General Erich von Manstein and Oberst Günther von Blumentritt. Rundstedt, the most respected of German senior commanders, was a withered 64-year-old aristocrat with a penchant for detective stories. The senior officer of the Wehrmacht, Rundstedt had recently been recalled from retirement by Hitler to lead the campaign. He left most of the work to his two subordinates, Manstein and Blumentritt.

Manstein was still only in his early fifties, but with his beaky nose, heavy eyebrows and grey hair, looked considerably older. He had spent most of his career in staff work and had worked his way up to become head of the operations section of the General Staff. But after the ousting of Blomberg and Fritsch in 1938, Manstein was moved sideways to an obscure divisional command, thanks to his lack of enthusiasm for the Nazis. A brilliant strategic thinker, Guderian described him as 'our finest operational brain'.[3] The Stug assault guns were his brainchild.

The finished plan these men produced bore all the traditional hall-marks of the German General Staff. The overall operational goal of Fall Weiss (Case White) was to destroy the Polish Army west of the Vistula. The plan called for a double envelopment of the Polish Army, with the Germans catching the Poles in a double pincer movement from East Prussia and Pomerania on one flank and from Silesia and Slovakia on the other. The inner encirclement was to close about Warsaw and the outer ring on the historic city of Brest-Litovsk.

The plan called for two army groups to attack simultaneously. The Northern Army Group under Generaloberst Fedor von Bock was given two armies – the Third Army would attack from East Prussia and the Fourth Army from Pomerania. Guderian was given command of the new XIX Armeekorps containing the 3rd Panzer and two motorized infantry divisions. His Chief of Staff was General Walther Nehring, a partnership which was to prove very successful both in Poland and in France. Guderian's XIX Korps was subordinate to the Fourth Army commanded by the argumentative General der Artillerie Günther von Kluge and it was now that the legendary feud between these two men first began to fester. The Third Army also had an armoured component composed of various assorted units including several small SS units, panzer regiments and assorted ancillary formations; these were all grouped together as 'Panzerverbande Kempf' which had the strength of a reinforced panzer division.

In total, this army group had 21 divisions and 600 tanks. Northern Army Group's task was to link East Prussia and Pomerania by advancing across the Polish corridor and then get behind the Vistula to attack the Poles in the rear; they would then swing south to link up with the spearheads of Army Group South.

The Southern Army Group was placed under the command of Rundstedt and his able Chief of Staff, Manstein. It had the more important role and was considerably stronger than its northern counterpart, with three armies, the Eighth, Tenth and Fourteenth, a total of thirty-six divisions. This army group also contained the bulk of the German armoured and motorised forces – 4 panzer, 4 Leichte (a motorised infantry division with 2 armoured units) and 2 motorised infantry divisions, roughly 2,000 tanks in all. Von Reichanau's Tenth Army had Hoepner's XVI Panzerkorps containing the 1st and 4th Panzer divisions, Hoth's XV motorised corps (2nd and 3rd Leichte Divisions) and another motorised corps on its establishment. These forces were detailed for the thrust towards the Polish capital. The Fourteenth Army meanwhile had two panzerkorps. Southern Army Group's task was to defeat the enemy in the large bend of the Vistula and then dash for Warsaw, seize the Vistula crossings and link up with Northern Army Group, thus forming the outer edge of the great encirclement in the eastern part of the country.

The Germans attacked Poland with a total of 42 divisions: 24 infantry, 3 mountain, 6 panzer, 4 Leichte and 4 motorised infantry. The panzer divisions that participated in the campaign were the 1st, 2nd, 3rd, 4th, 5th and 10th, as well as Panzerverbande Kempf. In what was to be the world's first great tank victory, the Germans brought 2,600 panzers to bear in Poland, yet the vast bulk of the armour was made up of the obsolete Pz I and II light tanks. Of the more modern models, there were only 100 Pz IIIs and 210 Pz IVs available. There were also nearly 350 Czech AFVs employed. The total tank complement in each panzer division was in the region of 320, whereas the Leichte divisions were all below 150 tanks with the exception of the 200 vehicles of the mostly Czech-equipped 1st Leichte. The freshly raised 10th Panzer Division was initially allocated to army reserve.

The fully-mobilised Polish Army numbered 1.75 million men with another 500,000 in reserve. They had 39 infantry divisions, 11 cavalry brigades, 1 motorised brigade and 2 armoured brigades with which to counter the expected German assault. These were gathered into seven armies, five of which lay west of the Vistula. The Army had reacted to political and prestige pressures by trying to defend as much Polish territory as possible, when they would have been much better off pulling back to the Vistula – this reluctance to surrender anything voluntarily was to prove a fatal error, especially given the speed of the German assault.

Although impressive in manpower terms, the Polish Army suffered terrible deficiencies in modern weaponry, in particular their lack of any significant mobile units. The Poles could only raise about 700 tanks, 450 of which were tankettes, mere tracked machine-gun carriers. They also had a number of obsolete French tanks or variations on British models which were formed into light tank battalions or companies and parcelled out to the infantry; only one of their cavalry units was motorised. For communication the Army was dependent on the civil telephone and telegraph system and the Luftwaffe soon bombed this into oblivion. Their artillery and anti-tank defences were hopelessly inadequate. Significantly, the newly founded Polish army was French-taught and so hardly likely to be imbued with the new doctrine of mobility and speed.

One Polish army stood opposite East Prussia and for political reasons, a large army was placed in the disputed corridor separating Germany from East Prussia; it is estimated that as much as one-third of the Polish Army was in this corridor when the German spearheads sliced through it. The Poles placed another army in the Poznan province to bar the direct route to Warsaw, but this substantial force was soon bypassed by the German attacking prongs and found itself isolated. South of the Poznan army were three more Polish armies arrayed from Lodz to the Carpathians; ironically one of these was commanded by a Polish General Rommel. The Poles opted to thinly defend the entire German border, rather than create a central mobile reserve.

The nature of the Polish topography was such that a concerted attempt to defend the many river lines, mostly running north–south, could have delayed the Germans long enough for the Allies to stage a holding attack, however the Polish general staff preferred to distribute their available resources as widely as possible rather than fight delaying actions. This would probably have made no difference anyway as their French and British allies showed no stomach for launching a full-scale offensive in the West.

At 0445 hrs on 1 September 1939, the five German armies struck Poland simultaneously from the north, south and west as the attack opened along the 2,600-km (1,750-mile) border. The Luftwaffe attacked enemy airbases and quickly eliminated any effective countermeasures by

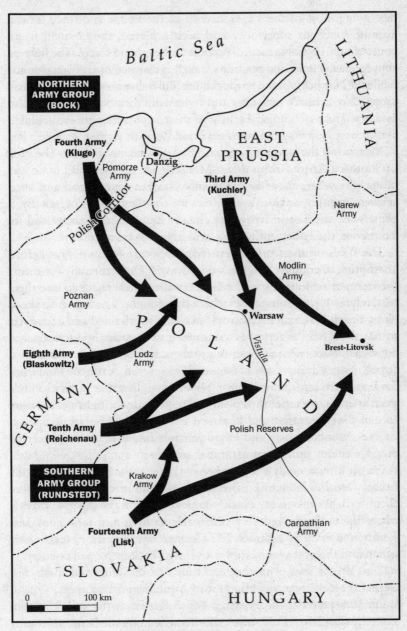

Fall Weiss, September 1939

destroying most of the 1,000 aircraft of the Polish Air Force on the ground. Once air superiority had been achieved, the German flyers concentrated on giving tactical support to the ground forces. The fighters shot up enemy units and positions as well as carrying out reconnaissance while the bomber units, in particular the Stuka dive bombers, hit tougher targets like artillery positions and repeatedly dive-bombed the Polish infantry. The psychological effects of these new tactics are incalculable and went a long way to insuring a rapid German victory.

Meanwhile the German vanguard had crossed into Poland. The staff of Southern Army Group under Manstein set up their HQ in an old monastery where they lived spartanly on stew, army bread and hard sausage, waiting anxiously for news on the fighting's progress. By 5 September, the Tenth Army was already halfway to Warsaw and its neighbour, the Fourteenth Army, was about to take Krakow.

The Poles on the frontier resisted stubbornly for two days before attempting to conduct a fighting withdrawal. Unfortunately for them, the German armoured spearheads were already racing deep into their rear, effectively trapping them where they fought. The Polish Krakow Army began to retreat eastwards, but it was overhauled and destroyed by Kleist's XXII Panzerkorps (containing two panzer and four leichte divisions). Suddenly the Poles found there was nowhere to retreat to. Supply routes and communications were severed, seriously hindering the Polish attempts at resistance. Hitler brought terror tactics to bear in an attempt to shatter the Polish will to prolong the fighting. Refugee columns were strafed and harassed by the Luftwaffe while towns, villages, wooded areas and any other features that offered cover to possible enemy units were saturated with fire.

On the afternoon of 8 September, tanks from the Eighth Army's 4th Panzer Division launched an attack on the suburbs of Warsaw. Over 50 of its 120 tanks were quickly knocked out in the narrow streets, where the tanks proved very vulnerable to both anti-tank guns and determined infantry assaults. The Germans were quick to learn their lesson and the unit was hastily withdrawn back into open country. It was an object lesson on the limitations of the tank and made the Germans forever wary of committing armour in urban areas.

On 10 September the bypassed Polish Poznan Army and remnants from the Corridor forces struck southwards along the Bzura river into the open flank of the German Eighth Army. The Germans were forced to respond and began withdrawing armoured divisions from less sensitive parts of the front to contain the Polish thrust. Rundstedt and Manstein were however playing for keeps and rather than launching an all-out assault with the risk of driving the Poles east, decided to draw them into battle with the Eighth Army while strengthening the encirclement about them.

The brilliance of Manstein first became apparent here as he forced the Poles into a situation where they were attacked from the very direction in which they hoped to break out. He ordered that the Tenth Army's XVI Panzerkorps, currently tied up in the Warsaw suburbs, wheel around and attack the Poles from the east – thus presenting the hapless defenders with a reversed front. He also had two reserve divisions attack from the west and a corps from Northern Army Group helped to complete the encirclement.

After heavy fighting the 1st Panzer and the 1st, 2nd and 3rd Leichte divisions again closed the ring of steel around the Pomoroze and Poznan armies. It was the largest ever encirclement at that time, although minuscule by the standards later set in Russia. The Battle of Bzura led to the capture of 9 Polish infantry divisions and 3 cavalry brigades, while elements of 10 further divisions were destroyed. When the Poles surrendered on 17 September, the Germans took 52,000 prisoners. This encirclement at the Bzura river was followed by the reduction of a pocket at Radom, which contained a further 60,000 Polish troops.

The men in the field had effectively overruled the Supreme Command, something that wouldn't be allowed to happen in future campaigns. The OKH had ordered the Tenth Army to advance straight over the Vistula, as they believed the Poles were retreating south. But Rundstedt and Manstein knew that the main Polish armies were still west of the river and could be trapped there.

Meanwhile in the north, Guderian's XIX Armeekorps had moved into Poland on 1 September under the cover of a heavy mist – he had placed the 3rd Panzer on his right flank to make the main thrust across Tuchel Heath while the two motorised divisions played a less important role. Almost immediately he nearly became a victim of the overactive artillery of the 3rd Panzer division when his armoured command car was bracketed by heavy calibre shells, whereupon the nervous driver drove the half-track into a ditch and bent the front axle. Guderian had to return to his command post to get a new vehicle and to have a quiet word with his overeager artillerymen – being the first corps commander to follow the tanks onto the battlefield in an armoured command vehicle had its risks.

However Guderian's steely nerves easily overcame this inauspicious start and his corps quickly pushed on into Poland. On the way they overran the Guderian family's old Prussian estate where the Panzer General's father had been born and his grandfather was buried. The panzers also seized the town of Kulm, Guderian's own birthplace. On the second day Guderian's panzers ran out of petrol and ammunition and were temporarily stranded until supply columns could fight a way through to them.

His impatient nature was soon in evidence again as he pushed his troops ever forward. On the banks of the Brahe river, a young lieutenant told the Corps Commander that the advance had only stalled because there was no one to lead it as the Division's commander, General-leutnant Geyr von Schweppenburg, was nowhere to be found. Guderian took the cue and personally led a panzer regiment across the river, seizing the far bank by coup de main. His sudden appearance in the thick of the fighting came as a shock to a group of staff officers hiding behind an oak tree and the whole incident did little for relations between Guderian and his divisional commander. Guderian then ordered his reconnaissance elements to force a passage across the Tuchel marshes through to the Vistula; by reaching this river he intended to cut off the Poles still opposing the Fourth Army.

Everywhere his unique leadership style and forceful personality were brought to bear. Disheartened and panicky commanders were firmly told to settle down and seize their assigned objectives. One commander of a motorised division told Guderian that his men were being forced to withdraw by Polish cavalry; when an incredulous Guderian regained the use of his voice, he asked the commander if he had ever heard of Pomeranian grenadiers being broken by hostile cavalry. The chastened commander agreed to hold his positions. Attacking forces that became bogged down were swiftly told to probe forward and find a fresh *Schwerpunkt* (point of maximum effort); tired troops were reinvigorated by the presence in the front line of such an energetic senior commander.

By 1 September his corps had managed to surround the opposing forces and it was during this series of engagements that one of the most illustrative events of the campaign occurred when tanks of the

3rd Panzer Division, were charged by the Polish Pomorska Cavalry Brigade wielding lances and sabres. Whether it was an act of supreme heroism or because the dragoons believed the tanks to be wood and canvas mock-ups like earlier German tanks, the result was the same. The cavalry was cut to ribbons and the last vestiges of the old way of waging war fell away.

Within the next few days the troops defending the Polish corridor separating East Prussia from the rest of Germany were completely surrounded. All that remained was for the pocket to be reduced, a task best left to the infantry. At this point Hitler himself visited Guderian and was amazed by the success the panzers had achieved. He was particularly impressed by the sight of a smashed Polish artillery regiment and said to Guderian, 'Our dive bombers did that?' Guderian proudly replied, 'No! Our panzers!'[4] The scale of German casualties was in stark contrast to Hitler's memories of the trench warfare of his youth. XIX Armeekorps had suffered less than 1,000 casualties in a week of heavy fighting, while Hitler recalled his own First World War regiment losing 2,000 men in its first day at the front. Events were bearing out Guderian's belief that tanks were a life-saving weapon.

On 6 September, Guderian's Armeekorps crossed the Vistula. He made his HQ in a castle that Napoleon had stayed in before the 1812 Russian campaign – the marks made by Napoleon's spurs were still visible on the wooden floor and Guderian slept in the same bed the Little Emperor had used. While there the tank commander had enough confidence in his staff to be able to take time out for deer-hunting, bagging a large twelve-pointer. Guderian now received orders to transfer his XIX Armeekorps from the Fourth Army to the mainly infantry Third Army. Aghast at the prospect of being held back by the pace of the infantry, he appealed to von Bock for permission to allow his armoured and motorised elements to carry on alone. Guderian argued that only if the motorised troops were left to their own devices could the Germans hope to prevent the Poles from falling back behind the River Bug and establishing a line of defence there. Bock agreed and reorganised the Corps accordingly, getting permission from OKH to place it under direct army control. Guderian relinquished command of one of his motorised divisions in return for the 10th Panzer and set Brest-Litovsk as the Corp's objective. By giving Guderian a free hand, von Bock had effectively created the first independent tank army.

Guderian's first task was to force a crossing of the Narev river and smash through the Polish defence line, which the troops achieved near the town of Vizna. Guderian promptly crossed the river, but was disappointed with the poor results achieved by his men once they had forced the crossing. Again he personally led a reconnaissance patrol to examine the Polish defences. On his return from the front line he issued orders for the tanks to be ferried across the Narev post-haste. By evening he had overrun the Polish defenders on the far bank and issued instructions for his remaining forces to cross the river by whatever means available in order to consolidate the gains.

Guderian's Armeekorps raced for Brest-Litovsk, ignoring attacks from the east and covering 300 km (200 miles) in just 10 days. So rapid was the advance that the Panzers surprised and destroyed one Polish tank unit as it was still being unloaded at a railway siding. On another occasion Guderian was completely separated from his staff. A rumour gained currency that Schnelle Heinz was encircled by the Poles in a small village and the General was both surprised and edified to see a motorcycle unit operating on their own initiative come streaming into the village to 'rescue' him. The advance continued to Bielsek and from there Guderian laid plans for the capture of his ultimate objective – Brest-Litovsk. On the way he screened infantry along a forested area into which the Poles had retreated as he didn't wish to be distracted from his primary goal. In addition he was aware that an assault on the forests would tie down his corps and render void the advantages of armour.

A surprise assault on the fortress of Brest-Litovsk was foiled by the Poles using an old Renault tank to barricade the town gates. Several other assaults also failed, but the town was eventually captured on the 17th when the Poles attempted to sally out and cross a bridge over the Bug. Once in possession of the city, Guderian established his headquarters and set about making contact with the XXII Panzerkorps of Southern Army Group advancing to meet him from the south.

At this point XIX Armeekorps was once again subordinated to Kluge's Fourth Army and the two men lost no time in resuming their bitter differences. Kluge wanted to disperse the divisions along three separate axes of advance. Needless to say any attempt to dilute the power of his hammer irritated Guderian immensely and a serious crisis of command was only averted by the news that the Russians were invading to the east and Brest-Litovsk was now within their sphere of operations.

On 17 September, 35 Soviet divisions had begun to trundle across the 1,300-km (800-mile) long border between Poland and Russia, sealing that unhappy country's fate for the next fifty years. The following day Guderian's corps made contact with the first units of the XXII Panzerkorps south of Brest-Litovsk, effectively ending Polish resistance, for the entire Polish Army was now trapped within the double pincer foreseen in the original plan. XIX Armeekorps moved out of the city on the 21st and the following day the corps was disbanded, as the campaign was to all intents over. Warsaw stubbornly held out until the 27th and the last Polish troops surrendered on 6 October.

Guderian's XIX Armeekorps had suffered only 650 dead along with 1,586 wounded and missing – just 4 per cent of its total strength. Guderian took the opportunity of his time off to visit Prussian relatives and his birthplace in Kulm. The Panzer General wasn't the only member of the Guderian family to fight in the Polish campaign: his eldest son, Heinz Günther, was the adjutant of a panzer regiment while his younger son, Kurt, was a second lieutenant in the 3rd Panzer, one of the divisions in his father's corps. Both sons came through unscathed, Heinz winning the Iron Cross along the way. Guderian senior was decorated with the Knight's Cross himself in October.

It had taken the Germans just five weeks to smash the large Polish Army and inflict 750,000 casualties on them in the process. The Germans themselves had suffered relatively small losses of 8,000 killed, 5,000 missing and 27,000 wounded, the majority of these in the infantry. The tank arm had suffered a reduction in strength of about 650 vehicles, a quarter of the strength committed. Of this total, one-third of these tanks were completely written off, one-third were beyond local repair and had to be shipped back to Germany and one-third were not worth repairing.

The Polish campaign heralded a new style of warfare. Although not a classic Blitzkrieg, it proved the theories of the tank school and in particular those of Guderian. The two decisive arms were also the Wehrmacht's newest: the Panzerwaffe and the Luftwaffe. Despite the fact that both utilised weaponry that had been in existence since the First World War, it was the revolutionary application of these, in conjunction with the traditional German emphasis on seeking victory at the planning stage, that ensured overwhelming success.

The Polish Army was beaten almost as soon as hostilities opened and not because they lacked valour or were hopelessly outnumbered. Rather the roots of their defeat lay in the fact that they expected an entirely different attack to that which Hitler's new army unleashed. Once news of the assault filtered through to the West both the French and British estimated that even unaided the Poles could be expected to hold out over the autumn and winter. Indeed, had the French attacked as promised within a fortnight of mobilising, they would have missed the boat. At that stage the Germans were in a position to rush troops back to the west as the Polish operations were virtually complete.

The tank gamble had paid off; prior to the campaign no one could have been certain how they'd perform. Fortunately for the Germans, the Polish plain was ideal tank country, even though the roads were poor. Timing was also vital – the rains of autumn would have turned everything to mud. As it transpired, the whole world was surprised at the pace of the German success. Never before had a campaign on such a scale been conducted so rapidly; the mechanised Tenth Army had covered 250 km (140 miles) in the first week. The tanks tore open the Polish front and penetrated deep, overrunning the Polish armies before they could even fully mobilise. The pace of the German advance also made Polish central control impossible. For the first time, big self-sufficient tank formations were used in war to devastating effect. The new German methods were marvelled at – but as we shall see, not studied closely enough – by Germany's European neighbours.

The Panzer arm had not escaped unscathed from the conflict. At any given time up to a quarter of their machines were unavailable for action due to breakdowns, enemy action and routine maintenance. The Pz Is and IIs proved the most vulnerable, particularly in built-up areas and when they met proper anti-tank defences. Their combat effectiveness had been flattered to a large extent because the Polish Army was neither morally prepared nor materially equipped to counter any tanks, regardless of their quality. Hitler's penchant for vast numbers of vehicles, regardless of their quality, paid handsome dividends in Poland but his more perceptive panzermen saw that an urgent overhaul and reorganisation of their units and equipment was necessary if they were to have any hope of beating their Western adversaries.

Other lessons garnered from the campaign showed the leichte divisions falling between two stools – failing to function properly either as armoured or motorised infantry divisions. In short they were as cumbersome to command, victual, manoeuvre, equip and staff as full panzer divisions, yet they packed less than half the armoured punch. The munitions industries were incapable of producing a sufficient number of medium tanks to equip even the original five panzer divisions so these new formations drew heavily upon the resources of the former Czech Army. Indeed without these extra tanks, it is highly unlikely that Hitler's next scheme, an attack in the West, could have succeeded. Tank production was now pushed up to 125 vehicles per month.

There was one kind of experience the Panzermen didn't get much of in Poland – tank-to-tank combat. The Poles had distributed their tanks in small units amongst larger infantry units, as was the case amongst most other contemporary armies, which left them open to complete destruction when they came into contact with concentrated panzer regiments. The only well-equipped Polish tank unit was overrun and destroyed in its assembly area before it could offer any semblance of defence. At the time this lack of practical testing of their methods and equipment against other tanks worried the officers of the Panzerwaffe, although as events unfolded it proved not to be a serious shortcoming.

One of the German Army's strong points was its ability to learn from both its successes and its mistakes. In this regard subtle refinements to their day-to-day organisation and procedures were made. The identification markings with which their tanks went to war proved an easy marker for enemy gunners and had to be camouflaged during the campaign. As soon as the hostilities had ceased the brilliant white cross was replaced with the distinctive, but less visible black-lined white cross – the 'Balkenkreuz' remained in use until the war's end and became the trademark of the Wehrmacht.

The 88 mm flak anti-aircraft gun was formally reclassified as a dual-purpose gun following its success under combat conditions at knocking out Polish pillboxes and other 'hard targets'. The mighty '88' could lob a 16-lb shot at a velocity of 3,700 feet per second and was the most effective tank killer of the war, remaining in service until 1945. No Allied or Soviet tank was immune to its penetrative power even at tremendous ranges and it quickly became the most feared German weapon amongst enemy armoured units.

The Panzerwaffe had come through its baptism of fire with a reputation as a war-winning weapon. The tactics and theories promulgated by its exponents, in particular Heinz Guderian, in the pre-war years had been vindicated. The most significant achievement of the Panzerwaffe in this campaign was in convincing the officers of the older arms of the true value of the new weapons. The campaign had also bolstered the self-confidence of the Panzertruppen's officers and men and they were never again to exhibit the hesitancy they had occasionally shown in Poland.

The Polish campaign also served to strengthen the hand of Hitler, both over the public and the Army. He now saw himself as a latter-day Bismarck, conducting intricate diplomacy and lightning wars with equal facility. He had shrewdly assessed the nature and intentions of his foes and had been proven right over his cautious generals. Hubris was not far away.

Despite their success, the leaders of the Wehrmacht still looked on with apprehension at the situation in the West. The French and British had declared war on Germany two days into the Polish invasion and the German generals were amazed that the Allies hadn't moved on the Rhine while the vast bulk of German forces and all available tanks were occupied in the East. The generals hoped that their devious leader would now sue for peace, but yet again they had grossly misjudged the Bohemian Corporal.

CHAPTER THREE

Sickle Cut through France

Knights of our times ... Tank units, mobile, fast and hard hitting, and directed by wireless from headquarters, attack the enemy. This armoured machine paves the way to victory, flattening and crushing all obstacles and spitting out destruction.

Signal, 1940

ALTHOUGH Britain and France had declared war on Germany in September 1939, nothing much happened on the Western Front until the Germans invaded France in May 1940. This was the period known to the Germans as the Sitzkrieg (sit-down war) during which time both sides faced each other across the frontier, the Allies waiting for the Germans to make the first move. The Germans for their part were surprised that the French had not attacked while the bulk of the Wehrmacht was engaged in Poland. Indeed not only had the Germans stripped the West of all of their tanks and almost all of their infantry, they had no defence line worthy of the name to delay any French thrust. But the French chose instead to renege on their military pact with Poland and do nothing to help their ally.

The French did launch a half-hearted attack from the Saar with nine divisions on 9 September, in what was to be the only major French offensive of the war. But these divisions were ordered to halt after just three days and were withdrawn completely by early October, largely due to an unwillingness to provoke the Germans. The Western Front then settled into a period of prolonged inactivity, broken only by oc-casional artillery duels and the continual patrols mounted by each side to discover the strengths and dispositions of the other. Activity in the air was limited to reconnaissance and leaflet dropping, both sides wary of encouraging retaliation on civilian centres.

At least part of the reason for French inactivity can be attributed to their Commander-in-Chief, the 68-year-old General Gamelin, a relic of the First World War with an over-inflated reputation. He seemed to regard his real enemy to be not the Germans, but his own government. Gamelin set up headquarters in a thirteenth-century castle without radio or telephone communication and admitted it normally took forty-eight hours for his orders to reach the front. He was also on poor terms with his chief of staff. Clearly the French High Command was neither technically nor psychologically prepared for the pace of the battle ahead.

The Germans had used the winter of 1939–40 to convert the four Leichte divisions to full panzer status, thus forming the 6th, 7th, 8th and 9th panzer divisions. The general shortage of tanks meant that once upgraded, they were equipped with only one tank regiment whereas the earlier divisions all had two and about half of the 220 tanks each of these new divisions contained were Czech-built. There were now ten panzer divisions. The process of replacing the obsolete Pz Is and IIs with the new Pz IIIs and IVs was also accelerated, but the low numbers of tanks being produced meant that relatively little progress had been made on this by May 1940.

On 1 March 1940 Hitler issued a directive for the occupation of Norway and Denmark which he codenamed Fall Wesserubung. It was a daring operation, devised from a Baedecker guide by General Nikolaus von Falkenhorst and the Kriegsmarine (German Navy) staff and conducted largely by naval forces landing infantry at the main ports. The attack was launched on 9 April and Denmark capitulated almost immediately with Norway subdued by early May. Although the Panzerwaffe played only a very minor role in the campaign, it is still worthy of a mention.

A special tank battalion, Panzer Abteilung zur besonderer Vervendung 40, was formed for use in Norway by taking one company each from the 4th, 5th and 6th panzer divisions. Two of these companies were initially used in Denmark and the bulk of the third was lost at sea when its transport went down. An experimental formation called

Panzerzug Horstmann was also dispatched to Norway, comprising three Neubaufahrzeug Panzerkampfwagen VI – these were prototypes sent with the specific intention of convincing the Allies that the Germans already possessed heavy tanks. With this purpose in mind, staged propaganda photographs were taken of the three tanks leaving the harbour. Whether the ruse worked or not must remain a matter of conjecture, as before the campaign had ended Hitler had struck in the West.

The total number of German tanks used in the northern campaign never exceeded fifty and was composed largely of obsolete Panzer Is and IIs. Despite the limited nature of the Panzerwaffe's participation in the Norwegian campaign, the Germans learned some valuable lessons. The prototype heavy tanks were found to be suitable only for supporting infantry operations and never went into production. Indeed one proved so heavy it bogged down at a fjord crossing and had to be destroyed by army engineers – it was replaced with a sheet-steel mock-up in order to maintain the subterfuge. Experience in dealing with mountainous terrain was studied and put to good use when the panzers struck in the Balkans a year later.

The Allies, while slow to honour their pact with Poland, had devised a plan to counter the likely German assault on France. The plan, code-named Plan D after the River Dyle, was to advance into Belgium to meet the invading Germans there. It was based on two simple premises: an expectation that the Germans would attack along the lines of the famous von Schlieffen plan which had come within an ace of success in 1914 and that the Allied southern front was adequately covered by the supposedly impassable Ardennes forest and the Maginot line fortifications. A German attack across the plain of Flanders offered ready access to France's greatest prizes, Paris and the industrial region near the Belgian border. To counter this expected revival of Schlieffen, the Allied plan called for a wheel-like advance along the Belgian border to establish a defensive line along the rivers Dyle and Meuse. The overall objective of Plan D was to gain time, not outright victory. The Allies aimed for a battlefield deadlock until their own armament production got into full swing and they could then launch a massive offensive of their own in late 1940 or early 1941.

The French Seventh Army was allocated the bulk of motorised units as it was expected to advance along the coast, at the rim of the imaginary wheel, and hence had the farthest to travel. The ten motorised infantry divisions of the British Expeditionary Force (BEF) occupied the centre of the front with the French First Army, to their south. Corap's French Ninth Army was at the hub of the wheel and was composed of second-rate reservists and older troops. Their advance was to be the shortest as these troops were not up to the rigours of the long forced marches expected of their northern comrades.

Little or no consultation was taken with the Belgian military, as the Belgians, keen to maintain a neutral stance, did not want to provoke the Germans with overtly belligerent behaviour – an attitude hard to reconcile with the fact that all her defences, including the fortress of Eben Emael, pointed toward the Reich. As a result no common defence plan, central command or framework for co-operation was agreed on for use in the event of a German attack. This unhelpful Belgian attitude to their own allies hampered the successful prosecution of Plan D, as the twenty-two Belgian divisions would be badly missed if they were destroyed in the initial stages of a German attack.

The French for their part had invested a lot of money and effort in the Maginot Line, the series of underground fortifications built along the central part of her north-eastern frontier during the 1930s. These forts were the physical manifestation of the French static warfare mentality. It is often said that generals always expect the next war to be fought in the same way as the last one and in the case of the French, this was certainly true. They anticipated the battle ahead would be First World War, Mark II with a deadlock on the battlefield forcing both sides to dig into defensive positions like the trenches of 1914–18. They seemed to have forgotten that Napoleon had once said that the side that stays within its fortifications is beaten.

Each of the large forts was the equivalent of a two-storey building sunken into the ground with only the big guns on its roof visible. They were designed to be self-sufficient and indestructible, the larger ones capable of housing up to 1,000 defenders for a prolonged period. Some were interconnected by tunnels and the guns were given a good range of fire, even capable of firing at neighbouring forts if they fell into enemy hands. This impressive piece of engineering formed a formidable obstacle stretching along the French border from Luxembourg to Switzerland. However it must be stressed that large parts of the line were less well defended and consisted of minor secondary works.

There was only one problem with the Maginot Line: it was clearly in the wrong place. No invader of France had ever followed the route it defended – from the time of the Romans they had always come further north. The Germans had come through Belgium in the First World War and even the Allies expected them to do so again in the coming attack. Why then was the Maginot Line not extended as far as the Channel coast?

The main reasons were political. For one thing, building a defensive line between Belgium and France would mean abandoning the Belgians to their fate. If it had been built, it would have left the Belgians to fight the initial German advance alone, while the Allies stood by and watched the Belgian Army's inevitable destruction from behind their defensive walls. More importantly, Allied military thinking was based on the notion of advancing into Belgium to meet the Germans there, thus keeping the fighting off French soil altogether. There were also the peacetime considerations of the detrimental effect such a barrier would have on trade, industry and communications.

Once war broke out, the French did begin work on extending the defensive line to the sea, but it was much too late by then and it didn't take the panzers long to breach these flimsy westward extensions when they met them in May 1940. In the end the Maginot Line proved more of a propaganda success than a military one. One commentator later stated that the Maginot Line did prove a formidable barrier, not to the Germans but to 'French understanding of modern war'.[1]

In September 1939, Hitler had ordered his army to produce a plan for the conquest of France. The work was allocated to the planning staff of the OKH (Oberkommando das Heer – Army High Command) led by Generaloberst Franz Halder, Chief of the General Staff. The bureaucratic, pince-nez-wearing Halder, a typical product of the German General Staff, looked and behaved more like a pedantic schoolmaster than a soldier. This colourless functionary had no real faith in the possibility of a successful Western offensive, and aided (or hindered) by a 58-page memo from Hitler, the OKH under Halder's guidance produced an unambitious plan which bore some resemblance to the Schlieffen Plan of 1914, but fell far short of promising the quick and decisive victory Hitler needed in France.

The plan proposed a strong right hook across Holland and Belgium led by Generaloberst Fedor von Bock's Army Group B. Holland would be overrun by Armee-Abteilung N (an army detachment – this was a small army made up of two or three army corps) while the three armies under von Bock were expected to engage and defeat the Allied armies in Belgium somewhere in the region of Liege. For this task Bock's Army Group was to receive eight of the ten panzer divisions and over half of the available forces in the West. At the same time Army Group A under Generaloberst Gerd von Rundstedt was to cover the southern flank of these operations using two armies and a single panzer division, but with little hope of getting much farther than the Meuse. Army Group C, commanded by Generaloberst Ritter von Leeb, was left to hold the Siegfried Line. Although the attack on Holland was repeatedly dropped and re-included over the coming months, the plan in essence remained the same.

Neither Hitler nor his army chiefs had any great faith in the 'Fall Gelb' (Case Yellow) plan. If the Germans failed to defeat the Allies outright in Belgium, all they could then hope for was to push them back to the Somme, at the same time aiming to seize as much of the Channel coast as possible for future operations by the Luftwaffe and Kriegsmarine. What was to happen after that was unclear, but it looked as if the battle would then settle into a protracted First World War style war of attrition, which the Germans knew from experience they couldn't win. Victory had to be quick if war in the West was to be viable.

The launch of Fall Gelb was postponed nearly thirty times, generally caused by poor weather prospects, but one wonders how much Hitler's basic dislike of the plan influenced these postponements. In the months before the attack he constantly sought modifications and improvements. Finally a new and radical plan came to his attention and he enthusiastically adopted that instead.

In October 1939 the Fall Gelb plan fell into the hands of General von Manstein, now Chief of Staff to Army Group A under his old boss, von Rundstedt, and he wasn't at all impressed. Manstein, who had ably proven his own planning credentials during the Polish campaign, remarked in his memoirs that he felt deep disgust that the General Staff could do no better than try an old formula, and even then on a less ambitious scale: 'I found it humiliating, to say the least, that our generation could do nothing better than repeat an old recipe, even when this was the product of a man like Schlieffen.'[2] By the end of the month he had formulated an entirely different plan.

Manstein was of the opinion that what was required was a decisive result from the campaign, not merely grabbing as much of Belgium as possible – he wanted to defeat the Allies completely. The strategic surprise so obviously lacking in Fall Gelb could only be attained by attacking through the Ardennes. With these ideas in mind, he proposed a feint attack in the north through the Low Countries and Belgium, as the Allies no doubt expected, by Army Group B. The new *Schwerpunkt* would now however lie along the front of Army Group A, reinforced with an extra army and most of the armour. Army Group C would continue to harass the Maginot Line and man the Siegfried defence line. Once the Allies had been lured north into Belgium to meet the threat of Bock's armies, phase two would be set in train. Rundstedt's forces would strike out for the Meuse and once that obstacle was overcome, would thrust in the direction of the Channel coast, thus severing the Allies' communications and supply lines and trapping their best troops in a pocket.

Manstein conferred with Guderian when the tank expert's new command, the XIX Panzerkorps, was transferred to Army Group A on Hitler's order to conduct an attack south of Liege. Guderian assured him that the terrain through the Ardennes was not in fact tank proof as all serious military experts assumed. He had personal experience of the Ardennes and the Meuse river valley from the First World War and study of the maps did nothing to discourage his view. He therefore became an enthusiastic supporter of Manstein's plan, realising that the panzer divisions were the ideal force to deliver the surprise blow needed. Armed with this assurance, Manstein now attempted to get his plan adopted.

Although in essence events evolved as Manstein had foreseen, the real struggle for France was in getting the Supreme Command to accept his proposals. Manstein bombarded the OKH with a whole series of memoranda, all countersigned by von Rundstedt, but to no avail. Halder and the Army's weak-minded Commander-in-Chief, Generaloberst Walther von Brauchitsch, lacked the imagination to appreciate the subtle genius of the plan. Manstein's persistence eventually led to him being sidelined to command an obscure infantry corps, which later backfired on the arch plotter Halder and his vacillating Commander-in-Chief.

On 10 January 1940 German plans received a serious setback when a Luftflotte II liaison officer was forced to land his plane in Belgium during a storm. In strict contravention of standing orders, he carried a full set of plans detailing Fall Gelb. Despite his frantic efforts to destroy the documents, they were captured relatively intact and sent post haste to Paris and London. In any event, the Allied High Command chose to dismiss them as a deliberate plant and made no effort to change their dispositions, but the Germans couldn't have known this and had to assume that the element of surprise was lost.

Only now were conditions ripe for the adoption of the Manstein plan. On 17 February Manstein and all other newly appointed corps commanders were summoned to meet Hitler for lunch. As they rose to leave, Hitler asked Manstein to remain and expound on his ideas for a thrust through the Ardennes. Manstein outlined his ideas succinctly, calling for a shift in emphasis to Army Group A, which would then attack across the Meuse towards the lower Somme, while Army Group B attacked the Allies frontally in Belgium. Once Army Group A reached the Channel coast, the Allied forces would then be surrounded and destroyed. He argued that for this Rundstedt now needed three armies: one to intercept the Allied forces driven back by Bock; a second to cross the Meuse at Sedan and destroy any French forces massing for a counter attack and a third to cover the southern flank of the Group. He also insisted that Guderian's XIX Panzerkorps was insufficient to force the Meuse crossings and demanded the motorised infantry of Wietersheim's XIV Armeekorps to reinforce them.

Hitler was attracted to his proposals for three reasons. Firstly, they were audacious and appealed to Hitler's liking for the unorthodox; secondly they tied in with his earlier calls for an attack south of Liege; and thirdly they were in complete contrast to the proposals of the hated General Staff. Whatever his shortcomings as a warlord, Hitler can never be accused of lacking imagination and a taste for novel schemes. Manstein himself received precious little credit for his masterstroke; he was to command a mere infantry corps in the second wave of the attack while Hitler later claimed the idea for the plan as his own.

On 20 February Manstein's Sichelschnitt (Sickle Cut) was officially adopted, although not without much opposition from within the High Command. The pedantic Halder declared the plan 'senseless' and wanted the panzers to wait on the Meuse till the infantry and artillery caught up for what he called 'a properly marshaled attack in mass.'[3]

Guderian was violently opposed to this. The vain and ambitious General Bock, appalled at the erosion of his Army Group, developed an irrational jealousy of Rundstedt that was to have dire consequences for the entire Wehrmacht within eighteen months. Even Rundstedt seemed doubtful that his Army Group could carry out its task and uncertain about the capabilities of tanks. In fact there was so little enthusiasm for the plan among the High Command that Guderian states in his memoirs that only three people believed it would actually work – himself, Manstein and Hitler.

On the eve of battle the German Army in the West comprised 136 divisions. These forces were opposed by 135 Allied divisions: 94 French, 10 British, 22 Belgian and 9 Dutch divisions. There was rough parity in the numbers of troops, about 2.5 million men each. The Germans were outnumbered however when it came to most important weapons: in field artillery pieces they had 2,500 versus the French's 10,000 and in tanks they fielded 2,600 to the French 4,000. The only place the Germans had superiority was in the air where they could pit 5,500 planes against the Allies' 3,100.

Of course as it turned out the tank was to be the crucial weapon in this campaign – not so much because of their quantity or quality, but because of the way they were handled. The BEF, though small, was entirely motorised and the French had a total of 7 armoured divisions; these were the 3 Divisions Légères Mécaniques (DLMs), mechanised cavalry divisions which carried out the traditional roles of cavalry, and the 4 Divisions Cuirassées Rapides (DCRs) which acted as infantry support units. There were also 25 independent light tank battalions engaged in infantry support. In total 1,300 of France's tanks were concentrated within these armoured divisions, which were spread across the front in line with the fatal French reluctance to concentrate their armour.

The French main battle tanks included 300 massive Char B1 heavy tanks, bigger and better armoured than anything the Germans had and carrying two guns, a 47 mm in the turret and a low-velocity 75 mm in the body of the tank. They proved almost impossible to destroy and the Germans who encountered them dubbed them *Kolosse*; their only vulnerable point proved to be a small ventilation grill in the side – it took a steady and calm gunner to hit it at close range. The French were also able to field over 250 Somuas, widely regarded as the best tank in Europe at the time and the model for the American Sherman; like the Char B1, it mounted the superb 47 mm gun and at least 55 mm of armour. The French also had plenty of light tanks, including 800 Hotchkiss H35s or H39s, nearly 1,000 Renault R35s and about 2,500 of the tiny First World War vintage Renault FTs. All these light tanks were armed with 37 mm guns and mainly used for infantry support.

The Char B1 was the only French tank with four crewmen. The Somua had three, all the rest only two. This proved to be a major disadvantage, especially as many of the French tanks incorporated a one-man turret where the commander was expected to choose targets and then load, aim and fire the gun all by himself; in the German turrets there were three men to carry out these tasks. Also, very few of the French tanks had radios, making formations hard to control in battle.

The French Army had neglected higher formation staff training for tank officers such as was needed for handling several divisions at once. This was in keeping with their belief that tanks should function either as infantry support or in the traditional cavalry roles. The French had completely failed to grasp the possibilities offered by tanks deployed independently and in concentration, instead sticking to the tired old formula of 'penny packeting' their armour.

There was no armoured division in the BEF, but the British did have almost 450 tanks in France, including about 150 A10 and A13 Cruisers and 75 of the heavy A12 Mark II Matildas, which proved virtually impenetrable to the German PaKs (Panzerabwehrkanone – anti-tank guns) because of their 75 mm (3-inch) armour. All these tanks used the same high-velocity 2-pounder (40 mm) gun. The BEF also had around 200 Mark II machine-gun tanks.

The Germans had a total of 2,600 tanks available for the attack, but these were all organised into ten panzer divisions and not frittered away in penny packets like the Allied tanks. This was in keeping with Guderian's adage that 'You hit with your closed fist, not with your fingers spread.' Concentrated together for an attack en masse, tanks could punch a hole right through the enemy front and then keep going. Of this tank total, 525 were Pz Is armed only with machine-guns and 955 were Pz IIs mounting a weak 20 mm cannon. These obsolete light tanks were really only a match for the lightest Allied armour, such as

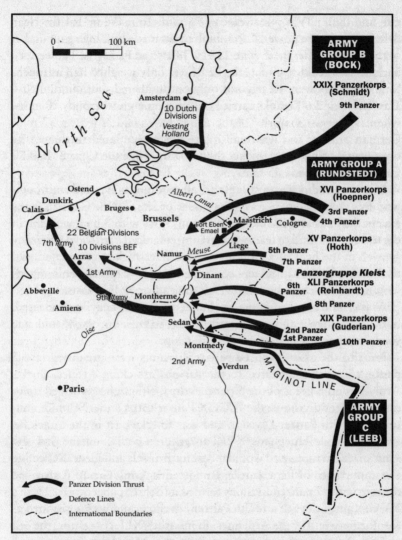

Sickle Cut – Blitzkrieg in the West, 10–15 May 1940

the Renault FT, but they did have the effect of terrorising infantry, who at that time had no adequate weapons for defending themselves against tanks.

Of the more modern German tanks, only 350 Pz IIIs and 280 Pz IVs were available for the attack on France. The Pz III carried a 37 mm gun and the Pz IV a poor velocity 75 mm. To make up for the clear deficiencies in gun power, Czech-built tanks made up a high proportion of the Panzerwaffe: there were 228 Pz 38(t)s and Pz 35(t)s. These tanks had the same calibre gun as the Pz III, yet only weighed half as much. So the panzers were clearly not only outnumbered, but outgunned – 1,500 of their 2,600 tanks carried only machine-guns or puny 20 mms, whereas the vast majority of the Allied tanks had at least a 37 mm. German armour too was inadequate when compared to that of its opponents, being never thicker than 30 mm while the Char Bs had 60 mm and the Somuas 55 mm.

One-way radio was available to all medium tanks and unit commanders possessed two-way sets to issue orders. All the German tanks except the Pz Is and IIs had 4- or 5-man crews with 3 men working in the turret. This kind of teamwork greatly enhanced battlefield efficiency as even in the heat of action no one felt overworked or isolated. On the battlefield the tanks were controlled by 135 Panzerbefehlswagens (command vehicles), built either on the Pz I or Pz II chassis.

As is clear from the figures, the Panzerwaffe was heavily outclassed, both qualitatively and quantitatively and so their success would ride solely on their men, tactics and leadership.

Prior to the assault the 10 panzer divisions were organised into 5 panzerkorps and allocated to the various attacking Armies. Bock's Army Group B got 2 of the 5 panzerkorps, although this added up to only 3 panzer divisions: the XXXIX Panzerkorps under Schmidt contained the 9th Panzer Division and was to take part in the attack on Holland, while Hoepner's XVI Panzerkorps contained the 3rd and 4th Panzer Divisions and would thrust for Brussels and Liege. Reflecting the importance of its new role, Rundstedt's Army Group A received the remaining 7 panzer divisions formed into three panzerkorps. Hoth's XV contained the 5th and 7th Panzer Divisions and was positioned at the northern end of the Ardennes. Reinhardt's XLI, containing the 6th and 8th Panzer Divisions, took up the centre. Most hopes were pinned on Guderian's XIX which was positioned at the southern end of the Ardennes and was made up of the 1st, 2nd and 10th Panzer Divisions as well as the crack motorised infantry regiment, Gross Deutschland.

Guderian's Panzerkorps and Reinhardt's Panzerkorps were both placed under the command of Panzergruppe Kleist, along with General Gustav Wietersheim's XIV Armeekorps, which contained 3 motorised infantry divisions. This Panzergruppe had 1,200 tanks, including the largest share of Pz IIIs and IVs and the first Schutzenwagens (armoured half-tracks for carrying infantry), and formed part of Generaloberst List's Twelfth Army. General der Kavalerie Ewald von Kleist, an efficient but cautious officer, had commanded a Panzerkorps in Poland, but as an old cavalryman was not known as a follower of the new school of tank theory. His appointment was made in an effort to reign in what the OKH saw as Guderian's impetuousness, an expectation Kleist certainly fulfilled during the campaign.

All in all, Rundstedt's Army Group A had 7 panzer divisions, 3 motorised infantry divisions and 35 ordinary infantry divisions, while farther north the reduced role of Bock's Army Group B meant that it had 3 panzer divisions, 1 motorised infantry division and 24 ordinary infantry divisions.

Early on the morning of 10 May 1940, Sitzkrieg gave way to Blitzkrieg. Late on the 9th the codeword 'Danzig' had been flashed to the German units waiting at the frontier and they had begun to move west, heading for Holland, Belgium and Luxembourg. At 0530 hrs the invasion of France began when Generalleutnant Guderian took the 1st Panzer Division across the Luxembourg border – the attack that had been postponed so many times was finally under way. To be close to the fighting, Hitler had moved to a new headquarters nearer the frontier, which he called 'Felsennest' (Eyrie).

Even though all the really significant events were happening in the south, for the first few days all eyes were on the north, just as the Germans had intended. The German attack in Holland and northern Belgium was likened by Liddell Hart to a matador's cloak, the intention of which was to dazzle the bull, or in this case the Anglo-French armies, so that they didn't see the real thrust coming.

First the Luftwaffe launched surprise raids on fifty Allied air bases. This was followed up on the 10th by Fallschirmjägers (paratroops) being dropped into Holland in a daring attack with the objective of capturing and holding the bridges on the Maas over which the 9th Panzer Division would move on its way to Rotterdam. They succeeded and by the 13th, Hubicki's panzers had reached the Dutch city. On the 11th, glider-borne Fallschirmjägers had landed on the roof of Eben Emael, the much-vaunted Belgian fortress near Maastricht, quickly putting it out of action. The road to Brussels and Antwerp was now open for Hoepner's XIV Panzerkorps.

Of course events in the north were just a feint, a mere side-show put on to persuade the Allies that this would be the *Schwerpunkt*, the point of main German effort. It worked brilliantly and the Anglo-French armies moved north to meet Army Group B, aided by the fact that the Luftwaffe purposefully didn't attack them on the way. Meanwhile the seven panzer divisions of Army Group A that had assembled on the Luxembourg frontier over the previous days were now threading their way through the Ardennes on their way to the Meuse, 70 miles away. The 1,500 tanks that made up the three panzerkorps stretched back one hundred miles from the frontier.

According to Oberst Günther von Blumentritt, Rundstedt's chief planner, the Germans saw the advance through the Ardennes as more of an approach march than an operation. Staff officers had had to put in a huge amount of preparatory work, poring over maps and aerial photos to make out what passable roads existed and then designating specific routes of advance for each division. Once they did get moving, effective traffic management was essential to keep the armoured train moving smoothly and quickly on the steep, narrow and winding roads. Despite all the planning, inevitably there were traffic jams, delays and stoppages, one of which lasted a whole day and was only sorted out when an officer went up in a plane to act as an aerial traffic warden.

But contrary to Allied expectations, the Ardennes, while steeply hilled, densely wooded and serviced by only a few narrow roads, was far from impassable as the panzers were quickly proving. Following on after the panzers came the three motorised infantry divisions under General von Wietersheim and thirty-five ordinary infantry divisions, the latter marching cross country in order to leave the few roads solely to the vehicles. Eighty battalions of motorised infantry took part in the invasion, yet only two of these were equipped with the newly-built 251 half-tracks, all the rest travelling by truck. The infantry were also supported by four 6-gun Stug batteries.

For the purpose of movement the panzerkorps were divided into three layers, the first two made up of armour, the third of motorised infantry. It must have been quite a sight to behold, this cavalcade of tanks trundling through the scenic countryside, followed up by the ganglia of supply in lorries and horse-drawn wagons, and flanked on either side of the road by grey-clad infantry marching through the woods. Allied pilots did spot the armoured columns and reported them to their superiors, but inexplicably were given no orders to attack.

As they had expected, the Germans met very little resistance as they travelled through the Ardennes, easily brushing aside the weak opposition of the Belgian Chasseurs Ardennais and two French cavalry divisions. The panzers moved with all possible speed, because the whole plan pivoted on their getting across the Meuse before the Allies realised what was going on. The defenders had mined, blocked or demolished many of the approach roads, but while these caused some delay to the onrushing tanks, they failed to hold them up for very long.

In those early days Guderian's greatest fear was not of enemy attacks on the ground, but from the air. He knew that bottled in as tightly as they were, with their movements channelled by the few available roads, the armoured columns were extremely vulnerable to air attack. But no air attacks came in those early days and didn't begin until the Germans had already reached the Meuse; by then the planes were already too late and suffered heavy losses as a result. Still the Allies had not realised that this German armoured thrust in the south was the *Schwerpunkt* of their whole attack and represented a deadly danger to their armies in the north.

Despite the clear lack of opposition, the natural caution of Guderian's commander, von Kleist, asserted itself on the 11th when he ordered that the 10th Panzer Division change its direction so as to meet a reported force of French cavalry. Guderian, unwilling to dilute his forces by one third just to meet a hypothetical threat, ignored the order. The French cavalry never appeared, but this was just the first of many halt orders Guderian was to face along the way.

By the evening of the 12th, the three panzerkorps were ranged along the eastern bank of the Meuse on a 64-km (40-mile) front stretching from Dinant to Sedan. They were surprised to discover how relatively feeble the French Meuse defences were, having expected extensive field fortifications bristling with heavy artillery and well manned by troops. On paper indeed the Meuse looked well defended, with 150,000 troops housed in concrete blockhouses along a 150-km (95-mile) front. But in reality these defenders were inferior troops of poor fighting quality, consisting mainly of elderly reservists and soldiers unfit for more active service, all the better divisions having been sent north to meet the

German threat there. Those left behind lacked modern weaponry, in particular anti-tank and anti-aircraft guns.

The weakness of the Meuse defences meant that the panzers would be able to start crossing the river almost straightaway instead of having to wait for the infantry corps to come up and launch an attack; this could have taken as long as a week, a pause that the French were counting on and during which time they could have brought up reinforcements.

By the evening of the 12th, Guderian's Panzerkorps had reached the Meuse valley and captured Sedan, scene of another French military disaster in 1870 when they were roundly beaten by the Prussians. Now another Prussian was on the verge of inflicting a second painful defeat. Guderian and his trusty Chief of Staff, Nehring, set up their headquarters in a nearby hotel, but were soon forced to abandon it when an enemy air attack brought a stuffed boar's head mounted on the wall crashing down within inches of the shaken Corps Commander.

Kleist ordered him to attempt to cross the river with his panzer divisions the next day. Guderian now altered and reissued orders from war games at Koblenz so as to minimise delay and the night preceding the attack was spent in bringing the artillery into position. The Germans had practised river crossings with tanks on the Moselle in Germany, but not while under hostile fire. No one really knew what to expect the next day, but the whole operation pivoted on the panzers getting across the river quickly.

At 1600 hrs on the 13th the Germans opened up on the defenders with artillery and Guderian positioned his Pz IVs and 88 mms so as to fire directly into the French concrete blockhouses that dominated the heights on the other side of the river. Then he called in waves of Stuka dive-bombers to terrorise the defenders. Guderian had requested the commander of the Luftwaffe's Third Airflotte to launch continual attacks for the entire duration of the Meuse crossing, rather than just a large, one-off attack, thus giving the attackers continual air support while keeping the defenders' heads down. As a result, twelve squadrons of dive-bombers were used in the Sedan sector and they continued to fly missions all that crucial day. In this way, aircraft took on the role more traditionally filled by artillery.

Meanwhile the panzer divisions' engineers laboured to build pontoon bridges. Guderian went to the crossing place of the 1st Panzer Division and crossed the river himself in an assault boat. On the opposite bank he met Oberstleutnant Hermann Balck, commander of a Schutzenregiment (rifle regiment), who greeted him with the words: 'Joy riding in canoes on the Meuse is forbidden!'[4] echoing Guderian's own words during a practice run on the Moselle. Balck and his men had formed the first German bridgehead across the Meuse, crossing the river in rubber boats under cover of the air attack and seizing enough ground to allow the engineers to begin building a pontoon bridge for the tanks.

Balck, like Guderian, was a Prussian with proud military antecedents. He had distinguished himself in the First World War as a company commander on the Western and Eastern fronts, winning the Iron Cross First Class and being wounded seven times. Retained in the Reichswehr after the war, he had twice turned down appointments to the General Staff, preferring to remain as a front-line officer. During the Polish campaign he'd been responsible for refitting and reorganising the panzer divisions and was to prove an inspired panzer commander himself.

Elements of the Gross Deutschland (GD) Regiment, the most pre-stigious unit in the German Army, crossed the river and headed for the Marfee Heights, a commanding position held by the French. Guderian's attack was aimed specifically at the junction of two French armies, the Ninth and the Second, always the weakest point in any defensive line. The morale of these garrison troops soon collapsed under the continual bombardment. The French 55th Infantry Division was routed and went into headlong retreat, telling stories of thousands of German tanks, even though Guderian's panzers hadn't even crossed the Meuse yet. So far the tank was having more effect on morale than it was actually having as an offensive weapon.

The 7th Panzer, one of the two armoured divisions in Hoth's Panzerkorps, had been able to skirt much of the forest and reached the river near Dinant on the afternoon of the 12th, finding when they got there that the retreating French cavalry had blown up all the bridges. The commander of the 7th was an obscure 48-year-old Generalmajor who was later to become very famous: Erwin Rommel. An ambitious and tough Swabian from a modest, non-military background, he had won Imperial Germany's highest award, the Pour le Mérite, for his exploits as an infantry commander at Caporetto in the First World War. The textbook he wrote based on these experiences, *Infanterie Grieft An* (Infantry Attacks) so caught Hitler's eye that he made

Rommel commander of his bodyguard battalion during the Polish campaign. As a reward, Hitler had granted Rommel one of the much-desired panzer commands for the coming campaign in the west.

Although he'd been an ardent infantryman all his career and had only taken over the panzer division the previous February, Rommel had extensively drilled and exercised his new division in the months leading up to the attack and had mastered all the necessary techniques. During the battle of France he was to prove a natural tank commander. His was one of the 4 panzer divisions created during the winter of 1939 by the conversion of the 'light divisions'; it had a complement of about 220 tanks, half of them Czech-built.

By the 12th Rommel was on the bank of the Meuse, personally directing the building of a pontoon bridge. Small-arms fire from the defenders on the opposite bank was proving dangerous so he gave orders that they be plastered with fire and nearby houses set alight to provide a smokescreen. He then crossed the river himself in a rubber boat and personally led a battalion assault. When French tanks attacked, Rommel and his men drove them off with small arms and flare pistols. He was to continue to show reckless courage and disregard for enemy fire throughout the campaign, just as he had in the First World War; both Rommel's adjutant and a battalion commander were to be killed by gunfire while standing next to him, events which added to his aura of invincibility.

Early on the 13th, some of his motorcyclists crossed the river via a stone weir and put the French defenders to flight. Then on the 14th, using a cable ferry and the bridge he'd built, Rommel began moving tanks over the Meuse, under the protective guns of a few Pz IVs. At least one tank went to the bottom of the river, but by the day's end thirty were across. That same day, Rommel got into trouble when his command tank came under heavy fire and crashed down a slope within easy range of the enemy. He quickly abandoned the Pz III, bleeding profusely from a facial wound caused by a shell splinter hitting the tank's periscope. On the 15th, Rommel's 7th Panzer Division began to thrust west, bypassing the French defenders, and on the first day covered 48 km (30 miles).

Rommel was to successfully employ several unorthodox techniques during his advance west. For one he indicated the route of his advance with 'DG7' signs marking all the relevant roads so that slow and straggling units could catch up with the vanguard, even though this was strictly prohibited by the High Command. He also ordered his panzers to fire while on the move, even when there was nothing to fire at, another activity frowned on by his superiors, but as Rommel had observed, 'the day goes to the side that is the first to plaster its opponent with fire'.[5] Sometimes he even chose to continue the advance at night, a risky activity, but one which paid off.

Rommel had instinctively grasped the techniques of tank warfare and the new demands it made on a commander. He realised that the Divisional Commander's place was not back in his HQ miles from the front, but at the head of his troops, giving direct orders on the ground. As a result he rarely saw his divisional staff, who sat in HQ far in the rear, wondering where their commander was and getting the odd radio message from him. To simplify radio traffic he agreed a 'line of thrust' with his operations officer and artillery commander, which they then marked on their maps. This made it easier to specify any particular location along the route of advance.

Reinhardt's Panzerkorps had fared less well than its neighbours. The approach roads of the 6th and 8th Panzer Divisions were extremely narrow and twisting, causing massive traffic jams, and the troops had met particularly fierce enemy resistance which held them up for three days. On the 13th, some of Reinhardt's riflemen reached the river at Montherme and tried to cross. However they ran into withering fire from the defenders and there was no hope of getting tanks across, at least for the time being.

By the afternoon of the 14th, Guderian's three panzer divisions were across the Meuse (the following infantry corps didn't reach there till the 15th). That same day the Allied air forces launched a heavy attack on his bridge, but the German flak brought down over 100 planes and the crucial bridge stayed standing. Now the broad, flat plain of northern France beckoned, ideal tank country that led directly to the Channel, 150 miles away. Guderian took the 1st and 2nd Panzer Divisions and headed west, leaving the 10th Panzer Division and the GD Regiment behind to guard his flank. By nightfall they had crossed the Ardennes canal and opened up a bridgehead 10 miles deep.

On that same night, the commander of the French Ninth Army, General Corap, alarmed by the breakthroughs achieved by Guderian and Rommel, gave orders that the Meuse be abandoned and the defenders withdrawn to a line farther west – a retreat which soon degenerated into a general rout. On the 15th Guderian had intercepted an order from the French Commander-in-Chief, Gamelin, which declared melodramatically 'The torrent of German tanks must finally be stopped!'[6], although at this stage the torrent was still only a trickle. Yet that same night Kleist tried to get Guderian to halt again so as to consolidate the bridgehead. Guderian would have none of it and a heated discussion ensued. Eventually Kleist permitted him to advance for another twenty-four hours and 'Hurrying Heinz' made the most of it, advancing a full 80 km (50 miles) farther west.

Reinhardt's Panzerkorps was still on the wrong side of the river by 15 May, bottled up in a Gordian knot of a traffic jam and pinned down by the French defenders. Fortunately for Reinhardt, the French Ninth Army began to withdraw and so early on the 15th the 6th Panzer Division broke through the French bunker line at Montherme and put the remaining defenders to flight. Eager to catch up with the other panzer divisions, it ploughed on west, covering a record-breaking distance in one day. On the way it overran and destroyed most of the disorganised French 2nd DCR Armoured Division, which had become cut off from its supply and technical support echelons, and scattered the remnants over 40 km (25 miles).

At this stage all three panzerkorps were racing side by side through the plain of northern France in a 65 km (40 mile) wide 'panzer corridor', Guderian having crossed the Meuse at Sedan, Hoth at Dinant and Reinhardt at Montherme. After clearing the water obstacle and breaking through the western extension of the Maginot Line swiftly and relatively painlessly, the seven panzer divisions now seemed to have an unstoppable momentum. The French defenders in their way, Corap's Ninth Army, were in full retreat and the Germans were to meet no really significant opposition in their race for the Channel. What little resistance they did meet on the way was spasmodic, weak and uncoordinated. When the panzers ran out of fuel, they filled up at French roadside petrol stations or were airdropped fuel by the Luftwaffe.

The French contemplated counter attacks, but trapped in a static warfare mindset, kept postponing them in the belief that the Germans would adhere to as sluggish a timetable as their own. That the German tanks crossed the river without waiting for several days for their artillery and infantry to catch up had come as a terrible shock to the French –

this was just not the done thing in their book of warfare. But their book was out of date, having been written in the trenches of the First World War. This was a new kind of war and the Germans were calculating their timetables by a new measure of speed – that of the tank, not the infantryman.

Again on the 17th, the Panzergruppe commander, General von Kleist, tried to put the brakes on Guderian, ordering him to halt his advance so that Wietersheim's motorised infantry could catch up. A furious Guderian, living up to his nickname 'Brausewetter', offered his resignation. Rundstedt sent the commander of the Twelfth Army, General Wilhelm von List, to mediate. It was pointed out to Guderian that the order came directly from the OKW (Oberkommando der Wehrmacht – Armed Forces High Command) where Hitler himself was worried about the vulnerability of the armoured columns as they raced west, leaving their flanks wide open and their reinforcements far behind. He feared a French counterstroke could sever the armour from its supplies and communications. Although Hitler had completely endorsed the Manstein Plan, including Guderian's proposed deep penetration by armour, he was now getting alarmed by its very success.

Guderian argued that the objective of Blitzkrieg was to reinforce success and so in line with his own maxim, *'Klotzen, nicht Kleckern'* ('Boot 'em, don't spatter 'em'), the panzers should continue to push west in concentration and at full speed, making the most of their early advantage. Knowing the French still embraced the outdated doctrine of positional warfare, he didn't believe they would attack until they knew his exact location, so the best thing was to keep moving. Guderian also knew that if the wedge driven by the panzers was deep and wide enough, they wouldn't have to worry about their flanks at all.

A compromise was reached by which Guderian was allowed a 'reconnaissance in force' which he interpreted as a continuation of the headlong dash west, while the motorised infantry would stay behind and hold Sedan. To prevent being issued any more senseless halt orders, Guderian laid down a telephone cable between him and his advance HQ, so the OKH could no longer fix his exact position by radio intercept. To his troops he sent: 'Fahrkarte bis zur Endstation!' (ticket to the last station), by which he meant keep going till the final objective is reached, in this case the Channel.

Now the French armoured divisions were thrown into the battle, but to little effect. The three DLMs had been sent into Belgium and were so badly mauled by Hoepner's XVI Panzerkorps that they had no more impact on the campaign. The four DCR's now entered the fray. Reinhardt's panzers had already smashed the French 2nd Armoured Division during its breakout from Montherme. Now early on the morning of the 15th, Rommel's 7th Panzer, along with the 5th Panzer Division fell upon the French 1st Armoured Division while it was still refuelling. By the evening the French were in full retreat, having lost 90 per cent of their tanks. Rommel continued his thrust westwards, leaving the 5th Panzer to finish off the French armour.

The French 3rd Armoured Division had been formed only six weeks before and was equipped with Hotchkiss H39 tanks with high-velocity 40 mm guns, as good as anything the Germans had. Ordered to Sedan on 12 May, it didn't get there until the 14th and then instead of counterattacking Guderian's very exposed flank, it formed itself into a 13-km (8-mile) defensive line of static pillboxes in what it called a 'defensive success'.

That left just the 4th Armoured Division, so new that its units were still only forming. It was commanded by France's leading tank expert, Colonel Charles de Gaulle, and was a rag-tag formation cobbled together from all the remaining armour the French could lay their hands on. Ironically de Gaulle was now moving towards the more professional army he'd written of in the 1930s. Badly mauled by the Luftwaffe while still assembling, the Division attacked near Marle on 17 May but was quickly brushed aside – Guderian didn't even bother reporting the incident back to headquarters. Yet this minor skirmish bulked large in post-war Gaullist propaganda.

So much for the French armour. Despite strong tank complements and some high-quality tank models, the French armoured divisions were disorganised, badly supplied, ineptly led and totally squandered in battle. In particular they lacked radio communication, infantry and supporting arms and seemed to be permanently short of fuel.

All this time Rommel's 7th Panzer were advancing well, from crossing the river at Dinant on the 13th to reaching Cambrai, scene of the first major tank battle of the First World War, on the 18th. The division was travelling too fast to take prisoner the huge numbers of French troops who were surrendering to them all along the way, although one French lieutenant colonel they encountered showed more fighting spirit; according to Rommel 'his eyes glowed hate and impotent fury and he gave the impression of being a thoroughly fanatical type'. Three times he curtly refused to accompany the Germans and so 'there was nothing for it but to shoot him'.[7] Once they reached Cambrai, Rommel's Division and the neighbouring 5th Panzer were ordered to stay there and protect the northern flank of Guderian and Reinhardt's Panzerkorps while the infantry caught up.

Three days after the meeting with List, Guderian's panzers had crossed the Somme and went on to take Amiens on the 18th and Abbeville on the 20th. A battalion from the 2nd Panzer Division travelled on to Noyelles and so became the first German unit to reach the Atlantic. The day before Weygand had replaced Gamelin as Commander-in-Chief, illustrating the state of crisis in the French military. It had taken the panzers just ten days to reach the sea, thus encircling a million Allied soldiers in the north – Guderian had ably proven his own maxim that the tank's engine was as important a weapon as its gun. The pocket – pressed from the east by Bock's Army Group B and flanked in the south by the panzers of Army Group A – contained nine British and forty-five French divisions as well as the entire Belgian Army. The trap had been successfully sprung. Now the second phase of Sichelschnitt was set to begin – that of destroying the enemy forces trapped in the pocket.

Meanwhile the British decided to counter-attack the long exposed flank of the German armoured thrusts. They assembled a motley collection of units including two infantry battalions, some field artillery and a tank brigade containing 16 Mk II Matildas armed with 2-pounders (40 mm) and 58 Mk Is armed with machine-guns; the French supplied 60 Somuas, the remnants of a light mechanised division. But the counter-attacking force was hampered from the start by a lack of maps and inadequate radio communication. It also lacked sufficient infantry and artillery support and had no air support at all. The British commander also made the elementary mistake of splitting his forces, deploying them into two separate columns with little communication between them.

Despite all these disadvantages, the force acquitted itself well in battle. On the afternoon of 21 May it attacked southward near Arras, clashing first with the motorised infantry of Rommel's 7th Panzer which was just preparing to move out. The Germans soon discovered that their 37 mm anti-tank guns were useless against the 3-inch armour of the Matildas and so had to send in their own tanks. The SS motorised infantry division, Totenkopf, which Himmler had recruited from the ranks of concentration camp guards, took fright and fled. Meanwhile Rommel brought 88 mm anti-aircraft guns to bear against the British tanks, personally directing the firing. After forty-eight hours, the doughty British withdrew, by which time they had lost nearly half of their tanks, but had inflicted about 400 dead and wounded on the Germans. Rundstedt later commented that none of the French counter-attacks carried as serious a threat as this one did.

Despite its failure, the Arras counter-attack bought time for the Allied divisions in the north by delaying the German advance. It also spooked the normally unflappable Rommel who reported he'd been attacked by 'five enemy divisions' and 'hundreds of tanks'. This in turn alarmed the OKW, who ordered Rommel to halt his division for rest and repairs. For a while the Germans feared the attack was the long-anticipated Allied counterstroke. Arras does show what a determined, well-led and properly supported Allied attack could have achieved even at that late stage, especially given the inadequacy of the German anti-tank weapons and the length of their exposed flank.

But it was soon too late for the Allies in the north to do anything. While the Arras fighting had been going on, Guderian had captured Boulogne on the 23rd and was heading for Calais. Dunkirk was now the only port left from which the BEF could be evacuated and the panzers would soon reach that too, cutting off their last hope of escape. Then on the 24th there came an event which was to have a major influence on the whole course of the war: Rundstedt ordered Guderian to halt temporarily so that the motorised infantry could catch up, whereupon Hitler stepped in, extending the order for three crucial days. The panzer divisions were told not to advance beyond the canal and that Dunkirk was to be left to the Luftwaffe, a decision Guderian attributed to Goering's vanity.

Halder noted in his diary that as the panzers approached Dunkirk, Hitler grew more and more nervous and inclined to 'pull the reins'. The Führer couldn't believe the operation really had been as successful as it seemed to be and kept anticipating a massive French counter-attack, which of course never came. Originally the panzers were to be the fast-moving hammer that would smash the Allied armies on the anvil of Bock's stationary armies, but the German attack now lost its velocity, with the panzers standing idly by for nearly three days, despite all their protests, as the BEF was busy being evacuated. After the war, von Thoma echoed the sentiments of most of the panzer officers present at Dunkirk when he angrily declared that Hitler had thrown away the chance of victory.

Debate has raged since about Hitler's controversial halt order at Dunkirk with various explanations put forward. One is that Hitler wanted to preserve the armour for the coming battles in the south; already Kleist's Panzergruppe had lost half of its tanks and the built-up areas around the port were bound to be costly for armour. Also Hitler was reluctant to send tanks into what he called 'the Flanders marshes' surrounding the port, claiming the terrain to be unsuitable for tanks, although panzer generals on the ground foresaw no great difficulty there. Goering, hungry for glory for his own arm, had given Hitler his personal guarantee that the Luftwaffe could destroy the Allied armies in the pocket all on their own. This boast proved impossible to fulfil, just as two years later when the Reichsmarshal promised to supply Stalingrad from the air, but as a top Nazi he held more sway over Hitler then did any of the panzer generals.

Another motive sometimes put forward is a political one: that Hitler had a grudging respect and admiration for Britain and so wanted to spare her honour for what he believed were the inevitable surrender negotiations by leaving her army intact. Whatever his motives were, the result of Hitler's halt order was that 340,000 Allies were successfully evacuated by sea between 28 May and 3 June, including the bulk of the BEF, although minus most of their equipment. It is also almost certain that if the panzers had been allowed to advance, very few Allied soldiers would have left Dunkirk beach. Of course at the time no one could have foreseen just how successful the evacuation would be. Just a few days after its completion Hitler himself conceded to Kleist that the halt order might have been a mistake, but asserted that the British would play no more part in the war.

The capitulation of the Belgians on the 28th opened up a 30-km (20-mile) hole in the British northern flank. Bock's ordinary infantry made for the gap with all possible speed, but they were too slow to get there before the hole was plugged by two British motorised divisions;

the Allies now had formed a strong defensive ring around the port of Dunkirk. The armour was moving again by 27 May, but against increasing resistance and in worsening conditions for tanks. Guderian's Panzerkorps found it hard going and so was withdrawn on the 29th for refitting, on Guderian's own suggestion. The Germans had little time for recriminations about the halt order, as there was still a lot of fighting ahead in the south.

The second phase of the attack was 'Fall Rot', the final conquest of France. After events in the north had seen 60 of the best Allied divisions beaten, it was largely a fait accompli anyway. The French were in a hopeless situation, having lost one-third of their army and with only 50 second-rate divisions left, barely 200 tanks and no air force with which to defend a front longer than the original one. As well as this, the French political and military command was in complete turmoil, with neither the will nor the ability to prolong the struggle for very long.

The campaign that followed proved to be of a much more conventional and traditional type than the radical Fall Gelb. It saw a reversion to the tried and trusted German technique of 'Kesselschlachten' (small encirclements) and greater involvement by ordinary infantry. The German forces redeployed swiftly along a 400-km (250-mile) front stretching from the English Channel to the Maginot Line and then began to push south. Guderian, as reward for his successful Channel dash, was given a new command, Panzergruppe Guderian, containing two panzerkorps, each one consisting of two panzer divisions and a motorised infantry division. These panzergruppen were armies in all but name, but were denied army status so as to maintain the traditional status quo and to keep the panzermen in their place. Guderian ordered a large white letter G painted on all his vehicles for identification purposes.

'Fall Rot' began on 5 June when the Germans attacked along the Somme and the Aisne and saw a few days hard fighting before the French defensive line was breached. But once it was, the Germans met less and less resistance as they moved south. The armour carved its way through France, leaving the defenders isolated in defensive pockets, which the infantry then finished off. On 14 June the Germans entered Paris, but it was not the vital objective it had been in the First World War. On that same day the Germans attacked the much-vaunted

Maginot Line, but from the rear, the kind of attack its designers had never anticipated. It was quickly breached, this outdated relic of static warfare in which the French had reposed so much hope and money, although 22,000 defenders held on impotently within its walls until 1 July.

From the 16th on, there was a general collapse of the French front. Marshal Pétain formed a cabinet and appealed for armistice terms. By 17 June, Guderian's 52nd birthday, his Panzergruppe had reached the Swiss border. In an impressive military manoeuvre the previous day, he had ordered two of his panzer divisions to make a 90-degree turn in a north-easterly direction into Alsace, thus encircling the 400,000 men of the eastern French armies. It was the kind of feat for which Montgomery and Patton would be 'acclaimed to the rooftops' in years to come, but which was merely routine to Guderian. Speaking of those famed Allied tank commanders, Guderian's biographer Kenneth Macksey wrote, 'It was to another that tribute should have been made for designing the methods which made their triumphs possible.'[8]

When Guderian first radioed the OKW to report his position on the Swiss border, Hitler radioed back: 'Your signal based on an error. Assume you mean Pontailler-sur-Saone,' unable to believe that Guderian had covered as much ground as he said he had. Guderian replied: 'No error. Am myself in Portarlier on Swiss border.'[9] In less than two weeks his Panzergruppe had captured 250,000 prisoners and a massive amount of enemy equipment. Guderian was now a hero back home in Germany and Goebbels persuaded the reluctant tankman to make a radio broadcast to the nation. Campaign films taken at the time were later turned into a documentary extolling Guderian and his Panzertruppen.

The campaign also brought more glory for Rommel. On 5 June he'd crossed the Somme, a decisive stroke which accelerated the French collapse, and had reached the sea near Dieppe on the 10th – his panzer regiment commander crashed through the sea wall in a Pz IV and drove down the beach until the waves were lapping around the tank's tracks. Rommel sent a laconic message back to the OKW: 'Am at sea.'

Rommel's panzers were the first German unit to cross the Seine and went on to cover 150 km (90 miles) in just four days. On 12 June St Valery fell to Rommel along with 40,000 Allied prisoners, the prisoners including 11 British generals and a French corps commander. Rommel's campaign ended on the 19th when he took the fortress of Cherbourg.

The total number of prisoners captured by the 7th Panzer was almost 100,000 and the Division had destroyed or captured a massive amount of enemy equipment, for a loss of just 42 of its own 220 tanks. The French campaign had made Rommel a legend and earned the 7th Panzer a nickname: 'The Ghost Division.'

On 22 June the French signed an armistice with Germany in the same railway carriage that had been used for the 1918 armistice. The panzers had pulled off a startling victory, but not without high cost to the Germans: 27,000 killed, over 100,000 wounded and 18,000 missing. The two newest weapons, the Panzerwaffe and the Luftwaffe, had suffered the heaviest casualties. Half of the tanks were out of action, either for good or until repaired. These figures prove that Blitzkrieg, while swift, was far from bloodless and also illustrate the fact that the campaign in France was no pushover for the Germans. Of course the losses they inflicted on the Allies were even higher: 100,000 dead, 250,000 wounded and 2 million either captured or missing. The tank had finally achieved its true potential.

The lightning victory won by the Wehrmacht can be attributed to an innovative plan – sublimely executed – combined with an enemy who was not so much incompetent as outmoded. The senior Allied commanders, and indeed many German staff officers like Halder, took it for granted that any war in the West must inevitably develop once more into static warfare. Such officers generally belonged to the older arms of service and believed that the defensive had finally overcome the offensive. They considered that modern artillery, with its creeping barrages timed and measured to fractions, machine-guns and pistols, gas, barbed wire and mines had all banished the infantryman from the attack.

They were partly right of course, but they failed to realise that the tank could be the new vehicle of assault. Everyone feared a return to the senseless slaughter of the Somme, but only one man, Manstein, had the vision to look for alternatives. Only one man, Guderian, had the expertise to execute that plan and only one man, Hitler, had the will to set it in train. The only believers in the Manstein plan were the same men who brought it success.

In short the Blitzkrieg in the West was proof that ingenuity, resourcefulness and audacity can sometimes be as decisive as firepower. The Germans' opponents had failed to counteract the threat of

Sichelschnitt because its unorthodox brilliance and speed was anathema to their concept of waging war. They believed that the pace of battle was dictated by the speed of marching infantry and the time needed to assemble vast supply dumps. The Allies were convinced that all they had to do was to hold out and eventually a resource-starved Germany would collapse, just as in the First World War. But in Hitler they encountered an enemy who had grasped that war can be a continuation of economics by other means. He realised Germany couldn't hope to win a trial of brute strength against the Allies, especially under the constant threat that the Russian Bear might pounce, and instead he leapt at the opportunity to strike a decisive blow.

The operation had carried grave operational risks, but the front-line commanders assessed correctly that the Allied command wasn't capable of carrying out the necessary countermoves. The Arras counter-attack showed what could have been achieved had the Allies been a little more flexible and a little less prone to farming out their armour in penny packets.

Blitzkrieg was never successful again. Ironically, its very success meant it couldn't work a second time. The vanquished assimilated its bitter lessons and began to develop tank forces of their own along the lines of the Panzerwaffe. The victory had been partly spoiled by Hitler's short-sightedness in halting the Panzers from cutting off the BEF at Dunkirk, yet paradoxically his support had allowed them to be in a position to overcome the world's best-equipped army in just six weeks. Hitler's flaws as a warlord were to become more and more evident as the war progressed.

The victory in France had one overwhelmingly negative effect: Hitler, claiming the operation as his own brainchild and feeling vindicated in his belief that he knew more than his generals, was now convinced that he was the greatest military genius of all time. As such he now took an even keener interest in the running of his armed forces, and in particular the Panzerwaffe. His patronage had brought them to their zenith and now his interference would lead to their nadir.

CHAPTER FOUR

The Greatest Gamble

When Barbarossa begins, the world will hold its breath!

Hitler during OKW planning conference,
February 1941

Now that Germany's frontier in the West was secure and with the British posing no threat to the Continent, Hitler felt able to look to the East. Ever the shrewd politician, he had managed to cajole Hungary, Romania and Bulgaria into alliances of various sorts with the Third Reich. Yugoslavia too, with its pro-Nazi King, seemed a safe bet to cover his southern flank and protect the Romanian Ploesti oilfields. However the Führer hadn't bargained for the actions of his closest ally, Mussolini. Miffed because Hitler had added Romania to Germany's sphere of interest without consulting him, the Italian Duce decided, in a fit of Latin jealousy, to invade Greece from his colony in Albania. But the Greeks doled out a sound thrashing to the Italians while at the same time across the Mediterranean the British were pushing the Italians from eastern Libya.

Worried about the effect these reverses might have on Mussolini's position back home, Hitler reluctantly decided to act. The resurgence of the British posed a considerable threat to Germany's interests if they again gained a foothold in the Balkans as they had in the First World War. Therefore he planned Operation Marita, the German invasion of Greece from Bulgaria. But before he could act, on 27 March the pro-British General Simovic overthrew the government in Yugoslavia. Hitler, sensing a threat to his long-awaited plan to invade Russia, reacted violently, issuing orders that Yugoslavia must be 'beaten down with merciless brutality in a lightning operation'.[1] This attack was codenamed in the British manner, indicating its objective – Operation Punishment – and was to run in conjunction with the invasion of Greece. Preparations were completed within ten days.

Generalfeldmarschall Siegmund Wilhelm List's Twelfth Army, which included Panzergruppe Kleist, would attack in the south while Generaloberst Maximilian von Weichs' Second Army invaded from the north. Subsidiary attacks were to be carried out by Italian and Hungarian armies. Belgrade was the victim of a terror raid by the Luftwaffe, while on the ground the Yugoslav Army was soon routed by the battle-hardened Wehrmacht. The panzers attached to Weich's army quickly outflanked enemy positions by overrunning passes through the mountainous terrain. Generalmajor F.W. von Mellenthin, who was a staff officer in Second Army, later described the campaign as 'virtually a military parade'.

Less than 600 German casualties were recorded in the swift subjection of Yugoslavia and once again the Panzerwaffe was the key to the rapid German success. Skopje fell to the 9th Panzer while the 2nd Panzer drove south in an effort to prevent any co-operation with the Greeks. The 5th and 11th Panzer detached themselves from Kleist's force and headed north to Nis. The 8th and 14th Panzer had captured Belgrade, Zagreb and Sarajevo by 15 April and two days later the country was forced to capitulate.

Greece proved a tougher nut to crack. Following the recent victory over the Italians, the bulk of her army was still located in the north. Further divisions were manning the Metaxas Line opposite Bulgaria and a second defensive line called the Ailiakmon Line covered the landings of a British and Commonwealth expeditionary force rushed from North Africa. Both of these lines rested on the Yugoslav border and were left hanging in the air when resistance there broke down. Nevertheless, when battle was first joined on the Metaxas Line, even List's elite Gebirgsjäger (mountain troops), were fought to a standstill. However a breakthrough came when the 2nd Panzer successfully outflanked the Metaxas Line by striking for the port of Thessaloniki during a successful night attack. Yet again the value of the indirect approach paid a handsome dividend as this move forced the now isolated defenders to surrender shortly afterwards.

Stumme's XL Motorised Corps levered the British from their defensive line and forced them back to Mount Olympus. As part of this operation, Oberst Hermann Balck commanded a Kampfgruppe drawn from the 2nd Panzer and on his initiative the line was widely outflanked and overcome. The key to this success was the use of panzer infantry in a role normally fulfilled by mountain troops. Afterwards Balck was full of praise for the fitness and determination of his troops in overcoming natural and man-made obstacles, commenting that the terrain really was passable only to infantry and tracked vehicles. As a result of his experiences in the campaign, Balck recommended the removal of all wheeled vehicles from the panzer divisions, but German industry simply wasn't capable of manufacturing enough tracked vehicles to fulfil this need.

The Greeks on the Albanian front were now in grave danger and were forced to retreat. They gallantly tried to stave off the Germans long enough to allow their British allies time to escape by sea. As the British withdrew to the south, they passed through the famous pass at Thermopylae, where twenty panzers from the 5th Panzer attacked in single file and were destroyed. Despite some heroics by Fallschirmjäger (parachute troops) on the Corinth Canal, the headlines were yet again the preserve of the Panzerwaffe. The 5th Panzer fought its way onto the disembarkation beaches where its foremost elements were forced to surrender to the determined defenders. Fortunately for them, release was quickly at hand because the Royal Navy was forced to leave the last of the defenders behind. The campaign concluded at the end of April with fewer than 5,000 German losses, while the Greeks had lost in excess of 300,000 killed, injured and captured. The bulk of the British forces had been evacuated by sea.

Once again the Panzerwaffe had decided the issue. In just three weeks Yugoslavia and Greece had been overrun, the British driven out of the Balkans and Germany's southern flank secured. Many commentators have put forward the view that the Balkans campaign delayed Barbarossa for several crucial weeks. However it is doubtful that the invasion of Russia could have taken place much earlier than it did because an exceptionally wet spring meant that the Bug and its tributaries were flooded over as late as the beginning of June.

What is certain is that the campaign added significantly to the wear and tear on the panzers. Almost one-third of Germany's tanks had participated in the Balkan campaigns and the going was so taxing that the tank units involved required a complete overhaul – but events in the East didn't allow for this. It is hardly surprising that when Operation Barbarossa was underway these same panzers suffered a particularly high attrition rate. But this factor too can be overstated as these tanks were all part of Army Group South, which only had a secondary role in the invasion of Russia.

Hitler's pathological hatred of communism, his fear of the potential threat Russia posed to the Reich and Germany's inability to bring Britain to terms all made a conflict between these two totalitarian states almost inevitable. Victory in the West had made a German attack on Russia a practicable proposition again by eliminating the threat of a two-front war. Hitler desired war with the Russian bear and his determination would lead to the greatest clash of arms the world has ever seen.

As early as December 1940, Hitler had laid out the general intention of Operation Barbarossa in his Directive No. 21. This stated:

> The mass of the army stationed in Western Russia is to be destroyed in
> bold operations involving deep penetrations by armoured spearheads,
> and the withdrawal of elements capable of combat into the extensive
> Russian land spaces is to be prevented.[2]

Yet the precise objectives of Barbarossa remained inherently vague and open to alteration. The broad aim of the campaign was to gain a line running from Archangel to Astrakhan, 2,000 km (1,200 miles) beyond the frontier, but beyond this the specific mechanism by which Russia was to be vanquished was never elaborated.

Even before battle was joined, Hitler fatally dissipated the Wehrmacht's strength by greedily reaching for too many objectives at once. Moscow as the centre of the country's communications, administration and industrial infrastructure was an obvious prime target and Army Group Centre was allocated that task. But Hitler's belief in the importance of the economic aspects of war meant that Army Group South was detailed to seize 'Russia's Breadbasket', the Ukraine, as well as the Donetz basin. At the same time the Führer's intense hatred of communism, as well as the political desirability of linking hands with the Finns, earmarked Leningrad, the birthplace of Bolshevism, as the goal of Army Group North.

Perhaps the factor that exerted the most insidious influence on Hitler was his fear of following in Napoleon's footsteps. He didn't want the

Red Army to be allowed to escape into the vast wastes of Russia without giving battle as had happened in the 1812 campaign. These historical fears conditioned Hitler's insistence upon destroying the Red Army in western Russia, and later manifested itself in his reluctance to strike for Moscow.

In reward for his triumph in France, Guderian had been made Generaloberst in July 1940. It was in November of that year that he first learned of Hitler's plans to invade Russia. As he wrote in *Panzer Leader*: 'when they spread out a map of Russia before me I could scarcely believe my eyes'[3] and he made no attempt to conceal his disappointment and disgust. Guderian, unlike the OKW, didn't underestimate the Russians. In *Achtung Panzer,* he had estimated that Russia possessed 10,000 tanks in 1937. By 1941, this figure had risen to 20,000, although admittedly a large proportion of these were obsolete. Back in 1933 Guderian had himself visited a Russian factory which was churning out 22 tanks per day.

Another ominous indicator of Russian tank strength had come during the spring of 1941, just months before the invasion. A Russian military commission had visited Germany and Hitler for some unknown reason had ordered that they be shown all the latest panzers. The Russians absolutely refused to believe the Pz IV was the heaviest German tank, suspecting the Germans were hiding their newer models; this suggested the Russians already possessed much heavier tanks themselves.

Hitler refused to countenance such ill omens and continued to lay plans for the invasion. At last fully convinced by the tank, he wanted production increased from 125 to between 800 and 1,000 tanks a month so that he could double the number of panzer divisions. The Minister for Armaments and War Production, Dr Todt, explained to the Führer that such a programme would cost 2 billion Reichmarks, require an additional 100,000 workers and technicians, and necessitate the reduction or cancellation of U-boat and aircraft production.

Not surprisingly this put Hitler off the idea of increasing tank production, but he decided to go ahead and double the number of panzer divisions anyway – which could only be achieved by halving the number of tanks in each division. During the autumn of 1940, eleven new panzer divisions were thus formed, pushing the total number up to twenty-one, the new formations being numbered the 11th to 20th Panzer inclusive and the 23rd Panzer.

Each division now only had one panzer regiment instead of two, while all the other elements of the division were the same size as before, which effectively meant that overheads were doubled, while the armoured punch was halved. Guderian, Manteuffel and von Thoma, all supporters of tank-heavy divisions, protested to no avail. The only factor that mediated this weakening somewhat was that Pz IIIs and IVs had at long last begun to replace Pz Is and IIs in the tank regiments.

Most of the infantry in the panzer divisions continued to be lorry-borne, with less than one-third being conveyed by half-track, the same ratio as in the French campaign. The panzer divisions' supplies also continued to be conveyed in over 2,000 truck types of varying national-ity, none of which had any cross-country capability. The new divisions were mostly equipped with captured French trucks which simply weren't durable enough for the conditions in Russia. There were also now thirteen motorised infantry divisions to follow up the advance of the panzers, but most of these remained lorry-borne.

A force of 7 infantry armies and 4 Panzergruppen was assembled for what was to be the greatest invasion in history. As with Fall Gelb, the OKH planners opted to maintain three Army Groups for the assault on Russia, each one advancing towards a separate objective: Army Group North under Generalfeldmarschall Ritter von Leeb was to attack from East Prussia and thrust through the Baltic states towards Leningrad. For this purpose it was given 23 divisions organised into 2 armies and 1 Panzergruppe – Hoepner's Fourth Panzergruppe con-taining 3 panzer, 3 motorised infantry and 2 infantry divisions. The Finns contributed 14 divisions.

Army Group Centre under Generalfeldmarschall Fedor von Bock was to thrust north of the Pripet Marshes and then follow Napoleon's route to Moscow, a journey of some 1,000 km (650 miles). Because it had the most important role, this was the strongest Army Group. It had 49 divisions and contained 2 armies and 2 Panzergruppen – Guderian's Second Panzergruppe with 5 panzer, 3 motorised, 1 cavalry and 6 infantry divisions, and Hoth's Third Panzergruppe with 4 panzer, 3 motorised and 4 infantry divisions.

Army Group South under Generalfeldmarschall Gerd von Rundstedt was to attack south of the Pripet Marshes and seize the Ukraine. It had 40 divisions, organised into 3 armies and 1 Panzergruppe – Kleist's First Panzergruppe with 5 panzer, 3 motorised infantry and 6 infantry divisions. This Army Group was to be supported by two Romanian armies, a Hungarian motorised corps and an Italian corps.

The invasion force contained 3,300 panzers, just one-third more than had participated in the French campaign. The majority of the tank force continued to be made up of obsolete, lightweight or Czech tanks: 410 Pz Is, 750 Pz IIs, 150 Pz 35(t)s and 625 Pz 38(t)s. Of the more modern medium tanks, only 965 Pz IIIs and 440 Pz IVs were available. Of the 21 panzer divisions now in existence, 17 would be involved in the initial campaign and fully 6 of these were equipped with Czech tanks. At this stage Stugs (assault guns) and Jagdpanzers (tracked tank destroyers) still played a relatively insignificant role, with just 250 Stugs supporting the advance.

Guderian's Panzergruppe contained 3 panzerkorps, the XXIV, the XLVII and the XLVI which together had about 850 tanks. Ironically, he had fewer tanks as a de facto army commander than he'd had as a mere corps commander in France the year before. He now led 5 panzer divisions, but with only half the numerical strength of the 3 he'd commanded in France and these were to be spread along a much wider frontage. But on the plus side, he did have more medium tanks.

According to the instructions of OKW, Guderian's Panzergruppe, in co-operation with Hoth's Panzergruppe on his northern flank, was to seize Smolensk, 700 km (410 miles) beyond their start line. And yet despite the tallness of this order, Guderian was deeply dissatisfied with the Smolensk objective and wanted to go even further – he strongly advocated a Panzer thrust all the way to Moscow. As he said to his closest officers:

> The objective of the German Panzertroops is always the enemy capital, they must always be given an objective whose name everyone knows and which has a magnetic attraction. Who has ever heard of Smolensk? Everyone has heard of Moscow.[4]

The largest invasion force in history – 3 million Germans and 1 million Axis soldiers – assembled itself on the Soviet frontier. The amount of equipment involved was staggering: 3,300 tanks, 7,000 field guns, almost 2,000 aircraft and 600,000 vehicles. Almost 90 per cent of the Wehrmacht was being sent into Russia. But the invasion force wasn't as well mechanised as is commonly believed – of the 150 German divisions in the invasion force, only 17 were armoured and a further 13 motorised. The rest of the army had no better mobility than Napoleon's Grande Armée of 1812. There were also over half a million horses, half of which would be dead before the year was out.

At 0315 hours on 22 June 1941, the day after Midsummer Day and the day before the anniversary of Napoleon's invasion, Barbarossa began with a massive artillery barrage. As soon as the infantry had overrun the Russian border positions and seized bridges and crossings, the Panzergruppen began to advance and strike deep behind the frontier. At the same time, the Luftwaffe struck at Soviet air bases and succeeded in destroying 1,500 Red aircraft during the course of the first day, the majority of these on the ground. So devastating were the Luftwaffe strikes that the Red Air Force was eliminated as an effective weapon until 1943.

It was Army Group Centre that made the most impressive progress in the initial stages with Guderian's and Hoth's Panzergruppen playing the leading role. Despite being opposed by 3 Russian mechanised corps, the Panzergruppen had sliced 320 km (200 miles) into Russia within 5 days to create the first great *Kessel* (pocket) at Minsk.

Guderian's first task when the invasion began was to retake the fortress of Brest, an objective which he had wrested from the Poles less than two years before and which had been handed over to the Russians as part of the post-war carve-up of Poland; now Guderian had to win it back. Despite the obstacle provided by the Bug river and the infantry's desire to win the first bridgeheads in the invasion, Guderian insisted that his Panzertruppen joined the assault in order to speed up the advance. He feared getting caught up behind the infantry and their supply echelons, as had happened in the second part of the French campaign. The Bug was crossed by specially-adapted 'Tauschpanzers' (diving tanks) of the 17th and 18th Panzer Divisions; these were Pz IIIs and IVs which had been waterproofed in preparation for the cancelled Operation Seelowe (Sealion), the proposed invasion of Britain. These tanks drove along the riverbed and the crew and engine received their air via a type of snorkel tube which became a feature of the later U-boats.

One of the 18th Panzer's tank battalions was commanded by the colourful Major Hyazinth Graf von Strachwitz. 'Panzer' Strachwitz, as he became known, was a Silesian nobleman who as a young Leutnant in 1914 had led a cavalry patrol to the very outskirts of Paris. This raid deep behind the French lines went on for six weeks until Strachwitz

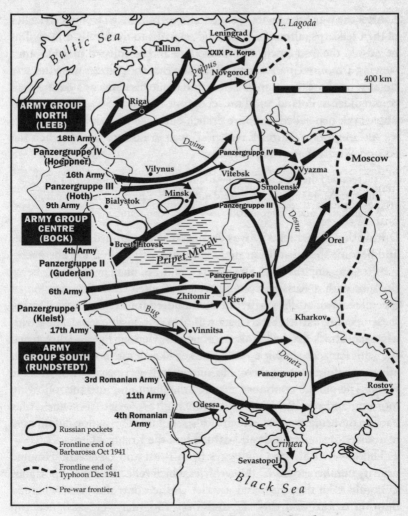

Operation Barbarossa, 22 June to 1 October
Operation Typhoon, 1 October to 5 December

was captured and sentenced to death. The sentence was revoked and
he spent most of the rest of the war in French prison camps. One
abortive escape attempt saw him fall from a mountain and become
seriously hurt. He was shipped to Switzerland to recover and convinced
the Swiss he was insane so as not to be sent back to France; as a result,
he was in an asylum at the war's end.

After the war, Strachwitz brought his expertise to the frontier struggles of the Freikorps, after which time he returned to the family estates. But he missed the excitement of military life and re-enlisted in 1934 after viewing armoured manoeuvres. Realising that the panzers were the new cavalry, he chose this branch to join and made his name as a daring tank commander in Poland and France; on one occasion Strachwitz and his single tank persuaded an entire French barracks to surrender.

Although the 'Panzer-Kavallerist' was in his late forties when the Second World War broke out, he

> still retained the dark moustache and the dashing good looks of a 1920s film star. More important, he had not lost the uncanny nose for danger which had made his reputation as a lucky commander.[5]

During the war Strachwitz was destined to be wounded fourteen times and become the most decorated regimental officer in the Wehrmacht.

After crossing the Bug, Strachwitz's unit became engaged in a fierce firefight with a Russian column which resulted in the destruction of several Russian artillery batteries and hundreds of supply trucks. During these opening battles, Strachwitz was also responsible for dealing with a Russian attack that had broken through the German line and threatened the 18th Panzer's supplies. His berserker-like charge broke the Russian advance before routing them. He immediately gave chase, firing all the while. The pursuit continued through the night and into the following morning and resulted in him overrunning the Soviet front line as far back as the artillery posts, which he also shot up. This action culminated in a series of similar raids and earned him the Knight's Cross.

There were only two highways from Brest and Guderian assigned priority numbers to his 27,000 vehicles which reflected their importance in combat; he thus enforced a strict traffic control system whereby fighting troops and their ammunition and fuel were assigned top priority on these roads. The infantry had to slog through the open terrain or along minor roads. One Luftwaffe communications officer, whose job it was to lay telephone lines, bemoaned his low priority to Guderian. The tank commander asked him bluntly, 'Can you shoot with your telephone poles?' When the Luftwaffe officer admitted he couldn't, Guderian roared at him, 'Then you will keep your third priority!'[6] The officer later shot himself, afraid to admit to Goering that he hadn't been able to make the Reichsmarschall's will prevail.

Guderian's route to Smolensk would carry him across several rivers as well as skirting the treacherous Pripet Marshes; he sent his cavalry division in to comb out this swamp. To guarantee the success of his drive, speed was essential in order to seize the vital bridges prior to demolition. Five days after the launch Guderian was crossing the Berezina river, but his rear was threatened by encircled Russian forces around Bialystok. As usual Guderian trusted his flank protection both to the speed of his advance and to the following infantry. As he said,

> We Panzertroops are in a fortunate position always to have open flanks. The security of the flanks is the responsibility of the trailing infantry. Panzertroops, therefore, don't have to worry about them.[7]

Two days into the invasion Guderian accidentally drove into a group of Russian infantry. He managed to escape, but the over-optimistic Russians announced his death over the radio, whereupon he assured them via German radio that reports of his death were greatly exaggerated. Earlier that day he had personally manned the machine-gun on his command vehicle to dislodge some Russians blocking the road ahead.

Von Bock had originally been instructed to seize Smolensk located along the main Moscow highway, but after three days Hitler interfered, insisting that Minsk be encircled by the panzergruppen while Bialystok in Poland was to be surrounded by infantry pincers. While these thoughts were in line with traditional German annihilation tactics, the Panzer leaders preferred rapier-like thrusts deep into the enemy rear. The Army Group's first attempt at encircling large enemy forces narrowly failed, but on 27 June, Panzergruppe Guderian effected a junction with Panzergruppe Hoth to the north and trapped over 300,000 Russians, along with 2,500 tanks, within the Minsk pocket. This was the first of many great German encirclements during the campaign.

It was at this point that the Russians chose to unleash their secret weapon, the formidable T-34 – the 18th Panzer was the first to encounter this tank and one panzerman described shells bouncing off the Russian tank 'like fireworks'. The panzers were shaken by the effectiveness of the T-34 and it was only its penny-packet deployment that saved the Germans from a sharp defeat on the Minsk-Moscow highway. In early July, Nehring, commander of the 18th, showed Guderian two T-34s that had become stuck in a bog and which the Panzergruppe commander photographed.

Three days into the invasion Army Group North had reported the first encounter with a massive and near indestructible Russian tank – the 40 ton KV-1 with frontal armour twice as thick as that of the Pz III and IV. Panzergruppe IV experienced a particularly nasty encounter with these armoured behemoths on 13 August when a panzer infantry regiment reinforced by 100 tanks and extra artillery encountered the KV heavy tank for the first time. The 100 panzers were unable to stop the Russian monsters and only 88 mm shells from the flak guns could penetrate them, eventually forcing their retreat. Many panzers were hit and several Czech 35(t)s were simply flattened by the Russian juggernauts. A 150 mm battery was also crushed in the onslaught and though it fired until the last moment, none of its shells penetrated the thick armour.

Another KV-1 managed to install itself in a commanding position dominating an important road and succeeded in cutting off German supplies for several days. Numerous attempts to knock it out failed, during which time several 50 mm Paks and an 88 mm were destroyed; despite registering 14 hits, none of the Pak shells penetrated the KV-1. Charges placed on the tracks failed to blow them off. In the end it took a feint attack by no less than 50 Panzers to distract the crew while an 88 was set up to shoot it up from the rear. The 88 pierced the armour with only three out of its fifteen registered hits, but finally succeeded in brewing it up.

The existence of the Russian medium T-34 and heavy KV-1 tanks came as a total surprise to the Germans; prior to the invasion they knew that the Russians would greatly outnumber them in tanks, but expected to encounter mainly light tanks or the massive and unwieldy multi-turreted landships which they dubbed 'Kinderschrecken' (Child frighteners). The Germans had believed that the quality of the Pz III and IV would balance out the differences in quantity, but now they were learning that the Russians not only had more tanks than the Panzerwaffe, but better ones too.

The T-34 went on to earn a reputation as the best main battle tank in use during the war with the possible exception of the Panther. It was armed with a 76 mm gun and a coaxial machine-gun, had a sophisticated Christie-type suspension system and armour so well sloped that it gave the equivalent protection of double the thickness of the 45 mm armour plate. One disadvantage was the two-man turret which meant the commander had to double as gunner. As the war progressed over 64,000 units were manufactured. The main improvement made was the introduction of an 85 mm gun in 1943, but otherwise it remained essentially unchanged.

The KV-1 was armed with the same 76 mm gun as its smaller family member and had no less than three machine-guns for close defence which made it difficult for infantry to knock it out. Its greatest advantage was massive 90 mm armour plate which made it almost impossible to penetrate and so the tank was really only susceptible to 88s and Stuka attacks – Rudel's JU-87 tank busters exacted a heavy toll as the campaign went on.

Both Russian tanks were powered by diesel engines. This gave them a greater range than their German opponents and reduced the fire hazard, but their belching exhausts made concealment a near impossibility. Both tanks also benefited from wide tracks that gave them a solid cross-country advantage over the panzers in conditions of mud, snow or ice.

The single greatest Russian achievement of the opening phase of the Russo-German war was the rapidity with which industry was relocated beyond the Urals and into Siberia. Over 1,500 factories had been moved by November and with the entire population mobilised, production quickly surpassed the older locations. Tankograd was the scion of several large industries, which were transported and amalgamated at Chelyabinsk and this new city was devoted to one single purpose – the mass production of the T-34. Throughout the war, the Russians simplified their production as much as possible, concentrating on the T-34 and KV-1 and their up-gunned successors as well as a limited number of self-propelled tank destroyers, all of which maintained a family resemblance.

Luckily for the Germans, Russian tank crews weren't as good as their tanks. Guderian commented that they were 'insufficiently trained, and lacked intelligence and initiative during the offensive'.[8] The Red crews made poor use of terrain and held too many firing halts. Often when a leader was killed, the rest of the tanks milled aimlessly around the battlefield, becoming easy prey for the agile panzers. Lack of radio was a huge problem and meant that communication on the battlefield was restricted to flags and hand signals. It also led to commanders becoming overly reliant on pre-rehearsed drills; as a result, when things didn't go according to plan, commanders were incapable of improvising as the Germans did.

The Russian mechanised corps, which contained two tank divisions and one motorised infantry division, proved unwieldy and hard to control in comparison to the panzer divisions. Also the centralised control system, coupled with fear of another Stalinist purge, paralysed commanders from corps level down and made them terrified of taking risks. Because of this poor command, the bulk of Russian tanks tended to be squandered in unco-ordinated piecemeal attacks.

Even more alarming than the Russian tanks was the Russian terrain. What had been marked on German maps as major roads turned out in reality to be nothing more than dirt tracks. And the choking dust thrown up was clogging tank engines and prematurely shortening their lives. Another disturbing factor was that after even a brief shower, the tracks that passed for roads turned to a sticky morass that made all movement impossible until the sun re-emerged. In these conditions the tanks were just about getting by, but the wheeled supply transport couldn't keep up.

Meanwhile the other Army Groups had also been making significant progress, although not as spectacularly as Centre. Army Group North's Panzergruppe commanded by Hoepner struck out of East Prussia and rapidly advanced along the Baltic coast towards Leningrad. Manstein's LVI Panzerkorps, which included the 8th Panzer, covered over 300 km in four days and managed to seize the Dvina bridges intact at Dvinsk. After five days the Corps was halfway to Leningrad and Manstein called the 'impetuous dash' of his panzers 'the fulfilment of all a tank-force commander's dreams'.[9] But these spectacular bounds forward were to be checked as Russian resistance stiffened. A Russian counter-attack isolated the Corps for several days and inflicted heavy losses on the 8th Panzer before eventually being overcome.

Reinhardt, the commander of XLI Panzerkorps (1st and 6th Panzer and two infantry divisions), ran into the strongest Russian defensive formations, the only two mechanised corps in the north-west front area. The battle was fierce, but the battle-hardened panzers eventually gained the advantage. By early August the German spearheads were on the Luga, only 100 km (60 miles) from Leningrad and three weeks later they and their Finnish allies had the city under siege, a siege which was to last for 900 days. The opening stage of the northern campaign was brought to a successful conclusion by the capture of over 20,000 prisoners from the debris of the Russian front. Army Group North was the only one to fulfil its objective.

Rundstedt's Army Group South faced the easiest going in terms of terrain; whereas the other two Army Groups had to endure swamps and forests, Kleist's panzers had the good tank country of the open steppes in front of them. Yet progress was slower than the other two because Army Group South faced some of the best-equipped and best-led Red Army units. As well as this, the Romanian southern wing proved incapable of keeping up.

One of the few competent Russian tank generals was Colonel-General Kirponos who commanded 6 mechanised corps. On 25 June these ran into the 600 tanks of Kleist's four panzer divisions and a tank battle raged for the next four days. Although heavily outnumbered, the panzers won out in the end, partly thanks to Luftwaffe support. The remaining Russian tanks retreated to Kiev, the capital of the Ukraine, and eventually ended up trapped there thanks to Stalin's insistence on holding the city. By 10 July Kleist's panzers were within a dozen miles of Kiev, but at this point were ordered south by Hitler where, with the help of two infantry armies, they succeeded in encircling 100,000 Russians in Uman by mid-August. The next great event on this front was to be the Kiev encirclement.

After Minsk, Guderian was faced with the option of either pushing on with the advance or waiting for the infantry to catch up. All of his superiors wanted him to wait, but Guderian estimated that if he waited the two weeks it would take for his infantry to catch up, his chances of successfully continuing the eastwards drive would shorten considerably. He knew that if he pushed on to the Dnieper straightaway, he could capitalise on the ill-prepared Russian positions. He got his way, provoking the classic remark from his arch-enemy and temporary superior, von Kluge: 'Your Panzer operations always hang by a silk thread.'[10]

Luftwaffe Oberstleutnant von Barsewisch was in charge of the Panzergruppe's reconnaissance planes and sometimes piloted Guderian himself. He was deeply impressed by the tank commander whom he described as 'a superman, a ball of energy'. Barsewisch wrote: 'When Guderian makes decisions it is as if the War God himself rides above Walstatt. When his eyes flash Wotan seems to hurl lightning or Thor swings the hammer.'[11]

Guderian again pushed forward and his panzers crossed the Dnieper in early July, prompting an unusually optimistic Halder to contend in his diary that the Russian campaign had been won in just fourteen days. Guderian continued his single-minded advance and relentlessly pushed his spearheads on toward Smolensk, which he encircled on 16 July with the aid of Hoth's Panzergruppe in the north, thus trapping 300,000 Russians and 3,000 tanks. Guderian's Panzergruppe had travelled the 660 km (410 miles) from Brest-Litovsk to Smolensk in just twenty-six days.

On 4 August, Guderian, Bock and Hoth attended a conference with Hitler at Army Group Centre's HQ. Although the three field commanders expressed their preference for pushing on to Moscow with all due speed, Hitler spoke of the importance of neutralising the Ukraine first. Guderian appealed for replacement tanks, but all Hitler would offer was 300 tank engines; he said he was keeping all the new tanks for fresh formations. He also made a telling admission when he remarked, 'If I had known the figures for Russian tank strength which you gave in your book were in fact the true ones, I would not – I believe – ever have started this war.'[12]

The account of Oberst von Barsewisch gives a vivid description of Guderian during the reduction of the Smolensk pocket. On 5 August, upon hearing a vital bridge was threatened, Guderian

> rushed immediately to the point, full of rage, and closed the gap with a battery of anti-aircraft artillery which he led personally into battle. There was this fantastic man, standing by a machine gun in action against the Russians, drinking mineral water from a cup and saying 'Anger gives you a thirst!'[13]

Once the pocket had been cleaned out by mid-August, Army Group Centre came to a halt at Smolensk. Moscow was now just 300 km (200 miles) away and Guderian was all for pushing on while the going was good. But Hitler had other ideas; he decreed that the infantry should continue to plod towards Moscow while the two Panzergruppen of Army Group Centre would diverge north (Hoth) and south (Guderian) to act as the outer jaws for encirclements by the neighbouring Army Groups. The Army Group was appalled. This operation would involve a south-western detour of almost 800 km to Kiev for Guderian's panzers. At the same time most of Hoth's tanks would be sent north in the direction of Leningrad. In Hoth's words, 'the panzer fist would be turned into an outspread hand'. Originally it had been envisaged that Army Groups North and South would support Centre, not vice versa.

Guderian didn't want to go to Kiev, believing it would senselessly delay the battle for Moscow and both Bock and Halder agreed with him. Even Brauchitsch, the ineffectual Army C-in-C, opposed the plan on the grounds that the Panzers needed maintenance, repair and refitting. Guderian flew in person to protest at Hitler's HQ at Rastenburg on 23 August but on arrival Brauchitsch ordered him not to broach the subject with Hitler. Needless to say, Brausewetter couldn't be kept at bay and he insisted to Hitler that the capture of Moscow was the key to the whole campaign as it would sever Russian north/south communications. At worst this would ease pressure on the other objectives, if not indeed guarantee their attainment. At best the capture of the capital could bring the whole campaign to a victorious conclusion. He pleaded that the diversion would merely wear out his panzers and prevent the successful follow-up attack on Moscow.

But there was no changing the Führer's mind. For the first time Hitler used what was to become one of his favourite arguments for justifying nonsensical orders: 'My generals know nothing about the economic aspects of war.'[14] Against all professional advice, Hitler ordered the panzers to diverge, claiming that the time for far-reaching operations was over and that from now on the Russians could only be defeated by a series of small battles of encirclement. The net result of Hitler's order was that Army Group Centre ground to a halt along the Desna until the end of September and the greatest opportunity for a swift victory was squandered. Jodl ascribed this decision to Hitler's 'instinctive aversion from treading the same path as Napoleon; Moscow gives him a sinister feeling'.[15]

Incidentally, this encounter turned Halder against Guderian for ever on account of what he regarded as the tankman's failure to stand up to Hitler; this was ironic coming from a man who frequently suffered nervous collapses in the Führer's company. In the weeks leading up to the Kiev encirclement, the highly-strung Chief of Staff noted in his diary that 'Guderian will not tolerate any army commander', that 'he throws out accusations and insults' at Bock and exhibited 'unheard of insolence!'[16]

Despite his original opposition, Guderian did a typically professional job. He pushed south from Smolensk on 25 August, with the tanks covering 100 km (60 miles) on the first day alone. Around the same time Panzergruppe Kleist struck northwards from Kremenchug. Resistance along the way was fierce, but on 16 September the pincers closed 250 km east of Kiev. They had succeeded in trapping no less than 665,000 Soviet troops, 1,000 tanks and 3,000 artillery pieces in what Hitler called 'the greatest battle in world history'.[17] The trapped Russians fought frantically to escape, 'ricocheting like billiard balls within the ring'[18] to use Halder's words, but Stalin had stubbornly refused withdrawal. It hadn't been an easy victory for the panzers – the 3rd Panzer had only 10 tanks left, 6 of which were Pz IIs.

The Kiev encirclement was over by 21 September and, great victory or not, it had delayed the battle for Moscow by two months. Even though this greatest of all encirclement battles had been a stunning defeat for the Russians, many historians believe it cost the Germans victory over Russia. Hitler had thrown away strategic success in favour of a tactical one. In the two crucial months that had passed, the Russians had had time to build up the defences in front of Moscow, constructing three long anti-tank ditches and sowing tens of thousand of mines along the natural invasion route. Also by now the full onset of the Russian winter was only a month away.

At the start of October, Army Group Centre's drive on Moscow began once again with Operation Typhoon. Army Group North was to settle for a mere investment of Leningrad for the time being and hand over most of its armour to Army Group Centre. Army Group South was to continue to push on into the Crimea and the Donetz basin. Hoth and Hoepner's Panzergruppen were now positioned on either side of Smolensk and only 300 km (200 miles) from Moscow; back in June it would have taken just 5 days to cover this distance. These 2 Panzergruppen were spread along a 240 km (150 mile) frontage and Guderian's Panzergruppe lay another 240 km (150 miles) south.

Panzergruppe Guderian was to attack towards Orel and Bryansk and was reorganised and reinforced for this purpose – XLVI Panzerkorps was handed over to Panzergruppe Hoepner, but in return Guderian received two army corps and XLVIII Panzerkorps. He still had XXIV and XLVII Panzerkorps and was also sent 100 replacement tanks.

Guderian decided to attack on 28 September, two days before the rest of the Group so as to try to close the gap with the other two panzergruppen. In an impressive feat, Guderian's Panzergruppe went from a position of containing the Kiev pocket on the 26th to swinging around through 90 degrees so as to attack north-eastwards on the 30th. On 1 October XXIV Panzerkorps took Sevsk, about 110 km

(70 miles) south of Bryansk. After moving through 200 km (130 miles) of woods in two days, the 4th Panzer arrived at the town of Orel, an important road and rail centre on the way to Moscow, on 3 October. The next mission was to follow the highway to Tula, which was 180 km (110 miles) south of Moscow.

The 6th of October was an eventful day: Bryansk, along with its bridges over the Desna, fell to XLVII Panzerkorps, the 4th Panzer ran into the 1st Russian Tank Brigade a quarter of the way to Tula and Guderian's Panzergruppe was renamed the Second Panzerarmee. But most significantly of all, the first snow fell that day in an ominous portent of what was to come. It quickly melted, turning the roads to what Guderian called 'canals of bottomless mud', but it was a warning to the Germans that they were fast running out of time to capture Moscow.

For Guderian's Panzerarmee most of the rest of October was taken up by an encirclement at Bryansk. The two panzergruppen north of Guderian were also making good progress. The pincers of Panzergruppen Hoepner and Hoth closed again at Vyazma-Bryansk, trapping another 600,000 Russians and 1,200 tanks. They also succeeded in smashing through two of the defensive lines in front of Moscow.

In the extreme south, Kleist's First Panzerarmee was moving towards the Sea of Azov and in mid-November launched its bid for Rostov. One of the key formations involved was a battle group drawn from the 14th Panzer. This formation was commanded by Willi Langkeit, the youngest major in the Panzerwaffe, and included the tanks of the 36th Panzer Regiment as well as motorised infantry.

On the morning of the 16th the Kampfgruppe set out across deeply frozen terrain. Langkeit overran two trench systems in quick succession and endured a shot from a Russian Pak which failed to explode. Two trench lines later and the Germans were in trouble, their forces spread across the battlefield and in danger of being destroyed piecemeal. Luckily, when the expected counter-attack materialised, it was led by lightweight T-26s which again hit Langkeit's machine without damage. Langkeit himself brewed up several of them before leading the panzers in pursuit of the broken enemy.

Forced to halt for the night the Kampfgruppe were kept bottled up in their tanks thanks to incessant harassing fire. When dawn broke the exhausted panzermen were met by almost 100 Soviet tanks, including many of the formidable T-34s and KVs. Langkeit ordered his panzers to hold fire until the Russians were within 600 metres in the hope that by then their shots would achieve better results. An attempt to outflank his small force was cut down by several Pz IVs, an engagement which led the Russians to reinforce their attacking units.

The new tanks were thrown into two successive frontal charges which the disciplined German fire control easily stopped. Twenty-five Russian tanks were left burning on the field before infantry too were sacrificed in a pointless frontal assault. Langkeit's men simply machine-gunned the masses in what was a classic example of Russian military inflexibility.

The following day saw his forces lured into a fire trap. As the panzers approached a village, Soviet tanks began to break cover en masse, but in a violent confrontation ten were knocked out for the loss of only a few panzers and the Russians withdrew. Langkeit laagered for the night and personally led the renewed attack the next morning. He rolled across a mine belt unscathed, though several following vehicles were destroyed, until his panzer was struck by Russian artillery fire.

His crew dead, Langkeit jumped from the burning tank and raced toward a Russian machine-gun nest which was firing at him. He killed the crew and routed the supporting infantry with only a pistol before hitching a ride on a Kubelwagen to direct the assault once more. His infantry cleared the village and on the 21st the battle group seized bridges across the Don and fought their way into the outer suburbs of Rostov. His booty in the preceding week included the impressive tally of 320 tanks, 70 guns of all types, an armoured train, a goods train, a plane and 2 river boats as well as 1,500 prisoners. Despite this, he was refused the German Cross in Gold.

All over the front, the mud got worse and worse. Wheeled vehicles could only move if pulled by tracked vehicles and this extra strain was burning out tank engines prematurely. There was a shortage of spare parts reaching the front as Hitler wanted them all for his new tanks. The Luftwaffe was kept busy dropping bundles of ropes to stranded vehicles so they could be pulled out. The Germans waited for the big freeze to begin – at least then the roads would be passable. And yet little preparation was being made for the coming winter – the vehicles had no anti-freeze and the troops no winter clothing. Guderian requested the latter be sent to the troops, but Berlin told him it would be issued in due course – in fact the necessary clothing didn't reach the Ostfront until 1942.

The road from Orel to Tula had become a ribbon of mud and progress was painfully slow. So-called 'corduroy' roads made up of tree trunks had to be laid for miles and petrol was in short supply. The maximum speed that could be achieved was 20 k.p.h. (12 m.p.h.), yet on 28 October Hitler ordered 'fast-moving units' to seize the Oka bridges. But as Guderian caustically remarked, 'There were no "fast-moving units" any more. Hitler was living in a world of fantasy.'[19] It wasn't to be the last time that the view from the Führer's HQ failed to tally with reality.

The superiority of the T-34 was becoming more and more apparent in the worsening conditions. A short-barrelled Pz IV only had a chance against the Russian tank if it attacked it from the rear and even then a lucky shot on the engine grating was needed to knock it out. Guderian sent a report on the subject to Army Group Centre, advising that a commission of tank experts and manufacturers be sent immediately to his sector. The resulting delegation arrived on 20 November where it saw destroyed tanks first hand and talked to panzer crews about future designs. The eventual result of this process was the Pz V, the Panther, but this wouldn't reach the front until July 1943.

Despite the tough conditions, Guderian was often in fine form during the drive for Moscow. Barsewisch describes him frightening

> some waddle papas of the infantry who have now come to know us and think our kind of war terrible. He derives from it a quiet and warm-hearted pleasure. 'You don't think you can secure 10 kilometres with a battalion? What a shame! Just think, I have 300 kilometres of open flank in which there is nothing and that does not bother me in the least. So, therefore, please. . .'[20]

On another occasion when his car got stuck in the mud, Guderian grinned, turned to Barsewisch and said, 'Well, my dear Herr von Barsewisch, we seem to be in the shit.'[21]

But for all his light-hearted banter, the tank commander was well aware of the seriousness of the situation he faced. On 6 November he wrote: 'the unique chance to strike a single great blow is fading more and more, and I do not know if it will ever recur'.[22] The next day his Panzerarmee began to suffer its first serious frostbite cases. On the 13th Guderian attended an Army Group Centre conference where the Second Panzerarmee was allocated a new objective: the city of Gorki,

400 km (250 miles) *east* of Moscow. Guderian told AG Centre's commander in no uncertain terms that this was completely impossible.

By mid-November, frost had set in everywhere and put an end to the muddy period until spring. The freeze meant that the offensive could resume until winter proper set in, but otherwise brought as many problems as the mud had. Tracks became worn down and the tanks skidded on ice, making steering impossible. Bridges broke and tanks crashed through the ice; as a result only the driver stayed in the tank when crossing a bridge and fords were used whenever possible. Tank camouflage had to be changed almost every day as weather conditions changed and so each tank carried a bucket of lime or chalk to darken or lighten the colour as required.

The cold was having an effect on both men and machines: gunsights were freezing; so was the water in the tanks' radiators, even when it had anti-freeze in it; oil was becoming viscous. Fires had to be lit under tanks before they could be started. A few panzers were started hourly and then the hot water from their radiators was pumped into the empty radiators of other tanks; in this way a whole regiment could be started within an hour.

On 17 November a German infantry division made contact with the first Siberian troops and was forced to retreat. German casualties on the Ostfront since June had reached three quarters of a million men, almost a quarter of the original invasion force. Guderian had lost half of his tanks. There was a great shortage of tanks and spare parts, but ironically not of crews, as casualties in the panzertruppen had been relatively light so far.

On 18 November the Second Panzerarmee attacked Orel as ordered. But Guderian had grave doubts whether the twelve and a half weakened divisions under his command would be strong enough to carry out this task. He pleaded with the AG Centre commander, General-feldmarschall von Bock, to have the Panzerarmee's task changed to something more achievable. Bock agreed to put Guderian's views to the OKW, but the reply that came back was that the mission stood. The town was eventually captured and the Panzerarmee moved on towards Tula where it became bogged down.

Meanwhile in the south the First Panzerarmee had captured Rostov on 21 November after fierce fighting. But little over a week later it was forced to withdraw from the city again. Hitler was infuriated and immediately replaced von Rundstedt as commander of Army Group South with Generalfeldmarschall von Reichenau, one of the few Heer officers who was an ardent Nazi. It was the beginning of the process by which Hitler was to replace almost all his capable commanders with second-rate yes-men.

Guderian's Second Panzerarmee made one last attempt to capture Tula because the advance couldn't advance either north or east until this communications centre and its airfield were in German hands. On 2 December Guderian launched his assault on the city with the 3rd and 4th Panzer Divisions and the Grossdeutchland regiment. The attack went ahead well despite the blizzard conditions, but the infantry failed to follow up and close the ring around the city. In light of the exposed position his troops were in, menaced in flank and rear, Guderian decided to withdraw the XXIV Panzerkorps into defensive positions. By now the temperature was 30 degrees below zero and frostbite was causing more casualties than the enemy.

The situation was as bad on the rest of the front. Hoepner's Fourth Panzerarmee and Reinhardt's Third were only 30 km (20 miles) from the Kremlin, but lacked the strength to push any further. A spearhead drawn from Reinhardt's Panzerkorps and commanded by Oberst Hasso von Manteuffel had established a bridgehead on the eastern bank of the Moscow-Volga canal, but were forced to withdraw on 29 November when counter-attacked. Units from the Fourth Panzergruppe penetrated into the suburbs of Moscow around the same time, but couldn't hold on there. The assault on Moscow had failed and soon it would be the Russians' turn to counter-attack.

For this purpose the Russians had assembled 1.5 million men in 328 divisions and they faced 600,000 Germans. Their massive counter-attack began on 5 December. As a result the leading panzer commanders, Guderian, Hoepner and Reinhardt (Hoth had been sent to command an army) were forced to abandon their attacks on the night of 5/6 December and withdraw their troops into shelter. First the Russians pushed back the Third and Fourth Panzergruppen 80 km (50 miles) back from Moscow before assaults began all over the front. German tank strength at this stage was reduced to just 1,000 – the 6th Panzer had no tanks left at all.

Guderian continued to bombard the OKW with realistic appraisals of the situation, but in their cosy and warm headquarters in East Prussia, they had no appreciation of the actual situation that prevailed on the front. On 14 December Guderian drove for twenty-two hours through a blizzard to attend a conference with the Commander-In-Chief of the Army, von Brauchitsch. The Generalfeldmarschall agreed that Guderian's Panzerarmee could withdraw to a line in front of Kursk, but a few nights later Guderian received a phone call from Hitler telling him that Brauchitsch had been sacked and forbidding any further withdrawals. The Führer also promised replacements but only a mere 500 men.

Since he couldn't seem to get through to Hitler through letters or phone calls, Guderian decided to travel to the Führer's HQ and tell him face to face what things were like on the Ostfront. He took a flight from icy Orel to the warmth of the Supreme Headquarters in East Prussia and arrived there on 20 December. That same day von Bock had reported himself sick and was replaced as Commander of AG Centre by Generalfeldmarschall von Kluge, a man on notoriously bad terms with Guderian.

When Guderian was received by Hitler, he noticed for the first time 'a hard, unfriendly expression in his eyes'[23] and so prepared himself for a stormy encounter. He told Hitler of his intention to withdraw the Second Panzerarmee and the Second Army to a defensive line along the Susha-Oka rivers and to overwinter there. Hitler said that he forbade any retreat. Guderian told him it was already underway and couldn't be halted till the troops reached the rivers. Hitler shouted that then the troops should dig in where they were, but Guderian countered by pointing out that the ground was frozen to a depth of five feet. Hitler then suggested they blow holes in the ground using their heavy howitzers, as he and his comrades had done in Flanders in the First World War. Guderian ridiculed this idea, and retorted that if he did this, instead of crater positions he'd have holes 'about the width and depth of a wash tub with a large black circle around it'.[24]

The discussions went on in a similar argumentative vein, with the two men failing to agree on a single point. When Guderian flew back to Orel on 21 December, he suspected his days as an army commander were numbered.

Meanwhile the Russians continued to attack. In a heated telephone discussion on Christmas Day, von Kluge accused Guderian of ordering the abandonment of the town of Chern, even though Guderian had just been following orders. Kluge hung up on the words, 'I shall inform the Führer about you.'[25] This was the last straw for Guderian and he sent off a telegram asking to be relieved of his command. But 'Kluger Hans' (Clever Hans) got there ahead of him and persuaded Hitler to transfer the tank commander to the officer's reserve.

On 26 December Guderian said farewell to his staff and left the Ostfront, arriving in Berlin on the last day of 1941. It would be 1943 before he held another command and by then the war would have turned irrevocably against Germany and the Panzertruppen. Guderian wasn't the only one to lose his command during December 1941 as, desperate for a scapegoat, Hitler sacked thirty generals. The three army group commanders also lost their jobs, as did the Army's Commander-in-Chief, with Hitler assuming the role of C-in-C himself from then on.

When the storm broke and Stalin unleashed fresh ski divisions and rugged Siberian units, the German front had been threatened with a rout. All the senior generals called for withdrawals but for once Hitler was right to insist on a no retreat policy. The Germans fell back in places, but quickly formed hedgehog positions around the main communications centres. In this fashion they managed to hold on until the Red wave ebbed and the front began to congeal again. During the retreat the 1st Panzer was cut off north of Moscow by a Russian attack and was forced to fight its way out. The tactics of indirect attack and breakout from an encirclement which the commander successfully employed became the hallmark of the Panzerwaffe in the coming years.

By the middle of December the whole front had changed over to the defensive and the panzers for the first time were required to play the role of fire brigade, a role that they were to play many times on the Ostfront over the next three and a half years. The panzer regiments were broken up into ad hoc task forces and held at strategic points behind the front, ready to intervene in the event of a Russian breakthrough. They soon proved themselves as adept in defence as in attack and it can truly be said that they were the backbone of the German front during that terrible winter. A number of innovative techniques were employed such as overrunning Russian assembly areas before they had the chance to attack and firing in salvoes to defeat the T-34s and KV-1s.

Understandably, the hard-pressed infantry wanted the tanks in the front line with them because of the sense of security the presence of armoured vehicles gave them, but this removed the tank's greatest advantage, its mobility, and made it little more than an armoured artillery piece. Because the ground was frozen solid, the tanks couldn't be dug in, but instead were piled up with snow, lumber, straw and hay. Snow fences were built to keep the few roads passable. Tank recovery became impossible and so instead mobile maintenance teams came to the tanks, moving on skis or sleds pulled by the ubiquitous panje horse.

Winter proved as terrible a foe as the Russians themselves. The failure of the OKH to supply the troops with the necessary winter clothing was a major blunder and one which could have been easily prevented – the Luftwaffe and Waffen SS were adequately supplied and in plenty of time. Conditions for the panzermen were no more pleasant than they were for the infantry, however much the Landser (infantry) envied them their steel shelters. Most of the German tanks relied upon a system to suck air for the engines through the crew area which in the excessive cold made life impossible for the operators unless they taped cardboard or wood over the intake ducts. Crews also insulated their bodies with newspapers and straw.

Some unlucky panzermen suffocated after lighting charcoal fires inside the confines of their tanks. Regular exercise was essential on long watches to prevent death. Alas for the crews, heavy overcoats were impractical within the cramped fighting compartment. Straw-lined pits beneath the tanks sufficed for beds, but two men had to stay in the tank at all times in case of sudden attack. Because the German tanks had no hatches underneath, the crew were exposed to gunfire when trying to get back into the tank in an emergency – a design flaw which also created difficulties in eliminating human waste.

As Marshal Winter tightened its grip, new measures had to be employed to keep the Panzerwaffe operational. Engines were started up every four hours and allowed to run for ten to fifteen minutes, which had the side effect of increasing fuel consumption; transmissions needed to be operated regularly to prevent shattering; iced-over surfaces in the compartment were a constant menace and required regular applications of salt which in turn accelerated corrosion.

Fan heaters were used to ready cold tanks for action but they required precious fuel. Batteries drained all too readily in the cold due to the demands of the engine and radio and, given their design and location, their replacement was a laborious task. The flywheel starters operated by a crankshaft were useful but not strong enough for incessant use. German Army lubricants were too viscous and froze, jamming transmissions and firing mechanisms. German tanks were simply not designed to cope with the extremes of the Russian winter and as such they suffered an enormous attrition rate.

The new conditions encountered by the Germans forced them to create new methods, equipment and tactics for overcoming the Russians. Hedgehog fortifications, new low-temperature lubricants and the use of the traditional Russian horse and cart were among the myriad of changes that the Wehrmacht was forced to adopt in order to survive that terrible winter.

Despite all the initial successes the Wehrmacht was a spent force by the end of 1941 and had to go over to the defensive. Even after killing and capturing over 3 million Russians, destroying 15,000 tanks and closing 9 immense pockets and 13 smaller ones, Hitler was still a long way from vanquishing his mortal enemy. The Russians seemed to have almost limitless supplies of men to draw from; as early as July Halder had nervously noted in his diary that the Russians disposed of far greater numbers than he had anticipated. In December, the Germans were dismayed to find a host of fresh formations arrayed against them. And not only did the Wehrmacht have to contend with hordes of Red Army soldiers, Russia's traditional ally, her climate, was also stepping into the fray.

Barbarossa failed quite simply due to inadequate planning and preparation. The Germans were unable to garner sufficiently accurate information on the Russian system, infrastructure and military apparatus on which to formulate a successful plan of attack. The primitive state of the roads alone came as a tremendous shock and went far towards costing the Wehrmacht victory – yet if all the German vehicles had been tracked they might still have taken Moscow despite all. The fact that Russia's railroads were of a different gauge to European ones also created terrible difficulties. Ironically, it was Russia's very backwardness which saved her from being overrun as quickly by Blitzkrieg as Western Europe had been.

The campaign plan itself was based on a whole succession of flawed premises. Russian equipment was both better and more numerous than had been expected. The stupendous scale of the country swallowed all the resources Hitler had devoted to his greatest gamble and stretched his forces to the limit. But here as ever the quality of the German soldier did much to compensate for these flaws. However, nothing could overcome Hitler's greatest error: repeated divergence of effort, both temporally and spatially. Imprecise and shifting aims cost the Germans dear.

Close though they came to pulling off a spectacular victory, the Wehrmacht was never able to surmount the punishing errors engendered by insufficient preparation. German military theory had always stressed that victory should be sought at the planning stage – instead some of its sharpest minds found only the seeds of defeat.

One new weapon system did perform particularly well during Barbarossa and led to a great expansion of the arm – the Sturmgeschutz (Stug) or self-propelled assault gun. During the First World War, the Germans had realised that the infantry needed some form of mobile artillery to accompany them during their attacks in order to destroy any obstacles in their path, such as enemy pillboxes and machine-gun emplacements. The infantry at that time didn't have the necessary firepower and conventional artillery wasn't adaptable or fast enough to fulfil this role. The solution adopted was the setting up of 'infantry escort batteries' – small artillery pieces which were pulled by horses or even men and manned by volunteer crews. They travelled into the attack with the infantry and could give immediate and accurate fire support wherever it was needed. As could be expected, these batteries suffered heavy casualties.

In 1935, Manstein, then an Oberst attached to the OKH, submitted a memo to the Chief of the General Staff, suggesting that the infantry escort batteries be revived in the form of Sturmartillerie units attached to each infantry division. These would be self-propelled (SP) guns on a tracked chassis and would carry the infantry attack forward by eliminating danger in their path through direct fire.

The concept wasn't universally embraced. Panzer officers in particular were not happy about the idea because they feared it would reduce the number of tanks being built. The infantry did welcome the idea, but they didn't possess the necessary technical skills to operate the SP guns. So in the end the Sturmartillerie came under the control of the artillery, although that branch didn't take on the new responsibility with any great enthusiasm. In fact very little effort was put into the development of the SP branch until it had clearly proven its value in battle.

The principal SP built was the Sturmgeschutz (assault gun) III or Stug III, which went into production in 1940 and was basically a turretless tank. The gun was fitted inside the body of the tank and so had a limited traverse of 25 degrees and an elevation of 30; this meant the Stug had to be pointed at its target and if attacked from a flank, the whole vehicle had to be turned around. But having no turret had its advantages too: the Stug had a very low profile at little over 2m in height, not much higher than a man, a useful feature when waiting in ambush. It was built on the chassis of the Pz III and had the same low-velocity, short-barrelled StuK L/24 75 mm gun as the Pz IV. It was chiefly intended for infantry support and so would mainly fire high-explosive shells, but to a lesser extent it was also expected to protect the infantry from enemy tanks. It was well armoured and in later versions the loader was given a machine-gun behind a protective shield for close-quarter defence.

During gunnery trials in 1937, the artillerymen who crewed the Stugs proved to be better gunners than the panzermen, being quicker to hit the target and requiring less rounds to get a killing shot. There were four men in the crew, as opposed to five in the turreted tanks; these were the driver, gunner, loader and commander and they worked in extremely cramped conditions, with the gun's breech barely 2 feet from their heads. Stug crews wore the same style of uniform as the Panzertruppen, but it was grey instead of black and the Waffenfarbe was the red of the artillery. Being a Stug crewman was the only way for an artillerymen to win the Knight's Cross.

Of the 6 Sturmartillerie batteries in existence by May 1940, 4 of them containing 30 Stug IIIs saw service in the French campaign and acquitted themselves well. The first Stug Abteilung (battalion) was organised in 1941 and these in theory had 18 to 30 SP guns. There were 11 battalions by Barbarossa – by the end of the war there would be 100. In 1943 the Stug Abteilungen were renamed as Stug brigades, without receiving any extra equipment. The establishment for a Stug brigade was 31 guns, but this was rarely achieved in reality. The Stug Abteilungen remained under the command of the artillery throughout the war, although Guderian tried and failed to get them put under his control while he was Inspector of the Panzertruppen. Only the Waffen SS and elite Wehrmacht divisions like the Gross Deutschland ever had Stug brigades permanently attached to their divisions.

The Stugs' effective range was 1,000m, although they could score success at greater distance, occasionally even up to 2,000m. Stugs fired while stationary and the preferred pattern was to fire and then move; in this way the enemy artillery couldn't hit them because they weren't in the same place long enough to draw a bead on. Ironically, given their original role of protecting the infantry, Stugs eventually had to be given infantry escorts to protect them from the opposing infantry and their anti-tank weapons. From mid-1943 they were fitted with *Schurzen* armour streets like other German AFVs to protect them from hollow-charge weapons.

After Kursk, the Germans were forced to abandon the offensive in favour of the defensive and the Stugs took on an important new role. The short-barrelled L/24 75 mm was replaced with either the long-barrelled L/43 or L/48 75 mm and these higher-velocity guns turned the Stugs into effective tank-killers. As Guderian wrote in 1943, 'Anti-tank defence will devolve more and more on the assault guns, since all our other anti-tank weapons are becoming increasingly ineffective against the new enemy equipment.'[26] The Stugs proved cheap and easy to build, each one costing only 82,500 RM and four Stugs could be built for the price of one King Tiger tank. They were as useful in defence as a turreted tank and as a result began to be used in Panzerjäger Abteilungs and even as replacements for tanks in the panzer divisions.

In total, 9,500 Stug IIIs were built during the war and 1,000 Stug IVs – the latter being built on Pz IV chassis. Over 1,000 StuG IIIs were also built carrying the 105mm howitzer – these were called Sturm-haubitzes (StuH) and were restricted to an anti-personnel role. By the end of the war, Stugs had destroyed over 30,000 enemy tanks, a rate that, gun for gun, was better than the panzer divisions.

The most famous Stug ace of all was Wachtmeister Hugo Primozic of the 667th Abteilung who managed to destroy twenty-four tanks in one day during an attempted Soviet breakthrough at Rzhev during September 1942. For this he was awarded the Knight's Cross. In December of that year, he scored his sixtieth kill and as a result received the Oak Leaves to the Knight's Cross, the first NCO to do so. As one lieutenant put it, 'Fighting in an SP is the nearest thing that contemporary ground warfare can offer to the soldier's concept of a knight in armour.'[27]

CHAPTER FIVE

High Water Mark on the Volga

We are in the position of a man who has seized a wolf by the ears and dare not let him go.

General F.W. von Mellenthin, 1943

THE Wehrmacht quickly put into practice the lessons it had learned during Barbarossa. For one thing the campaign had quickly exposed the inadequacy of the standard German anti-tank guns, the 37 mm and 50 mm Paks. These guns just weren't powerful enough to penetrate the armour of the Russian T-34 and KV tanks and their crews contemptuously nicknamed them 'door-knockers'. By now it was understood that kinetic energy was the real tank killer and that nothing less than 75 mm would suffice. As a result the 75 mm Pak entered service in late 1942 and remained in use till the end of the war. But Pak guns pulled by horses or trucks lacked true mobility and it was realised that what was really needed on the Ostfront was a self-propelled anti-tank gun.

The Tiger and Panther were still a long time off and in the meantime an immediate solution was need to swing the balance back in the Panzerwaffe's favour. As a result, the Pz IV and the Stug III began to be up-gunned with high-velocity 75 mm L/48s. It was also appreciated that the Pz Is, IIs and Czech tanks had reached the end of their service life and their obsolete chassis, along with French chassis, were quickly converted into Panzerjäger (tank destroyers) by the simple addition of 75 mm or Russian 76 mm guns surrounded by an open-topped, fixed superstructure of sheet armour. The result was vehicles such as the Marder family and the Nashorn – these stop-gap designs served well until the arrival of the second generation of tank destroyers in 1944, but had many disadvantages, such as the crews' exposure and the vehicles' very high profiles.

The demand for tanks continued to grow, without actual production increasing significantly. During 1942 each motorised infantry division received a tank battalion, although in reality these were often equipped with Stugs. In July 1942 the motorised infantry in each panzer division were renamed 'Panzergrenadiers' and in March 1943, all motorised infantry divisions, both Heer and Waffen SS, were given this new title. Several of these, in particular the Gross Deutschland (now a full division) and those of the Waffen SS, had more tanks than actual panzer divisions.

The formation of new panzer divisions also continued apace: during 1941 the 21st Panzer had been established for service in Africa and the 22nd was set up later the same year; while 1942 saw the establishment of four more: the 24th (formed from the last remaining cavalry division in the German Army, it still wore cavalry yellow as its Waffenfarbe rather than panzer pink), the 25th, the 26th and the 27th.

The motorcycle battalions included in each panzer division were disbanded, having experienced extremely heavy casualties during Barbarossa for very little gain. The surviving members were absorbed into the armoured car reconnaissance units.

The Germans also realised that what was really needed was a second generation of tanks. When war broke out in 1939, they had had no plans to build any tanks heavier than the Pz III and IV as these medium tanks were expected to fulfil all requirements. But after encountering the heavy tanks and modern anti-tank guns of the French, the British and later the Russians, it was realised that a heavy panzer was urgently needed.

On 26 May 1941, just a month before the opening of Barbarossa, Hitler met with two of his top tank designers, Porsche and Henschel, and gave them orders to design a new heavy tank for the Panzerwaffe. He had been impressed by the massive French Char B1s the Germans had met the summer before and by the British Matildas they were currently encountering in North Africa, and he realised that future tank models would need heavier armour and more powerful guns. The urgency of the project was accelerated that summer when the Germans encountered the Russian T-34s and KV-1s for the first time and were shocked to discover that their own Pz IIIs and IVs were simply no match.

The main design stipulations laid down were that the tank should have 100 mm frontal armour and a gun capable of penetrating 100 mm of armour at a range of 1,500 m. The tank could also weigh as much as 45 tons; up till then 36 tons had been the maximum weight allowed because this was all that European bridges could take. But the new tank was to have deep fording equipment to make it independent of bridges.

The boffins went to work. Dr Ferdinand Porsche created the innovative VK 4501(P) equipped with a longitudinal torsion bar suspension system and a radical petrol-electric drive train by which two engines drove electric motors connected to the tracks. But this drive train proved horrendously unreliable, took up half the hull and pushed the tank's weight up to 57 tons. The gun also had a serious overhang because it had to be set so far forward on the hull.

Meanwhile the other prototype, the VK 4501(H), was being built by Henschel und Sohn, an established heavy manufacturer based in Kessel. This firm specialised in heavy industrial and railroad equipment such as locomotives and so was ideally suited to build a heavy tank. The firm also had plenty of experience of tank-building as they had been building Pz Is, IIs and IIIs since the mid-1930s. Henschel had been working on a 30-ton tank chassis since 1938, the VK 3601(H), and after the May 1941 meeting, they quickly adapted this chassis for the new project. Their first running chassis appeared early in 1942 and mounted the 88 mm Flak.

The first prototypes were ready for inspection by the Führer on his birthday on 20 April 1942. The 10 km drive from the rail unloading point to the Fuehrerhauptquartier at Rastenburg didn't inspire much confidence in either prototype as they kept breaking down along the way. Henschel won the evaluation and was chosen to go into production, thanks to its superior manoeuvrability coupled with the numerous flaws in the Porsche design. It was also decided that the Panzer VI would be named the 'Tiger'.

The Tiger tank was built quickly because of the urgent need for a heavy tank in Russia and so there was little time for research and development. As a result almost all of its mechanical parts came from the VK 3601 chassis and the turret was fundamentally the same as the one on the Porsche tank. It was assembled in one of Henschel's three great assembly works in Kessel and was in production for two years from August 1942, during which time 1,350 vehicles were built. After August 1944 production was switched over to building the Tiger II or 'King Tiger'.

Each Tiger contained over 26,000 parts, took 300,000 man hours to build (twice as long as a Panther) and cost 250,000 Reichmarks; once weapons and radios were included the total cost per tank rose to 300,000 RM. In contrast a Pz IV could be built for just 103,500 RM or a Pz V Panther for 117,000 RM. Of course, the Tiger was never intended to be a mass-production, workhorse tank like the other two, but a specialised weapon: a *Durchbrüchwagen* or breakthrough tank.

The 88 mm KwK 36 L/56 was an accurate and powerful weapon that could destroy enemy tanks at distances of 1,500m and more. The Tiger itself proved frontally invulnerable to normal armour-piercing shells at ranges over 800 metres, including the American 75 mm and the Russian 76 mm tank guns. Allied tanks bearing these guns, such as T-34s or Shermans, only had a chance against the Tiger if they closed the distance quickly or if they attacked the Tiger's flanks or rear.

The Tiger was a massive vehicle: almost 3 m high, 8.5 m in length, 3.5 m wide and weighing in at 56 tons, twice as much as a Pz IV. Frontal armour was 100 mm and side and rear armour 80 mm. The hull itself was a square, heavily-armoured box with near vertical sides, which gave the Tiger its characteristic 'boxy' appearance. Its size meant that despite having a 650 bhp engine, the Tiger was still seriously underpowered with a poor power-to-weight ratio: every 12 horsepower had to move a ton of tank.

The Tiger was a sophisticated and technically complex machine that required regular preventative maintenance to keep it functioning properly. Tiger crews were the elite of the panzer divisions and were hand-picked from other units or from the Panzerschulen (Panzer schools). They had to be able to maintain the Tiger in the field themselves and so were given the *'Tigerfibel'*, a working manual on how to maintain and operate the tank. To hold their attention, the booklet was full of cartoons of scantily-clad women.

However, this great tank's debut was not very impressive. Hitler, as usual impatient to get his latest 'Wonderwaffe' into battle, over-ruled his senior officers who believed it would be better to wait until there were enough Tigers to make a real impact (he was to make the same mistake with the Panther at Kursk in 1943). Instead he hastily committed the new tanks to the battle around Leningrad. In August 1942, four Tigers of sPz. Abt. 502 were deployed in a forest south of Lake Ladoga. But the terrain didn't suit these armoured behemoths; narrow forest tracks were flanked on all sides by thick pine forest so that the Tigers could only move forward in Indian file. Even though frontal fire proved useless against the thick armour, the wily Russian anti-tank gunners successfully disabled the four Tigers by shooting at their tracks. The tank crews escaped, to return after dark to retrieve three of the Tigers; the fourth was firmly stuck in the mud and had to be blown up.

Just like Haig in 1916, Hitler had squandered the surprise value of a new weapon. It would have been much better to have spent the winter building up the numbers of Tigers, training the crews and devising new tactics and then to have launched a mass Tiger offensive in the spring of 1943.

Only a few elite divisions ever had a Tiger battalion permanently attached – the Gross Deutschland was one. Instead the Tigers were organised into special battalions called Schwere Panzer Abteilungen (heavy tank battalions), usually abbreviated to sPz Abt. These were held at army or corps level and were to be attached to other panzer units at the *Schwerpunkt* of a battle in order to perform a specific mission; they were not to be used to carry out tasks that the lighter tanks could do themselves. There were eleven Heer and three SS Schwere Panzer Abteilungs. Most saw action in Russia, although two were sent out to Rommel in Tunisia. Each Abteilung contained a total of forty-five Tigers organised into three companies.

The Tiger soon proved itself very hard to kill. One leutnant from sPz Abt 503 reported how during a six-hour tank battle around a Russian collective farm in February 1943, his Tiger was struck by 227 hits from anti-tank rifle rounds, 14 hits from 57 mm and 45 mm anti-tank guns, and 11 hits from 76 mm guns. Even though the tracks, suspension and road wheels sustained serious damage, the crew were uninjured and the Tiger still managed to cover an additional 60 kilometres under its own power.

The most common attack formation for the Tigers was the *Keil* or wedge, with the Tigers taking up the point of the wedge while the lighter tanks followed up behind or on the flanks. Another attack formation often used was the *Glock* or bell-shape in which the Tiger formed the clapper. The Tiger excelled at long-range defensive shooting from a hidden, hull-down position, but it proved less effective in the attack; on the open battlefield the Tiger acted like a barn door, drawing all the enemy fire. It was also vulnerable to flank attack. One Panzer officer from sPz Abt 506 advised:

> Because of propaganda in the newspapers, the Tiger has been touted as an invulnerable Rammbock [battering ram]. But it can be knocked out by T-34 tanks or 7.62 cm anti-tank guns from the rear at ranges up to 1,500 m. The strength of the Tiger is its long-range 8.8 cm Kanone, not its armour. It may not be used as a moving wall.

In 1944 Hitler declared: 'One battalion of Tigers is worth a normal panzer division.' The Tiger was indeed a very formidable weapon, both on the battlefield and in the effect it had on enemy morale; *'Tiger Schreck'* (Tiger Terror) was a recognised phenomenon and even though only 1,350 were built, the accounts of Allied soldiers give the impression that every German tank they encountered was a Tiger.

Despite the appalling ordeal of the previous winter, Hitler and his military advisors laid plans for a resumption of the offensive in the summer of 1942. The situation at the end of the Russians' winter counter-offensive, even in the light of all the privations suffered by the Wehrmacht, was far from unfavourable. Though the Germans had yielded vast tracts of land, their hedgehog tactics meant that they had maintained a grip on the vital communication points and tactically this left them in a strong position.

The Russians now occupied strips of territory between or behind the German garrisons and so were vulnerable to pincer attacks from two or more of the German hedgehog positions. Any pincer movements on these narrow salients would necessarily cut off a greater number of men and weapons than a frontal attack on a similar length of ordinary front because the Russians had had to employ a disproportionate number of units to hold their gains.

On the downside, total Ostfront casualties had already topped one million. The horrendous losses of the previous year meant that Germany was unable to conduct operations along the entire length of the front

Generaloberst Heinz Wilhelm Guderian – creator of Blitzkrieg, progenitor of the Panzerwaffe and Germany's finest soldier.

Generalfeldmarschall Gerd von Rundstedt was Germany's most senior officer. Held in great respect by all sides, this Prussian aristocrat was both eccentric and lazy, yet repeatedly proved his worth as an Army Group commander. His campaign in the Ukraine in 1941 was well conducted, but in France in later years his age deprived him of the vigour to command as effectively as energetic subordinates like Rommel and Model.

Hitler's Fireman – Generalfeldmarschall Walther Model first came to prominence as the commander of the 3rd Panzer Division during Barbarossa and made a name for himself as a superb defensive general in the bloody battles of the Rzhev salient. One of the few generals Hitler trusted, Model was expert at shoring up seemingly shattered fronts with scratch units and was called upon to do this both in the East and the West during 1944. Often dismissed as a mere Nazi General, yet Model's abilities were beyond doubt and his rank the just reward for success, not sycophancy. This Prussian remained true to his ideals and committed suicide rather than face capture after the collapse of the Ruhr Pocket in April 1945.

Generalfeldmarschall Ewald Paul von Kleist commanded the first ever Panzergruppe during the invasion of France. His hesitancy and caution earned him criticism from Guderian, but this Prussian cavalryman eventually overcame his initial reservations about panzer operations. He went on to command an exceptional campaign in the Caucasus which culminated in a superbly executed retreat and earned Kleist his baton.

General der Panzertruppen Hans Hube. Known to his men as Der Mensch (The Man), the one-handed Hube fought with distinction at Stalingrad before assuming command of the 1st Panzerarmee. His brilliantly conducted escape from Russian encirclement in 1944 ended in personal disaster when he died in a plane crash en route to collect his decoration for the feat.

General der Panzertruppen Hermann Balck. Balck's exploits as commander of the 11th Panzer marked him out as one of the greatest panzer commanders. He eventually rose to command an Army Group.

The Panzer-Kavallerist – Oberst Hyazinth Graf von Strachwitz. Strachwitz excelled at deep raids into the Russian rear and became the most decorated panzer leader in the Panzerwaffe when he relieved Riga in 1944 using just a handful of tanks. Panzer Graf's exploits were the stuff of legend and he attributed his success to a sixth sense for danger.

Generalfeldmarschall Erich von Manstein (*left*) talks to his troops after the fall of Sevastopol in 1942, a feat which earned him his field marshal's baton. Without doubt the war's greatest strategist, his restoration of the southern front and recapture of Kharkov after the Stalingrad debacle in 1943 stands as the finest act of generalship since Napoleon.

Guderian directs operations by radio from an armoured command vehicle. His experience in the Great War as a wireless post commander greatly influenced his recognition of the advantages of instant communication for mobile operations. The officer standing behind him wears the standard panzer uniform including the Tank Combat badge.

Rommel and General Fritz Bayerlein direct operations in Libya. Bayerlein went on to fight in Russia and eventually commanded the elite Panzer Lehr Division in Normandy and during the Ardennes Offensive. His unassuming manner belied an aggressive and capable panzer leader.

The Desert Fox. Generalfeldmarschall Erwin Rommel in the driving seat, his face showing the determination and dedication that made him a master of the battlefield. Unquestionably the greatest operational panzer commander, his flair for mobile warfare and conjurer's tricks led to a startling series of victories in North Africa. Confounded by Berlin's lack of interest in his theatre and by enemy superiority, his eventual defeat was inevitable. In France he brought all his famed energy to bear on strengthening the Atlantic wall, but once again the sheer weight of Allied material proved his nemesis. Disgusted at the conduct of the war, he paid the highest price for intriguing against his former master when he was forced to commit suicide.

Rommel in conference with his corps commander, General Hermann Hoth, in France during June 1940. Hoth later commanded Panzerarmees in Russia and led the unsuccessful attempt to relieve Stalingrad. Like Manstein, he favoured the old style Mütze (cap) which he is pictured wearing. This cap could be worn under the Stalhelm (steel helmet) and was used until the end of the war by panzer crews as the lack of a peak was useful in cramped tank interiors.

The Panzerwaffe's finest. Guderian and Rommel pictured together during a tempestuous conference in early 1944 at the latter's chateau HQ in La Roche Guyon, France. Guderian's thunderous expression is in stark contrast to the self-satisfied look on Rommel's face, suggesting the Desert Fox was getting his way. The two disagreed furiously as to the appropriate tank dispositions for meeting the Allied invasion and the failure to agree a single strategy for countering the invasion led to disaster. Hitler's eventual compromise on the positioning of the panzer divisions satisfied no one.

Saddle orders. Panzer troops confer over a map during the invasion of France. Behind them is a SdKfz 231 eight-wheeled armoured car. The sound training of all Panzertruppen allowed for the passing on of curt verbal orders. Long-distance tickets were issued whereby objectives were firmly set out, but the methods employed were left to individual units. Note the Panzermützen.

SS-Obersturmführer Michael Wittmann, the victor of Villers Bocage, in a posed propaganda shot. 'The Kill Rings' on the gun of his Stug represent his successes on the battlefield. When killed near Falaise in August 1944 Wittmann's final tally had reached 138 tanks and 132 anti-tank guns and other artillery pieces, making him the most successful tank ace of the war.

First in the line – the Panzer I. Even though obsolete at the design stage and armed with just two machine-guns, this tank was built in vast numbers and fought until 1942. After that many of its chassis were converted into command vehicles or Panzerjägers. The pennant features the Totenkopf insignia of the Panzerwaffe.

The stop gap design – the Panzer II. Although its armour and armament were woefully inadequate, the Panzer II was the mainstay of the Panzerwaffe until after the French campaign. Its chassis was later put to good use for the Luchs (Lynx) reconnaissance vehicle, the Marder II Panzerjäger and the Wespe self-propelled howitzer. A Panzer I can be seen in the background of this picture.

Czech surplus – the Panzer 38(t). After the seizure of the Czech armaments industry, Guderian pressed two of its tanks into service with the Panzerwaffe: the Pz 35(t) and the Pz 38(t). Of the two, the Pz 38(t) was by far the superior. Both suffered from their riveted construction, poor speed and inadequate armament. They were largely used to flesh out the compliment of the former Leichte divisions.

The main battle tank – a Panzer III advancing towards Bir Hacheim during June 1942. The Pz III gradually replaced the Pz II as the mainstay of the panzer divisions. Its strong basic design allowed it to be updated and up-gunned as the need arose, but by late 1943 its days were numbered and chassis production was turned over to the Stug III.

Up-gunned – a Panzer IV fitted with the long 75 mm gun and Schurzen armour sheets covering the tracks. This superb tank operated effectively in roles for which it wasn't designed for most of the war and was built in greater numbers than any other German tank. Prior to the emergence of the Panther, the so-called Pz IV 'Special' was the only tank capable of meeting the T-34 on anything like equal terms. Repeatedly up-gunned and up-armoured, it became the backbone of the Panzerwaffe and served until the surrender.

The workhorse – a Panzer IV with a short 75 mm gun. In the 1930s Guderian envisaged a medium tank for operating against soft targets like personnel and supply columns and the short-barrelled 75 mm Pz IV was the result. Unsuited for anti-tank actions, the short gun was gradually phased out and replaced with longer, more powerful guns.

Panzer V – the Panther. Without question the finest tank of the war, the Panther's long 75 mm gun packed almost as powerful a punch as the 88 mm. Its sloped armour owed more than a passing nod to the T-34 and effectively deflected most Russian shot. From late 1943 onwards it assumed the mantle of main battle tank. A total of 6,000 were built, half of which were destroyed in battle.

Panzer VI – the Tiger. Even though less than 1,500 were built, the Tiger was the most feared tank of the war. Intended as a breakthrough tank, it lacked speed but its splendid 88 mm gun more than made up for this. Its one vulnerable point was the relatively thinly armoured rear. The Tiger was only rarely employed directly within panzer division establishments and instead was normally utilised in Schwere Panzer Abteilungen (heavy tank battalions). Only the SS and the Gross Deutschland Division had organic battalions on their establishments.

Panzer VI Ausf B – King Tigers of sPzAbt 503 in France in late 1944 prior to moving to Hungary. The King or Königstiger was a combination of the best points of the Tiger and Panther. Its frontal armour was all but impenetrable and its long 88 mm gun was accurate up to 2,000 metres. Largely deployed in the West, Tigershreck took on a whole new dimension when this monster was unleashed. However, less than 500 ever entered service.

Marder III Panzerjäger mounting a captured Russian 76 mm gun on a Panzer 38(t) chassis. The Marder family were the German answer to an immediate need for self-propelled anti-tank guns. They were created by mounting a 75 mm or 76 mm gun behind an armoured shield on an obsolete tank chassis. Over 2,000 of the three Marder (Marten) variations were built. A closely related vehicle was the Nashorn (Rhino) which featured an 88 mm Pak on a Pz IV chassis.

The Hetzer. Towards the end of the war, the second generation of German tank destroyers came into production. The Hetzer or 'Troublemaker' was a neat combination of a 75 mm on the Pz 38(t) chassis. It proved a superbly effective weapon and exacted a heavy toll of enemy tanks. At little more than 2 metres in height, concealment was easy.

Guderian's Duck – the Jagdpanzer IV. Along with the Hetzer, this vehicle was the Panzerwaffe's main tank hunter as the war drew to a close. It mounted a 75 mm gun and was built on the Pz IV chassis. Over 1,000 were built.

and more alarmingly, she was forced to rely ever more on weak allied armies for flank defence.

Hitler's overriding concern at the start of the new campaign was the seizure of the oilfields in the Caucasus. He announced dramatically to his generals, 'If we don't take Maikop and Grozny, then I must put an end to the war.'[1] He also believed that the loss of these regions would quickly force the Russians to capitulate. Naturally, his soldiers were less well versed in these economic matters and had no choice but to accept his arguments. How wrong Hitler's economic assertions proved is shown by the Wehrmacht's resistance for a further three years even without the Caucasian oilfields.

Nonetheless, armed with these limitations the planners set to work. The campaign was not only supposed to gain a stranglehold on strategic resources, but additionally to inflict further crushing defeats upon the Soviets. Once again expectation was the father of failure as resources permitted at best the attainment of only one of these goals.

In the final draft of the plan, codenamed Fall Blau (Case Blue), Army Groups Centre and North were merely to hold their positions, with the exception of a small-scale offensive against Leningrad. Army Group South was to make all the running in the summer of 1942. The *Schwerpunkt* (point of maximum effort) was to be the strip of land separating the Donetz and Don rivers, with the ultimate objective being the seizure of the Caucasus. At this point the advance to Stalingrad was seen only as providing flank cover for the southern drive.

One million troops were assembled for the operation, organised into 65 German divisions and 25 Romanian, Hungarian and Italian divisions. Army Group South was divided into Army Group A and Army Group B. Army Group A under List was to strike deep into the Caucasus and capture the main oil supply regions. Its ultimate objective was Baku, the key Caucasian oil production centre, and for this ambitious programme it was given the First Panzerarmee, the Seventeenth Army and the Italian Eighth Army. As in Barbarossa, von Kleist commanded the First Panzerarmee which contained 3 panzer, 2 motorised and 11 infantry divisions. Seventeenth Army also had a panzer division.

Army Group B was commanded initially by von Bock but when he quarrelled with Hitler, he was replaced by von Weichs. The objective of this army group was to establish a defensive line stretching from Voronezh to Stalingrad so as to provide flank protection for the thrust on the Caucasus. It had four armies on its establishment: Hoth's Fourth Panzerarmee, Paulus' fateful Sixth Army, Second Army and the Hungarian Second Army. The veteran Hoth's Panzerarmee disposed of 3 panzer, 2 motorised and 6 infantry divisions. Sixth Army also had 2 panzer divisions.

Nine Panzer divisions were earmarked for the new attack and these were all brought up to an average of 140 tanks, bringing the total available to about 1,500. But the ten panzer divisions of Army Groups North and Centre received no replacements as a result and had less than 1,000 tanks left with which to cover their lengthy fronts. Worryingly for the panzer generals was the fact that less than 10 per cent of the tank force assembled were the so-called 'Mark IV Specials', the up-gunned version of the Pz IV; this was the sole German tank capable of meeting the famed T-34 on anything close to an equal footing.

Additionally, three of the panzer divisions were subordinate to infantry armies – a fact completely in contravention of successful panzer tactics. Hitler's Directive No. 41, which set out the objectives of Blau, even stated:

> It must not happen that, by advancing too quickly and too far, armoured and motorised formations lose connection with the infantry following them; or that they lose the opportunity of supporting the hard-pressed, forward-fighting infantry by direct attacks on the rear of the encircled Russian armies.[2]

Even the Panzerarmees were hamstrung to a great extent by their infantry components. Infantry made up more than half of the for-mations in the two Panzerarmees and these still depended on the horse as a prime mover. Had the available units been arranged differently, giving the Panzerarmees all the available tank divisions with the motorised infantry in support, the operation might have garnered more success. These fast mobile units could have been used for the penetrative stage of the attack and the immediate gains could have been held by motorised troops pending the arrival of ordinary infantry, leaving the panzers free to advance onwards.

In the months preceding the assault the Russians were duped into ex-pecting a renewed thrust for Moscow which helped attain tactical surprise when the real blow was delivered. Before the Germans could embark on a major new offensive it was essential that they carried out a spring-clean to tidy up their front and straighten the start line. Operation Fredericus was planned to reduce the Russian salient at Izyum in addition to capturing a bridgehead across the Donetz preparatory to the summer offensive. This salient was roughly 100 km square and was the result of Stalin's January offensive against Army Group South, which the First Panzerarmee and the Seventeenth Army had managed to contain.

In May Stalin bullishly ordered the immediate recapture of Kharkov by means of an attack from this salient; by so doing he was playing right into German hands. The Russian commander, Timoshenko, assembled 640,000 men and 1,200 tanks for the attempt to win back Kharkov, which began on 12 May, six days before Fredericus was scheduled to open. It succeeded in ripping a breach into the front of Paulus' Sixth Army and penetrated to within 20 km of Kharkov.

Some of the German commanders favoured the postponement of their offensive until this new threat was dealt with; Paulus in particular favoured giving ground. But Bock wanted to attack as planned and Hitler supported him. Halder for once showed a cool nerve and a shrewd assessment of the situation worthy of Manstein. He directed that the operation should open a day early and trap not only the Russians defending the salient as planned, but also smash the attacking forces.

Kleist's Panzerarmee struck south into the Russian salient before dawn on 17 May and four days later made contact with units of Sixth Army which had attacked the northern edge. In a victory worthy of the previous summer, the bulk of two Russian armies, 240,000 men in all, and most of their tanks, were trapped inside the 'Barvenkovo Mousetrap'. German confidence in the coming offensive was strengthened while Russian morale, somewhat restored by their successes during the winter, was shattered all over again.

The famous 'Panzer-Kavallerist', Oberst von Strachwitz, once again narrowly escaped death. As the ring was being closed around the Russians, part of the panzer regiment of the 16th Panzer Division found itself temporarily cut off as night fell. Strachwitz ordered a hedgehog defence formed and at dawn next day climbed a hill with a squadron commander and two artillery officers to carry out some reconnaissance. As the officers surveyed the surrounding terrain through their binoculars, Strachwitz suddenly shouted a warning to the artillery officers and pulled the squadron commander to the ground; immediately a Russian shell burst which killed the two hapless artillery officers – Strachwitz's legendary nose for danger had saved him once again.

Meanwhile Manstein's Eleventh Army in the Crimea had recaptured the Kerch Peninsula on 20 May. This meant that a foothold had been gained in the Kuban area across the Straits of Kerch, thereby applying leverage on the southern flank of the Caucasian attack. Manstein went on to storm the fortress of Sevastopol on 2 July, this success earning him his Fieldmarshal's baton and a transfer to Leningrad. The successful conclusion of these battles left the way open for Blau to begin.

The second German summer offensive began on 28 June 1942 when Fourth Panzerarmee, Second Army and the Second Hungarian Army deployed near Kursk, attacked towards Voronezh on the Don. Two days later Sixth Army attacked from the Kharkov area towards Stalingrad, while First Panzerarmee, Seventeenth Army and the Italian Eighth Army thrust in the direction of Rostov. Kleist's forces surged out of their assembly areas and swiftly overran the corridor separating the Donetz and Don, cutting the Rostov-Moscow railway in the process. Along the way they encountered T-34s dug in and camouflaged, but Russian crews still hadn't mastered the technique of fire and movement – they either stayed motionless until overrun or else moved too late. One panzer crewman described Russian tanks coming out of their emplacements 'like tortoises' and then trying to escape by zigzagging: 'Some of them still wear their camouflage netting like green wigs.'[3] Rostov fell to Kleist on 23 July and First Panzerarmee then drove southwards into the Caucasus.

On 10 August Kleist's tanks reached the vital oil centre at Maikop, 500 km south-east of Rostov, while other panzer units pressed on east into the Caucasian foothills. It was amongst the most spectacular advances in the history of warfare and entirely to the credit of Kleist. Gone was the hesitancy he had shown in France; the general selected as the first Panzergruppe commander as a counterweight to the excesses of the younger tank men had now become one of the prime exponents of panzer warfare.

Despite incredible early advances, the momentum of the First Panzerarmee quickly dwindled to just a kilometre or two a day. The sheer pace of the attack proved its undoing as the panzers outran their

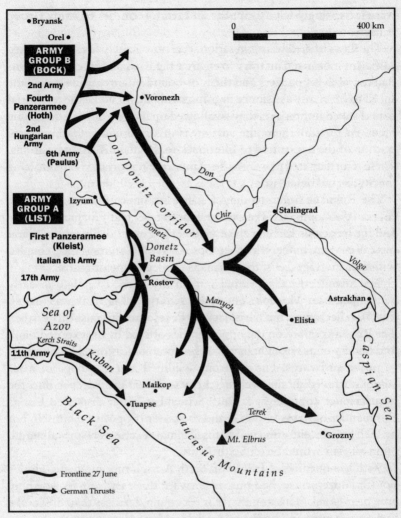

Fall Blau – German Summer Offensive, 1942

supplies and for days on end were halted while waiting for fuel to be delivered by Ju-52 or camel train. The tanks had eaten up the open, grassy plains, but ground to a halt once they approached the Caucasian mountains; here there were no road and rail links and the terrain was semi-desert. As the weeks passed, the demands of the Stalingrad front were increasingly felt as supplies and reinforcements to Army Group A decreased.

The flaws of army reorganisation were now acutely felt. Kleist lacked sufficient motorised infantry to encircle the Russian forces he had outflanked with his panzers and the foot-bound infantry units lacked the speed to be of any assistance in trapping them. So while the territorial gains looked impressive, they swallowed up many troops in defending them. At the same time the vast areas involved allowed a huge proportion of the opposition to filter back to the main Russian positions. These returning troops were to be of immense importance in reinforcing the Stalingrad defences.

The Russians began to offer a stiffer resistance once they had the cover of the mountains. The nature of the terrain greatly favoured defence and the tenacious Russian spirit made use of every defile, obstacle and piece of cover to hinder Kleist's troops. This stubborn resistance, coupled with fuel shortages, cost the Germans this leg of the offensive.

The advance finally petered out on the Terek river line in early September, near Mozdok. The strategic target of Grozny was just 80 km (50 miles) away, but Kleist lacked the resources to push any further. The Russians seized on the opportunities offered by his exposed flank and cavalry units wrought havoc on his communications. He continued to probe eastwards, but the front solidified and any hope of a resumption faded as the Wehrmacht was drawn ever deeper into the meat grinder at Stalingrad. On 9 September Hitler dismissed List as commander of Army Group A and took over the position himself, but by then his concentration was focused almost exclusively on Stalingrad. Soon all eyes would be on Sixth Army.

With the opening of Fall Blau, Sixth Army's running mate, Hoth's Fourth Panzerarmee, had pushed forward due east from its assembly area near Kursk. This impressive force counted no less than 800 tanks and assault guns and on the first day Hoth's panzers covered 30 miles, smashing through the Soviet lines between Kursk and Belgorod. After that they raced across the Don floodplain to the crossing point of that great river at Voronezh. This panzer advance was accomplished within just twelve days and for a while it seemed like Barbarossa all over again. But there was one important difference: there were no huge encirclements because the Russians were retreating across the Don in good order. So far only 150,000 Russians had been captured.

Upon reaching Voronezh, a young panzer officer seized a Don bridge and crossed into the town with only fifteen panzers. Eventually an entire division followed in his wake, seizing an unexpected but welcome bridgehead across the river. At this stage, Fourth Panzerarmee was relieved by Second Army and the Second Hungarian Army and began moving south-eastward down the Don towards Stalingrad.

Fourth Panzerarmee had pushed on to within 300 km of the city when on 13 July Hitler committed the first of his fatal errors during the campaign. Rather than allowing 'Papa' Hoth's powerful army continue towards Stalingrad in support of Sixth Army as originally planned, he decided to send these forces to aid Kleist in crossing the lower Don at Rostov. The reality was that Kleist had no undue difficulties in achieving a crossing until the tens of thousands of vehicles of the Fourth Panzerarmee rolled up and completely blocked all the routeways. In Kleist's opinion, Hoth's panzers could have taken the city of Stalingrad without a fight at the end of July, but the southern diversion allowed the Russians to gather enough forces there to put up a stubborn defence.

This decision was doubly damning as the thrust into the Caucasus was also delayed while Sixth Army became bogged down at Kalach. Yet again a fatal divergence of effort proved Hitler's undoing. Had the two Panzerarmees been allowed to stick to the original plan, Fall Blau might have succeeded. For the second campaign in a row Hitler foundered due to his inability to decide between psychological and political objectives on the one hand and economic ones on the other. He had already decided to run both stages of the operation simultaneously, whereas originally the Caucasian drive wasn't to begin until the Voronezh-Stalingrad flank line had been secured.

The drive to Stalingrad was the responsibility of the Sixth Army commanded by Generaloberst Friedrich von Paulus. Paulus was a capable planner, but not much of a battlefield general. Before being entrusted with one of Germany's strongest armies, he had served as an army chief of staff and as a senior staff officer in the OKW, but had never commanded any unit larger than a battalion. To one panzer officer he seemed 'more like a scientist than a general, when compared to Rommel or Model'.[4] He was so fastidious about cleanliness that he washed twice a day and wore white gloves to protect himself from dirt – it was a cruel irony that such a man should end up in the squalor of the Stalingrad *Kessel*.

Sixth Army made good progress as it rolled along the Donetz/Don corridor towards the industrial city on the Volga. The panzers advanced through endless fields of corn and sunflowers and it was good tank country except for the *balkas* (dried-out water courses). Luftwaffe forward air controllers with radios attached to the leading panzer divisions were able to quickly call in strikes by Richthofen's tank-busting Stukas whenever stiff resistance was encountered. The greatest difficulty was fuel – the panzers would often streak ahead and then grind to a halt for lack of petrol.

On 7 August the XIV and XXIV Panzerkorps joined hands in a pincer movement on the Don crossing point at Kalach, trapping 50,000 Russians and 1,000 tanks in the process. Stalingrad now lay just 60 km away. Much hard fighting remained to be fought in the Don bend before the city could be reached and it was late August before the Russians there had been defeated and bridgeheads across the Don secured.

On 22 August the 16th Panzer Division, 'the battering ram' of XIV Panzerkorps began to cross the Don with the intention of thrusting to the Volga, 60 km away. The commander of 16th Panzer was Generalleutnant Hans Valentin Hube, an unflappable old warhorse who frequently took naps during the course of a battle. A colourful figure whom his troops had nicknamed 'Der Mensch' (The Man), Hube slept in a straw-lined pit beneath his tank at night and wore a black metal hand as a replacement for the one he'd lost in the First World War.

Strachwitz, commanding a Panzer Abteilung, led the way for the whole division. He crossed the Don at dawn and raced across the fast-going steppe to reach the Volga by afternoon. He encountered little resistance along the way until he reached the soon-to-be famous airstrip at Gumrak and he quickly overcame this opposition by means of a combined tank and Stuka barrage. Strachwitz then became the first German to enter the city and reported a friendly welcome from the inhabitants.

The plan decided upon for the capture and reduction of Stalingrad was as ever a pincer attack. The Sixth Army would attack the city from the north-west while Hoth's Fourth Panzerarmee would strike from the south-west. On 3 September the two German armies met a few miles from the city centre, but no great encirclement was achieved

– the abrasive battles in the searing summer heat had sapped the strength of the offensive just as it approached its zenith.

It was now mainly up to the infantry to win the rest of the city as the panzers proved very vulnerable in street fighting to anti-tank rounds, grenades and even Molotov cocktails, particularly their thinly armoured rear decks. After weeks of brutal house-to-house fighting, 90 per cent of Stalingrad was in German hands by late October.

The panzers around the city had quickly become embroiled in a series of fire-brigade actions. Both Strachwitz and Willi Langkeit, commander of the 14th Panzer's tank regiment, excelled at lightning hit-and-run strikes and their panzers shot up Russian columns and reinforcements at every opportunity; at one stage Strachwitz even took to shooting up aircraft landing at a Russian airfield. During one two-day period wave after wave of T-34s and US Lend-Lease tanks attacked Strachwitz's panzers over the brow of a hill while the Germans waited on the reverse slope; not surprisingly given such tactical ineptitude, 100 Red tanks were brewed up. Shortly after this Strachwitz received the Oak Leaves to his Knight's Cross and was shipped back to Germany on account of his age. Langkeit spent most of his time shoring up threatened sectors within the city, rushing from pressure point to breakthrough zone and back.

Hitler quickly became frustrated with the length of time it was taking to capture the city as it had become a matter of political prestige to him to destroy the place that bore the name of his arch enemy. As a result he allowed the flower of the Wehrmacht and a large proportion of the Panzerwaffe to become drawn into a needless battle of attrition, where the gains could never outweigh the losses.

When Fall Blau finally ground to a halt, it left Sixth Army and Fourth Panzer Army still tied up in the fighting in and around Stalingrad and with no choice now but to overwinter there. The two armies were in a dangerous position, situated so far east with only weak forces to guard their flanks. The long northern flank along the Don was protected by the Third Romanian Army, one Italian and one Hungarian army. South of the city, the Fourth Romanian Army covered the open flank of the Fourth Panzer Army. Manstein remarked the situation was a 'a clear invitation' to the Russians to surround the forces at Stalingrad.

Halder's repeated warnings to Hitler about the dangers led to his dismissal on 24 September. His replacement was Kurt Zeitzler, a talented staff officer and Rundstedt's former Chief of Staff in the West; during the French campaign he had been the man responsible for organising the supplies for Kleist's Panzergruppe. Hitler correctly assessed that such a sudden promotion would curb any thoughts of dissent from his newest appointee, allowing him to conduct operations as he saw fit. Zeitzler, despite his administrative talents, was no politician.

With his military judgement as so often clouded by political concerns, Hitler and the OKW ignored the numerous reports from the Romanians on the Sixth Army's flanks that powerful Soviet forces were massing in front of them, even though the Luftwaffe issued similar warnings, as did General Hoth. No one was under any illusions as to the Romanians' fighting abilities if heavily attacked, especially by tanks. Their only anti-tank weapons were a few horsedrawn and outdated 37 mm 'Doorknocker' Paks.

Early on the morning of 19 November, the Russians took up their invitation and launched 'Operation Uranus', a plan to encircle Sixth Army. Over the previous weeks they had built up nearly one million men and strong mechanised forces behind the fronts north-west and south of Stalingrad. The main assault was launched on Sixth Army's northern flank by the South-west and Don Fronts with four armies, including a tank army. They first opened up with a massive artillery and rocket bombardment which went on for eighty minutes and shook the ground for miles around. It was the classic Soviet-style sledge-hammer-to-smash-a-nut: all this firepower was targeted on the second-rate Third Romanian Army.

After the barrage ceased, the Russians sent in wave after wave of snowsuit-clad infantry against the Romanian lines. The defenders fought back valiantly against the infantry, but when the Russians sent in the tanks, the Romanians, lacking anti-tank weapons, were quickly routed. The Soviet Fifth Tank Army and Fourth Tank Corps streamed through the two large holes they'd torn in the front and headed for the Don bridge at Kalach, with cavalry and infantry following in their tracks. Half a million men and 1,000 tanks under the command of General Vatutin attacked the northern perimeter that day.

It was several hours before Sixth Army HQ was informed of the northern attack and even then they were not unduly alarmed. They didn't order the 16th and 24th Panzer Divisions engaged in fighting in

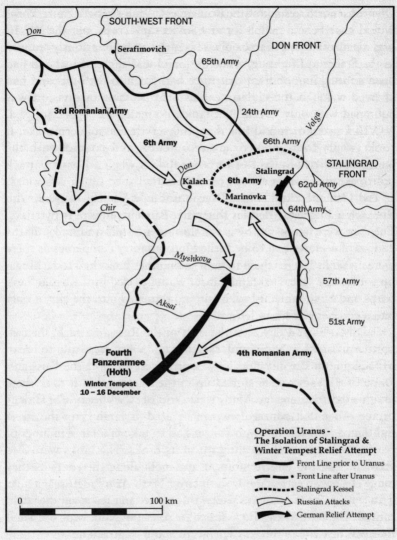

SOUTH-WEST FRONT

DON FRONT

Serafimovich

65th Army

Don

3rd Romanian Army

24th Army

6th Army

66th Army

Volga

Don

Kalach

6th Army

Stalingrad

STALINGRAD FRONT

Marinovka

62nd Army

64th Army

Chir

Myshkova

57th Army

Aksai

51st Army

Fourth Panzerarmee (Hoth)

4th Romanian Army

Winter Tempest 10 – 16 December

Operation Uranus - The Isolation of Stalingrad & Winter Tempest Relief Attempt

——— Front Line prior to Uranus

– – – • Front Line after Uranus

•••••••• Stalingrad Kessel

⇨ Russian Attacks

➡ German Relief Attempt

0   100 km

Stalingrad

the city to withdraw and prepare for a counter-attack. Instead they sent General Ferdinand Heim's XLVIII Panzerkorps – consisting of the 14th and 22nd Panzer Divisions and the 1st Romanian Panzer

Division – north to support the Romanians. A full-strength Panzerkorps would have been a match for any Soviet tank corps, but the XLVIII was a panzerkorps in name only. The 14th had been seriously reduced in the Stalingrad fighting, while the 22nd was short of fuel and had been so long immobilised that mice had got into the hulls and had chewed through the electric cables. The Romanian division was equipped with only Czech light tanks, no match for T-34s. In total, XLVIII Panzerkorps had less than 100 serviceable modern tanks. It took twenty-four-hours to get into action and contact with the Romanian division was lost for several days when a Russian attack destroyed the German liaison officer's radio.

The 14th and 22nd Panzer Divisions fought bravely as usual, with the 14th managing to destroy thirty-five Russian tanks over two days. But they were hampered by grave shortages of fuel and tanks. In the end surplus crews had to be turned into infantry companies as there were no tanks left for them to fight with; other tanks had to be blown up for lack of fuel. The 22nd Panzer was encircled by a Russian tank corps and by the time it broke out and retreated into the city, it only had a company of tanks left.

Finally, almost a day after the start of the Russian attack, the two panzer divisions in Stalingrad, the 16th and 24th, were told to break off fighting in the city and move north-west to meet the Russians. Some of the tanks were so tied up in the fighting that it took them another day to disengage. Many were short of crews because of Hitler's insane order that panzer crewmen be used as infantry in the street fighting; as a result the 16th Panzer had to take in a large number of Russian volunteers to fill the gaps in its ranks. The tanks were also short of fuel and had to stop off at depots along the route as they made their way across the Don to cover Sixth Army's left rear flank. This sending of the panzers westwards turned out to be another fatal mistake by Sixth Army HQ as it left the southern flank wide open and that was just where the Russians were about to attack next.

On the 20th the second part of the two-pronged attack was launched south of the city on the Stalingrad Front when three Soviet armies attacked. Their target was again the hapless Romanians, this time the Fourth Romanian Army. They awoke to 1,000 *Katyusha* rocket salvoes landing on their heads and suffered the same 'Panzerschreck' as their comrades in the north, with good reason – one Romanian regiment had only a single anti-tank gun with which to defend its 10-mile sector. They were soon put to flight and the Soviet Thirteenth Mechanised Corps was launched into the rear of the German Sixth Army, while the Fourth Mechanised Corps raced for Kalach and a meeting with the northern prong of 'Operation Uranus'. Once these two prongs joined hands on the vital Don crossing early on 22 November, the encirclement of Sixth Army was complete.

One of the last units to cross the Don eastwards during the great retreat was the 16th Panzer and the bridge was then blown up – the same bridge they'd crossed three months before when going east to attack Stalingrad. In the south, the only unit that had offered any real resistance was the German 29th Motorised Infantry Division, which managed to hold up the Russians for some time until forced to withdraw because the front had disintegrated all around them. This suggested that 'Uranus' could have had a very different outcome if the Russians had come up against Germans instead of Romanians and also that if the Stalingrad panzers hadn't been sent westwards, they could have had a real chance of smashing the southern arm of the encirclement.

The Germans were now trapped between the Don and the Volga in a *Kessel* that contained the entire Sixth Army as well as many units of the Fourth Panzerarmee. Five German corps, containing 20 German divisions, were trapped in the city, amounting to between 200,000 and 220,000 men in all. The pocket they were trapped in was only 50 km (30 miles) wide east to west and 40 km (25 miles) north to south, and they were surrounded by an enemy three times as strong. Three panzer divisions were trapped in the pocket, namely the 16th Panzer of Hube's XIV Panzerkorps (Hube had taken over command on 15 September when Paulus dismissed the previous commander, von Wietersheim) and also the 14th and 24th Panzer Divisions.

If the Sixth Army was ever going to break out of the encirclement, this was the best time, while the army was at its strongest and most mobile, and before the siege front solidified. On 21 November when the encirclement looked inevitable, General von Weichs, commander of Army Group B, requested that the Sixth Army be allowed to retreat 100 miles to the south-west. Hitler's reaction was to issue a *Fuhrerbefehl* ordering Sixth Army to stay put and informing them that they would be supplied by air during this 'temporary encirclement'. This was a fatal mistake, based on the ill-founded promises of Goering that the army could be adequately supplied from the air. On 22 November Paulus requested from the OKW 'freedom of action in an extreme emergency',[5] presumably to break out of the city if necessary, but Hitler refused, determined that what he called 'Fortress Stalingrad' must be held at all costs.

The Russians had used a total of 1,500 tanks in 'Uranus', the bulk of them T-34s or KV-1s. The operation wasn't a particularly risky one nor did the Russians suffer particularly heavy casualties, as they would have done if they'd encountered Germans instead of Romanians. The most striking thing about the operation was the way the Russians had used armour to effect deep penetrations, as the Germans had done in the great encirclement battles of the previous year and a half. As Manstein remarked, it was 'just as we had taught them to do'.[6]

It was a disaster for the Germans, but far from an unexpected one. Time after time the generals on the ground had warned the Supreme Command of the extremely dangerous position the Sixth Army was in, sitting immobilised so far east with nothing to guard its flanks but two weak Romanian armies. When the Russians did attack exactly in the way predicted, a scapegoat had to be found and it wasn't going to be Hitler and the OKW. It turned out to be General Heim, commander of the feeble XLVIII Panzerkorps, who was arrested for dereliction of duty, dismissed from the army and thrown in prison until 1943.

Certainly a more energetic officer like Balck would have made a better fist of things than Heim. It's also likely that a full-strength panzer-korps could have stopped the Russian attack on the north-western front in its tracks. Yet the real blame for the encirclement of Sixth Army didn't lie with Heim or the XLVIII Panzerkorps, but with Paulus, Hitler and the OKW. Paulus had ignored the danger signs and failed to maintain a strong and mobile panzer reserve; such a force could easily have broken the southern arm of the Russian encirclement in the early stages and then moved north-west to meet the main threat. With even just the lower arm smashed, the encirclement couldn't have succeeded. Hitler and the OKW, meanwhile, had disregarded repeated warnings about the dangerously exposed situation of Sixth Army.

On the second day of the Soviet offensive, Manstein was ordered to take over command of the newly formed Army Group Don, consisting of the encircled Sixth Army, the Fourth Panzerarmee and the Third and Fourth Romanian armies. Travelling down from Vitebsk in his luxurious headquarters train, and delayed along the way by partisan action, Manstein took the time to familiarise himself with the situation he would face. He realised his first task would be to try to extricate Sixth Army from Stalingrad and after that to prevent the entire German southern wing from being destroyed. Army Group A in the Caucasus was now also under threat of being cut off because there was a 250-km (150-mile) gap in the front between it and the *Kessel* which was screened by only light forces. It was a heavy task for the Generalfeldmarschall who had lost his son, Gero, in action less than a month before.

Manstein took over command of Army Group Don on 27 November, setting up his HQ at Novocherkask, near Rostov, where he posted Don Cossacks as sentries at the door. The units under his command that weren't encircled didn't amount to much: of the 22 divisions that made up the 2 Romanian armies, 9 had been completely wiped out by the Russian offensive, 9 had run away and only 4 were still fit for battle. All that remained of the Fourth Panzerarmee outside the *Kessel* (encirclement) was the 16th Motorised Division and the 18th Romanian Division. Even the Sixth Army came under his command in name only, with Hitler still maintaining absolute control over the immobilised army. He had even installed a staff officer with a radio at Sixth Army HQ so he could exert direct influence over Paulus at all times.

It was by now too late for Sixth Army to break out on its own. That risky operation might have succeeded in the very early days of the encirclement, but the Russians had quickly strengthened the siege front with all the forces they could lay their hands on, seven armies in total. Any breakout attempt would depend heavily on tanks, but during the first week of December the three panzer divisions in the pocket had lost half of their remaining 140 tanks in heavy defensive fighting and had very little fuel and ammunition left. The only hope now for the men in the *Kessel* was that a relief force could punch a way through to them and help them to break out. For this to be a viable option, the Sixth Army would have to be supplied with food, ammunition and fuel from the air until such time as the relief force could begin operations.

Originally the relief operation was to take place in early December, but delays in getting the relief force assembled put the start date off by almost two weeks. By that stage time was fast running out for the encircled troops. The Luftwaffe airlift was proving to be completely inadequate, chiefly because of bad weather and the resurgent Red Air Force. Goering didn't seem to care, having returned to *la dolce vita* in Paris. Inside the *Kessel*, food and ammunition stocks were so low that quartermasters calculated that there was only enough ammunition for one day's intensive fighting. With every day that passed the Sixth Army grew weaker and so the chances of a successful relief attempt grew slimmer. Intelligence had identified sixty major Soviet formations (regiments and larger units) in the ring of steel around the city.

On the first day of December, Manstein had given Sixth Army clear orders on what to do in the event of a relief operation: when they received the code-word 'Donnerschlag' (Thunderclap), they were to break out to the south-west and link up with the relieving force. Originally the relief force was supposed to include four panzer divisions, including Army Detachment Hollidt, a new formation set up in the sector of the Third Romanian Army and containing the reconstituted XLVIII Panzerkorps (with the 11th Panzer Division).

Manstein's original plan for Operation Wintergewitter (Winter Tempest) had envisaged a two-pronged attack to relieve Sixth Army, with two Panzerkorps attacking from two different directions simultaneously. The XLVIII Panzerkorps, only 65 km (40 miles) from the *Kessel's* western edge, would attack from the Chir front west of Stalingrad in the direction of Kalach. At the same time, the Fourth Panzerarmee, now reinforced by the LVII Panzerkorps, would attack from Kotelnikova, 160 km (100 miles) south of the city. The two forces would meet at the Mishkova River for the final push to the frightened city. But since 10 December, the Russians had been attacking all along the Chir front which meant that the XLVIII Panzerkorps could not break out of its bridgehead to participate in the relief attempt, but had to stay behind to bolster up the crumbling front.

That left just the Fourth Panzerarmee with the job of smashing the 100 miles to Stalingrad all on its own. It was expecting a lot from what amounted to two and a half panzer divisions. The strongest part of the relief force was the 6th Panzer Division led by Rauss, a division which had recently been refitted in France and was now fully up to strength with 160 Pz IVs equipped with long-barrelled 75 mms, as well as 40 Stugs. Even as it was detraining at the train station in Kotelnikova, it came under attack.

The second panzer division in the corps, the battered 23rd Panzer from the Caucasus, had barely thirty serviceable tanks to its credit. The third panzer division earmarked for the relief attempt, the 17th, brought from Orel and commanded by General Fridolin von Senger und Etterlin, was instead held in reserve behind the Italian Eighth Army on Hitler's orders, despite Manstein's opposition to this weakening of the strike force. The 17th Panzer wasn't finally allowed to join the operation until four days after it had begun, but as it turned out for once Hitler had been right in wishing to hold the division back. The Panzerarmee's flanks would be defended by the ever-unreliable Romanians.

One of the first Tiger battalions to be formed, Schwere Panzer Abteilung 503, equipped with twenty Tigers and twenty-five Panzer IIIs, was also to be added to the relief force. But it arrived late and the new tanks still suffered too many teething problems to achieve anything decisive.

The operational goal of Winter Storm was outlined concisely in Hoth's proposal of 3 December: 'Intention: Fourth Panzer Army relieves Sixth Army.'[7] Success depended on Sixth Army doing their bit to save themselves – they had to break out of the encirclement and fight their way south-west towards the Panzerarmee coming to relieve them. No one underestimated how difficult this would be – the besieged army would have to fight on all four sides at once as they pulled out of the city. Of the seventy tanks Sixth Army had left, there was only enough fuel for these to travel 20 miles; once this ran out, they'd have to hope that either the Fourth Panzerarmee was nearby or that they could be airdropped more fuel. It would be an extremely risky operation, but the alternative was even worse. Manstein had transport columns loaded with 3,000 tons of supplies and held behind the Panzerarmee, ready to be rushed to the besieged army as soon as the panzers had slashed open a corridor to them.

It took a week longer than anticipated to assemble the relief force, mainly due to transport problems and bad weather, and many of the divisions promised by the OKW either never turned up or were diverted along the way to stem some local crisis. On 12 December 1942, Hoth's Fourth Panzerarmee began to thrust north-eastwards through the driving snow. Initially the tanks made good progress, catching the Russians by surprise and travelling 50 km (30 miles) on the first day.

By the third day, so successful was Rauss' unguarded thrust that he managed to cross the Aksay river, assumed to be one of the most formidable obstacles in the path of the relief force. While the tank battles raged across the Aksay, a strong Russian tank force attacked the German bridgehead at the crossing point itself. The German 57th Panzer Pioneer Battalion resolutely defended their positions and in the words of Rauss: 'Each man became a tank buster. Just as fast as Russian tanks entered the village, they burst into flames. Not one escaped.'[8]

At this stage of the battle the Russians became so desperate in their attempt to stave off 6th Panzer that the Russian commander of the Third Tank Army was compelled to issue uncoded orders over the radio to speed up operations; this proved his undoing as the wily Rauss was able to dispatch locally stronger units to destroy the Russian armour in detail. The Austrian likened the fierce tank battles that 6th Panzer engaged in to 'a gigantic wrestling match'.

Rauss proved himself a master of the cut and thrust of tank battles. One of the tactics he used when the Russians managed to concentrate more powerful forces against him was to disengage and immediately attack the Soviets in the rear from another location. He was also a master at utilising terrain, and the topography of the ground before Stalingrad suited his purposes ideally as it was full of hills and hollows which were perfect for hiding tanks in. So successful were the Austrian's tactics that he created several 'tank cemeteries' wherein clusters of fifty to eighty Russian tanks lay knocked out.

From this point on however, the Russians kept throwing powerful tank forces against Hoth's panzers, most of them taken from the siege front at Stalingrad – this had the desirable side effect of weakening the *Kessel* which meant that Sixth Army's task of breaking out should be easier when the time came. However, it meant that progress became painfully slow as the Panzerarmee had Soviet tank corps after tank corps thrown in its path. Manstein requested that III Panzerkorps be added to the relief force, but Army Group A refused to hand it over.

By 19 December, one week into the operation, the Panzerarmee had formed a bridgehead on the northern bank of the Myshkova river, only 50 km (30 miles) from the southern side of the Kessel. The men in the *Kessel* heard the approaching guns and began to say to each other hopefully 'Der Manstein kommt!' It was the Sixth Army's best and only chance of escape and there wasn't a moment to lose. At 1200 hours on 19 December, Manstein sent an urgent appeal to Hitler's headquarters, requesting that Sixth Army be allowed to disengage from Stalingrad and break out to the south-west where it could join up with the Panzerarmee. He received no immediate reply, so at 1800 hours on the same day he sent Sixth Army direct orders to break out. By doing this he had transferred responsibility for the evacuation of Stalingrad from the commander of Sixth Army to himself, so now Manstein's head was on the block instead of Paulus'. Manstein believed that if the army did break out and evacuate the city, Hitler would have no choice but to accept it as a fait accompli.

But Paulus chose instead to obey Hitler's earlier order that Stalingrad could not be surrendered under any circumstances. Hitler, who had no intention of allowing Sixth Army to abandon Stalingrad, had agreed to allow the army to break out to the south-west only if it continued to hold on to the city, seemingly believing that the army could be in two places at once. His unrealistic notion was that the relief force could open and maintain a supply corridor to Sixth Army indefinitely, whereas in reality it was more a case of parting the Red Sea just long enough for the besieged army to escape.

However the really decisive events were taking place 200 km (125 miles) north-west of Papa Hoth's panzers. All the while 'Winter Tempest' was going on, the Soviets had been attacking west of the Don and along the Chir river front. Then on 16 December, the Russians launched 'Operation Little Saturn' when three Soviet armies attacked the Italian Eighth Army in Army Group Don's rear. There was no reserve now that 17th Panzer had joined the relief attempt and within two days the Italians were routed. A critical situation had developed on the entire German southern wing, for not only was the Fourth Panzerarmee in danger of being cut off, but if the Russians reached Rostov, they'd also trap the Seventeenth Army and the First Panzerarmee in the Caucasus. Manstein faced an agonising decision: call off the relief attempt or continue it at the risk of losing everything. He delayed till the very last moment and took every possible risk to give Paulus one last chance to break out, but the Sixth Army commander didn't take it.

Finally the threat to Army Group Don's left flank was so great that the relief operation had to be called off. On the evening of the 23rd,

Hoth's panzers were told to withdraw and to hand over one panzer division to the Chir front. The Panzerarmee had suffered a heavy mauling, with the 6th Panzer having lost over 1,000 men in a single day's fighting. The very next day, Christmas Eve, they were attacked by four Soviet armies and by Christmas Day, Hoth's Panzerarmee was in full retreat. Before 1942 was over, the Russians had retaken Kotelnikova, the start point for 'Winter Tempest'.

The 6th Panzer, returning to stabilise the crisis along the Chir, now fell victim to a planning failure. German tank tracks were too narrow for Russian conditions, but this was compensated for by the simple expedient of bolting on track extensions called *Ostketten* to give greater mobility over snow, mud and ice. Unfortunately these tracks were too wide for German rail cars and military bridges and the whole Division was held up for twenty-four hours while 160 tanks, Stugs and half-tracks had their *Ostketten* unbolted east of the Don and reattached once they'd crossed the bridge.

During all this time, the fighting on the Chir front had been fierce. The genesis of one of the Panzerwaffe's most successful partnerships began around this time when F.W. von Mellenthin was appointed as chief of staff to XLVIII Panzerkorps. In this capacity von Mellenthin first came into close contact with Hermann Balck, of whom he later wrote:

> he was one of our most brilliant leaders of armour. . . If Manstein was Germany's greatest strategist during World War II, I think Balck has strong claims to be regarded as our finest field commander.'[9]

The corps, which initially consisted of the 13th Panzer and the 1st Romanian Panzer, was reinforced in December with three new divisions including Balck's 11th Panzer – this was located in a defensive screen along the Chir river during the attempts to relieve Stalingrad and found itself attacked by the Soviet First Armoured Corps, which successfully forced a crossing of the river.

Balck at once rushed to meet the enemy corps and a tank battle raged at State Farm 79 which resulted in the Russian thrust being halted. Balck then had his Division form up during the night for a counter-attack to throw out the Russians for good. His plan paid handsome dividends as the Russians were routed in a surprise dawn assault while themselves preparing to attack. The panzers calmly moved along a column of truck-borne infantry and shot it to shreds, whereupon

Balck attacked the Russian armour in a concentrated, all-arms assault, resulting in over fifty Russian tanks being destroyed.

The Russians succeeded in establishing several bridgeheads across the Chir in early December and so 11th Panzer was forced to operate in the role of fire brigade, shoring up threatened stretches of the front. It was a role in which the Division and its energetic commander excelled. Balck ensured that at all times the panzers were free for their most important role – concentrated counter-attacks. He also relied mainly on saddle orders – orders delivered verbally and in person to the responsible officer – and restricted the use of uncoded transmissions to the minimum, thereby guaranteeing surprise.

During the attempt to relieve Stalingrad, XLVIII Panzerkorps was called upon to hold open the route to Kleist's armies in the Caucasus – had this failed, the Russians would have encountered little difficulty in hemming in and cutting off Army Group A, effectively destroying the German southern wing. Balck's first task was to destroy a Russian bridgehead at Nizhna Chirskaya before crossing the Don and joining Hoth's force to cover their flank. Just when Hoth was within reach of the city, the Russians attacked the Italian Eighth Army, forcing the withdrawal of 11th Panzer to repulse further attacks in the vicinity of Nizhna Chirskaya. Balck failed to eliminate this fresh crossing only because he was forced to rush to stem a further incursion upstream. He again forced his weary troops through a night march and with his remaining fifteen tanks fell in line with the advancing Soviet tanks, knocking out forty of them before the Russians realised that the panzers weren't in fact their own second wave. This feat was repeated a short while later and a further twenty-five Russian tanks were brewed up without German loss.

Despite these and other small tactical successes, Balck was forced to abandon his attacks on the Chir line and adopt a defensive approach. At this point the full scale of the calamitous failure of the Italians became apparent and XLVIII Panzerkorps were rushed west to save Rostov. The series of battles in defence of the Chir resulted in the destruction of some 700 Russian tanks – an impressive tally for one understrength panzer division and three scratch infantry divisions. These successes can be directly attributed to the leadership of Balck, who placed great stock in attacking unexpectedly with as much concentrated armour as he could amass. In this regard he himself noted:

For weeks on end the division moved by night, and before dawn was at the very spot where the enemy was weakest, waiting to attack him an hour before he was ready to move. Such tactics called for unheard of efforts, but saved lives, as the attack proper cost very few casualties, thanks to the Russians having been taken completely by surprise. The axiom of the division was, night marches are lifesavers.[10]

With the withdrawal of the Panzers, the fate of the Sixth Army had been sealed. There was no second relief attempt, even though Hitler talked of Operation Dietrich, a ludicrous plan to make another attempt from Kharkov in February using an SS Panzerkorps, by which time Sixth Army was no more, for it surrendered on 31 January 1943. But it hadn't all been in vain from a German point of view – by holding out so long, it had tied down ninety Soviet formations that would otherwise have been free to attack Army Group Don and Army Group A. The failed relief attempt had also inflicted a loss of 400 tanks on the Russians and this greatly aided the defence of Rostov, granting Kleist the reprieve he needed to extract his forces from the Caucasus in the New Year.

Many commentators doubt that the relief attempt could ever have succeeded in saving Sixth Army. Even if they had broken out, the weakened and starving soldiers might have been cut down in the snow long before they reached Hoth's panzers. If they had managed to link up with the Panzerarmee, it would have taken a tremendous effort to find their way west. But a breakout at least offered a fighting chance whereas staying in the *Kessel* meant starvation, surrender and, in the final analysis, almost certain death. Of the men encircled, about half died in battle or due to the effects of cold and starvation, while an additional 35,000 were airlifted out. That left 90,000 to surrender to the Russians – only 6,000 of them ever saw home again.

When Sixth Army surrendered, three panzer divisions, the 14th, 16th and 24th, were destroyed along with it. All three divisions were reformed from remnants that had been outside the city at the time of the encirclement and reconstructed around cadres of experienced men who had been airlifted from the pocket, men such as Langkeit and von Strachwitz, both of whom had been wounded. Other specialists like Hube had been flown out on 28 December on Hitler's express orders. In this way, Hitler afforded these divisions the rare opportunity to be destroyed more than once.

CHAPTER SIX

Sand and Steel

The desert is a tactician's paradise and a quartermaster's hell.

Rommel

IN February 1941 Hitler decided to commit German forces to prop up Mussolini in Libya. Il Duce had launched an ill-considered invasion of Egypt, but this was quickly rebuffed by the British who, though greatly outnumbered, were fully motorised and well equipped with tanks – the only significant motorised unit the Italians possessed was their brothel. In a two-month campaign the British had pushed the Italians out of Egypt and Cyrenaica (eastern Libya) and were now threatening western Libya. Hitler, worried about the effect on Italian morale if they lost this colony, decided to send in the Germans.

The original German forces to be dispatched for Operation Sonnen-blume (Sunflower) were just two divisions, the 15th Panzer Division and the new 5th Light Division, which was equipped with a Panzer regiment formed from units of the 3rd Panzer. Von Thoma, who had been sent on a fact-finding mission to Africa in 1940, had suggested that four panzer divisions be sent over, but Hitler, mindful of the looming Barbarossa, was unwilling to spare more than one of the precious armoured divisions for what he considered a side-show.

The 5th Light would start arriving in mid-February and the 15th Panzer in early March. Their mission was strictly limited: to halt the British advance into Libya and stabilise the front. To command this 'Deutsches Afrikakorps' (DAK), Hitler chose Generalmajor Erwin Rommel, erstwhile commander of the 7th Panzer. Apparently Manstein was also considered, but it was decided that he would be better employed in Russia. On 12 February 1941, Rommel arrived in Tripoli and overflew his new battleground for the first time.

What he saw below him was a forbidding and desolate landscape – miles of featureless, treeless desert as far as the eye could see. There was only one good road – the Italian-built Via Balbia which ran from Tripoli to the Egyptian frontier. But the desert did have one great advantage: it was a natural arena for tank battles. This would be a war of the machines in which speed and mobility held the key to success and in which non-motorised troops were just a burden.

Rommel later wrote that 'it was probably in North Africa that the war took on its most advanced form' and that the desert was 'the only theatre where the pure tank battle between major formations was fought'.[1] Certainly the rigours of the desert required unheard of exertions by the tank crews as they sweltered in their steel boxes in the terrible heat.

The bulk of the fighting was to take place in the 65 km (40 miles) wide coastal strip between Tripoli and Alexandria, most of which was good going for tanks. It was almost always possible to outflank the enemy on his southern flank, except where there were deep wadis or soft sand, such as in the area of the Qattara Depression 65 km (40 miles) south of El Alamein. For the next two years the desert war would rage back and forth across this narrow strip of coastline and would make famous the name of Rommel and his Afrika Korps.

While he waited for his tanks to arrive by sea, Rommel had dummy tanks built on Kubelwagen chassis to fool the British as to his strength. He realised there was very little to stop the British if they decided to push on to Tripoli, but unbeknownst to him, the best of the British units in North Africa had been shipped to Greece. Secretly Rommel was already thinking about a panzer drive to the Suez Canal, 2,400km (1,500 miles) away, even though his orders were only to hold Libya, not to engage in offensives into Egypt. He had been told by the OKW to stay on the defensive until the 15th Panzer arrived and even then not to push beyond Benghazi. But it wasn't in Rommel's character to stay on the defensive for very long and soon he was leading an extra-ordinary advance.

On 11 March the 5th Panzer Regiment disembarked in Tripoli with its 120 tanks (only half were Pz IIIs or IVs). Rommel held a military

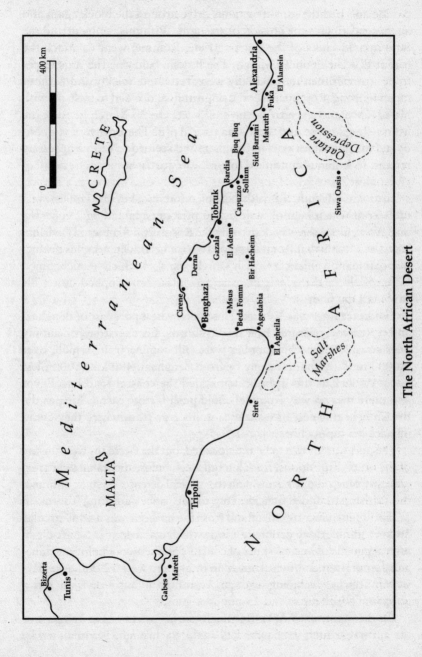

The North African Desert

parade and had the same few tanks drive around the block again and again so as to give the illusion of strength. With this regiment and the 80 outdated tanks of the Italian Ariete, Rommel went to attack the fort at El Agheila on 24 March. The British, believing the Axis forces to be stronger then they actually were, retreated quickly and without much fighting. Rommel, ever the opportunist, decided to push on with his advance and see how far he could get. On 30 March he took the Mersa Brega defile and Agedabia on 2 April. The British next abandoned the important port of Benghazi and seemed to be in a headlong retreat, so Rommel continued to push eastwards, hoping to seize all of Cyrenaica.

Next was Mechili, a British-occupied fort 160 km (100 miles) west of Tobruk which he took with 2,000 prisoners, including 2 generals, on 8 April, along the way destroying the British 2nd Armoured Division. It was at Mechili that Rommel gained two of his trademarks: his distinctive command vehicle, a British Dorchester 4x4 which he nicknamed 'Mammuth', and the pair of plastic goggles seen propped up on his cap in all the photos.

The next target was Tobruk. This was the best port east of Benghazi and if Rommel captured it, it would shorten his overstretched supply lines considerably – his supplies were still coming from Tripoli, over 1,600 km (1,000 miles) away or from Benghazi, 480 km (300 miles) away. As well as this Tobruk dominated the coastal road into Egypt and there was no way Rommel could push farther east as long as the British held this nest of resistance in his rear from where they could menace his supply lines.

The port was known to be well fortified, but the Germans were unsure of the exact dispositions. It took a full week before the Italians came up with the plans, despite having built the original defensive system, although the British had added considerably to this since capturing Tobruk in January. Ten miles (16 km) inland from the harbour was a semi-circular 50-km (30-mile) long perimeter, inside which was a deep anti-tank ditch, several minefields and two lines of concrete bunkers containing machine-guns, mortars and anti-tank guns. In total there were 12,000 defenders within Tobruk, including a tough Australian infantry division and a good number of tanks and 25-pounder guns.

On the night of 13 April Rommel sent his men to cave in a part of the anti-tank ditch so the panzers could go through. Before dawn he sent in twenty-five Pz IIIs and IVs of the 5th Panzer Regiment. They penetrated 2 miles without having to fire a shot, but as the sun came up, the panzers were hit with heavy fire from front, flank and rear. Within minutes half of the tanks were destroyed and the rest beat a fighting retreat. Another attack on the 16th was also repulsed with heavy losses for the Afrika Korps.

Earlier, Rommel had sent a force of armoured cars and motorised infantry past Tobruk and farther east where they'd succeeded in capturing Bardia, as well as the vital Sollum and Halfaya Passes into Egypt. But still Tobruk held out and there was no prospect of penetrating further into Egypt as long as it did.

Meanwhile back in Berlin, the OKW were getting worried about the way things were developing in Africa. Halder dispatched Paulus, Deputy Chief of the General Staff, to 'head off this soldier gone stark mad'.[2] He was there in time to see another assault on the fortress of Tobruk on 30 April. The 15th Panzer Division had arrived at last and drove a wedge into the defences, but failed in its efforts to expand the salient and by 4 May the attack had to be called off. The Afrika Korps had suffered 1,200 casualties.

On 15 May, the British commander in the Middle East, General Archibald Wavell, launched Operation Brevity, the first attempt to relieve Tobruk. The fifty-five Matilda and cruiser tanks committed succeeded in capturing Fort Capuzzo, Sollum and Halfaya Pass, but only temporarily, because Rommel quickly sent in the 8th Panzer Regiment and some 88s which soon succeeded in pushing the British back to the pass. On 27 May the 8th Panzer Regiment and a Kampfgruppe drove them out of that as well. In a little over three months Rommel had advanced 1,600 km (1,000 miles) and was now on the frontier with Egypt.

It was a situation the British just couldn't tolerate and Rommel knew they were bound to make a second attempt to relieve Tobruk. He now went on the defensive and began to fortify the Sollum and Halfaya Pass positions, including ordering a battery of 88s to dig in with their barrels at zero elevation so they could take on tanks. Tobruk had to be invested with troops to stop the besieged garrison from breaking out and all supplies going east of Tobruk had to make a dog leg south of the port, a serious nuisance until the Italians built a road.

At this stage the Afrika Korps had a total of 300 tanks, but 150 of them were obsolete Italian models which didn't see action in the coming battles. Of the German tank total, only 95 were Pz IIIs or IVs. The 15th Panzer with 80 tanks would man the frontier defences, while the 5th Light was held south of Tobruk, ready to intervene in a crisis and now led by the aristocratic General-Major Johann von Ravenstein, its previous commander having been packed off back to Germany by Rommel. With these preparations made, the Germans sat back and waited for the British to attack.

Wavell, under pressure from Churchill to attack quickly, drew up plans for 'Operation Battleaxe.' It would be a three pronged attack with the objectives of smashing the forces in the Sollum-Halfaya line, relieving Tobruk and then pushing the Germans as far west as possible. To strengthen the attacking forces, a British convoy carrying 240 tanks was pushed through the Mediterranean to Alexandria. The British assembled one armoured division and two armoured brigades, about 190 tanks in all, including 50 of the new Mk VI Crusaders, a fast tank with a 2-pounder gun that was roughly a match for the Pz III and IV. But the British plan had serious flaws: the heavy Matildas were too slow to keep up with the Crusaders and the crews hadn't received adequate training in the short time allowed for the build-up. Significantly, the British commander placed his HQ a five-hour drive away from the border with Libya – the British still hadn't assimilated the lesson that in highly mobile, fast-moving tank battles, the commander needs to be as close as possible to the fighting.

On 15 June, Battleaxe got under way with an attack by British tanks and Indian infantry on Halfaya Pass. They ran straight into withering fire from the 88s and suffered heavily in three failed attacks. But the British 7th Armoured Division did manage to take Capuzzo. Rommel counter-attacked with the 15th Panzer and 5th Light at dawn on the 16th, inflicting severe losses on the British tank forces. Then Rommel launched his masterstroke: he sent the 15th Panzer and the 5th Light across the British southern flank to cut into their rear, leaving them no choice but to withdraw or be trapped.

Battleaxe was a complete failure – the British lost over 90 tanks, including 60 Matildas and 30 of the new Crusaders. The Germans on the other hand had lost only twenty-five Panzers, being able to recover and repair three-quarters of their losses thanks to possession of the battlefield at the end of the fight. In the recriminations on the British side, Churchill replaced Wavell with General Claude Auchinleck, even though it had been Churchill who had wanted Battleaxe in the first place, not Wavell.

On the German side, the defeat of Battleaxe marked the beginning of the legends of both the Desert Fox and the 'tank-killing 88s' – the dual-purpose medium artillery pieces were a decisive weapon when used as part of the Panzerwaffe's Sword and Shield technique – they had a massive range, were very hard to spot when properly dug in and rarely missed their target. One British officer said that when an 88 shell scored a direct hit, it was as if the tank had been struck by a gigantic sledge-hammer. The tanks and anti-tank guns learned to co-operate closely, leapfrogging each other both in the advance and the retreat.

For the rest of the summer and autumn of 1941, Rommel waited in vain for the reinforcements he needed if he was to continue the advance into Egypt, but all he got were promotions and false promises. In fact no further German divisions were shipped out to Africa until the second half of 1942 – Russia was consuming everything. What Rommel got instead were some name changes and creative accounting to make his forces look bigger than they were. In July he was promoted to the rank of Panzer General and in August he was made commander of Panzergruppe Afrika, which consisted of the Deutsches Afrika Korps, the German 90th Light Division and six Italian divisions.

The DAK contained only the two panzer divisions – the 15th Panzer and the 5th Light, now renamed the 21st Panzer Division, even though it received no extra tanks or men. The DAK panzer divisions each had one panzer regiment with 194 tanks, as well as one motorised infantry regiment, an artillery regiment, an anti-tank battalion and an armoured reconnaissance battalion with 30 armoured cars. The establishment strength of each division was 12,500 men.

The DAK commander was General Ludwig Cruewell, with Oberst Fritz Bayerlein as his Chief of Staff. Bayerlein had just come from Russia where he'd learned all about mobile warfare from 'that master of the art, General Guderian'.[3] Bayerlein, a 'a stocky, tough little terrier of a man',[4] had fought in the First World War as a private and was destined to become one of the top German tank commanders of the Second World War.

A new German division, the 90th Light, was formed with what independent units could be scraped together in Africa; it had no tanks, but plenty of artillery, including an 88 battalion. The 6 Italian divisions under Rommel's command consisted of 4 infantry and 2 armoured divisions – the Ariete and the Trieste made up the XX Italian Motorised Corps. The total manpower of Rommel's three German and six Italian divisions was 119,000 men.

Rommel also received a new Italian superior that summer, General Bastico, whom he quickly nicknamed 'Bombastico'.

After the failure of Battleaxe, the front was quiet for a time as both sides raced to build up more men and weapons than the other. The German supplies, coming from Italy, had less distance to travel by sea than the British, but the inaction of the Italian Navy and the success of the RAF and Royal Navy operating out of Malta meant that many of the Axis convoys were going to the bottom of the Mediterranean, whereas British convoys through the Red Sea were relatively unmolested by comparison. By November 1941 Rommel had 260 German tanks, 150 of which were Pz IIIs and 50 were Pz IVs; he also had 150 Italian tanks, although these were close to useless. However the Panzer figures were nothing compared with the number of tanks the British had built up: 300 Cruisers, 300 American Stuarts and 170 Matildas.

The next British offensive, Operation Crusader, would be carried out by the Eighth Army, which had roughly the same number of men as Rommel's Panzergruppe, but with over 700 tanks ready for battle and 200 more in reserve, had substantially more armour than the Germans. The RAF also outnumbered the Luftwaffe by about ten to one. The Eighth Army was divided into two corps; the one with the bulk of the armour, XXX Corps, which included the famed 7th Armoured Division (the Desert Rats), would move around the southern flank of the Germans' Sollum-Sidi Omar defensive line and thrust north-west where it hoped to meet and destroy Rommel's armour. The second corps, XIII, would advance as far as the Sollum-Sidi Omar defences and pin down the German forces there until the tank battle was decided. While all this was going on, the Tobruk garrison was supposed to break out and move towards Sidi Rezegh, 10 miles east of Tobruk, where they would eventually link up with XXX Corps.

Crusader began on 18 November 1941, the same day Rommel returned from a visit to Italy. The British had successfully concealed their build-up and a torrential downpour the day before had grounded German reconnaissance planes. The battle would rage for two weeks and be so fast and furious that neither side was sure who was winning.

According to von Mellenthin, 'There has never been a battle fought at such an extreme pace and with such bewildering vicissitudes of fortune.'[5] To begin with the British seized the airstrip at Sidi Rezegh and Rommel had to break off his attack on Tobruk to go and meet them head-on. The 15th and 21st Panzer were sent to Sidi Rezegh on the 21st and inflicted severe losses on the British 7th Armoured Division, who contributed to their own defeat by dispersing their tank brigades so the concentrated panzers could take them on in detail. But the Germans too lost about half of the 150 tanks they'd thrown into the battle. At one point the fuel tanks of the 21st Panzer even ran dry and the tanks had to wait in leaguer until a fuel convoy arrived during the night. Bayerlein described the battle as a series of individual 'tank duels of tremendous intensity'[6] At the same time as this fierce tank battle was going on, the Tobruk defenders began their breakout.

Rommel came to the premature conclusion that XXX Corps posed no further threat and decided to launch a strategic raid into the enemy's rear. On the 24th he pushed on into Egypt with all his armour with the aim of destroying XIII Corps grouped in front of the Sollum-Sidi Omar defences. Rommel ended up having to spend the night in the 'Mammuth' with Cruewell after they lost their way while British forces moved around them on all sides, not suspecting the catch within their grasp – on the 29th they had succeeded in capturing von Ravenstein, commander of 21st Panzer. But meanwhile back at Sidi Rezegh, the British were far from beaten and had linked up with the Tobruk garrison. Rommel had to quickly abort his Egyptian raid and send the two panzer divisions back to restore the siege, which they achieved by 1 December 1941.

By now the Panzergruppe was seriously reduced in strength and no reinforcements could be expected before January, whereas the British continued to receive plenty of replacements. Rommel was faced with no choice but to retreat from Tobruk to Gazala, 60 km (40 miles) west, beginning on 7 December. The siege of Tobruk was finally lifted after eight months and the British kept advancing westwards. During December, the Panzergruppe was forced to fall back to Mersa Brega and then El Agheila, the points from where Rommel's offensive had begun the previous February. Despite the skill with which the retreat had been conducted, by the end of the month Rommel had lost 300 tanks (including Italian models) and suffered 38,000 casualties; 4,000

Germans and 10,000 Italians had been left behind in the isolated frontier positions at Bardia, Sollum and Halfaya.

During December 1941, the Germans in Africa were retreating to the west just like their Kameraden in Russia, and yet by the end of January 1942, Rommel was ready to attack again. Supplies had started getting through to the Afrika Korps at last – in early January fifty-five tanks were landed at Tripoli, giving the DAK a slight numerical superiority over the British. Rommel was also well aware that the British supply lines were now as overstretched as the German ones had been when the DAK was on the Egyptian frontier. On top of this, his command was now elevated from Panzer Gruppe Afrika to the impressive-sounding Panzerarmee Afrika, although he didn't receive any additional German divisions, still commanding the same three German divisions along with seven Italian ones.

By the fourth week of January the Afrika Korps had 110 tanks ready for action and 30 in reserve; Italian tanks totalled 90. Showing the cunning that earned him the name 'Desert Fox', Rommel sent convoys of trucks westwards so as to fool the British into thinking he was continuing to retreat. But instead he attacked on 21 January, catching the British by surprise and sending them into retreat. In hot pursuit the 15th Panzer covered 80 km (50 miles) in just four hours. By late January, he had recaptured Benghazi after mounting a feint against Mechili which drew most of the British armour away from the port.

By the first week of February, the British had dug in at Gazala, so Rommel halted the advance and took a month's leave. Back in Berlin, he tried to persuade Hitler to let him have three more divisions so he could conquer Egypt, but Hitler, too obsessed with events on the Ostfront to care much about Africa, agreed only to Operation Herakles, an invasion of Malta which would be launched in June. This tiny island had been a serious thorn in Rommel's side, with the RAF and RN stationed there constantly sallying out to menace his supply lines. The Panzerwaffe was ordered to establish a special-purpose tank battalion for use in the proposed seaborne landing; it was to be equipped with up-armoured Pz IVs and captured Russian KVs.

However, at this point Rommel, fearing a British attack before the island was taken, decided to return to Africa and push on with his advance. If he succeeded in taking Tobruk, he would then wait until

Malta was subdued before pushing on into Egypt. This turned out to be a tactical mistake as Malta was never taken.

Rommel's new offensive, Operation Venezia, got under way during the night of 26 May with the 3 German divisions supplemented by 3 Italian. Substantially outnumbered in tanks, infantry and artillery, Rommel had 320 German tanks (240 Pz IIIs, 40 Pz IVs and 40 obsolete Pz IIs) and 240 of the Italian 'self-propelled coffins'. In contrast the British could field 900 including 110 Matildas, 250 Crusaders and 200 of the new American-built Grants armed with long-range 75 mm guns. Only the long-barrelled Pz IVs were a match for the Grant, but the DAK had only 4 of them as opposed to 40 of the short-barrelled variety. The main tank of the panzer divisions at this point was the Pz III with the short-barrelled 50 mm. Of the tank-killing 88s, the Afrika Korps had just 48.

The British had built up a series of one-mile square strongpoints in their Gazala defences which they called 'boxes' and behind these, mobile reserves in the form of the 1st and 7th Armoured Divisions were waiting. In addition over a million mines had been laid down in extensive minefields.

Rommel's plan was a diversionary frontal attack on the Gazala Line by infantry, while his armoured and motorised formations (15th and 21st Panzer, 90th Light and XX Italian Motorised Corps), flanked the southernmost point of the Gazala Line at Bir Hacheim, and then swung back north into the enemy's rear around Acroma, in what he termed his 'risky right hook'. If it worked, the Gazala defenders would be trapped.

To make the frontal attack carried out by the Italian infantry seem bigger, Rommel employed his dummy tanks as well as aircraft engines mounted on trucks to throw up great clouds of dust. Meanwhile Rommel's motorised formations, consisting of 10,000 vehicles in all, moved through the night, skirted the British defences and then turned north towards the sea. But the next day the advance became stalled when the panzers ran into the new Grant tanks, which proved able to destroy the Pz IIIs and IVs at long range. When the panzer divisions went into leaguer for the night, a third of their tanks had been lost and the Afrika Korps was fast running out of food, ammunition and fuel because no supplies could get through to the 'Cauldron' they were trapped in.

After that first day's fighting Rommel knew his original plan had failed. He decided instead to move back west by going straight through the Gazala Line. But directly in his path was a minefield and one of the British 'boxes', the defenders of which put up a fierce defence. Rommel came to the tough decision that he would have to capitulate if they hadn't broken through by noon on 1 June. As Bayerlein described it, 'We were in a really desperate position, our backs against a minefield, no food, no water, no petrol, very little ammunition.'[7] On top of all this Cruewell was captured when his plane was forced to land behind British lines.

On 1 June, Rommel launched a furious final assault on the British box and just as noon approached, the defenders gave in – suddenly the balance had swung back in Rommel's favour again. He now chose to head south and attack Bir Hacheim, the southernmost stronghold in the Gazala Line. It surrendered on 10 June after fierce fighting and Rommel once again moved towards Tobruk. Halfway between Bir Hacheim and Tobruk he encountered the main centre of resistance in the Knightsbridge Box, where a large part of the remaining British armour was now located. The panzers attacked frontally and in flank and late on 11 June, the British abandoned Knightsbridge. Within days they were retreating back into Egypt, leaving the Tobruk garrison to its fate.

Rommel now crossed the Via Balbia and surrounded Tobruk. The attack went in on 20 June and the fortress fell quickly this time, now that the garrison had no hope of relief. The Germans captured about 35,000 prisoners and 2,000 vehicles and to crown his success, Rommel was elevated to Generalfeldmarschall at just fifty. It was the high point of his military career. Ironically, the low point was only months away.

With Tobruk in Rommel's hands, he now had the option of either continuing the advance into Egypt on the heels of the retreating British or staying on the defensive until Malta had been taken. In Rommel's opinion it was best to strike into Egypt immediately while the British were still disorganised rather than wait until they had had a chance to consolidate their defences. On the other hand, Rommel's superior, Generalfeldmarshal Albert Kesselring, C-in-C of all German forces in the South, favoured an attack on Malta first, but Rommel went over Kesselring's head and appealed directly to Hitler. He got his way; the advance into Egypt would continue. At the same time he was promised adequate supplies from the Italians.

On 23 June the Afrika Korps began to thrust eastwards again. Initially they made good progress, taking Mersa Matruh and advancing to within 80 km (50 miles) of Alexandria within a week. But by this stage both sides were exhausted; the DAK had just fifty tanks left and were halted by the British defences at El Alamein.

The Alamein line consisted of a 65 km (40-mile) long stretch of defensive 'boxes', a series of concrete blockhouses and earthworks protected by barbed wire and minefields. The gaps between the four main boxes were covered by mobile elements of the defending brigades and divisions. And the El Alamein position was one of the only defensive lines in North Africa which couldn't be outflanked – in the south it met up with the Qattara Depression, a sunken valley impassable to heavy vehicles. There was no way around it; if Rommel wanted to get to Alexandria and Cairo, he'd have to go right through the British defensive line. It would be the kind of static warfare battle the British excelled at and which nullified the Panzerarmee's great strengths of speed and mobility.

Rommel's plan of attack was formulated under several false premises. He incorrectly assumed that the British armour had eluded him and was already forming up as a reserve on the southern flank of the line when in fact it was only regaining the defences. He paused therefore to allow the slower Italian infantry to catch up. Additionally, he was unaware of the new box at Deir El Shein which lay across his proposed axis of advance.

He attacked on 1 July with the 90th Light, but met a fierce artillery barrage which rained down for two hours on the division as it, including Rommel and Bayerlein, lay on the open ground. The attack then ran into the new defensive box and the first day was spent in trying to overcome it. By 3 July they still hadn't broken through and Rommel called off the attack. The Afrika Korps was in a weakened state after five weeks of continuous fighting – the two panzer divisions had only 26 tanks left out of an establishment of 371 and all the Axis divisions were down to 1,200 to 1,500 men, only 10 per cent of normal strength.

Now it was the British turn to counter-attack and they kept it up for the rest of July, albeit with less vigour than usual. When Rommel diverted his pressure to the south, Auchinleck used the ever reliable Australians to launch an attack along the coast to crush the Italians. This forced Rommel to abandon his thrust and send mobile units north, a detour that stretched his tenuous supplies to the limit. Auchinleck now embarked on a series of attacks designed to keep the Germans off balance and force incessant fire brigade actions from the panzers. Again Rommel was aided by irresolute British leadership and poor communication between infantry and armour. German tanks, mines and 88s exacted a heavy toll; in one engagement the British lost 118 tanks to the Germans' 3.

The British now found that their position was a two-edged sword. It was as easy for Rommel to defend as it had been for them. His supply problems were easing daily and reinforcements were beginning to filter through. Auchinleck, a realistic and capable soldier, correctly assessed the flaws in his command structure and the exhaustion of his troops, and told Churchill he couldn't continue to attack without receiving reinforcements. Churchill promptly replaced him with General Alexander. At the same time he appointed an obscure lieutenant-general, Bernard Law Montgomery, to command the Eighth Army, but only after the man originally chosen for the task, General Gott, was killed in a plane crash. Both Eighth Army corps commanders were also replaced. Ironically the new men postponed going on the offensive for even longer than their predecessors.

Fighting ceased throughout August as both sides dug in and waited for men and material to build up. But the British were winning the battle of supplies. Rommel had been wrong to postpone the attack on Malta, because it was again proving a major thorn in his side. The RAF had regained air superiority, strafing Rommel's supply trucks as they moved along the coast road or sinking Axis convoys and fuel tankers on their way across the Mediterranean, thanks in no small way to information gleaned by the code-breakers of Bletchley Park.

The authorities in Berlin and Rome didn't seem to realise the importance of the coming battle, unlike those in London. What supplies did get through greatly favoured the Italians. Some supplies did eventually get through to the Germans – by late August they had 203 new tanks, in a consignment which included 75 Pz IIIs with 50 mm guns and 25 long-barrelled Pz IVs, the so-called 'Specials'. Fresh troops arrived to bring the depleted divisions closer to full strength, but by the end of August the Panzerarmee was still 16,000 men, 210 tanks and 1,500 other vehicles down on establishment strength. Fuel remained the most critical shortage – there was only enough for the two panzer divisions to travel 160 km (100 miles).

Rommel too was in poor shape, ground down by eighteen months in the desert as it had ground down an average of five generals per division. Even his legendary energy and robust health had begun to fail and doctors certified him unfit to command. Rommel agreed to go only if Guderian was appointed as his successor, but he received the following curt reply from the OKW: 'Guderian unacceptable' – the reason given was that Brausewetter's bad heart made him unfit for the tropics, but it was more likely that the tank expert was still out of favour in Berlin, fortunately for him as it turned out on this occasion. So Rommel decided to stay on in Africa himself and lead his men into a battle that he felt little confidence of winning.

Rommel had 4 German divisions (2 panzer – 15th and 21st) and 8 Italian divisions (2 armoured – Trieste and Ariete) under his command at this time, although the Italian divisions were in no way comparable with German or British divisions in terms of fighting ability or equipment. The Panzerarmee was at a decisive disadvantage to the British in terms of both weapons and men – 230 German and 280 Italian tanks faced 700 British and in troops the figure was 146,000 Germans and Italians versus 177,000 British. But it was in the air that the British had the most powerful advantage, with RAF aircraft outnumbering the Luftwaffe by five to one.

Rommel launched his last-ditch attack in what became known as the Battle of Alam el Halfa on the night of 30/31 August 1942, throwing all his armoured and motorised formations at the southern end of the El Alamein line. Strategic surprise was an impossibility but he hoped to attain tactical surprise through the rapidity of his advance and the overrunning of the Eighth Army's communication lines. If they could break through, they would then wheel north for the sea and try to force the British to engage in a mobile battle, something the panzers could always beat the British at. The Axis motorised infantry units were ordered to hold open the shoulders of the tanks' penetration while Rommel's panzers destroyed the British armour.

Thanks to effective and prompt code-breaking, Montgomery knew where the attack was going to be in the south and had prepared accordingly. The attack became mired in the deeper-than-anticipated minefields so that by dawn the panzers were barely extricated. The RAF began to attack the DAK columns as soon as light permitted and inflicted severe damage; Walther Nehring was an early casualty and command of the Afrika Korps passed to Bayerlein.

Rommel was now forced to wheel toward the unsuitable terrain along the Alam Halfa Ridge where rugged topography alternated with areas of soft sand, rather than further east as he had planned. Here he ran into 22 Armoured Brigade which was his equal in tank strength. The deciding factor in this battle was fuel, or rather Rommel's lack of it. As a result he couldn't press home his attacks and Monty, sensing the German offensive had run its course, rallied reinforcements to aid 22 Armoured. The ferocity of the British artillery and air bombardments, coupled with only having sufficient fuel for 100 km, forced Rommel to break off the attack.

By 3 September Panzerarmee Afrika had begun to withdraw, but Montgomery was afraid to pursue the Germans in strength in case it was one of the Desert Fox's ploys. Rommel retreated to high ground a short distance back and waited for the inevitable assault.

This battle was significant for several reasons: it heralded the advent of Monty and his cautious style of fighting which relied on ultra-orthodox methods coupled with overwhelming material superiority and close air co-operation; it was also the first major battle of the war where the issue was decided by simple defence rather than counter-offensive. Although the defeat was not crushing, it was nonetheless decisive as Rommel's wave had finally crested.

He relented to his sickness at last and departed for a rest cure in Germany on 23 September, being replaced in overall command by General Georg Stumme who was, like Rommel, a former 7th Panzer commander. Von Thoma assumed command of the Afrika Korps. Von Mellenthin too became a victim of tropical disease and dysentery forced his exit from the African theatre in September. The loss of so many senior officers experienced in desert warfare was a serious handicap to preparing a well-knit and effective defensive line.

Almost two months passed before the Eighth Army launched its next attack, with Montgomery steadfastly refusing to bow to Churchill's pressure for an offensive until every preparation was complete. His superiority in strength over the Axis forces was now overwhelming: 230,000 men to 80,000 (27,000 German); 1,000 tanks on the battlefield, 200 in reserve and 1,000 more in the workshops (including 250 Shermans and 170 Grants) against 540 (30 Pz IIs, 170

Pz IIIs, 40 Pz IVs and 300 Italian tanks); 1,500 aircraft as opposed to 350. Rommel's Pak strength was also effectively reduced as the new American tanks were invulnerable to his 50 mm Pak guns.

The attacks on Rommel's supplies were intensified to such an extent that tanker after tanker was sunk until the Panzerarmee was left with a mere three issues of fuel – 10 per cent of the minimum requirement for effective operations. The regular and adequate supply of ammunition, spares and food was also disrupted, spreading disease and demoralisation, particularly amongst the Italians. Ironically German reinforcements did begin to arrive, formations that had been earmarked for the attack on Malta – Ramcke's Parachute Brigade and the 164th Light. But these had no transport and proved more of a burden than a help in the desert conditions.

Montgomery also had the benefit of extremely precise details of the German dispositions and supply situation thanks to Ultra decoding. His plan, codenamed Operation Lightfoot, required a concentrated thrust near the coast, while at the same time diversionary attacks went in further south to provoke the panzers into burning up their precious petrol. As ever with the Englishman's plans, the result was a hard slogging match which Monty couldn't realistically lose, but which entailed much heavier losses than a more audacious approach might have sustained.

On 23 October 1942 the assault opened with a thousand-gun drumfire for fifteen minutes before the infantry advanced. The advance was slow however, as the British tanks became enmeshed in German minefields and it was the second day before they finally broke through. Stumme was an early victim of the assault – when his vehicle was bombed, he fell to the ground and died of a heart attack. Rommel was recalled by Hitler and arrived back in Africa in time to preside over a stubborn but doomed defence.

The German armour was sent hither and yon to meet new threats and became slowly ground down by the superior numbers of British tanks. However the attacking forces were tied down by a close-knit Pak front thanks to Montgomery's insistence on narrow frontage through lanes in the minefields. He tacitly admitted that the assault had fizzled out and planned the suitably titled Operation Supercharge whereby he regrouped the southern forces, including the Desert Rats, and attacked northwards on the 28th. Montgomery struck from the wedge he had driven in the German positions in the hope of trapping considerable elements of Rommel's northernmost units. He then planned to drive to the west to exploit any potential success. Again the mines foiled his aims and a vintage Rommel response in switching adequate covering forces to the precise trouble spot halted the attack. Despite the fact that the British had sustained higher losses than the Germans, panzer strength was ebbing at a proportionally greater rate because the British could make good their losses while the Panzerarmee had no prospect of reinforcement.

Montgomery accepted this rebuff and once again pushed to the west at the start of November. As before the Paks and mines wrought havoc with his forces, but the DAK lost so many of its tanks during the defence that it could muster only thirty. By this stage infantry losses were at 50 per cent and the number of German guns reduced by two-thirds. Now it fell to Rommel to make what must have been the most difficult decision of his career – he ordered his army to retreat to the Fuka position.

On 3 November, with the retreat already underway, Rommel received the infamous 'Victory or Death' exhortation from Hitler which required the holding of the El Alamein position to the last. The Swabian Field-marshal was stunned, but his long inculcated loyalty made him stop the withdrawal. The order was circulated to the main formation commanders prompting the plucky von Thoma to retort: 'I cannot tolerate this order of Hitler!'[8] and promptly withdraw to the Fuka position.

Thoma went forward the following day to personally verify whether or not he was being outflanked by British armour and when he failed to return, Bayerlein sought him out. He saw Thoma's knocked-out tank surrounded by converging British vehicles while the bellicose general stood erect alongside with his full medals on, waiting to be captured. Bayerlein returned to assume command of the DAK.

Hitler finally reconsidered his stand fast and allowed the Panzerarmee to retreat twenty-four hours later. By this stage the Axis front had been broken through, the British were streaming to their rear and Rommel had only 22,000 troops left. Thoma's kamikaze mission proved useful in that it forewarned Rommel of British attempts to outflank him and cut him off at the coast. That this attempt failed is solely due to Rommel's men extricating themselves skillfully from their positions and withdrawing swiftly westwards. Further attempts in the coming days failed because the British turned north too soon, thereby allowing the Axis rearguards to slip through the net. The booty captured by the Eighth Army amounted to only a few thousand prisoners and some tanks with empty fuel tanks, almost all of which were Italian.

The British pursuit after Alamein was marked by hesitancy (too narrow outflanking moves), poor planning (ammunition was deemed more important than petrol) and caution (they leaguered at sunset). Had they raced ahead of the panzers to Sollum, it is possible that the entire Panzerarmee would have been trapped.

On 6 November, the heavens opened and Rommel's escape was guaranteed by the difficult going, which provided a welcome respite for the beleaguered Fieldmarshal. Montgomery had given priority to the Desert Rats (7th Armoured) and the New Zealanders for the pursuit across Libya, but they missed Rommel's rearguards at Capuzzo on the 11th. At that point it became a chase rather than a hunt as Montgomery accepted that his opponent had escaped and so bided his time.

There was worse news to come for the Fox. On 8 November over 100,000 Allied troops were landed in Algeria and Morocco in Operation Torch. Rommel wrote in his diary: 'This spelled the end of the army in Africa.'[9] Soon the Axis would be sandwiched between enemies converging from both sides and the most Rommel could hope for now was to hold them off while evacuating his men by sea.

In the last week of November Rommel slipped through to the Mersa Brega position, 1,000 km (600 miles) west of Alamein. Hitler and Mussolini demanded Mersa Brega be held, but Rommel in return demanded fifty Panzer IV Specials and more 88s in order to be able to do so. Ironically, sufficient reinforcements and supplies were at last en route to Africa, but alas for Rommel, they were all destined for Tunisia. Now that it was clearly too late, ample reinforcements began to arrive, including the 10th Panzer Division, two Tiger battalions, a special Panzerabteilung and two motorised infantry divisions. It must have been particularly galling for Rommel when he had so often begged for just one more panzer division during periods when such an addition would have made a huge difference.

By 15 November, 15,000 Axis troops had arrived in Tunisia and had been placed under Nehring. Although outnumbered, the Germans halted the Allies' advance in early December and prevented them from taking Tunis, inflicting heavy losses in the process and giving the

Germans a chance to build up a defence line in the mountains. The forces in Tunisia were now named the Fifth Panzerarmee and placed under the command of Generaloberst Hans-Jurgen von Arnim, a stiff-necked, cautious old Prussian who'd commanded a panzer division and later a panzerkorps in Russia. Rommel took an instant dislike to him.

Upon reaching Mersa Brega, Rommel flew to Germany and demanded that the troops be allowed to fall back to Gabes in Tunisia so that they could be evacuated to Italy whereupon Hitler treated him to a vitriolic outburst that Africa must be held at all costs. Mussolini however was more realistic and gave him permission to prepare a fallback position. The British paused before assaulting the Brega defences, but on 12 December Rommel suddenly and unexpectedly pulled back to Buerat – a jump of some 400 km – whereupon Montgomery took another month to assemble the supplies he wanted for overcoming this new defensive line. This time he spared no effort in disguising the date of his attack and all preparations were carried out stealthily, but once again it was to no avail – when Monty struck, the Fox had already bolted his den.

Rommel, by now in a demoralised and defeatist state of mind, planned to withdraw into Tunisia regardless of what his masters desired and when the Italians requested a covering force to prevent the Allies seizing Gabes, he readily dispatched the 21st Panzer on 13 January 1943. This move left him with less than 40 Panzers against over 400 British and gave him a good excuse to pull back toward Tripoli. By now he was making the Italian infantry leapfrog back to his next intended line rather than risk leaving them behind as at Alamein. In the first week of February the Panzerarmee passed into Tunisia.

The delay imposed on Montgomery in resupplying for the pursuit allowed Rommel a chance to occupy what was possibly the strongest defence line in North Africa – the Mareth Line. This had been constructed by the French to prevent an Italian invasion of Tunisia and Rommel strengthened these emplacements. He also wished to fortify the Wadi Akarit line 60 km west, but was refused permission on the grounds that this would encourage further retreat. Nonetheless the Mareth position was tenable and the relentless retreat was over, at least for the time being.

The whole withdrawal had been a masterpiece. Like a boxer on the back foot but still punching, each backward step by the Panzerarmee was covered by a deadly Pak screen and the route of pursuit strewn with mines and demolitions. Rommel made full use of every suitable position to delay the Eighth Army's pursuit and even though armoured ripostes were an impossibility, his gunners and traps exacted a heavy tribute from the British. As Bayerlein remarked: '...the best thing Rommel ever did in North Africa was this retreat'.[10] Yet despite all of Rommel's skill, the cost had been heavy: over 30,000 Axis troops, 1,000 guns and 300 tanks had been lost. But the Panzerarmee was still in existence and now that his flanks and rear were relatively secure, Rommel's mind quickly turned to thoughts of the offensive.

At this point, out of favour with Berlin, Rommel was recalled from duty on grounds of ill health and ordered to hand over his command to von Arnim. The date of departure was left to his own discretion. His pause at Mareth and his proximity to supply depots meant that his forces increased to pre-Alamein proportions with about 30,000 Germans and 50,000 Italians. He had almost a hundred panzers fit for action and another thirty under repair. Rommel, though a sick man, was still capable of wreaking havoc and so he planned a strike against his green new enemy – the Americans.

Arnim had about 150 tanks. The two commanders agreed to hit the American First Army, but disagreed as to the attack's ultimate goal. Rommel called for an African Sichelschnitt which would break through the American line and then head north-west for the coast via Kasserine Pass and Tebessa. If this ambitious thrust into the American rear succeeded, it could possibly rout the Allies and drive them into headlong retreat into Algeria. Rommel would then be free to bring all his forces to bear on Montgomery's Eighth Army. However, all Arnim foresaw was a raid into the enemy rear to disrupt his offensive plans temporarily and it was this view that was adopted by the High Command.

The US II Corps was the initial target. Although well equipped, it had absolutely no combat experience and its incompetent commander lived in a luxurious bunker 100 km (60 miles) behind the front. The 21st Panzer had seized a foothold in the Faid Pass in January and on Valentine's Day 1943, the Fifth Panzerarmee sent battle groups from this division and the 10th Panzer to strike at Sidi Bou Zid. They surrounded Combat Command A (American armoured divisions were divided into three Combat Command HQs) from the US 1st Armoured Division, destroying forty tanks in the process and over the next couple of days the other two combat commands met a similar fate at the hand of the veteran panzermen.

Meanwhile, 50 km to the south Rommel and the DAK attacked through Gafsa in the direction of Kasserine. The combined effects of this twin strike panicked the Allied troops, especially the green Americans. However, command difficulties hampered the German plan; Ziegler, the general overseeing the battle, considered that as Arnim was nominal commander of the 21st, he ought to have the final say about its commitment and so it was the 17th before the Germans advanced to Sbeitla.

Rommel now pleaded for the 10th Panzer, but the vacillating and cautious Arnim was unwilling to part with it as he planned some inconsequential skirmishes in the north using this division. Rommel appealed to the Commando Supremo and these august armchair generals agreed to the attack through Kasserine, not west towards Tebessa as Rommel wanted, but northwards to Thala – straight into the arms of the Allied reserves. The new Allied commander had concentrated his armour near Thala as he expected Rommel to opt for the obvious course; it was lucky for the Allies that Rommel didn't get his way.

Rommel struck on the 19th, but Arnim temporarily withheld the 10th Panzer which weakened the attacking punch. The route to Thala required the forcing of a passage through the Kasserine Pass, but on the first day the Germans were repulsed. The following day they tried again using the belatedly arrived 10th Panzer and succeeded in storming the pass. The Fox was up to his old tricks again and sent prongs toward both Tebessa and Thala in order to keep the Allies guessing as to his real objective – one also suspects he was still toying with the idea of pursuing his original intention. The panicky Allies overestimated his strength and continued to withdraw steadily. Rommel infiltrated their Thala defences with an armoured column headed by a captured Valentine with the result that almost forty Allied tanks were destroyed for the loss of just twelve panzers.

However the offensive began to run down because of withering American artillery fire and reinforcements. The Allies blocked thrusts by the 10th and 21st Panzer on Thala and Sbiba and halted the DAK east of Tebessa. The attacking forces employed were simply too weak for a slogging match and their dangerously extended flank was vulnerable to a counter-attack which Rommel expected was imminent. On

22 February, Rommel and Kesselring decided to call off the attack in order to regroup for a strike against Montgomery's Eighth Army in the east. The panzers retreated skillfully back through the Kasserine Pass and the Allies were too disorganised to pursue them. Fortunately for the Allies, Rommel had finally shot his bolt.

For a cost of just 1,000 German casualties, Rommel had inflicted losses of 10,000 on the Americans, as well as destroying 200 tanks and 200 half-tracks. He had also given the Americans a short, sharp lesson in modern armoured warfare, but he was tormented by what might have been had he been given his way. Instead his superiors had turned a real strategic opening into a temporary tactical success. The pill was made even more bitter for Rommel when he was appointed supreme commander of Army Group Africa on the 23rd, even as his men were retreating through Kasserine.

Rommel had given the Amis a bloody nose. For his part, he was impressed with their ability to learn quickly from their mistakes. Additionally, they seemed to have inexhaustible supplies of every sort and intense air cover, realisations which made him extremely pessimistic about the outcome of the war and greatly influenced his actions in Normandy the following year.

Von Arnim meanwhile finally launched his cherished attack in the north. Codenamed Ochsenkopf (Bull's Head), the *Schwerpunkt* was directed at Beja with a battle group commanded by Oberst Rudolf Lang. For the purpose Lang had sPz Abt 501 with 14 Tigers at his disposal, as well as 40 Pz IIIs and 20 Pz IVs plus supporting units. His route took him into a series of narrow valleys which resulted in disastrous losses; on the first day he lost 40 tanks, although some were recovered that night. Nonetheless the delays imposed by stubborn Allied resistance allowed a tank killing zone to be prepared further back and when Lang's panzers finally smashed through, they were cut to ribbons by mines, hull-down tanks, artillery concentrations and fighter-bombers. As a result Beja earned the name 'Tiger Graveyard' while the hapless Oberst earned the equally chilling sobriquet of 'Tank Killer Lang'.

This unmitigated disaster was followed by Rommel's last battle in Africa when he launched the 10th, 15th and 21st Panzer Divisions against the Eighth Army's defensive positions at Medenine on 6 March. Montgomery had used his respite well and the German attack was ground to dust against his impeccably prepared positions. Rommel called off the attack after losing fifty panzers and immediately flew to Berlin to demand the evacuation of the Army Group by sea. Hitler refused and sent him on sick leave, while von Arnim took up the poison chalice of Army Group commander. There would be no escape – the famed Afrika Korps was left to face a bitter end. Rommel was never to return to Africa.

In late March, Montgomery pushed the Axis forces back to the Wadi Akarit line. Meanwhile the US II Corps under its new commander, Major General George S. Patton, attacked from the west – Lang's battle group managed to knock out over forty Allied tanks in a single skirmish at this time. Patton and Montgomery continued to compress the Army Group and by the time March closed, the Axis occupied little more than a beachhead in northern Tunisia. By this time, the Germans had only seventy tanks left and had to distil fuel from wine found in the cellars of Tunis.

The final Allied offensive began on 22 April and the Panzerwaffe launched its last brave, but doomed counter-attack in the green Tunisian hills on the 28th. The Allies soon broke through against weak opposition; the British headed for Tunis and the Americans for Bizerta. On 12 May 1943 the Axis forces in North Africa surrendered. About 150,000 German troops went into the bag, a figure comparable with the loss of the Sixth Army in Stalingrad just three months before. And as at Stalingrad, three of the best panzer divisions had been lost: the 10th, 15th and 21st.

What then was the true significance of the Desert War? To the British it was a key theatre if not *the* decisive one. The years 1940 and 1941 had seen a series of crushing defeats abroad and Churchill recognised the need for a morale-boosting victory. Additionally Africa was the only theatre where British troops could engage Germans; indeed after the fall of Singapore in early 1942, there was no other place to fight. For the Germans however it was a different story. Africa was seen as a minor affair, a sideshow. Rommel's men were there mainly for political reasons – to help Mussolini save face yet again. From Rommel's arrival his battles were very much the undercard to the main attraction: Barbarossa.

In many respects Rommel's own success was at the root of his problems. From the moment of landing, he achieved victories that seemed impossible given his available resources. But these victories against the odds produced unrealistic expectations of what his understrength forces could achieve and when they failed, the failure was often attributed to Rommel's defeatism.

The nub of the African campaign was the question of supplies. The British had the option of risking all and running convoys through the Straits of Gibraltar and a gauntlet of Axis air, naval and submarine attacks, or else travel the circuitous route around Africa; Churchill only opted for the former in times of crisis. The Axis communications were almost as thorny. The Allies maintained control of Malta and a strong air and naval presence in Egypt and Palestine. Initially Italian efforts to supply the African army were relatively reliable, but Malta's squadrons began to play an increasingly pivotal role in the Mediterranean. As the tide ebbed for Rommel, less and less supplies got through. The British virtually starved Panzerarmee Afrika of fuel by targeting every tanker that sailed from Italy, thus making the Eighth Army's job a lot easier.

Even those supplies that reached North Africa for both sides then had to be pushed forward to the front line. Here both armies faced similar situations depending on who was attacking and how far the battles raged from the rear echelons. Rommel has always been accused of paying insufficient attention to his supply problems, yet he was in no position to guarantee his needs were met. He had to rely upon the ordnance depots in Germany to move his munitions, spares and kit to Italy, whereupon their transport became the business of either the Italian Commando Supremo or Kesselring. Rommel could only demand what he needed, but he was helpless to guarantee its delivery across the Mediterranean.

It would be more accurate to accuse Rommel of attacking without having made sufficient provision for resupply during the offensive. Yet when one looks at the course of the war objectively it becomes readily apparent that had he waited for every last possible shell and pound of *Alte Mann* (Bully Beef), as did Montgomery, then quite possibly he would never have pushed far beyond Cyrenaica. The essence of his style relied upon striking unexpectedly in order to throw his opponents off balance. The nature of the desert communications required the establishment of large supply dumps behind the front lines and so a successful, sweeping attack had a strong chance of capturing the necessary supplies to continue the advance. The irony of many of Rommel's victories is that he pursued the British using their fuel and with supplies carried in their trucks.

From Rommel's perspective the most disheartening incident in the entire campaign was the rushing of the Fifth Panzerarmee to Tunisia to meet the US and British forces which had invaded Algeria. Had those forces been available to him a year earlier then he felt he could have pushed on to the Suez canal. He was further disillusioned by Hitler's stand-and-die order at Alamein and the Führer's refusal to allow Rommel's faithful 'Africans' to be evacuated to Italy. The experienced panzer crews that were senselessly sacrificed in Tunisia would have been invaluable in the defence of Europe.

Rommel's great legacy in Africa is that he achieved so much with so little. For the bulk of the fighting he had just two panzer divisions, the 15th and 21st and at no time did the DAK exceed 10 per cent of the Panzerwaffe's resources. That he held the British Empire at bay for so long and almost succeeded in driving them from Egypt is a testament to his initiative and drive. Had he succeeded, it is unlikely that Berlin would have had any ideas on how to exploit the victory.

CHAPTER SEVEN

Death Ride of the Panzers

The unfortunate and ruinous combat of 1943 had defeated all schemes to increase the fighting power of the panzer divisions. Only the quality of the individual tanks could be improved, but the total number dwindled steadily.

Guderian

A T the start of 1943 on the Ostfront, the Germans faced not only the loss of their Sixth Army in Stalingrad, but also the possibility that the whole southern front could collapse. Kleist's Army Group A, consisting of the First Panzerarmee and the Seventeenth Army, had remained in the Caucasus after Fall Blau ran out of steam and it was now in danger of being cut off by strong Russian forces pushing from the Don towards Rostov. With the Russians closing rapidly on the city from the north and Kleist still far to the east of that, Hitler reluctantly agreed to allow him to retreat, just one day after sending him an order to stay put. On 3 January, the Germans began to withdraw from the Caucasus.

It was to prove one of the most impressive retreats in military history. Kleist won a field marshal's baton for his skill in covering such a huge distance in winter and suffering relatively light losses while superior enemy forces pressed his flank and rear. With Manstein's Army Group South covering his flank, Kleist managed to withdraw his forces through the Rostov bottleneck before the Russians could cut them off and so reached the relative safety of the Dnieper. The operation was a fine testament to the effectiveness of elastic defence and Kleist's forces were still in good enough shape to contribute to Manstein's counter-attack in February.

The remnants of Sixth Army surrendered on 2 February 1943 – 120,000 Germans had died in the fighting and 90,000 more marched into captivity. Total equipment losses for this period included over 1,000 tanks and SP guns. Yet the situation wasn't as catastrophic as it had been just weeks earlier, thanks to Manstein's actions in aiding the remarkable retreat of Kleist's Army Group A from the Caucasus. Where before the annihilation of the German southern front seemed inevitable and with it certain defeat in the war, now there was at least a half chance of the front surviving.

The recapture of Stalingrad had been a great boost to Soviet morale and self-confidence and on 15 January they launched a massive attack west of the Don, again directed against lines held by German allies, this time the Hungarians. Just like the Romanians, the Hungarians were ill equipped to withstand tank attacks and quickly crumbled when Golikov's Voronezh Front and Vatutin's South-West Front swept over them. Soon a 300-km (200-mile) hole had been torn in the front and the German Second Army was forced to abandon Voronezh.

According to Manstein's calculations, the German divisions in the south were at this stage outnumbered eight to one by the Russians. It was also clear to him that the Russian plan was that the Voronezh Front would recapture Kharkov and when South-West Front reached the Dnieper, it would swing south towards the Black Sea in an effort to trap Army Group South. Yet Manstein was able to take a detached view of the impending disaster and assessed his strengths as threefold: he had space in which to manoeuvre, men who were qualitatively superior and he faced an enemy high command which lacked the experience and skill to conduct large-scale breakthrough operations. He also knew that the farther an offensive travelled, the weaker it became. Bearing these factors in mind, he sought an opportunity to exploit them.

Hitler, temporarily chastened by the recent Stalingrad debacle, met Manstein on 6 February in the latter's new capacity as commander of Army Group South, an amalgamation of Army Groups A, B and Don. Hitler was very reluctant to give up the coal-rich Donetz basin, which he considered economically vital to the German war effort, but after a four-hour discussion he finally gave Manstein permission to order a strategic retreat from the Donetz, to abandon Rostov and to regroup along a new front line. Manstein chose the Mius river, which ironically had been the jump-off point for Fall Blau only months earlier.

The Russian offensive made impressive progress throughout early February. Armee Abteilung Hollidt (Army Detachment – an ad hoc army-sized formation largely composed of scratch units) withdrew to the new line via Rostov and Armee Abteilung Kempf pulled out from Kharkov under severe pressure. Hitler was enraged when he heard this because he had ordered the city held at all costs, but SS-Obergruppenführer Paul Hausser, commanding the 1st SS Panzerkorps holding Kharkov, placed his faith in Manstein instead and withdrew. It is unlikely that a non-SS general who so blatantly defied the Führer's orders would have kept his command or for that matter his head.

On 16 February Kharkov, the Soviet Union's fourth largest city, was recaptured by the Russians. An incensed Hitler flew to meet Manstein at his southern headquarters in Zaporozhye. Manstein calmly told him that most of Army Group South was in danger of encirclement, but that there was an alternative: with all the available armour organised into five panzerkorps, he believed he could defeat the overextended Russian forces. Hausser's Panzerkorps would now actually serve a useful function in destroying the armies of Golikov and Vatutin once they had outrun their supplies and lost momentum. Hitler was told that there was no need to launch a costly counter-attack on Kharkov as it would 'fall like a ripe apple' when Manstein's stratagem reached fulfilment. Hitler reluctantly agreed to Manstein's plan – there wasn't much else he could do; by the time he flew away from Manstein's HQ, the Russians were only 10 km away.

According to Manstein's plan, the Hollidt and Kempf Army Detachments would hold the shoulders of the Russian attacks while First and Fourth Panzerarmees delivered the punch into their overextended flanks. Kempf held the area around Krasnograd with fresh reinforcements, including the Gross Deutschland Panzergrenadier Division. Hollidt held the Mius Line and covered First Panzerarmee's attack. Hoth's Fourth Panzerarmee consisted of the XLVIII Panzerkorps and the SS Panzerkorps contained the Das Reich and Leibstandarte Panzergrenadier Divisions, which had as many tanks as a full panzer division, including a Tiger company each. Mackensen's First Panzerarmee contained the XL and LVII Panzerkorps.

Russian tanks poured through the gap between the units commanded by Kempf and Fretter Pico and actually came within gun range of Manstein's HQ at Zaporozhye on 20 February. This was the signal for the ice-cold Field Marshal to begin his counter-attack. By now the Germans knew all about the dangers of overextended supply lines, having learned the hard way themselves over the previous two years.

The Russian lead tanks at this stage were running out of fuel and were outnumbered seven to one by Manstein's 350 panzers at the point of contact. The five panzer divisions of the Fourth Panzerarmee thrust north, severed the Russian tanks from their supply lines and established contact with Armee Abteilung Kempf. First Panzer Army also drove into South-West Front's flank and those Russian units not destroyed were thrown back across the Donetz with heavy losses.

During the counterstroke 'Panzer Graf' von Strachwitz commanded the Tiger battalion of the Gross Deutschland Division. He knew there was a Russian armoured column near one of the outlying villages around Kharkov, so rather than attacking at once, he secreted his Tigers in and around the village and decided to wait until dawn before engaging. So well hidden were the panzers that the Russians laagered there for the night little suspecting the trap. As planned, the 'Panzer Graf' opened fire at first light and the entire enemy force was destroyed. This latest escapade earned Strachwitz the Swords to his Knight's Cross.

Manstein had originally foreseen three stages to his attack. Firstly, the leading columns of the Russian spearhead were to be cut off and then either destroyed or repulsed beyond the Donetz; secondly, the Panzerarmees of Hoth and Mackensen were to turn north towards Kharkov and drive into Golikov's Voronezh Front, thereby retaking the vital communication and supply centre; this was achieved on 15 March in what Manstein was later to call the last major strategic German victory in the East. Along the way the panzers had smashed the Third Russian Tank Army, with help from the Stukas. Three days later a spearhead led by the Gross Deutschland recaptured Belgorod.

The third phase of the attack had envisioned a continuation northwards towards the Kursk salient, the Russian bridgehead formed during their recent offensive. The intention was to effect a junction with a proposed attack from Kluge's Army Group Centre, but the attack never happened, largely because of AG Centre's reluctance to participate, and in any event the *Raspituta* (spring thaw) soon intervened, turning everything to mud. Mobile operations were no longer possible and Manstein had no choice but to call off the third phase of the offensive.

But the first two phases had been startling successes – the two Russian fronts had lost 1,200 tanks and 70,000 men; 52 Russian divisions and brigades had been destroyed by Manstein's counterstroke. Just as significant was the blow to Stavka's (Russian High Command) con-

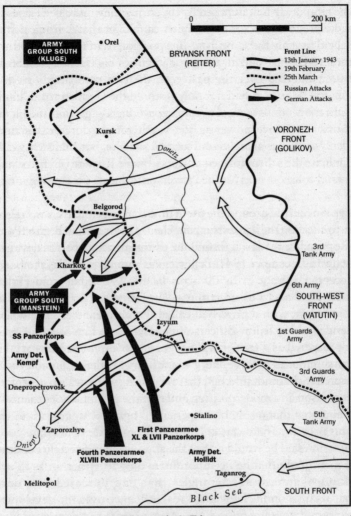

Manstein's Riposte

The Restoration of the Southern front and the recapture of Kharkov after the Stalingrad Debacle, March 1943

fidence in being able to conduct armoured operations as successfully as the Germans. Referring to the 'Miracle on the Donetz', von Mellenthin wrote: 'It may be questioned whether any achievement of Generalship in World War Two can approach the successful extraction of the Caucasus armies and the subsequent riposte to Kharkov.'[1]

The temporary halt imposed by the spring thaw gave both sides time to make preparations for the summer campaign ahead. Ironically both sides held roughly the same front-line positions that they had held at the start of 1942 – despite all the great victories and terrible defeats that had been inflicted over the past year, the two combatants were still stalemated. Manstein had not only restored the German front, but had gained a tremendous tactical victory, recovering lost ground and blunting the Soviet offensive power in the south for the foreseeable future. Suddenly the losses at Stalingrad seemed less dire. But Manstein's failure to eliminate the salient formed at Kursk by the Russian offensive was to have fatal consequences for the Panzerwaffe during the coming summer.

An event occurred around the same time that was to have a much more positive effect on the Panzertruppen. Heinz Guderian had been left sitting on the bench since his acrimonious dismissal after the failure to take Moscow in December 1941. Believing his campaigning days to be over, he accepted a grant of 2,500 acres in the Warthegau from Hitler in October 1942 and took up farming. The farmers of Schleswig-Holstein presented him with a prize bull called 'Panzergrenadier', but whether Guderian, whose fellow officers often referred to him as a bull, would have prospered as a farmer will never be known, for in February 1943 he was summoned to Rastenburg where he met Hitler's adjutant, General Schmundt. Schmundt told him that the Panzerwaffe was in urgent need of renovation and modernisation and that the panzer troops themselves had requested that a suitably experienced figure be appointed to carry out this process. There was only one real candidate: Guderian.

Guderian said he would accept the appointment if certain conditions were met: firstly that he be subordinate only to Hitler, so as to avoid the kind of internecine wrangles that had unseated him during Barbarossa; secondly, he wanted real influence over the development of armoured equipment and also control over the organisation and training of Waffen SS and Luftwaffe tank units. Unless he was given these far-ranging powers, Guderian felt the job would be toothless and he would not take it on such terms. Schmundt promised to bring his demands to Hitler's attention.

Guderian was soon summoned to the Führer's presence at Supreme Headquarters in Vinnitsa. He hadn't seen Hitler in fourteen months and was shocked at the Führer's visible deterioration and ageing. Hitler's first words were: 'Since 1941 our ways have parted: there were numerous misunderstandings at that time which I much regret. I need you.'[2] This admission was probably as close as Hitler ever came to an apology, a volte-face and a plea for help all at the same time. He agreed broadly with Guderian's requirements and sent the Panzer General off to prepare a draft of his duties.

Guderian was duly appointed Generalinspekteur der Panzertruppen on 1 March, a position he was to hold until his final dismissal in March 1945. As stated in the draft signed by Hitler, his job was to make the tank arm 'into a decisive weapon for winning the war'.[3] The post gave him the command powers of an army commander and made him the senior officer of armoured troops; he now had control over the training and organisation of all Panzertruppen, including Waffen SS, Luftwaffe and Panzergrenadier divisions as well as a strong influence over any technical developments in the equipment field. Most importantly of all, he was answerable to no one but Hitler, much to the OKH's displeasure.

With his characteristic energy, Guderian quickly set up office in Berlin and assembled a staff of officers who had recently left the front, and then only because of injury. As Chief of Staff he appointed Oberst Thomale, an ardent panzerman. At a conference in Vinnitsa Guderian presented his plans for 1943 and 1944 to Hitler and the OKW. His main goal was to rebuild the tank strength of the panzer divisions by increasing tank production and by putting an end to the endless frittering away of armoured resources. He wanted understrength panzer divisions withdrawn from the Ostfront for refitting and also hoped to build up a mobile reserve to meet whatever emergencies might arise in the East or the West. After a lively debate, there was broad agreement with his ideas, except for his demand that the assault artillery be placed under his command; these were the highly effective Stugs and they remained under the command of the artillery. An enraged Guderian saw this as an attempt to erode his powers.

He soon settled down to work. On 19 March he was present with Hitler at a demonstration of the Ferdinand tank destroyer and of Panzer IVs equipped with *Schurzen*. Guderian's keen eye noted with horror that the Ferdinand lacked a machine-gun for close-quarter combat against infantry. He also witnessed the firing of the 'Gustav', a massive 800 mm railway gun that took forty-five minutes to load. So he was surprised when an excited Hitler shouted, 'Listen to this! Dr Muller has just told me that "Gustav" could also be fired at tanks. What do you think of that?' To this ridiculous statement, Guderian dryly replied, 'It could be fired at them, I dare say, but it could certainly never hit one.'[4]

Establishment tables were drawn up for panzer and panzergrenadier divisions and although they remained largely ideal, they sought to keep as high a proportion of tanks and assault guns as possible. Guderian wanted fewer panzer divisions, but all with 400 tanks and a proportional amount of infantry, artillery, pioneer and signals in support. He maintained that watered-down panzer divisions required as many resources as full strength ones while packing a lesser punch. In addition, the large number of divisions diluted the available pool of trained men and dissipated the available equipment.

Guderian visited as many front-line tank units in the East and the West as possible to hear the experiences of tank men in battle, particularly with new vehicles like the Tiger. 'Hurrying Heinz' was beloved of the panzertroops and they were delighted someone was finally listening to them, especially as it was the man who had done so much to build up German tank forces in the first place.

He also enjoyed a close working relationship with Albert Speer, the Reichminister for Armaments, and together they achieved a remarkable increase in tank production, largely because they cut the number of types being built to concentrate on just the most important models. Guderian didn't get on quite so well with the rest of his colleagues though: after another frosty encounter with the super-sensitive and unstable von Kluge, the latter challenged him to a duel, with Hitler to act as his second. But Hitler forbade what would have been an interesting contest, especially in the choice of weapons.

Much of Guderian's time in 1943 was taken up with ironing out the many problems with what he called 'our problem child' – the Panther medium battle tank. This was Germany's long-awaited answer to the Soviet T-34 and was quite a radical departure from panzers to date, in appearance as well as in design. Whereas the Tiger looked like an extra large Panzer IV, the Panther looked like no previous German tank. It was the first panzer with sloped armour, by now known to deflect shells much more effectively than vertical armour. Weighing in at 45 tons, its 700-hp Maybach engine could propel it at a top speed of 50 k.p.h. (30 m.p.h.) and the large road wheels and sophisticated torsion-bar suspension system meant a smoother ride for the crew. Armed with an excellent 75 mm gun, two heavy machine-guns and protected by armour that was in places 100 mm (4 inches) thick, the Panther proved a very formidable fighting machine. Until mass-production was possible, the turn-out of the Panzer IV workhouse was accelerated and the monthly production of tanks brought up to almost 2,000 units.

The Panther was the result of the Guderian-inspired commission that had visited the Ostfront in November 1941 to examine the T-34. These experts had identified the most important features of the Russian tank, in particular the well-sloped armour to give maximum shot deflection and the wide tracks and large road wheels for improved cross-country mobility. As a result of this report the Waffenamt ordered Daimler-Benz and MAN to produce prototypes of a new medium tank incorporating these features. The tank should weigh 35 tons and have a high-velocity 75 mm gun. It was envisaged that each panzer division would have one battalion of Panthers and one of Pz IVs.

The two prototypes were ready by April 1942. Daimler-Benz chose the unimaginative option of simply copying the T-34 and so produced a tank with a turret far forward on the hull, jettisonable fuel tanks and a diesel engine. Oddly, considering his views on German superiority in all things and his contempt for the Russians, Hitler actually liked the T-34 style design. However Speer and the Waffenamt favoured the MAN prototype, partly because the T-34 would be hard to copy – particularly the aluminium engine block – but also because of fears that the Daimler-Benz tank would lead to misidentification on the battlefield. The MAN design was more in keeping with traditional German tank design – the turret was set well back on the hull, the engine was a Maybach petrol unit and the standard German internal layout was maintained.

The MAN design was accepted in May 1942 and at the same time frontal armour was increased to 80 mm and overall weight to 45 tons. Production began in December 1942 and during 1943 Daimler-Benz, Henschel and MNH also began building the Panther. The production target was 600 per month, but this was never achieved; instead an average of 154 Panthers per month were built during 1943 and 330 per month in 1944. Aircraft production was even cut back in favour of the tank and by the end of the war 6,000 Panthers had been built, half of which were destroyed in combat. Although the production figures were large by German standards, they were minuscule by Russian standards, so the Panther had to be qualitatively superior to the T-34, which it proved to be.

The Panther also turned out to be more than a match for the heavier and more expensive Tiger; its 75 mm gun had better armour-piercing ability than the Tiger's 88 mm despite a smaller shell and even though the Panther had thinner armour than the Tiger, the fact that it was sloped made it just as effective. The frontal glacis plate was sloped at an angle of 33 degrees, an angle designed to deflect shells right over the gun mantlet. The main gun was the Rheinmetal 75 mm KwK 42 L/70 which could penetrate 140 mm of armour at 1,000 m.

The Panther was able to destroy almost any enemy tank at ranges up to 2,000 m. It could destroy T-34s at 800 m whereas the T-34 had to come within 500 m of the Panther to shoot it up. Only late in the war was the Panther matched by the Russian Stalin tank with its 122 mm gun. American Army statistics estimated that it took five M4 Shermans or nine T-34s to destroy a Panther, although American bias must be suspected here as the T-34 was a far better tank than the Sherman. One of the most notable Panther actions occurred at the famous 'Barkmann's Corner' in Normandy during July 1944 when SS-Oberscharfuhrer Ernst Barkmann managed to knock out nine Shermans with his Panther during one day.

Along with the T-34, the Panther was the best tank of the war. It can also he considered the first main battle tank and it was to influence AFV design for many decades to come. A projected Panther II with an 88 mm gun and a Tiger II-style turret never got past the prototype stage. If the war had gone on, the Panther II and the Tiger II would have become the mainstays of the Panzerwaffe and would have shared many components.

Under Guderian, tank gunnery training improved greatly, allowing the panzers to score far more hits than their opponents. He also drew up the *Tigerfibel* (Tiger Primer) and the *Pantherfibel* (Panther Primer), humorous, cartoon-filled working manuals for panzer crews. Guderian's tenure saw many important technical advances such as the Tiger II, the Jagdpanzers and anti-aircraft tanks – the latter became particularly important once Allied bombing of Germany forced Luftwaffe units to withdraw from the various fronts in order to defend the Reich. For the same reason, valuable 88s were lost to the Panzertruppen because they were needed for AA duties back home.

Guderian also pioneered night-fighting tanks; he envisaged large-scale night operations by tanks as the only way to nullify the advantage of Allied air superiority. During the Ardennes offensive, several Shermans were knocked out in the middle of the night, much to the surprise of their crews. There were also reports of an entire British tank platoon destroyed during a short and one-sided night battle in April 1945. This was because a few Panthers had been fitted with a new night-fighting infra-red sighting device that could pick out enemy tanks up to 500 m away even in complete darkness. The area was then illuminated with flares and the tanks shot up. One thousand of the new IR devices were manufactured, but few saw service. It was a brilliant innovation, but as with so many German advances in weaponry during the war, it came too late.

The Generalinspekteur established the elite Panzer Lehr (Panzer demonstration) Division in France, which was commanded by General Fritz Bayerlein, Rommel's old chief of staff. This was created by gathering up the various demonstration units from the panzer schools and adding service and administrative units. This division was to be repeatedly smashed and reformed during the fighting following the D-Day landings.

If Hitler thought Guderian's days of arguing with his superiors were over, he was very much mistaken. The tank expert was soon at loggerheads with most of the high command, including Goering and Keitel. He was often the lone voice of reason at HQ. He opposed the sending of Tigers to North Africa and Sicily, where they were sure to be lost (and subsequently were) and the sending of the 1st Panzer Division to Greece when it was so badly needed in Russia. He turned down one of Hitler's pet projects, the gargantuan 'Mouse' tank, a 200-ton white elephant. He was the only senior officer to bluntly oppose the Kursk offensive and was to be proved right yet again. But most of the time his opinions were disregarded and he was denied the powers needed to make his will prevail.

Even after Manstein's brilliant manoeuvring had successfully shored up the Southern Front, the situation on the Ostfront remained extremely perilous. Although the map showed the Germans still holding a 2,400-km (1,500-mile) front line that extended from the Gulf of Finland to the Black Sea, on the ground their position was very precarious. The 160 battered divisions manning the Eastern Front were all seriously understrength and overextended. In the two years since the launch of Barbarossa, the Wehrmacht had suffered horrendous and irreplaceable losses in men and machines and by mid 1943 simply no longer had the strength to beat the Russians.

And as the Wehrmacht weakened, the Red Army grew stronger daily. Factories in the Urals were now turning out tanks at a rate of 2,000 a month and Russian infantry outnumbered German by four to one. American aid was pouring through Murmansk in huge quantities. The Red Army itself was beginning to exhibit a competence and skill it hadn't possessed in 1941 and 1942. Although the Germans maintained a qualitative superiority both in terms of men and equipment, this advantage was increasingly being overcome by the Russians' seemingly endless supplies of both.

After the German recapture of Kharkov in March, there was a long lull on the Ostfront while both sides waited for the ground to become passable again. Hitler, for political and prestige reasons as much as military ones, badly needed a victory in the East to avenge Stalingrad and, as he said, 'to shine like a beacon to the world'. So he ordered that planning begin for the by now traditional summer campaign; it was unthinkable to him that the Germans should go on the defensive this time and wait for the Russians to attack first.

But it was clear even to him that a summer campaign by the Germans on the vast scale of 1941 or 1942 was no longer possible. There were two alternatives. Manstein favoured what he termed a blow on the 'backhand', which involved waiting for a Russian attack before striking, as he had successfully done earlier in the year. He proposed as early as February that the Russians would most likely launch a pincer attack in the Donetz region as well as towards Kharkov. He envisaged an organised withdrawal from the Donetz and Mius to the lower Dnieper and the assembly of a strong reserve west of Kharkov to attack the flanks of the Russian thrust and destroy the units involved. But Hitler rejected this plan because as Manstein said: 'he was not the man to take a big risk in strategy'.[5]

The other possibility was a limited scale attack on 'the forehand', a powerful local offensive that would sap the Russian offensive capacity for the time being and maybe even allow the Germans to embark on a full-scale offensive of their own. At the very least a shortening of the front would allow the Germans to transfer forces to Italy and the Balkans in anticipation of the expected Allied invasion. This was the plan eventually adopted and was given the codename 'Zitadelle'.

A quick glance at the map supplied an obvious answer to the question of where to attack, but it was an answer as obvious to the Russians as it was to the Germans. This was Kursk, a Russian-held salient in the front, centring on the city of that name. The bulge in the German lines extended westwards for 160 km (100 miles), north to south for another 240 km (150 miles) and was sandwiched between two German-held salients, Orel in the north and Belgorod in the south. It contained five Soviet armies and could easily become the springboard for a Russian breakout westwards; the Germans knew from past experience how dangerous Russian bridgeheads could be. But a German pincer attack coming from north and south simultaneously could sever the bulge and leave the Russians within it 'in the bag'. This would decisively weaken the Soviets for the foreseeable future and buy the Germans time to reorganise and re-equip.

The plan itself was simple and to a well-tried formula: all available armour was to be concentrated in two giant pincers – Generaloberst Walther Model's Ninth Army (part of Army Group Centre) would drive southward out of the Orel salient at the same time as Generaloberst Hermann Hoth's Fourth Panzerarmee (part of Army Group South) drove north-eastward out of the Belgorod salient. The two jaws would come together east of Kursk, thereby encircling and destroying the Soviet armies within the bulge. This was the plan put forward in April by Generaloberst Zeitzler, Chief of the General Staff of the Army (OKH), and its main advocate. The encirclement and annihilation method had proved very successful in the past, in places such as Minsk, Smolensk and Kiev, where vast Russian armies had been destroyed as a result. In May, Hitler held a conference to discuss the plan with the relevant commanders. Present were Zeitzler, Speer, Guderian in his new role as Generalinspekteur, Model, Manstein, commander of Army Group South and von Kluge, commander of Army Group Centre.

Model, a fiery little man with an ever-present monocle, had made a meteoric rise from commanding the 3rd Panzer Division during Barbarossa followed by XLI Panzerkorps to his current position as an army commander. He was generally against the plan, arguing that air reconnaissance evidence clearly showed that the Russians had built strong defences in the very locations where the attack was to go in and furthermore had withdrawn their mobile formations, so as to reduce the spoils available to the Germans even if they did manage to capture the bulge. However, he did concede that an increase in the number of Panther and Tiger tanks might partially assuage these setbacks. Manstein spoke next. In his opinion the attack could have been a great success in April, but he was much more doubtful of a successful outcome now that the element of surprise had been lost. The mercurial von Kluge gave his general support to the plan, as long as its commencement was not delayed for too long.

Guderian was the only one who spoke out bluntly against the plan. He declared the attack 'pointless' and said it would only needlessly squander the armoured reserves the Panzerwaffe had so painstakingly built up, which in any case should have been preserved in readiness to repel the inevitable invasion in the West. Furthermore he pointed out that the Panther tank, the weapon on which Hitler was placing so much reliance, existed in insufficient numbers to be really decisive and anyway was still extremely unreliable. Speer agreed with Guderian on all these points. When the conference ended, Hitler seemed to be still undecided.

When Guderian met Hitler again in May, he tried once again to persuade the Führer to give up the idea of the Kursk offensive, asking:

> 'Why do you want to attack in the East at all this year?' Here Keitel joined in, with the words: 'We must attack for political reasons.' I replied 'How many people do you think even know where Kursk is? It's a matter of profound indifference to the world whether we hold Kursk or not. I repeat my question: Why do we want to attack in the East at all this year?' Hitler's reply was: 'You're quite right. Whenever I think of this attack my stomach turns over.' I answered 'In that case your reaction to the problem is the correct one. Leave it alone!' But despite all the misgivings, it was decided the attack would go ahead.[6]

Hitler's lack of any real enthusiasm or confidence in the plan was illustrated by the number of times he cancelled it. Originally it was to take place in the first week of May, but he then postponed it to wait for more tanks. In the end, the attack didn't take place until a full two months after the original date, even though both Manstein and von Kluge had advised against the attack taking place at all after mid-May. Ironically, Hitler's cautious indecision gave the Russians the time they needed to build up their defences. Eventually 5 July was the date set for the attack.

Why then did Hitler eventually decide to attack at all, in such a dangerous gamble which even if successful promised relatively little? General Warlimont of the OKW's Operations Staff put it down to the dictator's realisation that if he did not attack, he couldn't have avoided a large-scale strategic retreat on the Ostfront.

German preparations for Zitadelle were on a typically massive scale. Two-thirds of all the panzer and panzergrenadier divisions on the Ostfront were contained in the two strike forces that were to form the jaws of the pincer. In the north, Model's Ninth Army got 7 panzer, 2 panzergrenadier and 9 infantry divisions and in the south, Hoth's Fourth Panzerarmee received 10 panzer, 1 panzergrenadier and 7 infantry divisions. The Germans also employed Schwere Panzer Abteilungen equipped with heavy tanks like the Henschel Tiger or its Porsche variant. All of the divisions were brought as close as possible to full strength in terms of men and material. In total the attacking forces amounted to 900,000 men, 2,700 tanks and self-propelled assault guns, and 1,800 aircraft. The invasion of Russia had been launched with a similar concentration of armour two years before, but then the tanks were spread over a 2,400-km (1,500-mile) front; this time they were to be concentrated into barely 150 square kilometres (100 square miles).

The Wehrmacht placed a great deal of hope in a number of new weapons, chief among them being the Panther. As we have seen, Hitler had even delayed launching the offensive in the hope that more Panthers would be available, but in the end only 200 were ready in time for the battle. Ignoring Guderian's warnings about their unreliability, they were assigned to the Gross Deutschland. Another new weapon about to make its battlefield debut was the Ferdinand or Elephant. This 73-ton tank destroyer, heavily armoured, but woefully underpowered, was developed from Ferdinand Porsche's prototype for the Tiger tank. When his design was rejected in favour of the Henschel model, it was decided that the 90 chassis already built be altered to mount a fixed 88 mm gun. The resulting vehicles were formed into a special panzer regiment and assigned to Model's army.

Contrary to the usual perception, the bulk of the German tanks in action were not Tigers or Panthers, but up-gunned Panzer IIIs and IVs – 800 of the former and 900 of the latter, many of them equipped with *Schurzen* for extra protection. In fact, of the panzer total of 2,700, there were only 200 Panthers and 135 Tigers, 75 Tigers being organised into Schwere Panzer Abteilungen 503 and 505. In addition, the Gross Deutschland and the three elite SS Panzergrenadier Divisions, Liebstandarte, Das Reich and Totenkopf, each received a Tiger company containing 15 tanks. These heavy tanks, along with the 90 Ferdinands, were expected to act as breakthrough tanks, smashing holes in the Soviet defences through which the lighter tanks could then stream. Great numbers of outdated and obsolete models were deployed on both sides.

The Russians too had been busy. Aware of German plans due to Ultra's code deciphering and the Lucy spy ring, they knew where and when the attack was to take place. As a result, they had assembled 1.3 million men in 3 army groups or 'Fronts' as they termed them, along with 3,300 tanks, 20,000 artillery pieces (including 6,000 anti-tank guns), 1,000 rocket launchers and 2,600 planes. Even before battle commenced, the Germans were decisively outnumbered – a dangerous situation for an attacking force facing well-prepared defensive positions.

Stalin, like Hitler, wanted to attack first, but Marshal Zhukov, the Soviet Deputy Supreme Commander, had declared it would be pointless for the Red Army to go over to the offensive in the near future in order to pre-empt the Germans. Instead he believed it would be better to let the Germans smash themselves on the Russian defences and then by introducing fresh reserves, the Russians could go over to the offensive themselves. To this end, he began to fortify the Kursk salient in the months preceding the German attack, using hundreds of thousands of soldiers and civilians as a labour force.

As a result the Russians' real strength lay in the defences they had built up. Extending east to west for 160 km were six defensive belts, each of which contained a preponderance of troops, tanks and artillery. There was also a range of anti-tank obstacles ranging from several hundred thousand mines to deep anti-tank ditches. Each defensive belt was designed to be self-contained and self-supporting, with a maze of intersecting trench lines complete with pill boxes, dug-outs, bunkers, communications posts, supply depots and headquarters. Every hilltop, tree stand or farmhouse had been turned into a strongpoint. And behind each defensive belt was a manoeuvre zone for armour. The entire Kursk salient had been turned into a tank-killing zone.

The minefields themselves were even designed so as to channel the German armour into the anti-tank defences. The Russians had by this time adopted and refined the German idea of the *Pakfront*, a system which involved placing several anti-tank guns under a single commander who directed their fire. Its benefits were twofold: single targets were hit by anything up to a dozen shells, spelling an almost certain end to anything less heavily armoured than the Tiger, and in addition the volume of fire made it more difficult to pinpoint the position of any single Pak gun.

An 88 mm gun on the Panther chassis, the Jagdpanther was the best tank destroyer of the war. Hitler called it 'an armoured casemate'. Its well-sloped frontal armour offered excellent protection and its gun had a combat range of well over 1,000 metres. Fortunately for the Allies only 400 were ever built.

The Jagdtiger featured infra-red and optical equipment that wasn't surpassed until the 1960s. Its massive 128 mm gun was the heaviest anti-tank gun of the war and could take out any Allied tank at great ranges. The frontal armour was impenetrable, but the price paid for these advantages was an overtaxed transmission and poor manoeuvrability.

Early model Stug III mounting a short, low-velocity L/24 75 mm gun designed for infantry support. This was the same gun mounted on early Pz IVs and was known to troops as 'The Stump'. Later Stugs were up-gunned to the L/42 and L/60 guns which made them very useful in an anti-tank role. Eventually Stug production outstripped that of tanks.

A Stug equipped with a long 75 mm gun and Schurzen fires on Allied positions near Salerno in 1943. The assault guns excelled in the kind of defensive battles fought in Italy.

The SdKfz 250 Leichter Schützenpanzerwagen (light troop carrier) half-track could carry half a platoon and was issued to reconnaissance companies. It also served in an incredible variety of other roles ranging from command vehicles to ammunition carriers. The half-track pictured is the SdKfz 250/10 which mounted a 37 mm Pak.

Bring forward the Assault Artillery! A column of Stugs advance in Russia. Note the commander's scissors telescope.

A SdKfz 251 Mittlerer Schützenpanzerwagen (medium troop carrier) half-track towing a 105 mm howitzer ever eastwards in southern Russia. The versatility of the 250 and 251 half-tracks meant that there were never enough of them allotted for their primary role: the transport of panzergrenadiers into battle alongside the panzers.

The eyes and ears of the Panzerwaffe: a SdKfz 222 Leichter Panzer-spähwagen (light reconnaisance car) in the desert.

A panzer division's HQ staff study maps beside an SdKfz 251/6 Kommandopanzerwagen in the North African desert. This version of the ubiquitious SdKfz 251 half-track was fitted with powerful radios, cipher equipment, map tables and a bedstead frame aerial. The advantages of small mobile command posts such as these were ruthlessly exploited by the Panzerwaffe. Direct leadership from the front was a central tenet of Guderian's armoured theories from the start and efficient staff work often guaranteed victory even in the planning stage.

The SdKfz 234/2 'Puma' eight-wheeled armoured car with troops hitching a ride. The Puma mounted a 50 mm cannon in a turret originally designed for the proposed 'Leopard' light tank and reached the front in mid-1944. Production of this splendid vehicle was limited, but it showed where Guderian wanted to take his reconnaissance units.

Panzer artillery – the Wespe (Wasp), a 105 mm light howitzer on the Pz II chassis.

Panzer artillery – JU-87 Stuka dive-bombers prepare to attack Tobruk. The Stukas worked in close co-operation with the panzers in a ground support role by bombing and strafing troop concentrations, tanks and enemy strongpoints. Although slow and ungainly in the air, their accuracy and psychological effects made them one of the war's deadliest weapons.

Panzer artillery – the Hummel (Bumble Bee), a 150 mm medium howitzer on the Pz IV chassis, was used to support attacks with indirect fire.

37 mm Paks and crews in action. Contemptuously nicknamed the 'Door Knocker' by its crews because of its poor penetrating power, the 37 mm Pak's only real advantage was an extremely low silhouette. Until the 50 mm and 75 mm Paks were introduced in 1941 and 1942, the Wehrmacht had no worthwhile anti-tank gun apart from the 88.

A rare sight – a 37 mm Pak with a knocked-out Russian T-34 nearby. This brilliantly designed tank came as a terrible surprise to the Germans. Its sloped armour, wide tracks and 76 mm gun totally outclassed the Panzers until the Pz IV 'Special' appeared.

Tank killer – an unlimbered 88 mm gun fires during the battle for Mersa Brega in 1941. The 88 mm FLAK (Flieger Abwehr Kanone) was a vital component of Rommel's 'Sword and Shield' tactics; the panzers lured enemy armour into killing grounds covered by these deadly Paks. Usually they were dug in to hide their high profile, but in an emergency they could be fired from their trailer as in the case of the gun pictured. Modified versions of the '88' were incorporated into the Tiger tank and the Hornisse (Hornet), Nashorn (Rhinoceros) and Ferdinand Panzerjägers.

A battery of the deadly 88s in action in the anti-aircraft role for which they were initially designed. The high muzzle velocity and flat trajectory of the missile made this the hardest-hitting gun of the war.

The tools of Blitzkrieg. A panzer column watches as Stukas return from a raid. The combination of these two weapons proved an unstoppable team in the early war years.

Generalleutnant Baron Hasso-Eccard Freiherr von Manteuffel (*centre*), commander of the Gross Deutschland Panzergrenadier Division, pictured at his headquarters in south-eastern Germany during June 1944. Manteuffel commanded this elite division after service in Tunisia and a spell as 7th Panzer commander. He later commanded the 5th Panzerarmee during the Ardennes offensive in late 1944. His energy, aggression and ability placed him amongst the top panzer commanders. Also pictured are the division's regimental officers Oberst Willi Langkeit (*left*) and Oberst Lorenz. Willi Langkeit commanded the Gross Deutschland's panzer regiment. One of the most decorated regimental commanders of the war, this brave and talented soldier commanded an ad hoc panzer division as the war drew to a close and attained the rank of Generalmajor.

This Stug features extra wide Ostketten tracks which were designed to give the tanks a better purchase in winter conditions. One disadvantage was that they were too wide to cross German military rail bridges and this necessitated their laborious removal and refitting if tank units were moved by rail in winter.

Marshal Mud – a Stug struggles through swampy conditions on the Eastern Front. Terrain and weather conditions were as formidable an enemy as the Red Army and the marshes of northern and central Russia were a considerable obstacle to armoured operations.

Pioniers (combat engineers) at work constructing a pontoon bridge as a ta k crosses. The speed with which the Panzerwaffe could bridge defended river lines and ferry tanks across them was a decisive factor in both the French and Russian campaigns. Note the fascine of logs tied to the rear of the tank's turret.

Marshal Winter – a tank pulls a Stug from a snowdrift on the Eastern Front. The severity of Russian winters initially exacted a heavy toll on the Panzerwaffe, but by 1943 the Germans had adapted fully and wider tracked vehicles were coming on stream.

A German Panzer III passing through a destroyed French village along the Aisne on 12 July 1940. The 3-digit numbering system on the turret served to place each tank within the battalion. The first number referred to the company, the second to the platoon and the third was the tank's own number.

But even if the Germans managed to break through these six defensive lines, they faced another formidable opponent: the Russians' strategic reserve (the Steppe Front under Koniev) held 100km back and roughly the size of a German army group. Clearly, this was going to be no mobile, fast-moving battle of the kind the panzers excelled in, but a bloody First World War-style battle of attrition.

The area within which the offensive took place would normally have formed a natural battlefield for armoured operations. For the most part it was rolling plain, interspersed here and there with wheat fields and trees or cut by small streams and valleys. Overall the terrain was good going for tanks with few natural obstacles to mobility and such obstacles as did exist were all man-made. Into this natural amphitheatre would be thrown nearly 7,000 tanks and self-propelled guns in what was to become the largest tank battle in history.

At 0330 on the morning of 5 July 1943, the Germans commenced their offensive with a 45-minute artillery and 'Nebelwerfer' rocket bombardment of the Russian positions. Earlier, German sappers had begun to lift mines in the extensive minefields. However the Russians, fully aware of the exact timing of the attack thanks to prisoner inter-rogations, reciprocated by bombarding the German assembly areas. This delayed the advance of Ninth Army by an hour and a half, but the attack eventually got under way at 0700 hrs along a 55-km (35-mile) front. At the same time the Luftwaffe went into action, hoping to destroy the Red Air Force on the ground, as it had done two years before. The Germans gained some initial success in the battle for air supremacy, a struggle vital for the armour fighting on the ground.

In the north, the XLVII and LI Panzerkorps of Model's Ninth Army threw themselves against the Soviet defences, but made little progress. At the same time in the south, the XLVIII Panzerkorps and II SS Panzerkorps of Hoth's Fourth Panzerarmee attacked, screened by Army Detachment Kempf. The fighting was ferocious and went on all day in sweltering heat. Masses of infantry poured after the tanks and fought hand to hand. The Panzer crews were forbidden to leave their tanks even if disabled and ordered instead to continue firing as static gun-points; as a result they became easy prey to Russian infantry. So close were the combatants, that many tanks rammed each other and German tanks had to spray each other with machine-gun fire to dislodge Russian infantry trying to pump flame-throwers through the air intakes.

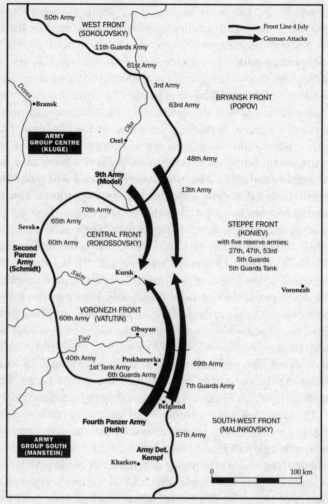

The Battle of Kursk, 5 July 1943

Overhead the two air forces fought aerial duels for supremacy. By the end of the day the battlefield was littered with burning wrecks and wreathed in smoke and dust.

The Germans attacked in 'Panzerkeil' or wedge formation, with the Tigers leading to prise open the front for the lighter tanks following, as they were practically invulnerable to enemy fire due to their thick frontal armour. They were followed up by the Panthers, Panzer IIIs and Panzer IVs, with about 100 metres between each tank. However the Russian anti-tank units found a weakness in the Tigers – their rear was much less heavily armoured. Consequentially they allowed the Tigers to break through before attacking them from behind.

After the first day's fighting, in the south, Fourth Panzerarmee had penetrated only 10 km (6 miles) into the Russian position. In the north, Ninth Army had been less successful, making no significant advance at all. Day two saw more fierce fighting. Hoth's army advanced another 20 km (12 miles) and managed to split the opposing Soviet army in two. In the north, Ninth Army continued to have a hard time: in the first forty-eight hours they had lost 10,000 men and 200 tanks and SP guns in what Model called 'a rolling battle of attrition'. The battle continued in like fashion for the next week.

The climax of the whole Kursk offensive took place around the village and collective farm of Prokhorovka in the south of the salient. This battle has traditionally been seen as a signal defeat inflicted on the panzers by the T-34s, but more recent scholarship shows that the Germans had fewer tanks than believed at the beginning of the battle and lost relatively few during it, while inflicting extremely heavy losses on the Soviets.

On 11 July, Hausser's II SS Panzerkorps, consisting of Totenkopf, Liebstandarte and Das Reich, had broken through the Russian defences after a week's heavy fighting. There on 12 July the 250 remaining tanks of the Korps (15 were Tigers and none were Panthers) met the 850 tanks (500 were T-34s) of the Russian strategic reserve in the form of the Fifth Guards Tank Army. The fighting raged all day in stifling heat in a killing ground of little more than 10 square miles. The combatants were so close to each other that artillery and air support had to cease fire for fear of hitting their own side. One panzer officer said the T-34s streamed all over the battlefield 'like rats'.

Even though the battle itself ended in stalemate and the Fifth Guards Tank Army may have lost as many as 650 of its tanks, it is still considered a Soviet victory in that the Germans withdrew without achieving their objective. The reason the panzers withdrew was not because they had been defeated, but because Hitler ordered them to. Although they had successfully penetrated 50 km (30 miles) and pushed the Russians back as far as Prokhorovka, they were unable to push them any further. Yet the Germans were not decisively defeated in this battle as previously believed, but simply ran out of time as Hitler's order to withdraw came before they had a chance to achieve a decisive result. Victory at Prokhorovka would have opened the way to Kursk and failure to capture it meant the inevitable failure of the whole offensive.

Meanwhile, there was further disaster in the north. Model's Ninth had only advanced about 16 km (10 miles) when on 15 July, the Russian West and Bryansk Fronts counter-attacked out of the northern edge of the Orel salient and struck at Second Panzerarmee, whose job it had been to guard Model's flank. As a result, Ninth Army had to go over to the defensive and so the German pincer lost its northern jaw. The planned encirclement was now an impossibility. Now the only hope was that Manstein's forces in the south could still be used to draw the Soviet mobile reserves into a battle of annihilation.

But then on 13 July Hitler summoned Manstein and Kluge to his headquarters where he told them that the Allies had invaded Sicily on 10 July and he was therefore calling off Zitadelle to send reinforcements to Italy and the Balkans. Manstein was furious; he believed Army Group South was winning the battle against the two Soviet tank armies and just needed time to finish the job. But his protestations were to no avail – Hitler ordered that the SS Panzerkorps be transferred to Italy. Manstein had no choice but to withdraw his forces to their start point in Belgorod. The Kursk offensive was over, but the fighting still raged as the Russian counter-attack progressed and was extended to the southern edge of the bulge. By 23 July Hoth had been driven back to his starting positions by the Steppe and Voronezh Fronts.

The failure of the Kursk offensive was to have a long-lasting and devastating effect on German fortunes in the East. The two pincer jaws which were supposed to meet at Kursk within five days never even came close; in the south, after ten days of fighting, Fourth Panzerarmee was halted after travelling just 32 km. Progress in the north was even worse; Ninth Army had advanced only 19 km. The Germans had advanced less than a quarter of the distance needed in order to achieve the encirclement.

In total, 50,000 Germans had been killed; also lost were 1,000 tanks and 1,000 planes, material losses which the Germans could ill-afford. The new weapons had proved a grave disappointment. Of the 200 Panthers that had started the battle, scarcely 40 were still operational by the end of the first day. Guderian, who visited the battlefield himself to talk to the tank crews, was proved right about the Panthers' mechanical unreliability – they suffered variously from suspension, transmission and engine problems, as well as a tendency to bog down because of too-narrow tracks. Even though the Panther went on to become one of the best tanks of the war, they were just not battle-ready by Kursk.

The 90 Ferdinands fared no better; with no machine-gun for self-defence, they had become easy prey to the Russian infantry. This deficiency in armament meant that once they reached the enemy infantry zone, they had, in Guderian's words, 'to go quail shooting with cannon'. Russian losses too had been heavy, suffering in the region of 500,000 killed and wounded and a reduction in tank strength of half. But the difference was that the Russians had ample capacity to replace their losses and soon did.

Each of the Germans' three successive summer campaigns on the Ostfront (Barbarossa, Fall Blau and Zitadelle) was smaller in scale and less successful than the one that preceded it. Kursk was to be the last large-scale German offensive in the East and from now on the Russians were in strategic control. Almost immediately the Russians embarked on a series of offensives of their own and the weakened German front collapsed. The Russians were to make good use of the initiative, gifted to them by Hitler's failed gamble, and would not stop now until they reached Berlin. It is interesting to contemplate what the outcome would have been had Manstein got his way, either in the original planning or at Prokhorovka. Could he have pulled off the Kharkov riposte on an even greater scale and could his mobile defence have forced a stalemate?

For the Panzerwaffe, the so-called 'Death Ride of the Panzers' meant the effective end of offensive operations in the East and a switchover to a defensive role. Never again would the panzers be used for deep and swift thrusts into an enemy front and to effect great encirclements; now their job would be to defend retreating armies from being completely routed and to inflict painful losses on a reckless enemy. To achieve this, new methods and new weapons would have to be developed. From now until the end of the war, the panzers would be used as a kind of 'fire brigade', sent here and there to bolster the front wherever it was about to collapse.

However, more significant than all the tactical or material losses suffered by the Germans as a result of Kursk, were the strategic ones. As Guderian wrote:

> Needless to say the Russians exploited their victory to the full. There were to be no more periods of quiet on the Eastern Front. From now on the enemy was in undisputed possession of the initiative.[7]

In future German strategy would be a purely defensive series of stop-gaps and improvisations to postpone the inevitable defeat for as long as possible.

In the wake of Zitadelle's failure, the Russians were soon on the offensive everywhere. On 17 July two Russian armies crossed the Mius river and pushed along the northern coast of the Sea of Azov. Their objective was to cut off Kleist's Army Group A on Manstein's southern flank. At the same time in the area of Army Group Centre, Kluge was being pushed back to Smolensk. By 5 August the Russians had recaptured Orel and Belgorod, the German start points for Zitadelle.

By the middle of August, the Germans in Kharkov were again in danger of encirclement, but Hitler, as in February, gave the order to hold the city at all costs. Manstein defied him and ordered withdrawal, unwilling to sacrifice six divisions for nothing. On 23 August, the city fell permanently back into Russian hands – Manstein's brilliant recapture of the previous March had proved just a postponement of the inevitable. Army Group South would soon have to retreat to the Dnieper or else stay put and face being encircled and destroyed.

Hitler and Manstein met on the 27th in the Ukraine where Manstein warned that the Donetz Basin could not be held with the forces available and requested both reinforcements and freedom to manoeuvre. Hitler for his part promised twelve divisions, but they never arrived. All the while Army Group South was coming under terrible pressure. The two men met again at Manstein's HQ on 8 September. This time Manstein bluntly told Hitler that two armies would be lost if he wasn't allowed to withdraw, namely Army Group A in the Crimea and Seventeenth Army across the Kerch Strait in the Caucasus. But again Hitler refused, unwilling to give up even an inch of ground uncontested.

On 15 September Hitler finally gave Manstein freedom to withdraw. By now the situation was critical along Army Group Centre's front as well, with Hoth's Fourth Panzerarmee pushed back almost to Kiev and Smolensk recaptured. In the Crimea the remaining Germans were about to be cut off. Manstein gave orders for the one million men of Army Group South, including 200,000 wounded, to fall back to the Dnieper in the hope that Europe's third largest river would provide a defensible barrier against Russian assaults. They adopted a 'scorched earth' policy along the way in the hope of delaying the following Russians.

Guy Sajer, a soldier with the Gross Deutschland, gives a vivid account of the retreat to the Dnieper in his classic if controversial Ostfront memoir, *The Forgotten Soldier.* He describes a chaotic operation that was only one step away from a general rout with fuel so scarce that horses pulled most of the equipment and whole regiments were annihilated when caught by Russian motorised forces. The Luftwaffe air-dropped parcels of rope so that the vehicles without fuel could be pulled by tanks, but there were no tanks left.

The scene on the eastern bank of the Dnieper was one of chaos and panic with the helpless Soldaten bombarded and strafed by Russian planes and menaced by Red tanks while waiting to cross over to the other side. Sajer did eventually get across the river and like most of his fellow soldiers, believed the western bank of the Dnieper would mean 'security and safety, a barrier between us and the Russians...the bulletins had been official: we would hold on to the Dnieper'.[8] By 30 September all the armies of Army Group South were on the Dnieper-Melitopol Line which they hoped to defend.

But Stalin, convinced that smashing Army Group South was the key to victory on the entire Ostfront, had different ideas and threw 80 per cent of the Russian armour and almost half of the Russian infantry against the Dnieper defences. The 500-km (300-mile) front was just too long for the Germans to defend and by the end of September the Russians had crossed the river in over twenty places, but so far in no great numbers.

Eventually two regiments got across the river north of Kiev and were quickly followed up by the Fifth Guards Tank Army. This bridgehead held on and in October was reinforced by the Third Guards Tank Army. The Russian tanks broke out of the bridgehead during a night attack in early November and by the 6th had pushed Hoth's Fourth Panzerarmee out of Kiev. As a result, Hitler transferred the battle-weary Hoth to the Führer Reserve and replaced him with the equally competent Austrian General der Panzertruppen, Erich Rauss, erstwhile commander of the 6th Panzer Division and the XLVII Panzerkorps.

Manstein concentrated his armour in the area of Zhitomir, a town due west of Kiev, with the intention of staging a concentrated armoured counterstroke in the direction of Kiev. Guderian independently suggested the same idea to Hitler and called for the stripping of all available Panzer divisions in the south from non-vital sectors like Nikopol, but Hitler declined, asserting that the Nikopol-Crimea region had to be held at all costs because its reserves of manganese were so vital to the armaments industry. He appointed General Ferdinand

Schorner to defend the Nikopol bridgehead. Schorner, an ardent Nazi and one of Hitler's favourites, was better known for his ruthlessness towards his own men manifested through drumhead court martials than for his skill as a general.

The assembly of the strike force near the town of Fastov was hindered by Russian attacks and the newly arrived 25th Panzer was rushed to the scene. This division had only recently been formed in Norway using occupation troops and captured equipment and in November was shipped to the Ostfront on Hitler's orders, despite Guderian's protests that the raw formation needed at least another four weeks for further training and equipping. This premature commitment in piece-meal fashion and without its commander, Generalmajor Schell, meant that the green division suffered such severe casualties that it had to be reformed almost from scratch – such were the difficulties Guderian faced in trying to rebuild an armoured reserve.

The XLVIII Panzerkorps played a big part in the subsequent fighting around Zhitomir and its battles are a good illustration of what mobile defence could achieve when the panzer divisions were in the hands of a superb commander – Balck had been appointed commander of the Korps in November, much to the pleasure of that formation's Chief of Staff, Mellenthin. The pair formed one of the most successful com-mander and chief of staff partnerships of the war.

Rauss opted to eliminate the Russian forces around Zhitomir before pressing on to Kiev and ordered Balck to recapture the town. For this purpose, XLVIII Panzerkorps was given five panzer divisions – 1st, 7th, 19th, 25th and the Liebstandarte; there was also a battle group from Das Reich. Balck's and Mellenthin's plan worked perfectly. While the other tank formations provided flank support, 1st and 7th Panzer recaptured Zhitomir on the night of 17 November. The Russian Third Guards Tank Army counter-attacked at Brussilov and Balck decided to try to trap it in a pocket. While the Liebstandarte held the Russians in place with a frontal attack from the west, 1st and 7th Panzer travelled along the Zhitomir-Kiev highway to outflank the Russians. At the same time 19th Panzer was pushing north-east.

As darkness fell on the 20th, 1st and 19th Panzer made the mistake of laagering for the night. Balck was enraged as he had expected the divisions to forego rest and repair until the encirclement was completed and he now ordered the divisional commanders to press on and close the pincers. This was soon achieved and by 24th November the Germans had eliminated the pocket, the booty amounting to 150 tanks, 300 guns and 3,000 Russian dead. Despite this victory, significant Russian forces escaped.

The next task of XLVIII Panzerkorps was an assault on the Soviet Sixtieth Army north of the Zhitomir-Radomyshl road as this was a danger to any thrust towards Kiev. One of the key formations, the 7th Panzer, was commanded by a fast-rising star of the Panzerwaffe – Generalmajor Baron Hasso-Eccard Freiherr von Manteuffel. A daring young tank leader, while commanding a division in Africa he had launched a successful counter-attack near Tunis which severed Allied communications. One of the few generals Hitler would listen to, by the war's end the little Panzer Baron was commanding a Panzerarmee.

Manteuffel's full strength 7th Panzer was to sweep around the Russian Army under the utmost secrecy and then thrust deep into the enemy's rear, while 1st Panzer and the Liebstandarte would roll up the Russian line from west to east. All preparations had to be done unobtrusively if the ploy was to succeed – bridges were surreptitiously repaired, divisions moved only at night and no formal orders were given.

At dawn on 6 December the three panzer divisions commenced the operation and everything ran like clockwork. The attack achieved complete surprise and soon 30 km of Russian front had been rolled up. One pocket led to the destruction of three and a half Russian divisions and the HQ of the Sixtieth Army was overrun. The attack also served to forestall a coming Russian offensive in the area.

Balck was next sent north-west to attack Russian forces arrayed near Korosten and believed to be about to make a breakthrough attempt. The 7th Panzer crossed the Irscha river near the town of Malin, while 1st Panzer and the Liebstandarte moved west before travelling north over the river. Soon 1st Panzer, 7th Panzer and the Liebstandarte had the enemy surrounded on three sides and so successful was the three-division assault that Mellenthin hoped for a 'miniature Tannenburg'.

But without knowing it, the three panzer divisions had trapped much greater forces than anticipated in the Meleni pocket and were soon rocked by the ferocity of the breakout attempts. The Leibstandarte alone knocked out almost fifty tanks. When Balck examined maps captured from a dead Russian officer and discovered that he had actually encircled three tank corps and four rifle corps, he realised he had bitten off more than he could chew. He was therefore forced to abandon the attack, but for the time being he had foiled a major attack aimed at recapturing Zhitomir.

As Balck's Panzerkorps withdrew, the Russians struck at Brussilov and scattered XXIV Panzerkorps. By the end of the year, the Russian offensive had succeeded in recovering all the ground Balck had seized over the previous months, including Zhitomir on 31 December. Yet during the battles of November and December, Balck's XLVIII Panzerkorps had succeeded in destroying two Russian armies, mauling a third and capturing or destroying 700 tanks. Single-handedly, the Panzerkorps had eliminated the Russian forces that crossed the Dnieper and its achievements suggest that had Balck's methods and Manstein's plans been adopted by Hitler, a strategic stalemate might still have been a realistic possibility. As an interesting footnote to these battles, Hitler was so impressed with the performance of the 7th Panzer that he asked Manteuffel to join him for Christmas and there presented him with an unusual present – fifty tanks.

By the end of the year, the entire northern half of the Dnieper was back in Russian hands and Manstein ordered First Panzerarmee withdrawn from the river on 29 December without waiting for Hitler's permission. Army Group Centre meanwhile had been pushed west of Smolensk. The Germans in the Crimea were also cut off and Schorner was looking to withdraw. Three days into 1944, the Red Army crossed the pre-war Polish frontier which meant that during 1943 they had succeeded in recapturing 100,000 square kilometres of their territory.

Many important places had been fought over and eventually lost by the Wehrmacht in the course of 1943: Kursk, Orel, Belgorod, Kharkov, Rostov, Kiev. The Germans had begun the year fighting on the Volga, but ended it fighting on the Dnieper; soon they would be fighting in Poland. The Kursk offensive had been the fatal gamble that triggered this general retreat. But more damaging to the Germans than all the ground they had lost were the irreplaceable losses: almost half a million German soldiers had been killed on the Ostfront during 1943.

When the year began, victory in the East was no longer a possibility, although stalemate was. But by the year's end, even stalemate was no longer on the cards, given the growing strength of the Russians. Now all the Germans could hope to do was to delay the inevitable defeat for as long as possible and to make the Russians pay a high price for every yard gained. This heavy task would fall mainly to the Panzerwaffe.

CHAPTER EIGHT

The Second Front

Believe me, Lang, the first twenty-four hours of the invasion will be decisive. . .the fate of Germany depends on the outcome. . .for the Allies as well as Germany, it will be the longest day.

Rommel to his ADC, April 1944

AFTER the victory in North Africa, the Allies' next target was what Churchill called 'the soft underbelly' of the Axis – Italy. On 9 July 1943, the Allies staged landings in Sicily. As it quickly became clear that the Italians had thrown in the towel, the Germans had no choice but to withdraw across the Straits of Messina to the mainland. Although the brunt of the fighting on the island was borne by the infantry, the inexperienced Hermann Goering Panzer Division, the 15th Panzergrenadier (formed from the remnants of Rommel's lost 15th Panzer), and the Tigers of Schwere Panzer Abteilung 504, were instrumental in allowing the evacuation to take place.

General der Panzertruppen Fridolin von Senger und Etterlin commanded the German forces in Sicily and then XIV Panzerkorps on the mainland. Talking to Liddell Hart after the war, he explained how the Tigers were particularly unsuitable in the olive tree-covered, mountainous terrain of Sicily because of their size and general lack of manoeuvreability, but that during the retreat they gave 'immeasurable service' as anti-tank guns and by providing 'a moral backbone for half-demoralised infantry'.[1]

The Allies swiftly pursued the retreating Germans across the Straits and invaded Italy on 3 September, seizing a foothold on the toe of the country. Several panzer units were involved in the containment of this beachhead, but little action of significance was undertaken by either side. The Allies next opted to outflank Kesselring's forces in southern Italy by means of an amphibious landing at Salerno on 9 September; it was here that the Panzerwaffe made its biggest contribution in the Italian campaign when the landings were met by the LXXVI Panzerkorps (16th and 26th Panzer), the Hermann Goering Division and two panzergrenadier divisions. So bitter was the fighting that the Allies considered re-embarking before massed naval gunfire eventually forced the panzers to pull back towards the north.

Generalfeldmarschall 'Smiling Albert' Kesselring was appointed commander of German forces in Italy. His brief was simple: defend every inch of Italy and tie down as many Allied troops as possible, while protecting the southern flank of the armies in Russia. He was fortunate in that the topography of Italy is ideally suited for defence as it essentially consists of a central mountain range, the Apennines, with many rivers draining from these peaks to the shores, thus creating innumerable natural defence lines.

The Allies found themselves held first at the Gustav Line south of Rome and later at the Gothic Line further north, and as a result it was May 1945 before German forces in Italy finally surrendered. Kesselring opted to defend the Gustav Line most truculently and entrusted its defence to von Senger und Etterlin. This line, which incorporated the famous Monte Cassino monastery, was held for months against all-comers by Fallschirmjäger. An attempt to outflank it at Anzio in January 1944 was swiftly contained.

Italy was essentially an infantry war, for mobile operations were to all intents impossible in the craggy peaks and rocky valleys. The Panzerwaffe's role was strictly in support of the defence and as the campaign dragged on, more and more panzer units were withdrawn to France and the Ostfront. However, the narrow defiles of central Italy did offer excellent opportunities for long-range defensive shooting and the superior optical equipment of the panzers coupled with their incomparable weapons and crews offered them a tremendous advantage over their opponents in this respect. On one occasion in June 1944, a single Tiger platoon knocked out or captured twenty-three Shermans. Stugs and Panzerjägers also played an important role as in this kind of defensive fighting turreted tanks offered no advantage.

The greatest threat the panzers faced in Italy came from Allied field artillery and ground-attack squadrons and so tank commanders made sure to change their position rapidly once spotted. Most tanks were held in reserve to counter possible Allied breakthroughs, but many were also dug in as strongpoints. One defensive innovation was the ground-mounted Panther turret emplaced on top of an underground steel shell. The low ground clearance of the 75 mm gun made it virtually impossible to spot and any hit was almost certain to disable the opposing enemy tank.

By and large, the Italian campaign was fought by infantrymen who bitterly contested each position and the Panzerwaffe never had an opportunity to influence events other than at a tactical level. During the whole campaign there were never more than three panzer divisions in Italy and for most of the time there was only one. Nonetheless, the Panzerwaffe knocked out hundreds of Allied tanks and helped tie down as many as eighteen Allied divisions until the last weeks of the war.

In November 1943, Rommel and his Army Group B staff were withdrawn from the Italian front and sent to France to prepare *Festung Europa* (Fortress Europe) for the coming invasion of the West. He was given responsibility for the coastal defences along the entire Atlantic seaboard and immediately threw himself into the task of making the reality of the so-called Atlantic Wall bear some relationship to the outrageous propaganda claims.

Although initially holding only an inspector's portfolio, in January 1944, Rommel was given tactical command of all the troops on the coast facing Britain. Overall command in the West continued to be held by Generalfeldmarschall Gerd von Rundstedt and the two field marshals worked surprisingly well together considering the vast differences in their backgrounds and leadership styles. The reserved and refined Rundstedt exerted a calming influence on the energetic Rommel, while the Desert Fox made up for the shortcomings of the older man's laissez-faire attitude.

Rommel told his officers that the main battle line would be the beach itself. His experiences in Africa and Italy had taught him that as soon as the Allies got ashore in substantial numbers, the battle was already as good as over and this conditioned his belief that 'we must stop the enemy in the water and destroy his equipment while it is still afloat'.[2] Rommel knew that the invasion would have succeeded if the Germans hadn't driven the enemy back into the sea by the fourth day at the latest.

In pursuit of this aim, he began constructing his 'Death Zone' – a fortified coastal strip, mined on both the landward and seaward sides and filled with troops, guns and, if he got his way, tanks. By the invasion date he had supervised the placing of over half a million beach and water obstacles and over 4 million mines. However, as Rommel believed the invasion would come in the Pas de Calais, the Fifteenth Army's sector was much better defended than the Normandy coastline held by the Seventh Army, the sector where the invasion actually fell.

In addition to his characteristic energy, another of Rommel's trade-marks soon surfaced – friction with colleagues. An acrimonious row erupted between the forthright Field Marshal and the equally resolute commander of Panzergruppe West, General Baron Leo Geyr von Schweppenburg over how the panzers should be employed in the invasion battle. Rommel believed as strongly as Guderian in the principle of the concentration of armour, but he had also experienced the paralysing effect of Allied airpower on armoured operations. As a consequence, he wanted the panzers held at the most likely landing points in order to counter-attack immediately once landings com-menced.

This view was the complete antithesis to that propounded by traditional German armoured theory. Geyr, with the full support of Guderian, was of the opinion that a strong central armoured reserve should be located well behind the front so that once the landings were made, a telling blow could be launched against the Allies in a mobile counter-attack. But Rommel believed that Allied air superiority would make it impossible to move the panzer divisions by daylight without suffering heavy losses and that parachute flares would make night marches almost as risky a proposition.

Rundstedt too preferred the notion of the great counter-attack, but Rommel would have none of it, declaring, 'You won't be able to fight a mobile battle because of the enemy warships' gunfire and their air supremacy.'[3] So vehemently did he argue that airpower was the dominant consideration that many generals suspected he had lost faith in armoured operations as a result of his North African experiences at the hands of the Allied air fleets. As he said himself to Bayerlein, 'the day of the dashing cut-and-thrust tank attack of the early war years is past and gone'.[4] His opponents were right to suspect he suffered from a new-found inferiority complex, but events showed his fears to be well founded.

The panzer controversy raged on. On 28 April, Guderian and Geyr visited Rommel's chateau HQ at La Roche-Guyon and in the word's of Guderian's staff officer, 'a decidedly tempestuous conference' ensued. Der Schnelle Heinz argued that the panzer divisions' greatest strength was their combination of mobility and firepower and that this would be lost if they were embedded in Rommel's defence system. Guderian wanted all the tanks concentrated in two groups north and south of Paris, well out of range of Allied naval gunfire and behind a definite Stop Line beyond which they wouldn't be allowed to advance. The Fox countered: 'If you leave the Panzer divisions in the rear, they will never get forward. Once the invasion begins, enemy air power will stop everything moving!'[5]

Early in May Hitler stepped in with a compromise that effectively cherry-picked the worst points of both options and satisfied neither side. Rommel was given the 2nd, 21st and 116th Panzer Divisions, while at the same time an OKW Reserve, the 1st SS Panzerkorps under Dietrich, was formed; this contained the Panzer Lehr and the 12th SS Panzer Division Hitler Jugend and couldn't be employed without Hitler's express permission. The remaining scattered armour was placed under Geyr's Panzergruppe West while still being subject to the formations in their immediate area. In Guderian's opinion, 'this dispersal of strength ruled out all possibility of a great defensive victory'.[6]

However, with hindsight it can be seen that neither Guderian's nor Rommel's plan was likely to have been successful and that the alternatives really only offered the panzers the choice between being destroyed by either the Allied air force or the Allied navy.

The illustrious 21st Panzer of Afrika Korps fame had been lost in Tunisia and rebuilt around a slim cadre of Rommel's 'Africans'. Equipped with 130 Pz IVs, it stood at Caen and so was the closest panzer division to the Normandy beaches; the 2nd and 116th Panzer were too far away to play any part in the immediate fighting. The OKW Reserve was also a formidable force: the elite Panzer Lehr commanded by Generalleutnant Bayerlein had been specially trained for anti-invasion operations and was equipped with 190 tanks, 40

Stugs and 600 half-tracks. Hitler Jugend, made up of fanatical Hitler Youth teenagers, had 180 tanks and would be commanded by SS Brigadeführer Kurt 'Panzer' Meyer from mid-June on, making him at thirty-three the youngest divisional commander in the Wehrmacht.

Rommel was also unsure as to where the landings would be made. Initially like most senior German officers he assumed that the invasion would come in the Pas de Calais as this offered the most direct route into Germany. However, as time progressed, he came to view Normandy as a possible landing location and managed to have the 21st Panzer located on the coast near Caen. He failed, however, to have a second panzer division located in the vicinity of St Lo. Yet again his intuition proved correct as these two towns covered the landing zone and immediate panzer attacks would almost certainly have scuppered the entire invasion.

For better or worse, the die was cast by early June and the Germans anxiously awaited the invasion. Of the 54 divisions stationed in France, there were 10 panzer containing a total of 1,500 tanks. These 10 divisions represented one-third of the Panzerwaffe, but 3 of them had no combat experience at all and several of the others were recovering from a mauling in the East. Half of them were also too far away to be quickly brought to bear in Normandy – 3 were in the south of France and 2 more were in Belgium. On top of this, the 116th Panzer (formed from the wreckage of the 16th Panzergrenadier Division) was to stand idle on the Channel coast until 19th July, awaiting a second invasion that never came.

On 6 June 1944, the long-awaited invasion of Europe began. The Allies chose five different landing beaches in Normandy and only the steep cliff-face at Omaha presented difficulties for the invaders. Elsewhere operations progressed as planned with beachheads quickly secured under the cover of intense air and naval bombardments. The lack of serious resistance in the early hours of the invasion came as a surprise to the Allied commanders, one reason being that Hitler had become convinced that the Normandy landing was merely a feint to draw away his reserves. Another reason for the unco-ordinated German effort was that many of the senior officers of the Seventh Army were away on map exercises as the meteorologists had predicted inclement conditions. Rommel himself had rushed off to Germany to plead with Hitler to adopt his plan for a dispersed counter-attack and to celebrate

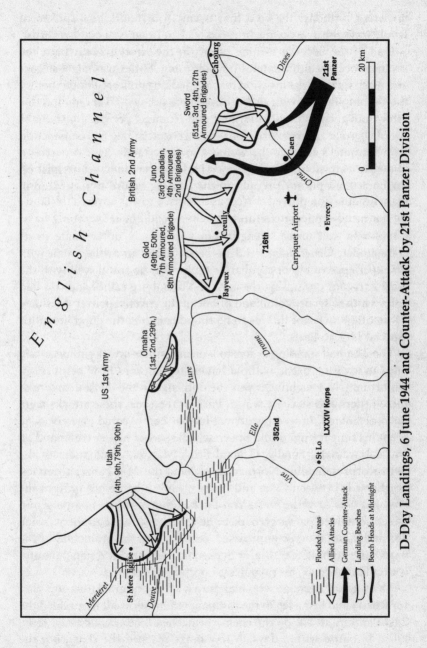

D-Day Landings, 6 June 1944 and Counter-Attack by 21st Panzer Division

his wife's birthday; the vital first twenty-four hours he'd spoken of would now ebb away while he raced back to organise a counter thrust.

One of the decisive turning points in the effort to beat back the invasion occurred that fateful June morning. Hitler was a late sleeper and when news of the invasion reached Jodl, he preferred not to bother the sleeping Führer with such troublesome tidings. To compound this error, Jodl then refused Rundstedt and Rommel permission to make use of Dietrich's Panzerkorps for a counter-attack. Taken in conjunction with Rommel's absence (he would almost certainly have ordered an immediate attack or at least phoned Hitler in person to get permission for one), the option of repulsing the landing before it was made in force quickly faded.

The nearest panzer division to the invasion beaches, the 21st at Caen, was well up to strength, but particularly unfortunate in its commander, Generalmajor Edgar Feuchtinger, an artilleryman with no experience of either combat or tanks. But he stood well with the Nazi Party for organising the annual Nuremburg rallies and this had helped him to secure command of one of the coveted panzer divisions. More often than not he was to be found enjoying the good life at his 'Special HQ' in Paris.

The 21st had standing orders to launch counter-attacks immediately once an invasion began without having to wait for OKW permission. Unfortunately, Feuchtinger was the only man in the division aware of these orders and since he was in Paris at the time, these attacks were unco-ordinated. Indeed his arrival further complicated matters as he spent his time trying to find out to which specific higher command he was subordinate. Finally, General Erich Marcks, commander of the 84th Korps defending Normandy, ordered the 21st Panzer to attack northwards between Caen and Bayeux while a battle group from the Division was to strike west. Von Luck commanded this battle group which contained panzergrenadier and reconnaissance battalions, some 88s and a battalion of improvised assault guns; the brainchild of the battalion's commander, Major Becker, he had fitted Russian guns and rocket launchers of his own design onto French tanks.

The veteran Marcks, who had drawn up the original invasion plan for Russia and lost a leg in the campaign that followed, himself led the 21st Panzer's attack on the enemy bridgehead; he was destined to be killed in battle within days. A few tanks reached the coast, but the

British anti-tank gun screens and pulverising naval gunfire exacted a heavy toll. Then an Allied supply drop that had gone off course dropped thousands of parachutes in the rear of the 21st and Feuchtinger, mistaking these for paratroopers, panicked and withdrew the Division. The 21st had only seventy tanks left, but its attack had prevented the Allies from capturing Caen. This was to be the only counter-attack by German armour during D-Day.

Ten hours into the invasion, the OKW finally allowed the Panzer Lehr and the Hitler Jugend to move towards Normandy, but the delay meant that at least part of the approach march had to take place in daylight, exposing the divisions to constant air attack by Allied fighter-bombers. The result was that Panzer Lehr didn't reach Caen until the afternoon of the 7th, losing eighty-five AFVs and five tanks along the way; Bayerlein was almost killed when his car was strafed.

It was 10 p.m. on D-Day before Rommel arrived back at his HQ and by then the Allies had landed 150,000 men in Normandy. Over the coming days the Allies quickly expanded their beachhead with the American and British armies meeting in the centre. Bayeux, 8 km (5 miles) inland, was taken. On 8 June Rommel tried to launch an attack between Bayeux and Caen with three panzer divisions led by Dietrich, but after a delayed start it ran into a combination of British armour and naval gunfire and ground to a halt. Allied bombing on the 10th scuppered plans for a second armoured counter-attack and from that point on, Rommel was forced onto the defensive. As he had predicted, it was clear by the fourth day that the Allied invasion had succeeded and the only possibility now was to try and contain the enemy bridgehead. To this end he established a deep defensive front around Caen.

Just as Rommel had feared, the whole campaign became subject to Allied air supremacy. On the 12th he informed the OKW that daylight movement in a zone stretching 100 km (60 miles) back from the coast was no longer possible. Reinforcements could move only at night and were often forced to make long detours to avoid blown bridges or damaged rails; in the rear partisans blocked roads and carried out ambushes. The supposedly mobile elements were tied down by Hitler's orders into a static defence and pounded to pieces by naval, air and ground fire. Fighter-bombers hit exposed tanks with cannon fire, bombs and rockets and even blew up the HQ bus of Panzergruppe West just one hour after Rommel and Geyr had left it. The Allies could fly with impunity for the Luftwaffe had all but ceased to exist, putting just two planes in the air on D-Day.

The arrival of panzer reinforcements was particularly badly disrupted by air attack. The OKW had ordered the 2nd Panzer moved to the front, but the Division had to make a 250-km (160-mile) detour because of blown bridges and took a week to fully arrive. The 2nd SS Panzer Division Das Reich, 720 km (450 miles) away in the south of France, didn't reach Normandy until the end of June. An SS Panzerkorps containing the 9th and 10th SS Panzer Divisions travelled from the Ostfront to France faster than it crossed France itself.

For the rest of June the Allies made numerous efforts to probe the German line for weaknesses and it was during one of these that a famous Tiger encounter occurred. Following one of Montgomery's probing attacks, the Panzer Lehr Division was separated from its neighbouring unit and a gap opened in the German line. Monty sent a spearhead from the 7th Armoured, the famed Desert Rats, through the village of Villers Bocage in order to trap and cut off the defenders of Caen. In response Dietrich sent the SS Schwere Panzer Abteilung 101 to plug the gap until 2nd Panzer could relieve them.

The four Tigers of SS-Obersturmführer Michael Wittmann's company drove toward Villers Bocage and from the commanding position of Hill 213 Wittmann spotted the British vehicles incompetently lined up nose to tail in the village shortly after dawn on 13 June. As a leading tank ace who had achieved 117 kills on the Ostfront, starting off in a Stug III during Barbarossa, Wittmann knew a golden opportunity when he saw one and wasted no time in seizing it.

Approaching the column stealthily in his Tiger, Wittmann pressed on unobserved past the stationary lead vehicles and then shot up three out of four Cromwells before proceeding into the village's main street. Several British shots bounced harmlessly off the Tiger's frontal armour. Wittmann was satisfied with his recce and reversed, only to have his tank shot in the back twice by the surviving Cromwell. Again the shells failed to penetrate and Wittmann quickly dispatched the British tank with an 88 shot.

The Tiger then engaged the forward elements of the column which were parked so close together that their main guns couldn't be used. His first shot was put into the only tank that posed a threat to the Tiger, the Firefly – a Sherman up-gunned with a high-velocity 17-pounder

(76 mm) gun. Wittmann then casually drove the length of the convoy shooting up each vehicle in turn and in five minutes destroyed no less than 25 tracked vehicles before withdrawing back to Hill 213.

Intense fighting continued around the village all day. At one stage Wittmann had to abandon his disabled Tiger and walk cross-country until he found a Panzer Lehr position. There he was given 15 Panzer IVs and returned to recapture the village in association with units from the 2nd Panzer Division. For the loss of just 3 Tigers, the Panzers destroyed 25 Cromwell and Firefly tanks, 14 half-tracks and 14 Bren-gun carriers at Villers Bocage that day and stopped the advance of the 7th Armoured Division in its tracks, thus saving the Panzer Lehr from encirclement. A grateful Bayerlein recommended Wittmann for the Swords to his Knight's Cross and the Tiger ace was promoted to Hauptsturmführer, at the same time turning down an instructor's position.

On 8 August he was killed during the defence against the Canadian Operation Totalize aimed at capturing Falaise. On this occasion Wittmann was without his usual crew and his unit of three Tigers was travelling along a road with Canadian units on one side and British on the other. Despite being exposed to the British, he concentrated on advancing toward the Canadians. He would no doubt have reacted differently had he suspected the British had a Firefly – this British tank apparently brewed up all three Tigers at a range of 800 m. Despite the Canadians also claiming this success, the British Firefly was the only tank present which was capable of knocking out Tigers at the range involved. There have also been claims that a rocket-firing Typhoon aircraft was Wittmann's nemesis.

Whatever hit Wittmann's Tiger, it was powerful enough to blow the turret right off and kill the entire crew. During his career, Wittmann had destroyed 138 tanks as well 132 anti-tank guns and other artillery pieces, making him the most successful tank ace of the war.

By the time the Allies captured the vital deep sea port of Cherbourg on 26 June, they had already landed a million men in Normandy. Hitler's plan was to separate the Allied armies by a thrust to the coast and then defeat the British Second Army, after which time he believed the American First Army would have no choice but to surrender. Unwittingly, this played right into the hands of the Allies; their plan called for the Americans to make the initial breakout while the British kept the German reserves occupied. With this aim in mind, Montgomery began a series of limited offensives to tie the Germans down.

The first of these attacks, code-named Epsom, was launched on 26 June with 600 tanks and 60,000 British and Canadian troops. The Canadians soon ran into the teenagers of the Hitler Jugend who distinguished themselves by their suicidal and fanatical resistance – their Divisional Commander was 'Panzer' Meyer, who after three years in Russia regarded the Allies as 'kleine fische' (little fish) and considered himself as 'Siegfried leading his warriors to their deaths in the best Wagnerian tradition'.[7]

Epsom was succeeded by Jupiter on 10 July which extended the scope of operations into the surrounding countryside. During these attacks Caen finally fell. These operations saw the Allies use their strategic air-fleet to great effect. Sections of the German front were carpet-bombed in order to soften them up for the ground attack and the panzers too fell victim to these; many units were trapped in their tanks until the barrages died down.

The Western Front began to lose its best commanders. On 3 July Rundstedt was replaced by Kluge as Commander-in-Chief West because, when the OKW Chief Keitel had rung him for advice on the French situation, Rundstedt had replied: 'Make peace you fools! What else can you do?'[8] Geyr was also sacked. The temperamental von Kluge was soon on equally bad terms with Rommel as he had been with Guderian, but it wouldn't be long before he was commanding Rommel's Army Group B as well. On 17 July Rommel's car was attacked by a fighter-bomber near a village named, with cruel irony, Sainte Foy De Montgomery. The Field Marshal was critically injured and never returned to active service. With Rommel's departure, the Germans had lost their best chance of delaying the Allied advance. By October he was dead, forced to commit suicide by a vengeful Hitler because of the peripheral role he had played in the plot to kill the Führer.

The day after Rommel's accident, Operation Goodwood commenced. Although Montgomery claimed after the war that this operation was never intended to break out, but was merely a diversionary attack to allow the Americans to do so, it is likely that Monty sought to keep his undefeated record intact by conveniently adjusting the record post-war. Even by the lavish Allied standards of material employment, this full-dress assault seems a little extravagant for a mere diversion.

On 18 July, three British armoured divisions attacked south-east of Caen with the aim of seizing Bourgebus Ridge and effecting a breakout from the Allied bridgehead, but Rommel had fully expected action in this quarter and so had laid his defence plans carefully and with great emphasis on depth. Opposing the British were three panzer divisions: the 21st Panzer, the SS Leibstandarte and the SS Hitler Jugend; this force was greatly strengthened by thirty Tigers and almost eighty well dug-in and camouflaged 88s.

The redoubtable von Luck was once again at the forefront of the German force opposing the attack and this time he enjoyed vastly strengthened forces. He now possessed Schwere Tiger Battalion 503, Becker's assault gun battalion, a Pz IV battalion, a battalion of Luftwaffe infantry, numerous 88s, assorted divisional artillery and his own Panzergrenadier Regiment 125. In accordance with Rommel's plans he had set up a 15 km deep defensive belt in the bocage country, well stocked with anti-tank guns, artillery and Nebelwerfers. All possible camouflage precautions were taken and these efforts were to be well rewarded as the British underestimated the strength of the defenders.

Prior to the attack, Sepp Dietrich pressed his ear to the ground in order to hear the British tanks rolling forward into position, a quirk he'd developed in Russia. However for all his Ostfront experience, Dietrich's Panzerkorps was soon to experience a terrible new kind of firepower. The British opened the attack with carpet-bombing by 2,500 planes and artillery drumfire from 1,000 guns, wreaking havoc on the German positions. A personal reconnaissance by von Luck in a Pz IV after the bombardments confirmed his worst fears – both battalions of tanks were out of action and many of his grenadiers were dead, wounded or simply stupefied by the ordeal. Some German prisoners were so deafened by the barrages that interrogation was impossible for hours afterwards. Several of the 60-ton Tigers had even been overturned in the explosions! Their company commander remarked that 'they had been spun through the air like playing cards'.[9]

Von Luck had opposed the positioning of the panzers so close behind his front line, but was overruled by a superior officer who hailed from the infantry. British tanks now swarmed through the gap blasted through his front line and von Luck's entire command was threatened. He scraped together whatever units he could for the fight-back, including a Luftwaffe 88 mm Flak battery who had to be persuaded at pistol point to shoot at tanks instead of planes. Von Luck used this battery to secure his flanks and it soon had over forty British tanks brewing up, an impressive toll for a Flak unit which had never shot at ground targets before.

Luck's countermeasures stalled the attack long enough for the two SS divisions to join the battle. By the following day many of his panzers were operational again and able to face Monty's renewed attacks which were now better supported by artillery and infantry. The British had learned a hard lesson the previous day and their advance was remarkably cautious. A few assault guns, Tigers and 88s again inflicted severe losses on the British and the offensive broke down. Over the three days the British had been roughly handled by the panzermen and over 200 of their tanks knocked out. Old Afrika Korps hands noted with some satisfaction that although Rommel had left the battlefield before Goodwood, his preparations had inflicted one last defeat on his old foe, Montgomery.

But Goodwood also had the adverse effect of concentrating even more German armour opposite the British and Canadians while only the Panzer Lehr and 2nd SS Das Reich opposed the Americans. Of the surviving 850 Panzers in Normandy, only 200 were positioned holding the American sector of the front while the remainder had been sucked in by Monty's attacks. Just as the western army was at its lowest ebb, disaster struck at Avranches on the last day of July. The Allied bridgehead in Normandy had become a festering boil which was about to burst.

Code-named Cobra, this operation required the Americans to advance southwards from the beachhead towards Avranches from where they would break out into Brittany. To meet the new threat, Kluge dispatched the 2nd and 116th Panzer from before the British positions. Montgomery immediately launched yet more holding attacks in an attempt to tie down all the available German reserves and these probes forced the hard pressed 21st Panzer and II SS Panzerkorps to their limit. The front had now been pushed as far south as Falaise and virtually all of the German armour was engaged there.

On 25 July, 2,000 American bombers dropped 4,000 tons of bombs on the Panzer Lehr's sector. Bayerlein described the devastating effect of the opening carpet-bombing:

> After an hour I had no communication with anyone, even by radio. My front lines looked like the face of the moon and at least 70% of my troops were out of action – dead, wounded, crazed or numbed.[10]

When ordered by Kluge's HQ to 'hold the line', Bayerlein replied, 'You may report to the Field Marshal that the Panzer Lehr division is annihilated. Only the dead can now hold the line.'[11]

On 30 July Patton's Third Army took Avranches, the gateway into Brittany and on the first day of August broke through into open country, diverging in various directions, including north towards the Seine. The US First Army all the while pushed on towards Mortain. Kluge was well aware of what was in the offing and saw that the entire Army Group B was about to be encircled. He pleaded with Hitler to allow the panzers to cover a retreat across the Seine, but to no avail. Rather he was ordered to assemble eight panzer divisions for an attack through Mortain to the coast at Avranches in order to close the gap and cut off Patton's rampaging army. Kluge knew he didn't have time to assemble the 8 divisions, so in the end he scraped together 4 divisions with a total of just 200 tanks – the 2nd, 116th, Das Reich and the Leibstandarte.

Unternehmen Liege opened at midnight on 6 August and won some minor initial successes including the recapture of Mortain. But the Americans had known the attack was coming and threw four divisions, including two armoured, in Kluge's path. The good flying weather also spelled disaster for the panzers who were hammered mercilessly by the Allied fighter-bombers. Two days later the Germans had been driven back to their starting point. A furious Hitler ordered Kluge to renew the offensive with more tanks and Kluge obediently prepared to do so.

But it was already too late to stem the tide. At this stage Montgomery's Twenty-first Army was pushing south to cut off the German's retreat to the Seine while Patton's Third Army was thrusting northwards to link up with the British. Kluge requested permission to re-deploy to meet this threat, but was ignored. As a result on 16 August the British and Canadian pressure from the north and the American pressure from the south and west trapped the Fifth Panzerarmee (formerly

Panzergruppe West), Panzergruppe Eberbach (the divisions at Mortain) and the Seventh Army in a pocket 40 km (25 miles) long and 25 km (15 miles) wide. The Falaise pocket contained some 100,000 men and by the 17th the only exit had contracted to just 10 km (6 miles) wide. Thanks to II SS Panzerkorps keeping the neck of the sack open as long as possible, 40,000 of the trapped men did manage to escape the trap minus practically all their equipment.

Kluge himself became a casualty of the disaster. Hitler already blamed him for not pushing the 'Liege' offensive hard enough and now his inability to be contacted while sheltering from an air attack convinced Hitler that he was negotiating a surrender to the Allies. Kluge was innocent of this allegation, but he was involved in the anti-Hitler plot. So when he was summonsed to Berlin on the 18th, he poisoned himself rather than face the Gestapo. Model now picked up the reins of complete command in the west until Rundstedt's return as OB West (Oberbefehlshaber – C-in-C West) in early September allowed Model to concentrate his prodigious energies solely on commanding Army Group B.

While these dramatic events had been unfolding in the north, the Allies had landed on the Mediterranean coast in the south of France on 15 August. Army Group G received permission to retreat and Generaloberst Blaskowitz expertly retreated along the Rhone to the German border, only to be scapegoated by Hitler on arrival and replaced by Balck. Clever defensive tactics by the covering 11th Panzer had allowed this retreat to pass off successfully.

Even Model, that master of creating a defence line from scratch, couldn't overcome the present crisis and so the remnants of the Western army were forced eastwards in full retreat. Army Groups B and G fell all the way back to the West Wall, the defensive line of 3,000 interlocking bunkers and pillboxes that ran along Germany's border with France and Holland. Since D-Day they had lost 300,000 troops and 2,200 tanks and assault guns; by 7 September Army Group B was left with just 100 tanks which were outnumbered twenty to one, but the West Wall offered some possibility of a temporary respite.

At this stage, Montgomery, recently promoted to Field Marshal and desperate to be the one to deliver the death blow to 'the German', came up with a risky plan that seemed to offer the possibility of a quick end to the war: a crossing of the Rhine in Holland, thus outflanking the West Wall, followed by a quick thrust into the Ruhr; without this industrial heartland, Germany could not expect to resist for long. The plan called for bridges over the Maas, the Waal and the Rhine to be captured by means of a bold airborne attack and held until the British XXX Corps came to pass over them.

On 17 September, Operation Market Garden began when 20,000 Allied troops were dropped into Holland by parachute or glider. The operations at Eindhoven and Nijmegen went well, but the forces at Arnhem had the misfortune to land almost on top of two very formidable opponents: Generalfeldmarschall Model and II SS Panzerkorps. The British paratroopers landed over 10 km from the Arnhem bridge they were supposed to seize and close to the hotel where 'Fireman Model' and his staff were breakfasting. Model instantly arranged for a counter-attack by SS General Bittrich's II SS Panzerkorps (9th SS 'Hohenstaufen' and 10th SS 'Frundsberg' Panzer Divisions) which was resting and refitting in the area after being shattered in Normandy.

The combative Field Marshal personally led and directed actions to prevent the encircled airborne infantry trapped in the *Hexenkessel* (witches' cauldron) from being relieved by the British XXX Corps. The paratroopers put up a resolute defence in holding the bridges, frustrating the efforts of the 9th and 10th SS Panzer who had to use ferries to bring the tanks over the Rhine. Meanwhile a battle group of Panthers and Tigers under the one-legged Moscow veteran Major Hans-Peter Knaust seized defensive positions at Nijmegen and with the help of Student's First Parachute Army, prevented the link-up with XXX Corps.

Monty called off Market Garden on 25 September. His only ambitious plan during the course of the war had failed – for once he had abandoned his usual cautious formula of building up overwhelming superiority on land and in the air before attacking. Lacking the verve of a Rommel or the strategic ability of a Manstein, it is no surprise he failed to pull it off. Of the 10,000 men dropped on Arnhem, only 2,000 managed to return from the mission. The Germans had inflicted 13,000 casualties on the paratroopers and their relief force and suffered only 3,000 themselves in what was to be one of the last victories of the Panzerwaffe in the West.

As October rolled in, the situation in the West was still grave but not as catastrophic as two months earlier. Units had recovered much of their strength and despite all available new Panthers and Panzer IV's being sent East to counter the catastrophic events there, the West rebuilt itself to a strength of almost 500 Panzers, Jagdpanzers and Stugs. Hitler had decreed that as the West was on the defensive it should get most of the Jagdpanzer and King Tiger production.

At this stage, Model's front line was largely along the Rhine. So rapid had been the Allied advance that major ports like Antwerp fell into their hands almost without damage. They were now lined up in front of the West Wall and building up supplies for an assault on Germany in the spring. As the winter began to exercise its grip, both sides paused to prepare for the coming battles for the Rhine and the Ruhr.

It never occurred to anyone on the Allied side that Germany would be capable of launching a major offensive in late 1944. Most of France had been liberated and the Americans had penetrated into Germany itself in the Aachen sector while the British were in Holland. On the Ostfront the Russians were massed on the borders of East Prussia. During the summer of 1944 alone, the Germans had lost 1,200,000 men.

The loss of the Romanian oilfields and the effect of the Allied air campaign against the synthetic oil industry left the Reich with a severe fuel shortage. On the other hand, the intensive Allied bombing had not significantly reduced arms production. In fact German war production was the highest it had ever been, largely thanks to the efforts of Reichsminister Speer: 19,000 AFVs were produced in 1944, which included 4,000 Panthers, 5,700 Stugs and 3,600 Panzerjägers.

By the autumn of 1944, 10 million Germans were under arms in 327 divisions and brigades; of this total, there were 31 panzer divisions and 13 panzer brigades. During the summer, Hitler had launched a campaign to comb out what he called 'the rear area swine', a process which produced 18 new divisions, 10 panzer brigades and almost 100 infantry battalions. On the map table in the Führer's HQ, the German Order of Battle still looked impressive, but in reality every division was seriously understrength and the green new formations couldn't be equated with the battle-hardened divisions of old.

Despite all the mounting evidence to the contrary, Hitler continued to regard himself as a military genius and believed he could still win the war. He took particular heart from the example of his great hero,

Frederick the Great, who at the Battle of Rossbach and Leuthen had defeated an enemy twice as strong, as a result of which the coalition against Prussia had fallen apart. Encouraged by this historical precedent, Hitler aimed for a military victory to shatter the Allied coalition. This would leave the way open for a negotiated peace with the British and Americans and then the German forces in the West could be transferred East to attack the Russians. So, against all expectations, he decided to launch a great counter attack in the West.

Hitler still regarded the Westfront as more important than the Ostfront because in his mind an enemy on the Rhine was more dangerous than an enemy in East Prussia. The plan for Wacht am Rhein (Watch on the Rhine) as Hitler originally dubbed it or Herbstnebel (Autumn Fog) as it became, originated during the daily conference in the Wolf's Lair on 16 September. Guderian, Keitel and Jodl were all present and the latter was giving a briefing on the situation on the Western Front.

Suddenly Hitler cut Jodl short and there followed a few minutes of dramatic silence. Then the Führer announced in a loud voice: 'I have just made a momentous decision. I shall go over to the counterattack!' He pointed to a map and said, 'here, out of the Ardennes, with the objective – Antwerp!'[12] The plan as it developed had two phases: in phase one, the Germans would attack through the thinly-manned Ardennes-Eifel sector and cross the Meuse between Liege and Namur. In phase two they would swing north and seize their ultimate objective: the port of Antwerp, the main supply base for British operations. The Meuse was to be reached within two days and Antwerp within a week. The four Allied armies trapped north of the Bastogne-Brussels-Antwerp line could then be destroyed. Hitler spoke of 'another Dunkirk' that would force the British off the continent and out of the war.

It was ironic that Hitler should return to the scene of the greatest German victory of all – Manstein's Sichelschnitt. Now he was trying to pull off a second Ardennes stroke. But circumstances in December 1944 were very different from those in May 1940 – for one thing the Germans would face much stiffer resistance on their way to the Meuse than the Belgian Chasseurs, and also, they had lost air superiority, crucial in any large-scale movement of armour. To neutralise this latter disadvantage, the offensive could only take place when bad weather had grounded the Allied planes.

The attack would be spearheaded by two Panzerarmees: the Fifth Panzerarmee, commanded by General der Panzertruppen Hasso-Eccard Freiherr von Manteuffel and the Sixth SS Panzerarmee, commanded by SS-Oberstgruppenführer Josef 'Sepp' Dietrich. The Seventh Army, under General der Panzertruppen Erich Brandenberger, would be largely infantry and would guard the Panzerarmees' southern flank. Dietrich's SS Panzerarmee would be on the northern flank and would make the main thrust to Antwerp; this was mainly for political rather than military reasons – if there were any kudos to be won, Hitler wanted them to go to the SS, not the Heer. The Heer Panzerarmee was placed in the centre and was supposed to capture the vital road and rail centre of Bastogne and then support Dietrich on the drive to Antwerp. Thirty divisions were initially earmarked for the operation, including twelve panzer. There would also be plenty of artillery and Nebelwerfer batteries.

The plan for Wacht am Rhine or the Battle of the Bulge as it became known to the Allies, was almost entirely Hitler's own. Manteuffel told Liddell Hart after the war: 'The plan for the Ardennes offensive was drawn up completely by OKW and sent to us a cut and dried Führer order.'[13] As a result the plan had all the signs of being drawn up by a military amateur and it is impossible to see how it could have succeeded. The military professionals were dismayed when they heard the exact details for it was clear to them that they'd never reach Antwerp and that all the counter-offensive would produce was a long and narrow salient into the Allied lines. The Allies would throw everything they had at this salient and then the Germans would either have to withdraw or be pinched off and trapped in a pocket.

That wily old soldier, von Rundstedt, whom even the Allies regarded as one of the best in the world, was staggered by the plan. When Model, commander of Army Group B, first saw it, he declared, 'This damned thing hasn't got a leg to stand on!'[14] Even Dietrich, no great military brain himself, thought the plan was a joke when he first heard it.

As the two senior commanders in the West, Rundstedt and Model knew that the forces available weren't strong enough to carry out such an ambitious plan and both men drew up alternative ones with the more modest objective of a double envelopment of Liege which would have had the effect of easing the pressure on Aachen. But Hitler, always favouring the 'Big Solution', rejected their plans as too conservative. From then on von Rundstedt played only a figurehead role in Wacht am Rhine, even though the Americans persisted to call it 'von Rundstedt's battle'. Instead Hitler appointed Model to see the original plan through.

Preparations began with the attack originally expected to take place in November. Divisions were withdrawn from the front for refitting and fuel and ammunition were stockpiled. Since early August, the West had been given priority for all new tanks coming off the production line and now this was extended to include SP guns and artillery. Of the eighteen new divisions produced during the previous summer, fifteen had already been sent to the East. So in early September Hitler tasked Goebbels with scraping up enough men to form twenty-five more Volksgrenadier divisions; these poorly trained and badly equipped units of elderly reservists and teenagers didn't have a very high fighting value and lacked heavy weapons such as SP guns. Many redundant Kriegsmarine and Luftwaffe men were also drafted in as infantry replacements.

Ten new Panzer brigades were formed – SS-Standartenführer Otto 'Scarface' Skorzeny, the man who'd sprung Mussolini from captivity at Gran Sasso, was given Panzer Brigade 150. His far-fetched mission was to sow confusion and chaos behind the Allied lines using English-speaking Germans wearing American uniforms and to seize two Meuse bridges. Panthers had sheet metal welded on to make them look like American tanks, but according to Skorzeny they would have deceived only 'very green troops, at night and when seen from a great distance'.[15] Not surprisingly this mission was a failure, although the Americans did become convinced that Skorzeny was out to kill Eisenhower. A few hundred Fallschirmjäger led by Oberst Friedrich von der Heydte, the 'Rosary Para', were also dropped in front of Dietrich's Panzerarmee, but the expected link-up never occurred and most of the parachutists went into captivity.

Throughout the period of the build-up, Patton's Third Army continued to attack in the Aachen sector in what Rundstedt feared was a prelude to a thrust into the Ruhr. Even though he was expressly forbidden by Hitler to use the divisions earmarked for Wacht am Rhein in the fighting, he was forced to do so anyway. He also had to allow other divisions to be withdrawn for refitting in preparation for the offensive. There was no choice but to postpone the attack until December.

The final order of battle was drawn up. In the first wave would be 13 infantry and 7 panzer divisions, a quarter of a million men in all. But overall tank strength was low – between them the two Panzerarmees had only 900 tanks and 200 SPs. There were 250 Tigers, including 150 of the new King Tigers, and the remainder of the tank force was divided equally between Panthers and Pz IVs; 5 more divisions as well as 450 tanks and SPs would be held in the OKW reserve to be committed to the battle when needed. To build up the attacking force, the rest of the Western Front had been reduced to just 400 tanks and SPs. The advance would be supported by 1,900 artillery and Nebelwerfer pieces and Goering, in a typically gross exaggeration, promised 1,000 planes, including 100 jets. The greatest shortage would be fuel; even though 10 million litres (two million gallons) had been carefully stockpiled, each tank had only enough petrol to travel 150 km (100 miles) and that was calculated on the basis of good roads, not cross-country.

Dietrich's Sixth Panzerarmee contained 5 infantry divisions and 4 Waffen SS Panzer divisions – the 1st SS Leibstandarte, the 2nd SS Das Reich, the 9th SS and the 12th SS Hitler Jugend. Sepp Dietrich, a hard-drinking former sergeant, was one of Hitler's cronies from the Beer Hall days and this, rather than any military qualifications, was the reason why he had been elevated to command an army. Rundstedt described him as 'decent, but stupid'.

Manteuffel's Fifth Panzerarmee had 3 panzer divisions (2nd, 116th and the Panzer Lehr under Bayerlein) and 4 infantry divisions. He also had the Führer Begleit Brigade in reserve which contained 3 Panzer-grenadier battalions and a Panzer IV battalion taken from the Gross Deutschland. Manteuffel was still only 47 and had risen from com-manding a division to an army in just one year, but in his case the rapid promotion was well deserved.

Brandenberger's Seventh Army held just four weak Volksgrenadier infantry divisions, had no tanks and very few anti-tank guns. Manteuffel's request that it be given a panzer division was refused. Its mission was to cover the Fifth Panzerarmee's southern flank, yet it was supposed to keep up with the tanks on foot.

The German guns and Nebelwerfers opened up at 0530 hrs on 16 December 1944 and the bombardment went on for an hour and a half. Then the infantry went in, followed by the tanks, along a

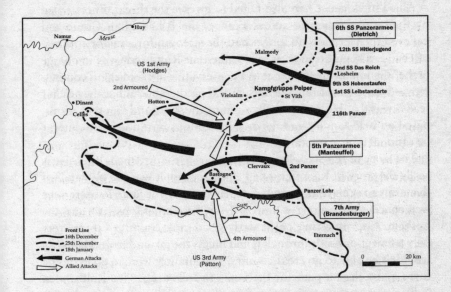

Wacht Am Rhein
Hitler's Second Ardennes Stroke, 16–25 December 1944

135-km frontage. Initially the Germans spearheads made good progress in their drive to the Meuse. On the first day the Allies believed it was just a localised spoiling attack to draw forces away from Aachen, but all the same Eisenhower sent two armoured divisions, one from the south and one from the north, to hold the shoulders of the German offensive.

On the section of front chosen, 200,000 Germans faced 84,000 Americans. The Germans had punched through a part of the front thinly manned by only four green or burnt-out American divisions, and had also managed to achieve almost complete surprise. The build-up to the attack had been skilfully done: radio silence was strictly observed and the noise of engines was shrouded by planes flying overhead or by artillery fire; tanks and other vehicles moved singly along straw-lined roads, often at night, and then hid in the dense forests. Bad weather had kept Allied reconnaissance planes out of the air so they had no warning of the build-up.

Allied intelligence had also failed to foresee the threat. Encouraged by their rapid advance across France, the Allied High Command believed the Germans no longer had the strength for a major counter-offensive. They also took at face value that Rundstedt was in charge of the Western theatre and that as a conservative old soldier, his counter-moves would be rational, defensive and predictable. What they didn't realise was that Hitler was really running the show and that his actions, based on wild fantasy and his own mysterious intuition, would never be rational and predictable.

The story of the Sixth Panzerarmee during the Ardennes offensive is really the story of Kampfgruppe Peiper, because it was the only unit of that army to achieve any significant penetration. The Sixth Panzerarmee was concentrated along a narrow front between Monschau and the Losheim Gap. It wasn't particularly good tank country – there were only a few poor roads through it and unless the ground froze, the tanks wouldn't be able to go cross-country. The infantry were to go in on the first day to clear a path for the tanks to follow up. Five Rollbahnen (advance routes) were designated for the tanks' advance to the Meuse and it was hoped that a speed of 30 k.p.h. (20 m.p.h.) could be achieved.

But progress for the Sixth Panzerarmee was slower than anticipated. The Volksgrenadier divisions performed poorly and the Americans put up a stubborn defence, jamming Dietrich's right shoulder. Sixth Panzerarmee was held up at Monschau, at Elsenborn ridge and then at the small town of St Vith, just 19 km (12 miles) behind the front line and a vital road and rail junction on the way to the Meuse. Without possession of the town, supplies couldn't reach the attacking armies by rail. Here Dietrich ran into the 7th Armoured Division, one of Eisenhower's reinforcements, and was forced to take a less direct route to the river. St Vith, supposed to be taken on the second day of the offensive, wasn't finally captured until the 21st and then only with the help of Manteuffel and the Führer Begleit Brigade. By the 20th Dietrich's advance had fizzled out and Model decided that the main effort of the offensive be passed to Manteuffel who had made much better progress than his neighbouring Panzerarmee. From now on Dietrich would support Manteuffel.

One Waffen SS unit did achieve some progress. Spearheading the 1st SS Panzerkorps was the 1st SS Panzer Division, the Liebstandarte Adolf Hitler (LAH). At the forefront of the LAH was Kampfgruppe Peiper. This ad hoc battle group was led by 29-year-old SS Obersturmbannführer Jochen Peiper, a fanatical officer who'd once been Himmler's adjutant and who'd proven himself a ruthless commander on the Ostfront. He'd won the Knight's Cross for his actions at Kharkov in 1943 and because he drove his men so hard, his units always had very high casualty rates. In Russia, Peiper's unit had earned itself the nickname of the 'Blowtorch Battalion' because of its propensity for burning down villages. When in November 1944 the Chief of Staff of Sixth Panzerarmee asked Peiper how long it would take to move a tank regiment 50 miles in winter conditions, Peiper tried it himself in his Panther, travelling the full distance in one night.

Kampfgruppe Peiper's (KG Peiper) mission was to reach the Meuse before the bridges could be blown up and then hold them until the rest of the SS Panzerkorps arrived to cross over them. He was to travel the 125–150 kilometres (75–95 miles) of tortuous, winding roads to the Meuse as quickly as possible, avoiding resistance along the route when he could. It was made clear to him that nothing should be allowed to delay the lightning advance, including the taking of prisoners. For the task Peiper was given the bulk of the 1st Panzer Regiment of the LAH, which included 2 tank battalions containing 35 Panthers and 35 Pz IVs, a battalion of mechanised infantry, a battalion of engineers and a Schwere Panzer Abteilung with 25 King Tigers.

It was the kind of impossible mission that the Waffen SS habitually took on, in the process suffering casualty rates no Heer unit would have tolerated. Peiper faced a ridiculously tall order – not only had he to seize the Meuse bridges intact, but also any other bridges on the route as he was given no bridging equipment with which to ford rivers. He had only enough ammunition for five days and petrol was so short that he would have to raid American fuel dumps along the way.

On the first day of the offensive, Peiper watched impatiently as the weak Volksgrenadier divisions tried to break through the American lines. They made little progress and Peiper, eager to be underway, decided to take his Kampfgruppe into action regardless at dawn on the 17th. The first thing they ran into was a massive traffic jam, through which Peiper drove his vehicles ruthlessly. He soon found to his anger that the road hadn't been cleared of mines as promised and lost some of his vehicles as a result. Soon KG Peiper had pushed itself into the gap between retreating American convoys and was on its way to Bullingen, a big fuel dump. After that they headed for the stone bridge over the Ambleve river at the small town of Stavelot, just 67 km (42 miles) from the Meuse. Here they ran into an American roadblock and Peiper decided to wait till the next day to take the town. Already the strict timetable was falling apart and he sensed that the German forces that were supposed to be behind him weren't following up at all.

On the 18th Peiper took Stavelot and left some of his men behind to hold the town while he drove on towards the village of Trois Ponts where three bridges crossed the Ambleve and Salm rivers. On the way there he went right past a million-gallon fuel dump without knowing it and missed out on enough fuel to supply the whole SS Panzerkorps; when he got to the village, he found American engineers had blown up the bridges. Lacking the necessary equipment to build his own bridge, Peiper could do nothing but curse the Americans for the delay and look for somewhere else to cross – after the war he told his captors he believed he could have reached the Meuse on that same day if the Trois Ponts bridges hadn't been blown up.

Peiper detoured to La Gleize and crossed the Ambleve there, by which stage he'd lost twenty of his tanks to mines and aerial bombing and fuel was running low. Then he discovered he couldn't cross the Ourthe and Lienne rivers either because the ubiquitous American engineers had blown those bridges too, so he returned to La Gleize. Meanwhile in his rear the Americans had retaken Stavelot and blown up the Petit Spa bridge along which all of Peiper's supplies had to come.

Peiper was now in real trouble – by 20 December he had only thirty tanks left and practically no fuel. Supplies had been airdropped, but 90 per cent of it fell behind American lines; an attempt to float supplies down the river failed. On 21 December the remainder of the LAH was ordered to move up and reinforce KG Peiper's position, but they couldn't get through. Stoumont, just beyond La Gleize and about 60 km west of the start-line, was as far west as KG Peiper ever got. Here it was blocked by an American counter attack and at the same time the Americans struck at La Gleize and Trois Ponts. Peiper withdrew to La Gleize and by the 22nd was encircled in that village and under heavy artillery fire.

He sent a radio message to the LAH's commander on the 23rd: 'Almost all our Hermann [ammunition] is gone. We have no Otto [fuel]. It's just a question of time before we're completely destroyed. Can we break out?'[16] The reply he received was that he could break out, but only if he brought all the vehicles and wounded with him –

which was patently impossible without fuel. Peiper decided to break out on foot anyway and ordered the radio car blown up to prevent counter orders arriving.

At 0200 hrs on Christmas Eve, Peiper and 800 of his men set off on foot, leaving behind 300 men to act as a rearguard as well as their 30 remaining tanks, 70 half-tracks and 2 artillery batteries. On Christmas morning they reached the German lines where Peiper collapsed from exhaustion, not having slept for nine days. The mission of KG Peiper had been a complete failure; in little over a week it had lost over 3,000 men and 95 tanks and had achieved nothing besides advancing farther west than any other unit in Dietrich's army. After this failure, Model switched the Sixth Panzerarmee to supporting Fifth Panzerarmee's northern flank. For his part, Peiper received the Swords and Oakleaves to his Knight's Cross.

KG Peiper had certainly embodied Hitler's exhortation that the offensive be waged ruthlessly in a wave of terror. Accustomed to the brutal warfare of the Ostfront where the Geneva Convention meant nothing and prisoners were seldom taken, the Waffen SS applied the same ruthless methods in the West. During the Ardennes offensive, Peiper's men murdered several hundred POWs and civilians, of which the Malmedy Massacre is the most infamous. Peiper, Dietrich and seventy-three former members of KG Peiper were tried for these crimes after the war. Although it was never proven that Peiper was personally present at any of the killings, he did know what his men were doing but took no measures to stop them. He was released from prison in late 1956 and went to live in a small French village in the early 1970s. He died on Bastille Day in 1976 when French Communists firebombed his home. His charred body was found with a gun by its side – Jochen Peiper had died as he had lived.

At the same time as Dietrich was being held up in the north, Manteuffel was attacking in the south with more success. The little Panzer Baron attacked along a broad front and dispensed with the kind of lengthy artillery bombardment that usually gave the game away; instead he sent in small *Sturm* (assault) detachments to infiltrate the American lines. Ramps were laid down on the dragon's teeth anti-tank obstacles so the tanks could clamber over them and searchlights were used to illuminate the darkness. On 19 December Manteuffel's Panzerarmee surrounded two American regiments in the Schnee Eifel and forced 8,000 men to surrender – the largest number of Americans ever to surrender on a single day in the European theatre.

By the 19th Manteuffel's XLVII Panzerkorps spearhead was at the outskirts of Bastogne. This city was the main road and rail junction leading to the Meuse, but Manteuffel failed to capture it because the American 101st Airborne Division got there first. Instead Manteuffel encircled the city on 21 December and moved on towards the Meuse, but Bastogne remained a boil on his communication lines that couldn't be lanced. He was also worried that Brandenberger's Seventh Army wasn't advancing fast enough to cover his southern flank.

Bastogne and its defenders has entered American folklore, particularly Brigadier McAuliffe's famed reply of 'Nuts!' when asked to surrender, but it is wise to put this minor encirclement in perspective. The Americans in Bastogne were encircled for less than a week and always knew that relief wouldn't be long in coming. Contrast this with the encirclements that occurred to both sides on the Eastern Front, such as the Cholm pocket where 4,000 Germans held out for three and a half months against 128 Soviet assaults, suffering 1,550 dead in the process. Against that background, Bastogne hardly seems an example of superhuman endurance.

After the war Manteuffel suggested that Hitler had always wanted to see a Heer Panzerarmee and a Waffen SS Panzerarmee competing against each other. If he did, he got a pretty conclusive answer as to which was better during the Ardennes offensive. Manteuffel's Panzerarmee knifed 100 km (60 miles) deep into the American lines along a 50-km (30-mile) front, while its running mate, Dietrich's Panzerarmee, made no significant penetration at all, with the sole exception of Peiper's doomed Kampfgruppe. The Heer's success can be at least partly attributed to the fact that it was led by an efficient professional soldier rather than a Nazi party hack elevated far beyond his competence.

A week into the operation it was clear that the initial German momentum was beginning to run out. Bastogne, St Vith and numerous other local engagements had sapped the Panzerarmees' strength and put them way behind schedule. They still hadn't reached the Meuse and yet Hitler's unrealistic plan had originally envisaged them in Antwerp within a week. On Christmas Eve, Manteuffel rang Jodl and told him that Antwerp was now out of the question, but that he could still reach the Meuse and then swing north, thus trapping all the Allied armies east of the river. This was more or less a reversion to Rundstedt and Model's 'Small Solution', which at least offered the prospect of a significant victory. But Hitler, still believing he could push his armies across the river by sheer willpower, shot down Manteuffel's plan.

Manteuffel continued to push on towards the Meuse, even though his tanks were short of fuel and his supply lines overextended. The 2nd Panzer Division pushed further west than any other unit in the offensive when it reached Celles on the 24th, only 6 km (4 miles) from the Meuse and not far from Dinant, the very place where Rommel had crossed the river with his 7th Panzer Division in 1940. Manteuffel pleaded with the OKW for reinforcements so he could widen his narrow 8-km (5-mile) wide salient; three divisions were promised but it was too late. The 2nd Panzer wasn't to repeat Rommel's illustrious feat because it was blocked and cut off by the American 2nd Armoured Division before it could reach the river.

On 19 December the Allies finally woke up to the threat the German offensive posed and began to prepare for a counter-attack. Field Marshal Montgomery was given command of all Allied forces north of the German salient and American General Omar Bradley commanded all forces in the south. The Third Army under Patton would strike north against Manteuffel's flank and the First Army under Hodges would strike south against Dietrich's. Monty, ever cautious, wanted to allow 'the German' to run his course before counter-attacking, pedantically declaring: 'you can't win the big victory without a tidy show'.[17]

On 23 December the weather cleared for the first time in weeks. Now the Allied fighter-bombers were able to take off and the German armour was exposed to air attack. Goering's promised air support had of course never materialised. On Christmas Day and the day following it, the Germans suffered a series of reverses – the Seventh Army was driven back, the ring around Bastogne was broken by Patton and the 2nd Panzer Division, trapped in the Celles pocket, had to break out and pull back with the loss of eighty tanks.

Hitler planned to see in 1945 with a bang. Just before midnight he began Operation Nordwind when eight German divisions attacked the US Seventh Army in northern Alsace. It was supposed to ease the pressure in the Ardennes, but had little effect. In addition Hitler's 'Great Blow' was struck on 1 January 1945 when the Luftwaffe attacked Allied air bases, destroying 200 Allied aircraft at a cost of 300 Luftwaffe planes.

The full-scale Allied counter-offensive in the Ardennes was launched on 3 January 1945 by two American armies and a British corps. The Germans, exhausted and short of fuel, were pushed back, suffering heavy losses in the process because Hitler wouldn't sanction a withdrawal. But by 8 January, he was left with no choice and reluctantly ordered troops to be withdrawn from the rapidly shrinking Bulge. At Houffalize on 16 January, one month after the start of Wacht, Allied troops from the First Army in the north met up with troops from the Third Army in the south. The Germans were more or less back where they'd started and by the end of the month the Allies had won back all the territory lost in the offensive.

The Germans had inflicted 81,000 casualties and tank losses of 800 on the Americans, but in return suffered 100,000 casualties themselves. As well as large quantities of half-tracks and artillery, 500 irreplaceable panzers had been lost in Hitler's last great gamble. In a futile battle he had senselessly thrown away the armoured reserves painstakingly built up by Guderian, reserves that would have been much more fruitfully employed in the East. In Rundstedt's opinion, Wacht am Rhein became 'Stalingrad No 2', and according to Manteuffel, from then on Hitler directed 'a corporal's war. There were no big plans – only a multitude of piecemeal fights.'[18] Wacht am Rhine probably prolonged the war by as much as six weeks, but it threw away the last of Germany's strength and meant that there could be no significant opposition to the massive Russian offensive of January 1945.

The Americans still take great pride in the Battle of the Bulge, mainly because it was the largest battle they were ever involved in. But the Wehrmacht, just five months away from utter defeat, wasn't the force it once had been. The Bulge hardly ranks on the scale of a Kursk or a Stalingrad and cannot be considered a great military feat by either side. It is really notable only for being the last major German tank attack. General Adolf Galland, commander of the Fighter Arm, considered that the Luftwaffe received its death blow in the Ardennes offensive – the same thing can probably be said of the Panzerwaffe.

The final verdict on the western 'Death Ride of the Panzers' can be left to Speer: 'The failure of the Ardennes offensive meant that the war was over. What followed was only the occupation of Germany, delayed somewhat by a confused and impotent resistance.'[19]

CHAPTER NINE

The Skies Grow Dark

It is no longer important to capture such and such a position. The essential thing is to give the enemy no respite. The Germans are running to their deaths.

Marshal Rokossovsky, 26 July 1944

A T the beginning of 1944 the 11 German armies in Russia had been pushed back to the Carpathians and the old pre-war Russo-Polish border. Facing them was a combined Russian strength of 58 armies, 7 million men in all. After the many rebuffs of 1943, the military outlook for the Wehrmacht in 1944 was very grave indeed. They were soon to face Stalin's 'Ten Blows'. The early blows drove the Germans back from Leningrad, liberated the Ukraine and the Crimea and pushed back the Finns; the sixth blow was to be the most terrible of all for it smashed Army Group Centre.

As Rommel had commented in his diary, the skies over Germany had indeed grown dark – dark with Allied bombers. The air war interfered with munitions production and troop movement to a certain extent, but its most baleful influence as far as the Ostfront was concerned was in drawing away the Luftwaffe to defend the Fatherland. Close tactical support by fighters, bombers and ground-attack aircraft had always been a central tenet of German armoured theory. Although the Red Air Force wasn't particularly efficient, they now roamed ever more freely without encountering any significant opposition, which simply added to the handicaps under which the Panzerwaffe was now forced to operate.

Another consequence of the Luftwaffe's decline was that the panzer divisions were required more and more to provide their own anti-aircraft protection, yet another drain on limited resources. This requirement led to the production of fairly ineffectual vehicles such as the Flakwagens – AA guns mounted on half-track chassis such as the SdKfz 251.

Just as decisively, the Western bombing campaign required the diversion of thousands of Germany's only true 'miracle weapon', the superb 88 mm dual-purpose gun. This was the one anti-tank weapon which remained unmastered throughout the war. The Schild und Schwert (Shield and Sword) technique which Rommel had perfected in France and Africa, was equally effective on the Ostfront in the hands of officers like Model and Balck who used these guns as an anvil onto which the enemy armour was driven by means of carefully planned attacks to the enemy's rear. Deprived of so many of the mighty 88s, the defence of the Ostfront was rendered incalculably more difficult.

The Western Allies' policy of supporting Stalin's armies reached its peak in 1944. The Russians preferred to manufacture their own weaponry, since in almost every case, from machine-pistols to tanks, they were superior to those of the Allies. None the less, the Red Army received over 12,000 tanks, most of them Shermans, which Russian tank crews considered poor substitutes for T-34's. But inferior or not, these Lend-Lease tanks still had to be knocked out by the Germans. Indeed all the impedimenta of modern warfare from rations to rails poured into the Soviet Union from 1943 on, and played a key role in the defeat of the Wehrmacht.

The poor state of Red Army communications was greatly helped by the one million miles of telephone cable and the tens of thousands of radios provided by the Allies. Possibly the most vital Allied contribution to the Red Army was the 400,000 vehicles dispatched, including jeeps, trucks and half- and fully- tracked troop carriers which greatly extended Russian mobility. The massive breakthrough operations of 1944 and 1945 could not have been as rapidly exploited without the mobility conferred by these vehicles. Whole mechanised corps were raised to accompany the tank armies and the tactical advantage hitherto enjoyed by the Germans in dealing with inadequately supported tank attacks was now nullified. It was no longer possible to separate the Red infantry from the tanks and then defeat each in turn. From now on the Germans had to contend with the Russian version of Panzergrenadiers. Oddly, the Russians never developed an armoured personnel carrier of their own during the war, perhaps because of their lack of interest in saving the lives of their troops.

Between January and April 1944, the Germans on the Ostfront claimed 12,500 Russian tank kills and yet continued to lose the war, a fact which illustrates the overwhelming odds they were now facing. During 1944 the Russians built a total of 29,000 tanks, assault guns and tank destroyers, including 11,000 of the up-gunned T-34s with the 85 mm gun and 2,000 IS-2 heavy tanks carrying a 122 mm gun against which even the Tigers were vulnerable. A fair proportion of tank kills were now being won by the ordinary infantry, upon whom the burden of tank destruction began to fall more and more as the number of German tanks decreased. The infantry had been equipped with effective personal anti-tank weapons such as the Panzerfaust and Panzerschreck and any soldier fortunate enough to single-handedly destroy a tank using just infantry weapons was awarded the Tank Destruction Badge.

Early in the Russian campaign it had been realised that the ordinary infantry needed a weapon with which to fight tanks, otherwise they would continue to be dependent on the Panzerjägers or Stugs for anti-tank defence, and in the absence of such armoured support would be very vulnerable to enemy tank attacks. Conventional ordnance proved ineffectual against armour and so hollow- or shaped-charge projectiles were employed; these had first been used during the capture of the Belgian fort of Eben Emael in May 1940 and worked by propelling a spike of molten metal into the target. The main defence against such a weapon was to cause the warhead to explode prematurely and this was the reason behind the *Schurzen* (skirts) applied to German tanks from 1943 on. Magnetic hollow-charge grenades were issued to grenadiers during the autumn of 1942, but once anti-magnetic paste like the German Zimmerit was applied to tanks, these kinds of grenades became largely obsolete.

The Panzerfaust (tank fist) was introduced in 1942 – this was a disposable, single-shot, anti-tank grenade projector. The steel tube contained a charge that propelled a 44 mm hollow-charge anti-tank grenade against the target and by the end of the war the Panzerfaust had a range of 150m, five times the original range. They were light, cheap and powerful enough to allow a single infantryman to knock out an enemy tank. The weapon could also be used in an anti-personnel role and against enemy strongpoints. By the end of the war over 8 million Panzerfausts had been produced, with 3.5 million produced during the winter of 1944/45 alone. In March 1945 the Wehrmacht possessed 3 million Panzerfausts.

The Panzerschreck (tank terror) was a variant of the American Bazooka and was more powerful than the Panzerfaust. This was a reusable piece of anti-tank ordnance with a range of up to 400m. Nicknamed 'Ofenrohr' (stove pipe) by the grenadiers, it was operated by a gunner and a loader, and fired an 88 mm hollow-charge rocket projectile. It entered service in December 1944 and was issued to Panzerzerstörergruppen (tank destroyer groups), but only 25,700 had been delivered to the front by the war's end. The Germans also experimented with an anti-tank guided missile, the X-7, but the war ended before it could be put into use.

At the same time the Germans were developing new types of tracked tank destroyers to combat the newer Russian tanks. By late 1942 it was realised that new varieties of Jagdpanzer (tank destroyers) were needed to replace the towed anti-tank guns and makeshift open-topped vehicles. The first vehicle in this second generation of tank destroyers was the Ferdinand or Elefant; these consisted of the ninety chassis built by Porsche for the Tiger project fitted with an 88 in a fixed turret. Unlike its predecessors, the Ferdinand had a completely enclosed structure, thus protecting the crew. Although they performed poorly in battle, along with the Stugs their design pointed the way to future tank destroyers; a limited traverse gun did away with the need for a rotating turret and meant the gun could be mounted inside the body of the tank, thus making for a lower profile or silhouette.

Two vehicles were to become the mainstays of German anti-tank defence from 1944 on – the Jagdpanzer IV and the Hetzer. Both vehicles proved very effective tank destroyers with two great advantages: they packed a hard-hitting gun and their low height at little over 2 m, not much more than a man's height, made them easy to conceal in ambush.

In December 1942 it was decided to build a Jagdpanzer based on the Pz IV chassis mounting a 75 mm gun to replace the outdated, open-topped Marders in the Panzerjäger Abteilungen (tank destroyer battalions). The Jagdpanzer IV went into production in January 1944 and continued in production until March 1945, by which time 2,000 had been built. The gun could only traverse 10 degrees right or left of a central line and was set in a thick and well-sloped frontal armour plate.

The Jagdpanzer IV first saw service in 1944. Originally it was equipped with the L/43 or L/48 gun, but from August 1944 onwards it was equipped with the 75 mm L/70, the same gun as the Panther. Crews gave the vehicles the affectionate name of Guderian Ente (Guderian's Duck) because they had a tendency to be nose-heavy. As the war continued they were commonly used as replacements for tanks in the panzer divisions.

The Panzerjäger 38(t), better known as the Hetzer (Baiter or Troublemaker) was based on the still plentiful Czech 38(t) chassis and mounted the same 75 mm gun as the Pz IV, namely the L/48. This gun had only a limited traverse: 5 degrees to the left and 11 degrees to the right. The Hetzer went into production in April 1944 and stayed in production until May 1945, by which time 2,600 had been built. They were mainly used to equip the Panzerjäger Abteilungen of panzer and panzergrenadier divisions.

The Hetzer was a capable little vehicle that looked like a miniature Jagdpanther. It had a number of unusual features: for example, the gun was off-centre, being mounted far to the right – this caused problems for the gunner and loader who sat on the left of a gun designed to be loaded from the right. As in all the turretless tanks, crew conditions were extremely cramped. There was a remote-controlled machine-gun on the roof which was operated from within the tank. After the war the Skoda and Praga plants continued to build Hetzers until the early 1960s and the Swiss Army kept Hetzers in service until the early 1970s.

Another important Jagdpanzer, although built in much smaller numbers than the other two, was the Jagdpanther. This was probably the best tank destroyer of the war and has influenced design until the present day. Based on the Panther chassis, it mounted an 88 mm L/71 gun, the same as the Tiger II. This gun was mounted in a 'saukopf' (pig's head) mantlet set in a well-sloped 80 mm frontal plate and had a traverse of 13 degrees left or right. The Jagdpanther went into production in January 1944 and in total 415 were built. The 5-man crew included 2 loaders. Hitler called the Jagdpanther 'an armoured casemate' and predicted it would prove superior to the King Tiger. The vehicle possessed all the advantages conferred by the excellent Panther chassis and the hard-hitting power of the 88. It was heavier (46 tons) and taller (2.72 m) than the Hetzer or Guderian's Duck, but made up for this with its thicker armour and superior firepower.

The first Jagdpanthers reached the front in June 1944 and were organised either into independent Schwere Panzerjäger Abteilungen or were placed in panzer divisions. One sPz Abt saw service in the Normandy battles, where it exacted a heavy toll from the Allies in the Bocage country. Fifty-one Jagdpanthers took part in the Ardennes offensive. But they arrived too few and too late to have a really decisive impact.

The Jagdtiger was a tank-destroyer version of the King Tiger mounting a 128 mm L/55 gun in a fixed turret; this was the largest gun fitted in a production vehicle during the Second World War and allowed the Jagdtiger to penetrate 178 mm of armour at 1,800 meters, which in essence meant there was no tank it couldn't destroy. The Jagdtiger could easily brew up Shermans at ranges beyond 2 km and its own 250 mm thick frontal armour was practically impenetrable. It was also the only German tank to require a six-man crew because the shells were so big, they had to be split and handled by two loaders.

Weighing 70 tons and standing nearly 3 metres tall, the Jagdtiger wasn't exactly inconspicuous, nor did it have the excellently sloped frontal plate of the Jagdpanther; it looked more like an ordinary King Tiger with a rigid turret and a longer gun.

The Jagdtiger really was just another example of Hitler's senseless desire to want everything built bigger and heavier. Only eight-five were ever built, just enough to equip two Panzerjäger Abteilungen – one of these fought in the Remagen bridgehead and the other in Operation Nordwind. Jagdtiger production ceased in February 1945.

The Jagdpanzers shared a low profile and a high-calibre gun with only limited traverse. Being unable to rotate the gun meant that the whole vehicle had to be pointed towards the target; this would have been a serious disadvantage in a mobile battle, but by 1944 the Panzerwaffe's days of mobile battles were over. Now they were fighting on the defensive and the Jagdpanzers were ideally suited to this role. Their low profile meant they could hide in an ambush position and by the time the onrushing enemy realised they were there, it was already too late. They were also cheaper and easier to build than turreted tanks and eventually even began to replace tanks in the panzer divisions.

Concurrently with the development of these new defensive weapons, Hitler insisted on the creation of a new generation of turreted tanks.

In August 1942 the Waffenamt requested that work begin on a more heavily armoured version of the Tiger. Unlike its predecessor, it would carry a sloped frontal plate like the T-34 and the Panther and would mount the 88 mm L/71 gun, rather than the shorter 88 mm L/56 installed on the Tiger. As with the Tiger, both Porsche and Henschel submitted prototypes and as before, Henschel won. Production of the Tiger II, or Königstiger (King Tiger) as it came to be unofficially known, began in January 1944 at Henschel's plant in Kassel.

The resulting tank looked more like the Panther than the Tiger, having a sloping frontal plate and a rounded turret – not at all the boxy, vertical-sided appearance of the Tiger. It also shared many parts with the Panther, including cupolas, engines and road wheels, because it was intended that the Tiger II would share as many parts as possible with the proposed Panther II.

The King Tiger was a huge beast: 34 feet long (10 m), 12 feet wide (4 m) and weighing in at close to 70 tons, making it the heaviest production tank of the war. The turret armour was 7 inches thick. The 88 mm L/71 was almost 21 feet (6 m) long and weighed 20 tons, more than the entire weight of the original Pz IIIs and IVs. It was a highly accurate and effective gun capable of knocking out Shermans, Cromwells and T-34/85s at ranges of up to 3,000 m. It was also superior to the Russian JS II armed with the 122 mm. The frontal armour plate was 150 mm thick and set at an angle of 40 degrees which made it impervious to almost every weapon; in fact there is no record of a Tiger II's frontal armour ever being penetrated in combat.

The Königstiger's very wide tracks went some way towards neutralising the huge weight and it also carried a more powerful 700 b.h.p. engine than its predecessor, but its power-to-weight ratio was still poor at just 10 hp per ton. The drive train was constantly overtaxed and there were frequent engine fires. Worst of all was fuel consumption: the tank burned up 500 litres of fuel every 100 km, a serious problem considering the fuel shortages the Germans were facing from 1944 on.

As with its predecessor, the Königstiger was formed into independent heavy tank battalions, the Schwere Panzer Abteilungs, each battalion of which contained forty-five Tiger IIs, or else into regiments in a few elite panzer divisions. The Königstiger first saw action near Minsk in May 1944 and two companies of sPz Abt 503 fought in Normandy. Some 489 Königstigers were built, less than 100 of which were destroyed in battle. The Allies had nothing that could combat it, but like so many German advances in weaponry, the Königstiger came too little, too late. Interestingly the last German tank destroyed in the Second World War was a Tiger II of sPz Abt 503, blown up by its crew in Austria on 10 May 1945.

On 5 January 1944 General Koniev launched an attack on the town of Kirovograd using the 2nd Ukrainian Front in a plan to encircle the town within a double envelopment. His opposing force was XLVII Panzerkorps under the auspices of the Eighth Army. This Panzerkorps included the 3rd, 11th and 14th Panzer, but they were all seriously understrength and combined could barely muster 150 tanks and assault guns. In contrast the Russians disposed of over 600 such vehicles. German infantry strength too was at a low ebb and in all respects they were heavily outnumbered, a common occurrence at this stage of the war.

After heavy fighting, XLVII Panzerkorps was driven through the town and cut off in the northern suburbs. The area was stubbornly defended and the resistance hindered Russian hopes of a resumption of their westward advance. During the night of 8 January, the Panzerkorps HQ was wiped out by Russian tanks and the commanding officer forced to take to the steppes in his underwear. His last order had been to hold Kirovograd at all costs.

Generalleutnant Bayerlein, commanding the elite 3rd Panzer, chose to ignore this order and opted to effect a breakout from the north-west. He rallied his troops with the stirring words:

> We are completely surrounded by the Russians. The last instructions received 15 hours ago, were to hold Kirovograd under all circumstances. That is now senseless. Kirovograd sounds like Stalingrad and I do not wish my troops to suffer the fate of the Stalingraders. We will break out tonight and operate against Kirovograd from the outside.[1]

Rommel's erstwhile chief of staff then divided his troops into five Kampfgruppen and took personal command of the remaining twenty-five tanks. In temperatures of minus 40 degrees, the panzers assaulted the Russian ring, covered by artillery and aided by infantry and pionieers. Bayerlein's tanks instantly overran ten Russian Pak guns and cleared the path for his other columns to follow. Once outside the

Soviet ring, he set up defensive positions and proceeded to raid Russian strongpoints about the town. His precipitate breakout and his raids to divert the Russians' attention allowed the trapped defenders to launch their breakout attempt against depleted Russian forces. The trapped units managed to break out and return to the main German lines on the 9th, where they linked up with relieving forces including the Gross Deutchland.

After this battle the Russians forced a breach westwards around Vladimirovka in mid-January, but ran straight into the freshly detrained 3rd SS Panzer Division Totenkopf who sealed off the breakthrough. The Russians had received a rough handling from the panzer divisions and were left with grievous gaps in their infantry ranks in addition to the loss of over 450 tanks.

The downside to the success of the XLVII and XLVIII Panzerkorps in the early months of 1944 was that it led to the creation of a German salient between Kirovograd and Zhitomir; this was held by the XLII and XI Korps containing ten divisions including the 5th SS Panzer Division Wiking. This salient offered a soft target for the Russians and they swiftly enveloped it with a concentric attack by the 1st and 2nd Ukrainian fronts. By 6 February the defenders were enclosed within a ring of steel variously called the Cherkassy or Korsun pocket. Three days later the Russians sought surrender terms but General Stemmermann, commander of the 50,000 men trapped in the pocket, bluntly refused to parley. Rather he opted to attempt a breakout to the southwest where he would meet up with the relief force, General Breith's III Panzerkorps, consisting of 16th and 17th Panzer, the Liebstandarte and Schwere Panzer Regiment Bake.

Bake's regiment was the spearhead for the relieving attack. This heavy panzer group was formed in January 1944 and contained sPz Abt 503 with 30 Tigers, a 50-strong Panther battalion and a battalion each of Stugs and Pionieres. Its commander, Oberstleutnant Dr Franz Bake, was a panzer veteran who had fought in the tank battle of Cambrai in 1918, and won the Tank Destruction Badge three times during the Battle of Kursk for brewing up tanks with Panzerfausts. The regiment had soon proved its worth when thrown into action near Vinnitsa to head off 5 Soviet tank corps; during five days it managed to destroy 270 tanks and 160 guns at a loss of just 5 of its own tanks.

By mid-February the 50,000 trapped Germans were defending an area 15 km by 10 km and the end was close. Manstein travelled to Uman in his command train to supervise operations. Stemmermann made his break on the night of the 16th with 35,000 men; the wounded had to be left behind. Towards midnight the group moved off, but at dawn were spotted and bombarded by Russian artillery. The infantry, rallied by mounted officers and fighting with a fury born of desperation, overcame the Russian defenders. Meanwhile III Panzerkorps was slicing a way through to the pocket, coming within 12 km (8 miles) of it in the end. The last tanks were used to bridge the final stream and Group Stemmermann linked up with III Panzerkorps later that morning. The six and a half rescued divisions were completely lacking in heavy equipment and had to be withdrawn for refitting. About 30,000 men rejoined the German lines, 5,000 having been killed by artillery fire, run over by tanks or cut down by Cossacks. Stemmermann himself died fighting in the rearguard.

The indirect result of the Korsun breakout operation was the stripping of resources from the Dnieper bend. The weakened defence of Nikopol allowed Malinovsky to successfully force its abandonment on 8 February. The Reich had lost its best source for manganese ore. The loss of Nikopol merely heralded a series of enforced withdrawals over the coming weeks and Hitler's insistence on rigid defence resulted only in producing a greater loss of terrain than would have been required had Manstein been allowed a free hand to practice elastic defence.

Throughout February, Manstein's Army Group South continued to be pushed gradually westward. Manstein estimated that at this period the Soviet tanks corps Army Group South were facing possessed an average of between 50 and 100 tanks each, whereas the corresponding number for panzer divisions was just 30 vehicles. And although Russian armoured losses in the south continued to be extremely high, they had received 2,700 replacement tanks since July 1943, whereas Manstein's command had received only 870.

As ever Hitler continued to decree this point or that town as inviolate bastions or strongholds, without any regard for their actual defensibility. As a result of this kind of intransigence, it wasn't long before the First Panzerarmee, including Panzer Regiment Bake, found itself trapped. Toward the end of March the 1st Ukrainian Front crossed the Dniester river and reached the Carpathian foothills, thus encircling Hube's First Panzerarmee which was engaged with the 2nd Ukrainian Front. Hube's army contained 9 panzer, 1 panzergrenadier and 10 infantry divisions as well as several smaller units like Bake's regiment.

Having foreseen this kind of development, Hube had already evacuated all his non-fighting personnel to the rear. Fuel was carefully rationed, non-essential vehicles destroyed and extensive use made of the panje horse and cart. Manstein began to bombard OKW with requests for permission to allow the army to break out almost as soon as the Russians closed the ring – eventually Hitler gave his approval.

Hube had two main avenues of escape open to him. To the south lay the most accessible route via his bridgehead across the Dniester at Hotin; this offered good going and the chance to regroup in Romania, but for those reasons it was also likely to be the one most closely defended by the Russians. The alternative was to attack to the west, but this involved the crossing of three tributaries of the Dniester – the Sbrucz, the Sereth and the Strypa – and fighting a way through two Soviet tank armies. In its favour the western route offered the shortest distance to the new German line then forming and the army would be able to assume its place there almost as soon as it broke clear of the Russians.

Manstein in any event ordered Hube to break out to the west as he foresaw that the southern route would merely postpone an eventual final encirclement and destruction of the army. He also decided to build a relief force around Fourth Panzerarmee with which to effect a junction with Hube. He demanded reinforcements from Hitler and eventually received II SS Panzerkorps which contained the 9th SS Hohenstaufen and the 10th SS Frundsberg Panzer Divisions. Along with two infantry divisions, this relief force would attack eastwards to cover Hube's breakout and, as March drew to a close, was brought to its jump-off positions at Tarnapol, 200 km (125 miles) away from the encircled army.

As his first objective Hube set out to convince the Russians that he would opt for the southern route. A scheme incorporating false radio messages and rerouted vehicle activity succeeded brilliantly and managed to disperse the Russian strength by convincing them to go on a 'wild panzer chase' to the south. To sustain his wandering pocket Hube divided his panzers into three groups: two attack forces spearheaded by Panther battalions would attack north and south while a rearguard was formed containing most of the Tigers. Morale in the pocket was greatly aided by regular air supply and evacuation of the wounded.

The breakout began on the night of 27/28 March and was greatly aided by a blizzard which helped to obscure the army's movements. The initial assault was conducted by the Panthers of the two strike forces and crossings across the Sbrucz were quickly secured before the panzers struck out for the Sereth. This initial success was greatly assisted by the deceptive measures of the previous days, but Koniev, quick-witted as ever, soon realised his error and ordered the Fourth Tank Army to attack the Panzerarmee's flank between the two rivers on 30 March. Hube's panzers met this army head-on and inflicted a sound beating on it, while the remainder of the army continued to cross the Sereth.

Once Hube's men had escaped across the first two rivers, Koniev opted for a pincer attack against both German flanks, coupled with an assault against the rearguard. In April the weather broke and a thaw reduced the Panzers' manoeuvrability. However Koniev was distracted by the relieving attack of II SS Panzerkorps, which had managed to make radio contact with Hube thus greatly facilitating co-operation between the two formations.

On 15 April the panzers of Hube's two attack forces got across the Strypa, the final river in the Germans' way. A day later his vanguard met the vanguard of II SS Panzerkorps at the Strypa river where the weary troops rejoined the main defensive line. The Russians were deprived of their prey yet again and suffered a bloody nose into the bargain, for during the breakout the First Panzerarmee had destroyed over 350 Russian tanks and 40 assault guns. For his pivotal part in the operation Hube was promoted to Generaloberst and awarded the very rare Diamonds to the Knight's Cross, but on 21 April this immensely talented soldier was killed in a plane crash while travelling to have the decoration bestowed upon him. Only his black metal hand was recovered from the wreckage and this was granted a full state funeral. The Panzerwaffe had lost one of its finest officers just as his star was beginning to wax.

Three weeks before Papa Hube's death, Hitler finally rid himself of his 'finest operational brain' – Manstein. Their personal and professional relationship had gone from bad to worse over the previous few months. Manstein continued to agitate for operational freedom of movement in the south, which Hitler took to mean withdrawals. In a stormy conference in January, the Field Marshal had bluntly told Hitler that the current disastrous situation was 'also due to the way in which we are led'.[2]

On 30 March, both he and Kleist, commander of Army Group A, were collected by Hitler's personal Condor plane and flown to the Berghof. Here they were awarded Swords to their Knight's Crosses and relieved of command. Hitler sought to justify himself to Manstein by saying that 'the time for grand-style operations in the east is now past'[3] and that what was now needed was gritty defence. As a consequence, Army Group South became Army Group North Ukraine, with newly promoted Generalfeldmarschall Model as its new commander. Kleist's Army Group A became Army Group South Ukraine under Schorner. These appointments were a tacit admission from Hitler that the war was as good as lost for both of these officers specialised in last-ditch defence.

Manstein's last words to Hitler before he left the Berghof were a characteristic understatement: 'I trust, mein Führer, that the step you have taken today will not have any untoward effects.'[4] Manstein left his HQ at Lwow on 3 April 1944 and returned to Germany. Although Hitler had promised to re-employ him, Manstein never again held another command. Gone was probably the only man who could have still imposed a stalemate on the Ostfront, if granted freedom of manoeuvre. In the words of Mellenthin, he was 'the one man whose strategic genius might have frustrated the Russian masses'.[5] Mud now brought a temporary end to the ten months of continuous fighting in the south, but this respite turned out to be just the calm before the storm.

On 22 June 1944, the third anniversary of the opening of Operation Barbarossa, one of the seminal events of the Second World War began to unfold. Code-named Bagration, this Russian offensive was to begin the final smashing of the German front. Although largely ignored by Western historians, this offensive and its associated operations were of even more decisive importance in terms of Germany's eventual defeat than the Normandy landings. Bagration heralded a whole series of overlapping offensives that ranged from the Baltic to the Carpathians and the cascading effect of these attacks kept the Germans permanently off balance and prevented them from ever stabilising the front. When these offensives finally broke down, Eastern Europe had changed hands and the Wehrmacht's next battle would be for the Reich itself.

Early in June flak gunners had shot down a Soviet reconnaissance plane flying over Army Group Centre and captured the pilot, a Soviet air staff officer. Found on him were plans that clearly showed the next Russian attack would come against Army Group Centre. But Hitler refused to give any countenance to this intelligence scoop or to alter his dispositions accordingly because he and his cabal of advisers were convinced the next blow would come in the Ukraine. Stavka (Russian High Command) had other ideas and divined that the real weakness in the German dispositions was the overstretched Army Group Centre. They planned to attack this sector of the front with the ultimate aim of driving a wedge between Army Groups North and Centre, perhaps even cutting off the former entirely. The ultimate destination of the Russian armour was therefore the Baltic coast.

At this stage Army Group Centre was thinly stretched across the 250,000 square miles of Belorussia between the Baltic and the Pripet Marshes. The Crimea had been lost in May. Considered German military opinion also favoured the evacuation of Army Group North entirely as it served no strategic function whatsoever since all hope of taking Leningrad had faded. This would have shortened the front considerably and freed troops for other areas. Hitler needless to say rejected this out of hand claiming that their presence in the Baltic states tied down large Russian forces and kept Finland in the war. As usual his intransigence was about to breed a new disaster.

After Kluge was injured in a car crash, Generalfeldmarschall Ernst Busch took over Army Group Centre. Of all the wartime field marshals, Busch was the most unsuited for senior command. This mediocre officer's rapid rise can be put down more to his being a fervent Hitler supporter than to any military prowess, but even he could see that his front would bear the brunt of the next Russian offensive. He asked to be allowed pull AG Centre back behind the Berezina river in order to confound the Red Army's preparations and protect his men from the ferocity of the initial assault. If the Russian blow was allowed to fall on thin air, Busch believed an immediate counter thrust à la Kharkov could be launched. But typically Hitler refused to allow any withdrawal.

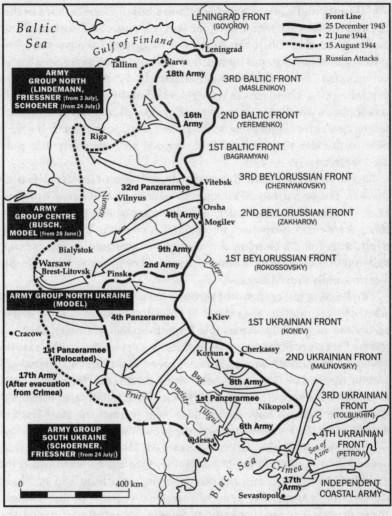

Ostfront 1944
Operation Bagration and the Collapse of Army Group Centre

Facing the 700,000 men of Army Group Centre were 3 Russian fronts of 166 divisions containing 1.25 million troops. The Germans were heavily outnumbered when it came to the decisive weapons – tanks, artillery and aircraft – for example, 900 panzers faced 4,000 Russian tanks. The attack began with a terrible bombardment from

30,000 guns and Katyusha rockets; thousands of Germans died in this opening artillery barrage alone. The survivors were so disoriented and disorganised that when the Russian armour and infantry were unleashed, they failed to put up much resistance. At the same time a pre-emptive strike by the Red Air Force effectively eliminated the Luftwaffe from the skies. These strikes were followed up by swarms of ground-attack planes which shot up supply and armoured columns and inflicted severe casualties on infantry, artillery and headquarters. For the first time in the war the Russians had attained air superiority and they used it effectively.

Bagration quickly turned into the single biggest German defeat of the war. The overstretched German front collapsed so quickly that no hope of reforming a tenable defensive line was possible and the German forces were either swept back into Poland as far as the Vistula or swiftly overrun. A full 25 German divisions were destroyed in the carnage and 400,000 men killed, wounded, captured or missing. Army Group Centre simply ceased to exist.

The Russian tanks streamed through the gaps torn in the front and advanced relentlessly, regardless of loss. Russian tanks even drove across the supposedly impassable Pripet Marshes via newly laid log roads. Every breakthrough was ruthlessly exploited and the rate of advance was not allowed to suffer. Instead resistance was bypassed and the trapped German units held within double envelopments – one to tie down the encircled units and the second to rebuff relief attempts. Clearly the Russian tank commanders had learned the hard lessons doled out by the Panzerwaffe over the previous three years.

In the first week the Russians advanced 250 km (150 miles) and opened up a hole 400 km (250 miles) wide in the German front. By the 27th Vitebsk was cut off, thus opening up a huge gap in Third Panzerarmee's front. The Panzerarmee, now reduced to just a single corps, was soon pushed back into Lithuania. A great pincer movement closed around Minsk in early July, trapping 100,000 troops. By the middle of July the Soviet spearheads were deep into north-eastern Poland and perilously close to East Prussia. The Russians now shifted the thrust of their attacks from the centre to the two flanks with attacks in the south and north.

As soon as the extent of the catastrophic collapse of Army Group Centre became apparent, Hitler sacked the hapless Busch and on

28 June appointed Walther Model to command this as well as his own Army Group North Ukraine (the name reverted during this period to Army Group South). Model was the perfect man for the job, Mellenthin describing him as 'an alert, dapper, fiery little man, never separated from his monocle' and 'a soldier of great driving power and energy'.[6] Guderian called him a 'bold, inexhaustible soldier' and the best possible man to carry out the difficult task of reconstructing the front.

Model's abrupt, impatient and ruthless style cajoled and bullied shocked staffs into action and his common touch with the troops, whom he visited incessantly, helped galvanise their morale. His energy was legendary and he flew across the battlefield every day as well as visiting every unit he commanded. During one Russian bombing of his headquarters, he dryly ordered that only General Staff officers with red stripes should take cover while he calmly sat out the air raid himself as he lacked the requisite britches. He also liked to engage the troops in choral competitions in which he participated himself.

Model quickly identified the many weak points in the front and shored them up as best he could, although without much success. He was able to transfer precious reserves from his other Army Group to AG Centre, with his main aim being to close the dangerous gap the Russians had opened between Fourth Army and Third Panzerarmee. In addition, to which, in the area of Army Group South a new gap had been punched between First and Fourth Panzerarmees. Model intended to plug this gap with the hastily reforming Seventeenth Army and until it arrived, the job of staving off any further Russian penetrations fell to the 24th Panzer Division. The divisional commander achieved this by creating several battle groups which adopted successful hit-and-run tactics until Seventeenth Army was firmly in place. However as this battle reached its critical phase the Führer had even more pressing business for his Fireman Field Marshal to deal with and Model was appointed C-in-C West in the middle of August.

When Bagration erupted, the XLVIII Panzerkorps, still commanded by that ablest of Panzer leaders, Hermann Balck, was located in the vicinity of Lemberg and Tarnapol, about 150 km north of the Carpathian mountains. The Panzerkorps' front lay along the Strypa river and it contained in the region of ten divisions, including an artillery division and several smaller independent infantry units; the Korps' former panzer divisions, the 1st and 8th now lay in reserve.

In preparation Balck had made plans to drive back the Russians in a series of small attacks designed to disrupt their offensive preparations, as well as to rearrange his own defensive positions. As the meticulous von Mellenthin acerbically notes, however, Model's uncompromising attitude created additional difficulties. Model had decreed that the front line was to be maintained and manned fully even at night and also wanted the entire front similarly manned and armed. Balck, in line with Busch, wanted a forward line of outposts with a main defensive line further back, out of artillery range. In addition he wanted his own artillery concentrated for more effective counter fire and the available panzers held ready to be used as a mobile fire brigade to meet any Russian breakthrough. After much argument, Model finally gave way but the Russians struck before the German artillery had been fully regrouped into Pak fronts. At least the infantry were spared the fate of their comrades in Army Group Centre, but Balck's defence plans were seriously hindered.

On 14 July, the Russians struck in the south with the long-anticipated Galician offensive. The pattern was identical to that of a month earlier – a violent but brief artillery firestorm followed by air and ground attacks. Balck's preparations paid off however and the Russians only managed to break through in two sectors. He immediately ordered his two reserve panzer divisions to counter-attack. The 1st Panzer met with success, but the commander of the 8th disobeyed Balck and used a main road for his approach route instead of forest tracks. As expected the Red Air Force hit hard and the exposed division was shot to pieces. Balck was justifiably enraged and after the war commented that 'It's interesting to note, incidentally, that this fellow was a highly rated General Staff officer. Clever, but unfortunately not very practical.'

Balck sent von Mellenthin to assume temporary command of this division with orders now to assist the encircled XIII Korps in the northeast. The XLVIII Panzerkorps was separated from these 40,000 men by strong Russian forces and von Mellenthin expected a hard fight. Instead he discovered that only half an hour before the attack was to begin, the Panzer Regiment commander ordered the covering infantry to pull back and reform in full view of the enemy. An incensed Mellenthin instantly relieved the errant regimental leader, but it was now too late to attack because the Russians, forewarned of the attack, had strengthened their positions. Fortunately, the surrounded men still managed to break out independently by charging at the Russians armed with only small arms and berserker rage.

Nonetheless the German line was untenable and XLVIII Panzerkorps was driven south into the Carpathians. By the first week of August the Russians had seized Lublin and the troops of Koniev's front had reached the Vistula. Both the First and Fourth Panzerarmees were in full retreat when Balck and his 'clever general staff man', von Mellenthin, were transferred to assume command of the latter on 28 July. Koniev was relentlessly attacking Fourth Panzerarmee at this time in the hope of splitting it from First Panzerarmee. Fourth Panzerarmee's previous commander, Rauss, was transferred to command Third Panzerarmee in the north.

The Russians concentrated on capturing bridgeheads across the Vistula in early August. Most notable amongst these was the major one at Baranov, but several smaller ones were also seized. While the German infantry fought a resolute defence to contain them, Balck concentrated both his III and XLVIII Panzerkorps against the bridgehead and managed to reduce it considerably. Guderian praised his actions highly, but regretted that the Russians could not be entirely wiped out. Balck also met with success at some of the smaller Russian crossings and the skilful use of the panzer units in attack managed to wear down the Russian defenders.

On 28 July, the Russian armoured spearheads reached Brest-Litovsk in Poland, the point from where Barbarossa had begun three years before. But as it reached the Vistula, the Soviet offensive finally began to run out of steam. In early August they were forced to a standstill at the gates of Warsaw by five panzer divisions: the 4th, 19th, 3rd SS Totenkopf, 5th SS Wiking and the Hermann Goering Panzer Division. But the Russian halt on the river for the next six months was as much due to the need to rebuild supplies for the final offensive as to renewed German resistance. By the time Bagration finally ground to a halt it had advanced 720 km (450 miles) in a month and utterly destroyed Army Group Centre.

On 20 July, during the height of disasters in both the East and West, a group of officers led by Colonel Klaus von Stauffenburg attempted to blow up Hitler at his military headquarters at Rastenburg in East Prussia. The bomb narrowly failed to kill the Führer but the bruised and shaken warlord quickly exacted a terrible revenge on the plotters, and indeed anyone who fell under the slightest suspicion. Among the victims was General Erich Hoepner who had commanded one of the four Panzergruppen during Barbarossa; he was heavily implicated in the plot and was executed.

But the most illustrious victim of Hitler's paranoia was Rommel. So popular was he with the masses that the plotters had pencilled him in as the new chief of the armed forces, even though the Field Marshal himself had played only the most peripheral role in the plot. Betrayed by the tortured ravings of an injured plotter, he was visited while recuperating at his home in Ulm by two Nazi lapdogs, Generals Burgdorf and Maisel. They offered him the option of a discreet suicide or the humiliation of a People's Court trial, after which his family too would fall victim. Rommel, ever the consummate father and husband, opted for the former and swallowed a phial of poison. The official report stated he died of a brain haemorrhage induced by his recent wounds and the Field Marshal received a full state funeral.

On the day immediately after the explosion Hitler sacked Kurt Zeitzler and as a mark of disgrace he was forbidden to wear his uniform. Guderian was appointed in his place and was told in no uncertain terms that his post involved merely the transmission of Hitler's orders to the Ostfront, preparing daily reports and offering suggested operations. He was to have no executive powers and as Guderian soon found out his advisory role was an empty shell too – Hitler had his own schemes and didn't like them tempered by professional realism.

Guderian and many of his fellow officers roundly condemned the plot, despite being wholly opposed to the methods of the Third Reich. These officers, largely engaged in fighting the Russians, were of the opinion that to strike at the nation's leader while the country fought for its existence was treasonable and betrayed the men fighting and dying in the field. They also feared that even a temporary paralysis of leadership could result in a Russian breakthrough.

Guderian found the OKH control centre in a chaotic state. He came across just one sleeping private in the office block and when he lifted a phone and gave his name to the female switchboard operator, she screamed and hung up. As he recalls in a masterpiece of understatement in his memoirs, when he assumed his new post on 21 July, 'the situation on the Eastern Front was far from satisfactory'.[7] Nevertheless the energetic Panzer General quickly got the machine in running order again, although he soon discovered that Hitler would allow him only the most limited powers of decision.

Hitler himself succinctly summed up the events of the previous weeks when he commented during one of his interminable conferences: 'I really can't imagine a worse crisis than the one we had in the East this year. When Field Marshal Model came, Army Group Centre was nothing but a hole.'[8] This remark came only days after the severing of what remained of Model's re-established Army Group Centre from Army Group North and just hours before the Poles of Warsaw rose up in open rebellion. However, by the end of August the front in the south had more or less been re-established. This was the moment chosen by Stavka to unleash yet another offensive.

On 20 August this new offensive opened against Army Group South Ukraine. Two Russian fronts poured into Romania and despite vociferous assurances of loyalty by the Romanian dictator, Marshall Antonescu, his troops defected five days later. Antonescu himself had suggested a shortening of the German lines, but Hitler had forbidden Freissner, the Army Group's commander, from withdrawing until clear evidence of an impending Russian attack was available. But the attack came as a surprise and when the Romanians turned their guns on their erstwhile allies, the ensuing confusion prevented the Wehrmacht from holding any bridges across the Danube. As a result, no fewer than 16 German divisions were struck from the order of battle. The important Ploesti oilfield was also lost to the Wehrmacht.

The Bulgarians also chose this time to defect and Guderian ruefully bemoaned the sending of eight-eight Pz IVs and fifty assault guns to them just a few days earlier. Army Groups E and F in Greece and Yugoslavia were now in danger of being cut off. To complete the bleak picture, in the north the Finns concluded an armistice with the Russians in early September, releasing even more Russian troops for action against Army Group North.

In early August the Russians encircled the Latvian port of Riga, thereby cutting off the only supply line to AG North, now commanded by Schorner. Guderian was in favour of evacuating the Baltic states altogether, but when Hitler forbade this, he made plans instead to re-establish communications between Army Groups North and Centre by means of a local offensive – XL Panzerkorps, containing the 4th, 5th, 14th and Gross Deutschland Panzer Divisions and fielding 400 tanks and assault guns, would attack from the west while a special battle group under none other than the colourful Panzer Graf Von Strachwitz would attack from the north.

Recently promoted to Generalmajor, Strachwitz had been sent to Army Group North in April to assume command of the 1st Panzer Division. In addition he was made senior panzer officer within the Army Group and as such also commanded two further panzer divisions and an anti-tank brigade. While this sounded like an impressive force, Strachwitz soon discovered that in fact none of his units was available. Using what odds and ends he could scrape together plus ten panzers and fifteen troop carriers that Guderian managed to reroute to him, he was soon back in business. During this period he quickly resumed his old tricks and his exploits included calmly radioing intended times and locations of attacks to the Russians and then shooting up their clumsy attempts at trapping his units. He also made a raid deep into the Russian rear – up to 150 km – shooting up everything in sight before returning to his lines unscathed.

The job now entrusted to him was on a much greater scale, but he still approached it in his own inimitable manner. Advancing under the cover of a heavy artillery barrage with only the reinforcements sent by Guderian, Strachwitz managed to storm several Russian positions, including a guarded bridge, on his way to his first objective, the town of Tuccum. At the town perimeters he encountered a Russian tank battalion which he had destroyed with the aid of well-directed gunfire from the pocket battleship Lützow in the Baltic.

At this point he had only three tanks left, the rest having been sent back to escort prisoners or guard various points along his route. With these three vehicles he now planned to raise the siege of Riga. En route he stumbled across two Russian infantry divisions and a tank corps who surrendered to him in the mistaken belief that they were surrounded. Strachwitz assigned five of his transport lorries to guard the Russian force and moved on with his three tanks. By the time he reached the centre of Riga, only Strachwitz's own Tiger remained, the other two tanks having been left behind on guard duty along the way. His remaining grenadiers now dismounted from their lorries to engage the Russian units in the vicinity and he drove on alone into the city centre. There he was greeted by several generals who hailed him as a Leutnant since he wore no lapel badges. In late September XL Panzerkorps, aided by the heavy guns of the cruiser *Prinz Eugen,* broke the ring around the town.

Strachwitz's excursion had resulted in the capture of 18,000 prisoners and 30 batteries of artillery, while his medal collection also increased as he added the Diamonds to his Knight's Cross. But shortly after this award, the Panzer Kavallerist was so seriously injured in a car accident that he wasn't expected to survive. He did however and saw out the war raising and leading tank destroyer brigades. Having exhausted all his nine lives, Strachwitz surrendered to the Americans in Bavaria in May 1945.

But it wasn't long before Army Group North was finally severed from the rest of the Wehrmacht for ever because on 10 October the Russians renewed their Baltic offensive with three Fronts. One of the Fronts reached the sea near Memel while the other two cut off Riga. Schorner had accelerated the defeat by concentrating his armour in the wrong place, contrary to Guderian's specific orders. The thirty-three surviving divisions of AG North were trapped in the Courland peninsula with resupply now only possible by sea. Some of the divisions were evacuated, but the remaining sixteen, which included the 12th and 14th Panzer, stayed put and managed to hold out till the end of the war. Guderian was particularly angered by the loss of panzer divisions so desperately needed in the final battles for Germany itself.

On 20 October Germany's last ally, Hungary, was finally exposed to the Russian steamroller. The exploits of 'Scarface' Skorzeny, who kidnapped the Regent and spirited him away in a rolled-up carpet, prevented the Hungarian Government from defecting like the rest of Germany's Balkan allies and meant that the Hungarian army fought alongside the Germans until the end of the war. This allowed the Germans to conduct a better organised defence there than was possible elsewhere and as a consequence slowed down the Russian advance that seemed so inexorable everywhere else.

Generaloberst Freissner, the capable commander of the recently renamed Army Group South, now based in Hungary, set to work in repulsing the Russian thrust. In the area around Debrecen he massed the 1st, 23rd and 24th Panzer Divisions and, using typical Panzerwaffe hit-and-run tactics, wore down the Russian spearhead until a large pocket was formed which Sixth Army reduced. Up to three Russian corps were destroyed in this manner. This proved one of the few reassuring feats of the year, but like so many apparent victories of the Panzerwaffe it merely set the stage for an even greater defeat. By the end of the year Budapest, although under siege, was still in German hands and this encouraged Hitler to order another one of his fatal divergences in 1945.

On the Ostfront, the year 1944 was a momentous one. That the Wehrmacht survived it and continued to keep the fighting largely on foreign soil was due in great measure to the tenaciousness of the Landser and the relentless energy of the Panzers. The operational pattern of the year is largely repetitive: a Russian attack is predicted; various staffs draw up a plan to counter it; Hitler automatically rejects any measures that involve a retreat to shorten the line or the adoption of mobile defence which he regards as a euphemism for retreat; when the attack begins the available panzers are rushed to defeat a Russian break-through or to relieve encircled units. All the while no reserves can be spared and any available troops are immediately committed to the maelstrom.

From Guderian's perspective the latter months of the year entailed frantic attempts to reconstitute the Ostfront only to see it crumble time and again. Hitler and the sycophants who surrounded him refused to believe that the Russian front was the decisive one, so obsessed were they with plans for the West. As a result, all of Guderian's attempts to siphon off even slender reserves were frustrated repeatedly and all available materiel continued to be diverted to the West. It was only the personal rapport between Guderian and the Armaments Minister, Albert Speer, that ensured basic supplies to the East. In the final months of the year, less than half the total tank and assault gun output was sent east. Guderian's efforts to establish a strong line of defensive fortifications in the East were also stymied by Hitler who believed this would only encourage his generals to retreat.

The almost unanimous consensus amongst the German generals was that the forward defensive line ought to consist of outposts while the main line should be located at least 12 miles further back, putting it safely out of artillery range. Infantry was to be used to hold the lines while artillery and armour were to be used in concentration at the decisive points. In this way even scarce resources could be stretched to the utmost. The Russians lacked the ability to quickly adapt their plans and the Germans found that a timely withdrawal completely upset the Russian timetables.

But Hitler's ideas were a little different – hold everything! Even though he was attracted to technology and new weapons, his military outlook continued to be deeply influenced by his time in the trenches. Despite the success of Manstein at Kharkov in 1943 and a multitude of similar smaller engagements, he never fathomed the benefits of an elastic defence conducted by tanks. He continued to think in terms of fixed defended lines and yet at the same time never permitted the construction of rearward defences, believing his generals would instantly withdraw to them. It was during 1944 that these attitudes of Hitler had the most disastrous effect, both in the East and the West.

Another one of his vices showed itself when he resorted to creating new units rather than refitting battle-worn ones. During the year thirteen new panzer 'brigades' were formed which were in reality barely of regimental strength. Again they served only to dilute the scarce resources available to the hardened Panzer veterans and their combat effectiveness was minimal as they lacked the requisite cohesion and training. The inevitable result was excessively heavy casualties.

The Ostfront had cost Germany a million casualties during the summer of 1944. When Hitler had commented during the previous year that the troops weren't of the same calibre as the men of 1941, Model caustically replied, 'The reason is because the men of 1941 are dead. Their graves lie strewn across the whole of Russia.'[9] No army, no matter how resilient, could survive such haemorrhaging for very long. The end was in sight now. All that remained to see was who would overrun Germany first.

CHAPTER 10

Twilight of the Gods

Since midnight the guns have been silent.

The last OKW communique, May 1945

As 1945 began, Germany was anticipating another massive Russian assault – the Red Army had been sitting on the Vistula since July, giving them plenty of time to build up their forces. Guderian's 'Foreign Armies East' intelligence staff had identified 225 infantry divisions and 22 armoured corps between the Baltic and the Carpathians, the bulk of them in three main attacking groups in the Baranov bridgehead, north of Warsaw and on the East Prussian border. Guderian's staff estimated that the Russians would have an advantage over the Germans of 11:1 in infantry, 7:1 in tanks and 20:1 in guns. In anticipation of this attack, Guderian wanted forces withdrawn from the West and assembled into a strong reserve army in the East, ready to engage in a mobile battle with the Soviets once they broke through.

Guderian travelled to Hitler's Supreme Headquarters on Christmas Eve, 1944, hoping to convince the Führer to abandon the failed Ardennes offensive and transfer those forces to the Ostfront. His mission was a failure. When he outlined the enemy dispositions and strengths, Hitler declared the figures a Russian bluff and shouted, 'It's the greatest imposture since Ghengis Khan! Who's responsible for producing all this rubbish?'[1] He even contended that the Soviet tank formations had no tanks. SS Chief Himmler, now commanding the Training Army, declared his own conviction that there was nothing going on in the East. Guderian spent a 'a grim and tragic Chrismas Eve' in the company of these buffoons with their 'ostrich strategy'.

On Christmas Day Guderian learned that Hitler was transferring SS Obergruppenführer Gille's IV SS Panzerkorps with its two SS Panzer divisions from north of Warsaw to Budapest where they took part in a failed night attack to relieve the city on 1 January. This transfer just served to further dilute the panzer reserve Guderian had assembled to combat the coming Russian offensive – a reserve that now consisted of twelve and a half panzer or panzergrenadier divisions for a front 1200 km (750 miles) long.

On New Year's Eve, 1944, Guderian tried again to convince Hitler. Although the powers of the OKH Chief had become so reduced as to only have jurisdiction over the Ostfront, Guderian had persuaded Rundstedt to hand over four divisions from the West. But once again his plans were stymied when Hitler diverted these divisions on a wild goose chase to try and raise the siege of Budapest. He was to do the same thing with Sepp Dietrich's 6th SS Panzerarmee when that formation was withdrawn from the Ardennes. Meanwhile he continued to refuse the withdrawal of the twenty-six divisions of Army Group North trapped in Courland where they were serving no purpose at all.

On 9 January, just three days before the Russian offensive began, the OKH Chief made one last-ditch effort to convince Hitler of the deadly threat to be faced and to gain permission to pull back Army Groups A and Centre. A heated showdown followed. Hitler, on reviewing Guderian's estimates of Russian strengths declared them 'completely idiotic' and ordered the compiler, General Gehlen, committed to an asylum. Guderian stoutly defended Gehlen as one of his best staff officers and angrily told Hitler, 'If you want General Gehlen sent to a lunatic asylum, then you had better have me certified as well!'[2]

When he had cooled down, Hitler thanked Guderian for building up such a relatively strong reserve. To this Guderian bluntly retorted, 'The Eastern Front is like a house of cards. If the front is broken through at one point, all the rest will collapse!'[3] Hitler's parting words were that 'the Eastern Front must help itself and make do with what it's got'.[4] Guderian returned to his headquarters at Zossen expecting the worst.

By this time the Russians had accumulated a great abundance of men and materiel in their bridgeheads and had even laid down their own broad-gauge rail tracks so as to be able to keep the advance supplied.

Three of Russia's best commanders, Zhukov, Koniev and Rokossovsky, would each command a Front in the coming offensive. The Fronts of Konev and Zhukov amounted to 2.2 million men, 6,400 tanks and 46,000 guns. The initial objective of the offensive was to overrun Silesia, one of Germany's last remaining industrial regions, but the true target was Berlin, 500 km (300 miles) away.

The offensive was launched on 12 January 1945 when Koniev's ten armies, including two tank armies, burst forth from the Baranov bridgehead along the Vistula – now would Germany reap the failure of Balck to reduce it the previous summer. Two days later the fronts commanded by Rokossovski and Zhukov joined the fray. Guderian's proposal that the Germans withdraw from the Vistula and build their main defence line 20 km (12 miles) behind the front line, thus allowing the Russian blow to fall on thin air, was turned down by Hitler who refused to give up even that much ground without a fight. As a result everything was overrun in the initial Russian breakthrough. A furious Hitler declared, 'Who was the half-wit who gave such idiotic orders?'[5] Only when the minutes were read aloud to him did he realise it was himself.

Seven German divisions were belatedly rushed to Silesia, but the 300-km (200-mile) breach was too wide to fill. On the 17th Warsaw finally fell – Hitler's rage at the loss meant Guderian was interrogated for hours by the Gestapo Chief and several of his staff officers were sacked. On the 20th Koniev's forces penetrated Silesia and the Russians set foot on German soil for the first time. Six days later the Russians reached the Gulf of Danzig, cutting off all the German forces into East Prussia – the nineteen infantry and five panzer divisions of Army Group North fell back to Koenigsberg and were encircled. By the end of the second week Koniev had got across the Upper Oder in several places in the vicinity of Breslau while Zhukov's forces drove down the corridor between the Vistula and the Warta. On 31 January Zhukov reached the lower Oder near Kustrin, just 65 km (40 miles) from Berlin. The ill-starred Army Group Centre had again been shattered – this time for ever. However, after their triumphant rampage across Poland, the Russian spearheads now encountered stiffening resistance from desperate Germans benefiting from a shorter front line.

The German front-line positions had quickly dissolved under the weight of the initial Russian assault. Fourth Panzerarmee's mobile reserves, consisting of Nehring's XXIV Panzerkorps, were overrun while the Panzerarmee itself virtually disintegrated. Nehring was forced to form a wandering pocket based on the remnants of his Panzerkorps and assumed command of disparate elements cut off by the Russians as he retreated. Originally located near Krakow, he headed westwards towards Lodz. Forced by Soviet attacks to repeatedly reroute, he eventually regained the main German lines and linked up with the Gross Deutschland Korps on 22 January after an eleven-day, 250-km trek.

Nehring's order of the day succinctly summed up his Panzerkorps epic battle, while also encapsulating in many respects the entire German Ostfront experience:

> little or no rest coupled with shortages of ammunition and fuel, but with frost and snow in abundance, along frozen roads, against a stronger and more speedy enemy, traversing difficult country and crossing rivers which had no bridges. . . none of these could stop our determination to defeat the enemy wherever he was met.[6]

The Gross Deutschland Korps (containing the elite, eponymous Division and the Hermann Goering Panzer Division) had been located in East Prussia at the start of the attack where it was commanded by the redoubtable von Saucken. But Hitler insisted that this powerful panzer force be sent south to Kielce in Poland, leaving East Prussia to its own devices, a fact that deeply pained the Prussian Guderian. As it happened the formation spent over a week in transit, frequently loading and unloading its tanks while the Russian behemoth trundled ever forward across western Poland. However, once the row about its deployment had been resolved, the Korps wasted no time in making its presence felt, managing to gain time to allow encircled forces in the Vistula bend to escape.

During all this time battles almost as fierce were going on in Hitler's Berlin bunker between the dictator and his resolute Army Chief of Staff. As the catastrophe unfolded, Guderian proposed the creation of a new Army Group Vistula, which he hoped to construct from troops withdrawn from the West including Sepp Dietrich's 6th SS Panzerarmee, as well as Ostfront veteran units. This new formation would be used to spearhead an OKH offensive. Alas Hitler now had another of his 'inspired' moments and decreed that 'Treuer Heinrich' (Loyal Heinrich) Himmler would take command. Guderian used all his persuasive powers to try to persuade Hitler to install a professional army officer instead of this 'military ignoramus', but to no avail.

Hitler also ordered that the staff be drawn from the SS since the Army could no longer be trusted – as a result the newly created Army Group Vistula's HQ's signal service failed to function and its inexperienced staff officers were in no way equal to the huge task that faced them. Himmler, who had taken the job because he wanted to win the Knight's Cross, soon proved himself a completely incompetent commander, giving up vital positions along the Vistula in panic, including Kulm, Guderian's birthplace.

This blunder was followed by Hitler's decision to send the 6th SS Panzer Army to Hungary. So, as carefully as Guderian made plans to save his homeland, its leader casually dismantled them. As Alan Clark observed: 'As we watch this man, a superb technician struggling with worn out machinery and malicious individuals, it is impossible not to feel sympathy for him.'[7]

In early February Guderian again asked Hitler to evacuate the divisions trapped in Courland so they could play a role in the defence of East Prussia. A furious row ensued. As Speer described it:

> Guderian opposed Hitler with an openness unprecedented in this circle. Probably fired by the effects of the drinks he had had at Oshima's, he threw aside all inhibitions. With flashing eyes and the hairs of his moustache literally standing on end, he stood facing Hitler across the marble table. . .Hitler appeared visibly intimidated by this assault.[8]

But Guderian tells how his Chief of Staff, Thomale, pulled him backwards lest he be physically assaulted by the raving despot.

Guderian had noted that the Russians were inclined to take greater and greater risks, secure in the belief that victory was close at hand. Zhukov force's had left an exposed salient on the Oder between Frankfurt and Kustrin and the OKH Chief believed a two-pronged counter-attack with pincers converging from the north and south could sever it. He could sense that the Soviet attack was running down and that a sharp riposte would startle the complacent Russians and delay the final assault on Berlin. But Hitler would agree only to a single thrust from the north.

A stormy conference took place in the Führer's bunker on 13 February. Guderian wanted his principal assistant, General Wenck, to take charge of the attack instead of the incompetent Himmler. For two hours Hitler ranted and raved at him:

> His fists raised, his cheeks flushed with rage, his whole body trembling, the man stood there in front of me, beside himself with fury and having lost all self-control. . . he was almost screaming, his eyes seemed about to pop out of his head and the veins stood out on his temples.[9]

But Guderian remained 'cold and immovable' and continued to argue with 'icy consistency' until finally Hitler gave in and agreed to Wenck's appointment.

Guderian opted for a limited offensive in the Arnswalde forests using the three and a half panzer divisions of Rauss' 3rd Panzerarmee; to this he added the two refitted panzer divisions from the West. Despite this, all did not augur well. All the divisions were severely understrength, the troops and equipment were worn out and fuel was at a premium thanks to incessant Allied air attacks on the synthetic oil plants and the loss of all the oilfields save the minor ones in Austria and at Lake Balaton in Hungary.

Operation Sonnenwende (Solstice) began early on 16 February by which time only half the troops earmarked for the operation had arrived. The Russian formation set to meet this last substantial German offensive was the Forty-seventh Army which lacked effective armoured support because the tanks had been drawn into reserve for reorganisation and refitting. As a result the desperate Panzermen initially made good progress against their surprised foe. Speed was of the essence as the lack of supplies precluded any extended operations and there was little hope of being able to deal with any Russian counter moves.

It seemed the Germans were about to inflict a serious tactical setback on the Russians when disaster struck on the 17th. Wenck had orders to report in person to Hitler every night which involved a 300 km round trip. The exhausted Wenck fell asleep at the wheel of his car and was critically injured when it ran into a bridge. Krebs, a staff officer with little command experience, took over and the attack fizzled out after another two days. Gone was the last chance of any respite and the road to Berlin was now wide open.

By the third week of February the Russians had closed up along the banks of the Oder and the Neisse. As with Bagration when it reached the Vistula, this new offensive had finally run out of steam. The Soviets had travelled over 400 km (250 miles) during the sweep from the Vistula and now came to a temporary halt on these river lines while waiting for the Western Allies to make their breakthrough over the Rhine.

In March the last great panzer battle took place, although not in Poland or Germany, but Hungary. In mid-January the 4th SS Panzerkorps had narrowly failed to relieve the besieged garrison trapped in the Hungarian capital, Budapest. At this point Hitler decided to employ Sepp Dietrich's Sixth SS Panzer Army in Hungary rather than in Poland where it was badly needed, trying to justify this to Guderian on economic grounds by claiming that the insignificant Hungarian oilfields were vital to the Reich's war effort.

The Western air forces hindered the transfer of the Panzerarmee back east and this in conjunction with the constant change of destination of these units meant that it was mid-February before the Army finally received orders to attack. The 1st SS Panzerkorps (Liebstandarte and Hitler Jugend) was immediately employed in a spoiling attack on a bridgehead held by the elite Soviet Sixth Guards Tank Army and an infantry army. The well-equipped and motivated SS men, fresh from the Ardennes offensive, quickly destroyed the bridgehead and pushed the Soviets back behind the Hron river, inflicting almost 9,000 casualties in the process. One direct result was the immediate easing of pressure before Vienna as the Russians drew off troops to shore up the Hungarian front.

With this preparatory work completed and the rest of the army in place, plans were finalised for the last major Wehrmacht offensive – 'Fruhlingserwachen' (Spring Awakening). This attack by the Sixth SS Panzerarmee in conjunction with Balck's Sixth Army comprised 10 panzer divisions, 5 infantry, 2 SS cavalry and 4 Stug brigades as well as several Tiger battalions – a powerful concentration at this stage of the war. The German attacking strength amounted to an impressive 400,000 men and almost 900 tanks and Stugs. For a change, the Russian opposition was almost numerically identical. Both sides mustered about 900 tactical support aircraft.

The offensive was designed to destroy the Russian 3rd Ukrainian Front under Tolbukhin situated between Lakes Balaton and Valencei, and was to be flanked by the Second Panzerarmee, which despite its name, lacked any tanks, and a Hungarian army of dubious loyalty at this stage of the war. Tolbukhin's trump card lay in the fact that

Bletchley Park had intercepted information detailing the German intentions which allowed him to build up that Russian speciality – defence in depth.

On 5 March Army Group E began a diversionary attack to draw off Russian reserves. The two assault armies, Balck's Sixth and Dietrich's Sixth Panzerarmee, joined the battle soon after under cover of a short artillery firestorm. Thanks to the spring melt and the marshy terrain, the ground was completely unsuitable for panzer operations and the attack suffered as a result. After four days Dietrich had advanced 30 km (20 miles), but still hadn't broken through. Both sides had thrown in their last reserves, but Stavka had sensibly withheld further reinforcements until they were sure Dietrich had shot his bolt. On the 16th the Russians finally countered and as usual concentrated on the weak German ally. The Hungarian Army was quickly smashed and the German command had no option but to withdraw and attempt to reform a tenable line.

Once again Balck showed his mettle and took over the front between the two lakes, the two SS Panzerkorps being sent north to fill the gap left by the Hungarians. Balck managed to repulse attacks from the Russian Sixth Guards Tank Army and withdraw safely, albeit separated from the SS Panzerarmee. The Panzerwaffe's last major offensive had been costly with over 40,000 casualties and the loss of 500 tanks and Stugs, losses which could no longer be borne. On 25 March three Soviet armies smashed through the gap between Balck and Dietrich's armies and didn't stop till they reached Vienna.

Even as the Panzerwaffe fought its last battles, its creator was playing his final part 'in the gigantic drama of our destruction'.[10] Guderian's final months as Army Chief of Staff were busy ones as he travelled ceaselessly between his headquarters and Hitler's bunker, becoming in Kenneth Macksey's words, 'a lonely and abrasive figure among frightened sycophants'.[11] One achievement was ridding the Ostfront of its military ignoramus – Guderian tracked Himmler down to a clinic where the ailing Reichsführer was receiving treatment for a head cold and convinced him to relinquish his command. In late March Generaloberst Heinrici took over Army Group Vistula.

But the tensions between Hitler and his Chief of Staff continued to grow. Hitler was furious with the failure of an attempt to relieve the fortress of Kustrin on the Oder. From its inception Guderian hadn't cared much for this venture and let the attack fizzle out at the earliest opportunity. More seriously in Hitler's increasingly paranoid view, Guderian had tried to persuade the spineless Ribbentrop and Himmler to seek an armistice with the West. He had also conspired with Speer to prevent Hitler's demolition order from being enforced.

On 28 March after another series of furious rows, the Führer told his Chief of Staff, 'Generaloberst Guderian, your physical health requires that you immediately take six weeks convalescent leave.'[12] Guderian knew it was hopeless to protest. As he left the bunker for the final time, Hitler's parting words to him were, 'Please do your best to get your health back. In six weeks the situation will be very critical. Then I shall need you urgently.'[13] In six weeks the war was over and Hitler was dead. With Guderian's departure the sole voice of reason in the bunker was gone and at this point any semblance of a coherent front disappeared. From now on Götterdämmerung (the Twilight of the Gods) reigned supreme.

Guderian spent a month in a Munich sanatorium receiving treatment for his heart trouble and at the the start of May travelled to the Tyrol to join the staff of his Panzertruppen Inspectorate. Along with this staff he went into American captivity on 10 May.

The story of the panzers during the last months of the war is mainly the story of single, understrength divisions and smaller units engaged in fierce local battles in a futile effort to stem the Russian advance. Several short-lived, ad hoc panzer divisions were formed during this period. These units, with names like Clausewitz, Jutebog, Feldherrnhalle II and Kurmark, were never actually larger than regimental battle groups and often contained just a handful of tanks and assault guns. Yet against all the odds, when led by inspirational commanders, these units could still achieve minor tactical victories – Kampfgruppe Langkeit and the subsequent Kurmark Division are good examples of what the panzers could achieve even at this late stage.

When Zhukov's First Byelorussian Front first struck towards the Oder line, the German command decided that the threat would most effectively be countered by strong battle groups. As a result several smaller units were amalgamated into a single unit under Langkeit's command. While this group and others assembled, it was hoped that the Russian onslaught could be contained by defensive emplacements located between the series of lakes east of the Oder.

The High Command assumed that the Russians would be channelled into the areas between the lakes which would then become ideal tank-killing fields; alas for the High Command's illusions, only rudimentary work had been carried out on these defences as the Nazi party officials in charge of the work had fled leaving the defence of these incomplete foxholes and slit trenches in the incapable hands of elderly Volksturm, boys and injured Landser.

When Langkeit received orders to form his all-arms battle group he found he lacked both artillery and panzers. He overcame these deficiencies by the simple expedient of requisitioning them from depots and factories and appropriating them from less wilful commanders. At this desperate stage of the war his booty included charcoal gas-fuelled tanks and others that lacked turrets or guns. Despite these problems, by 27 January his command was ready to march toward Frankfurt to intercept the Russian spearheads near Stettin. Movement was greatly hampered by the sub-zero conditions and the resultant icy roads. Along the way Langkeit sent out reconnaissance teams to find trapped units and to liaise with a nearby SS panzerkorps.

His troops captured the town of Pinnow against fierce Russian opposition – they hadn't even known it was in enemy hands till they got there as higher command had little or no intelligence available on Russian movements and positions. Later that day reports from Langkeit's reconnaissance troops indicated that the Russians were outflanking him, at which point his troops linked up with some of the encircled SS and Wehrmacht units. The scene was one of utter chaos – the SS commander, Bittrich, was unaware of the location of his units. Langkeit took every available armoured unit under his own command and directed the remainder of the troops to break out towards Frankfurt. He then ordered his badly dispersed units to fall back on Reppen in an attempt to prevent the threatened Russian encirclement from materialising. His columns became inextricably mixed up with fleeing refugees en route and as a result were split in three: the Reppen garrison and two separate columns were on the highway to Kunersdorf, one column was trying to return to Reppen and another was attempting to shrug off the refugees in order to attack the Russian armour. During this confusion the Russians cut the highway behind Kampfgruppe Langkeit, trapping them.

On the 30th Langkeit concentrated his remaining panzers into two groups and charged the Russians, but the mass of refugees hindered his plans and the attack failed amid the carnage wrought by the Russian armour and guns. The following day at Reppen the news was better after an ill-advised Russian tank and infantry sweep was cut to shreds by the gritty panzergrenadiers, a Russian tank battalion and an infantry battalion being completely destroyed as a result. Despite this tactical reprieve Langkeit, assessing that the defenders were spent, called on the Reppen garrison to destroy what they couldn't carry and to attempt to rejoin him along the road.

Langkeit opted to try a breakout through the woods along the roadside. Despite help from the tankbusting Stuka ace Rudel, his units were once again in trouble, trapped between columns of desperate refugees and Russian armour. By 2 February the situation was critical. The Germans were low on ammunition and the Soviet ring was tightening. Langkeit played his last card and the following day redirected his *Schwerpunkt* back onto the road. A strong rearguard dug in to hold the Russians in the woods while his panzers vainly attempted to smash through the Russian roadblocks. His panzer-grenadiers also tried their luck and charged the Russians with such ferocity that a battalion destroyed their opposition in hand-to-hand combat. The Russians countered with every available man and Langkeit instantly noticed the slackening at the road defences so he immediately assembled his few surviving Hetzers and panzers and smashed open the road to Kunnersdorf. His column poured through the gap. Outside Kunnersdorf they encountered a Russian armoured unit – with the intoxicating frenzy of near freedom the panzers charged and smashed the Russian tanks; his panzergrenadiers continued to hold open the corridor until thousands of refugees and troops had escaped towards Frankfurt.

Langkeit reassembled his men in that city and there was informed that his Kampfgruppe had been upgraded in status to become the Kurmark Panzer Division. He received more tanks and artillery as well as fresh troops and was immediately sent east of the Oder. While there Langkeit fought so well that his army commander had him promoted to General and he went on to win the Panzerwaffe's highest award – the Panzerkampfabzeichen in gold, awarded for in excess of seventy-five successful tank actions. He surrendered in the end to the Americans on 7 May with the remnants of his division.

Upon his release from captivity in 1951, this brave and modest soldier joined the Frontier Defence Force where he formed and led the special boat patrols.

At the start of March 1945 Germany's enemies were arrayed along two great rivers – the Rhine in the West and the Oder in the East. While the Russians waited on the Oder-Neisse line, the Western Allies were to storm the Rhine. On 7 March the US First Army seized the railway bridge at Remagen intact in a coup de main and secured an important bridgehead. On 22 March Patton's Third Army managed to cross the river almost unopposed to establish a second bridgehead at Oppenheim. When Hitler called for panzer reinforcements to meet this stroke, he was told that there were just five tanks available and these were in a depot 150 km (100 miles) away.

All the while Montgomery had been cautiously building up over-whelming supplies for his river-crossing at Wesel. On the night of 23 March, after a prolonged drumfire from 3,000 guns, 25 divisions began to cross the river. The only opposition they faced were 5 weak and exhausted German divisions and the bridgehead quickly swelled. Yet displaying excessive respect towards an already beaten enemy, Monty refused to advance eastwards until he had 1,500 tanks massed on the eastern bank.

Once the Allies finally began advancing from the Rhine, they met only the lightest opposition. Their breakout trapped Model's entire Army Group B within the Ruhr region on 1 April, one-third of a million men in total including the remnants of the Fifth Panzerarmee. Permission to withdraw was refused and the troops were ordered to stand and die. In addition they were ordered to destroy all the factories in this great industrial region. Model, a man often dismissed as a Nazi general, now showed his true face by flatly refusing to destroy what remained of the Ruhr.

Von Mellenthin described the scene vividly:

> The fog and cold of winter still hung over the land, and the gaunt and broken cities of the Ruhr formed a fitting backdrop to the last act of this tragedy. The great heaps of coal and slag, the shattered buildings, the twisted railroad tracks, the ruined bridges, all made their contribution to the gloomy scene. I have seen many battlefields, but none so strange as the great industrial complex of the Ruhr during the final dissolution of Army Group B.[14]

Model assembled all the available panzers (Panzer Lehr, 9th Panzer and the 3rd Panzergrenadier Division) under Fritz Bayerlein's LIII Panzerkorps and ordered these forces to break out and establish contact with Army Group G. The initial attack was repulsed so Bayerlein personally assumed command of his old Panzer Lehr and forced a passage. At this point the rains of the previous days cleared and the panzers were destroyed in a maelstrom of air strikes. The survivors were forced back into the pocket, each division now with a strength of less than thirty tracked vehicles.

Model's Army Group fought on valiantly for eighteen days before Model ordered the troops to surrender. Humanely, he dissolved the Army Group and demobilised his youngest and eldest troops. True to his soldierly creed, the man who had criticised Paulus two years earlier for allowing himself to be captured alive, now fell on his own sword – on 18 April Model shot himself. The surrender of Army Group B was the second largest surrender in history and over one-third of a million troops, including twenty-four generals went into the bag, one of them being that quintessential general staff officer, Generalmajor F.W. von Mellenthin.

On 11 April the Western Allies reached the Elbe, just 100 km (60 miles) west of Berlin. But instead of taking the Reich's capital, it was agreed Berlin would be left to the Russians while Eisenhower sent Patton south on a wild goose chase to the fantastical 'Alpine Redoubt' which Goebbels had announced would house the last defenders of the Reich. It was now the Russians' turn to attack. On 16 April Koniev and Zhukov broke out of their bridgeheads on the Oder and the Neisse and struck at Army Group Vistula with over 3,000 tanks. By the 25th Zhukov and Koniev had encircled the city and on the 27th joined hands with the Western Allies on the Elbe.

The battle for Berlin proved every bit as fierce as the battle for Stalingrad. Every available man was sent to defend Berlin, equipped with anti-tank weapons ranging from Panzerschrecks and Molotov cocktails to vintage rifles and the occasional 128 mm Jagtiger. Units of cripples, boys, veteran infantry, hardened front-line troops, factory workers, party functionaries and even women marched forth to join battle with the Russian Bear for the last time. Panzerfausts, the only weapon still being produced, were liberally handed out to untrained civilians who managed to destroy hundreds of Russian tanks with them. Hitler even ordered a 'tank destroyer' division set up which consisted of brave men on bicycles who attacked T-34s and Stalin tanks with grenades.

The result was never in doubt. Hitler unrealistically ordered the 'Steiner Attack' to relieve Berlin, but this SS General commanded a mere five shattered SS panzergrenadier divisions and his troops – many of them foreign – were only too anxious to desert rather than face Russian capture. The attack never materialised as even Steiner's remaining loyal troops were fighting for their lives in small local engagements. Hitler then commanded Wenck to abandon his battle with Eisenhower's troops to the west and march to relieve Berlin. Wenck obeyed but marched with leaden steps. This relief attack never got going either, for on 30 April Hitler committed suicide in his Berlin bunker and on 7 May 1945 Germany surrendered unconditionally to the Allies. The Thousand Year Reich was over.

Captivity and possible trial awaited the panzer leaders. Manstein was put on trial at Hamburg in 1948. The Field Marshal helped to successfully defend the General Staff and the OKW on the charge of being a criminal organisation, but was sentenced to eighteen years imprisonment himself after what was widely regarded as an unfair trial; Churchill even sent a cheque to aid his defence. Manstein was released in 1952 due to poor health and in 1955 he published his memoirs of the war entitled *Verlorene Siege* (Lost Victories). In 1956 he became a senior advisor to the newly created Bundeswehr at the request of the West German Chancellor Konrad Adenauer. He lived in Bavaria until his death in June 1973.

Manteuffel became a member of the West German Bundestag from 1953 to 1957 as a representative of the Free Democratic Party. He died in the Tyrol in Austria in September 1978. Von Kleist was taken prisoner by the British, but he handed over to the Soviets in 1948, dying in a Russian camp in 1954. Mellenthin went to live in South Africa and wrote the influential *Panzer Battles*. Along with Balck, he then participated in seminars with senior NATO officers in the late 1970s and early 1980s. Rundstedt died in an old folks' home in 1953.

When Panzer Graf von Strachwitz was released from prison, his wife and youngest son were dead and his estates had been confiscated. He went to Syria at that government's invitation in order to help organise their army and agriculture, but a coup forced him to flee. He returned to Germany penniless in 1951 and died shortly afterwards.

Once the Cold War began, the Western Allies decided to exploit the knowledge of their former enemies, especially their experiences in Russia. In 1946 the Americans assembled 200 generals and staff officers in a camp at Allendorf for interview by the US Army's Historical Section. Halder co-ordinated this massive historical study and many former Wehrmacht officers contributed to the project, including Bayerlein and Rauss. Guderian was to be a co-ordinator as well, but the bad blood between him and Halder made this impossible.

Although never charged with any crime, Guderian was held in American captivity until his 60th birthday in June 1948. Throughout his imprisonment, his bearing was 'dignified and soldierly' and he passed the time playing bridge, tending the camp vegetable patch and contributing to the historical study. His captors described him as a 'very kindly man, cheerful. . .with an excellent sense of humour.'[15] The head of the American War Department Interrogation Committee said the best way to produce a good war history would have been to install him on somebody's porch for 'a summer of casual conversation'.[16]

Upon his release in June 1948, Guderian retired with his wife Gretel to a small house where he gardened with enthusiasm and planted a forest. In 1950 he published his war memoirs, *Erinnerungen eines Soldaten* (Memories of a Soldier), which came out in English in 1952 as *Panzer Leader*. The book became an international bestseller and sold over a quarter of a million copies in ten languages, including Russian. Generaloberst Heinz Guderian, father of the Panzertruppen and last Chief of Staff of the Wehrmacht, finally redeemed his ticket to the Endstation on 14 May 1954 at Schwangau bei Fussen, fourteen years after his breakthrough on the Meuse.

The following October Germany was admitted into NATO and the German Army was re-established under the title 'Bundeswehr'. With the Bundeswehr came the re-establishment of the Panzerwaffe – if during the Cold War years, the Third World War had broken out, the panzers no doubt would have been the bulwark against a Russian invasion of Western Europe.

Conclusion

Dann ist unser Panzer ein ehernes Grab (Then our tank
is an honourable grave)

Last words of the Panzerlied

A T the end of the war, all of Germany lay in ruins. The long, unequal
struggle was over and all that remained of the German Reich
was ashes, corpses and twisted steel. The grotesque dreams of a dictator
had reaped their inevitable and bloody harvest. Hitler died by his own
hand on 30 April 1945 and it was strangely fitting that eleven days
later the last German tank to be destroyed in the war was blown up by
its own crew. It comes as no surprise that Hitler's most effective weapon
had not survived him for long.

Many of the Panzertruppen's finest men were strewn in lonely graves
all over Europe and Africa. Those who survived had disappeared into
Russian gulags or were languishing in Western cages, stripped of all
vestiges of their former rank and glory. In the eyes of the victors, what
formerly had been signs of honour were now badges of shame.

So intrinsic to the Nazi war effort were they, that for the coming
years the Panzerwaffe was denigrated as a leading instrument of
German militarism and its reputation tarnished by the evil regime it
had served. However, with the onset of the Cold War, the Western
Allies clamoured to coerce the expertise of their former enemies in
armoured operations.

The Panzerwaffe had made armoured forces the spearhead on every
battlefield and the decisive arm of war. They had almost slain the
Russian Bear, but failed to deliver the final coup de grace. Now the
West wanted to assimilate their hard-won knowledge in anticipation
of a future contest with the same enemy. For their part, the Russians
sought to build on the bloody lessons suffered at the hands of the
Germans.

The Panzers' elan in the attack and their resolution in defence led to the creation of new tactical doctrines studied with zeal by both East and West. In the heat of battle the panzers had forged the sword and shield into a cohesive combination and in post-war Europe, the Americans and British chose the shield and the Russians the sword. Soon German tanks were once again expected to be the first line of defence against the possibility of an onslaught from the East.

For three years the panzers were the undisputed masters of the battlefield and it was only by adopting their methods and employing hugely superior numbers that the Allies managed to beat them. Despite grievous losses over the final years, the panzers never really suffered the cumulative deterioration in the quality of its men and machines that affected other German arms such as the Luftwaffe. Nor was there one final catastrophic defeat. In fact, it could be argued that the Panzerwaffe of May 1945 was stronger in many ways than it had been in September 1939.

Their resiliance was renowned – battle-weary units could be withdrawn and refitted within days and returned to the battle to real effect. Such was the strength of quality in depth that badly mauled and decimated formations continued to offer stiff resistance long after the enemy expected their collapse. Ad hoc units under energetic commanders were frequently thrown in at moments of crisis and performed superlatively.

The esprit de corps, skill and initiative of individual crews were never attained by their enemies. Their superior tactical awareness, fire discipline and use of terrain staved off the eventual defeat for as long as possible. In the final analysis, it was the sheer weight of enemy men and materiel that swamped them. In the East it was the immense hordes of Russian tanks and in the West it was the overwhelming Allied air superiority that told against the panzers. Numerically, the Germans were never on equal terms, but to the final day were still attaining small tactical victories in the face of overwhelming odds.

The advent of the Panzerwaffe sparked a revolution in warfare. The one constant was their ability to adapt to changing circumstances on the battlefield. The Panzerwaffe of 1945 was very different in equipment and practice to that of 1939. Guderian successfully amalgamated traditional German military practices of planning, staff work and training with new technology and methods. The pace of panzer operations was ideally suited to the traditional German flexibility of command and encouragement of initiative.

When the final surrender document was signed, over a million men had passed through the ranks of the Panzertruppen, at least a quarter of whom were killed. Fifty thousand armoured vehicles lay wrecked or smouldering on the battlefield of Europe and the face of warfare had been changed for ever.

One can't help wondering if Guderian and his panzer generals, as they whiled away the years in post-war captivity reliving their old campaigns, rued the lost opportunities that had cost them victory. Would Guderian have found comfort in the ultimate vindication of his methods, when shortly after his death the new German Army, the Bundeswehr, reformed the Panzerwaffe like a phoenix from the ashes? Though their exploits were fleeting, the panzers' legacy endures. *Klotzen, nicht Kleckern*!

Appendix I

Comparative Ranks

Formation	Wehrmacht	SS	Soviet Union	United States	Commonwealth
Army Group	General-feldmarschall	–	Marshal	General	Field Marshal
Army Group/Army	Generaloberst	SS-Obergruppenführer	Colonel General	General	General
Army/Corps	General der (Arm of Service)	SS-Obergruppenführer	General	Lieutenant General	Lieutenant General
Corps/Division	Generalleutnant	SS-Gruppenführer	Lieutenant General	Major General	Major General
Division/Brigade	Generalmajor	SS-Brigadeführer	Major General	Brigadier General	Brigadier
Division/Brigade	–	SS-Oberführer	–	–	–
Division/Brigade	Oberst	SS-Standartenführer	Colonel	Colonel	Colonel
Regiment/Battalion	Oberstleutnant	SS-Obersturmbannführer	Lieutenant Colonel	Lieutenant Colonel	Lieutenant Colonel
Battalion/Company	Major	SS-Sturmbannführer	Major	Major	Major
Company	Hauptmann	SS-Hauptsturmführer	Captain	Captain	Captain
Company/Platoon	Oberleutnant	SS-Obersturmführer	1st Lieutenant	1st Lieutenant	1st Lieutenant
Platoon	Leutnant	SS-Untersturmführer	2nd Lieutenant	2nd Lieutenant	2nd Lieutenant

Appendix II

Panzer Division Establishment – 1935

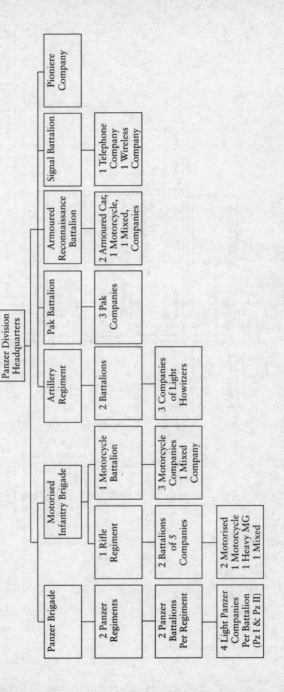

Panzer Division Establishment – 1940

Divisional Headquarters

Panzer Brigade
- **2 Panzer Regiments**
  - **2 Panzer Battalions**
    - 2 Light (Pz I, II & III) Companies
    - 1 Medium (Pz II & IV) Company

Rifle Brigade
- **Infantry Regiment**
  - 3 Battalions of 5–6 Companies
  - 2/3 Infantry, 1 Mixed, 1 Motorcycle, 1 MG Companies
- **Motorcycle Battalion of 4 Companies**
  - 2 Motorcycle, 1 MG, 1 Mixed, Companies
- **Heavy Infantry Gun Company**

Artillery Regiment
- **2 Light Battalions, 3 Batteries of 4 Guns Each**
- **1 Heavy Battalion, 3 Batteries of 4 Heavy Howitzers**

Armoured Reconnaissance Battalion of 4 Companies
- 2 Armoured Car, 1 Motorcycle, 1 Mixed. Pioniere Platoon

Pak Battalion
- 3 Light Companies 12 Guns
- 1 Heavy Company 6 Guns

Flak Battalion 3 Companies
- 2 Light Companies 12 guns
- 1 Heavy Company 9 Guns

Signals Battalion 2 Companies
- 1 Wireless Company 1 Telephone Company

Pioniere Battalion of 6 Companies
- 2 Motorised, 1 Armoured, 2 Bridging, 1 Light

Supply & Administrative Echelon

Panzer Division Establishment – 1942

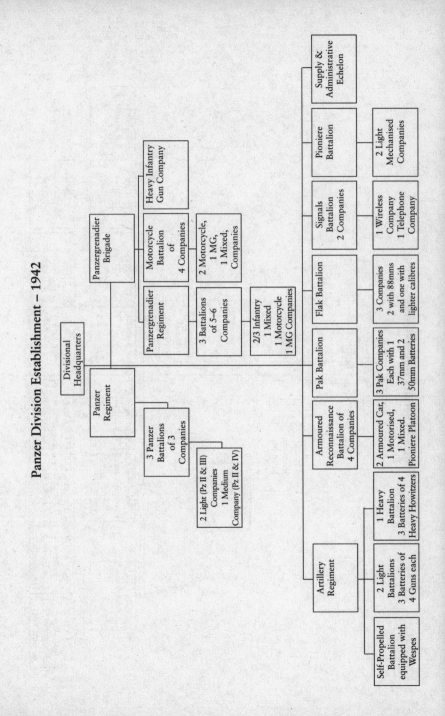

Panzer Division Establishment – 1944

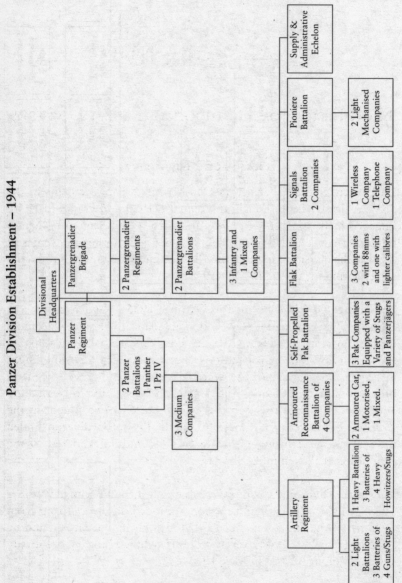

Appendix III

Short History of the Important Panzer Divisions

Heer Panzer Divisions

1st Panzer Division. Formed in October 1935 using elements of the 3rd Cavalry Division. Fought in Poland in 1939 and France in 1940. Engaged in Russia between 1941 and early 1943. Sent to France to refit and then returned to Ostfront in late 1943. In the later stages of the war the division fought in the Ukraine and Hungary before finally surrendering in Austria in May 1945.

2nd Panzer Division. Formed in October 1935 – Guderian was the Division's first commander. Saw action in Poland and France, becoming the first division to reach the Atlantic. Fought in the Balkans campaign in 1941, followed by participation in Barbarossa. The Division fought in Russia until January 1944 when it was sent to France to refit in preparation for the coming Allied invasion. Saw action in Normandy and was almost destroyed in the Falaise pocket. Also fought in the Ardennes offensive and advanced further than any other division. Ended the war as the Thuringen Panzer Brigade and surrendered to the Americans at Plauen in April 1945.

3rd Panzer Division. 'The Bear Division'. Formed in Berlin in October 1935. Fought in Poland and France. Stationed on the Ostfront from 1941 to 1945. Was commanded by Model during Barbarossa and by Bayerlein from late 1943 to early 1944. Fought in Hungary, eventually surrendering in Austria in May 1945.

4th Panzer Division. Formed in 1938. Fought in Poland and France.

Fought on the Ostfront between 1941 and 1944. Trapped in the Courland peninsula in 1944, the Division was evacuated to West Prussia at the start of 1945 where it surrendered in April.

5th Panzer Division. Formed in 1938. Fought in Poland and France and in the Balkans campaign of 1941. Stationed on the Ostfront from 1941 to 1944. Trapped in Courland peninsula, surrendered in East Prussia in April 1945.

6th Panzer Division. Formed in 1939 from 1st Leichte Division which had fought in Poland. Fought in France in 1940 and in Russia between 1941 and 1942. Refitted in France and returned to the Ostfront in late 1942. Was commanded by Rauss for a period. Remained there until the end of the war, fighting in Hungary and Austria, and eventually surrendering in Czechoslovakia.

7th Panzer Division. 'The Ghost Division'. Formed in 1939 from the 2nd Leichte Division which had fought in Poland. Fought in France in 1940 under Rommel's command. In Russia 1941–2. Then sent to France on occupation duty. Returned to Ostfront late 1942. Fought in the Baltic states and surrendered in East Prussia in April 1945.

8th Panzer Division. Formed in 1939 from the 3rd Leichte Division which had fought in Poland. Fought in France in 1940 and the Balkans in 1941. Stationed on the Ostfront from 1941 to 1945. Fought in Hungary, eventually surrendered in Czechoslavakia.

9th Panzer Division. Formed in 1940 from 4th Leichte Division which had fought in Poland. Fought in Holland and France in 1940, and in the Balkans in 1941. Campaigned in the Soviet Union from 1941 to 1944. Sent to France to refit in 1944 and opposed invasion of Normandy. Also fought in the Ardennes offensive. Surrendered after being trapped in the Ruhr pocket in April 1945.

10th Panzer Division. Formed in 1939. A battle group from the Division fought in Poland. Fought in France in 1940 and in the Soviet Union from 1941 until 1942. After refitting in France, was sent to Tunisia in late 1942 and surrendered with the rest of the Axis forces in North Africa in May 1943. Was never reformed.

11th Panzer Division. Formed in 1940. Served in Soviet Union from 1941 to 1944. Commanded by Balck during the Chir river battles in late 1942. Sent to France in 1944 to refit. Covered German withdrawal from Southern France and manned West Wall. Surrendered in Bavaria in 1945.

12th Panzer Division. Formed in 1940 from the 2nd Motorised Infantry Division. Fought on the Eastern Front from 1941 to 1945. Trapped in the Courland pocket in September 1944 and held out there until May 1945.

13th Panzer Division. Formed in 1940 from the 13th Infantry Division. Sent to Romania to protect Ploesti oilfields in late 1940. Served on the Ostfront from 1941 till the war's end. Destroyed during the defence of Budapest and reformed as Feldherrnhalle II. Final commander was Oberst Bake.

14th Panzer Division. Formed in 1940. Fought in the Balkans in 1941 and in Russia between 1941 and 1943. Was one of the panzer divisions lost at Stalingrad. Was reformed in France in late 1943 and returned to the Ostfront where it remained until the war's end. The remnants were evacuated from Courland by sea in the dying days of the war.

15th Panzer Division. Formed in 1940. Sent to Africa in early 1941 as part of Rommel's Afrika Korps. Fought on there until Axis surrender in May 1943. Reformed later that year as the 15th Panzergrenadier Division.

16th Panzer Division. Formed in 1940. Fought in the Balkans in 1941 and then in Russia from 1941 to 1943. Commanded by Hans Hube. Was lost at Stalingrad. Reformed in France and served in Italy before returning to the Ostfront in late 1943. Surrendered in Czechoslovakia in May 1945, some units to the Russians, others to the Americans.

17th Panzer Division. Formed in 1940. Served on the Ostfront from

1941 to 1945. Was part of the relief force that tried to break the Stalingrad encirclement. Was destroyed in April 1945.

18th Panzer Division. Formed in 1940. Commanded by Nehring from 1940 to early 1942. Fought on the Ostfront from 1941 to 1943. After suffering heavy losses the Division became the 18th Artillery Division in late 1943.

19th Panzer Division. Formed in 1940. Served on the Ostfront from 1941 to 1945. Remnants encircled near Prague at the end of the war.

20th Panzer Division. Formed in 1940. Fought on the Ostfront from 1941 to 1945. Surrendered near Prague in May 1945.

21st Panzer Division. Originally formed as 5th Leichte Division and sent to North Africa in February 1941. Converted to full panzer division in July 1941. Commanders include von Ravenstein. Fought in Africa until Axis surrender of May 1943. Reformed in France and fought in Normandy and at the West Wall in 1944. Was transferred to the Ostfront at the beginning of 1945 and surrendered there.

22nd Panzer Division. Formed in 1941 and fought on the Ostfront for most of 1942. Disbanded in January 1943 due to heavy losses.

23rd Panzer Division. Formed in 1940 but not completed until 1941. Served on the Ostfront from 1942 to 1945. Surrendered in Hungary.

24th Panzer Division. Formed in 1942 from the 1st Cavalry Division. Sent to the Ostfront in 1942 and lost at Stalingrad. Reformed in France, then sent to Italy. Returned to the Ostfront in late 1943 and ended the war in East Prussia.

25th Panzer Division. Formed in 1942. Fought on the Ostfront 1943–4 and sent to Denmark to refit. Returned to the Ostfront in late 1944 and was destroyed in Austria in 1945.

26th Panzer Division. Formed in 1942. Fought in Italy between 1943 and 1945, and surrendered there at the war's end.

27th Panzer Division. Formed in 1942, but sent to the Ostfront before complete. Dispersed during the Stalingrad operations, the Division had ceased to exist by the start of 1943.

116th Panzer Division. 'The Greyhound Division'. Formed in 1944 from remnants of the 16th Panzergrenadier Division. Fought in Normandy and suffered heavy losses escaping from the Falaise pocket. Fought in the Ardennes offensive. Surrendered in April 1945 after being trapped in the Ruhr pocket.

Panzer Lehr Division. Formed in late 1943 from demonstration units of the panzer schools. This elite division was specifically intended for anti-invasion operations. Fought in Normandy and the Ardennes offensive – Bayerlein was commander during these battles. Surrendered in April 1945 after being trapped in the Ruhr pocket.

Gross Deutschland Panzer Division. Originally elite motorised infantry regiment. Became panzergrenadier division in mid-1942 and elevated to full panzer division status in late 1943. Commanders include von Manteuffel. Along with other armoured units, became full corps in late 1944. The Gross Deutschland served in Poland and France and on the Ostfront from 1941 to 1945. Surrendered in East Prussia in May 1945.

Hermann Goering Panzer Division. Luftwaffe formation. Originally raised as Panzergrenadier division in mid-1942. Elements were lost in Tunisia in May 1943. Fought in Italy 1943–4 and on the Ostfront 1944–5.

Waffen SS Panzer Divisions

1st SS Panzer Division Liebstandarte Adolf Hitler. Originally Hitler's bodyguard regiment, it fought in Poland, France, the Balkans and Russia. Commanded until 1943 by Sepp Dietrich. Became panzergrenadier division in mid-1942. On occupation duties in France 1942–3. Returned to the Ostfront in the spring of 1943. Transferred to Italy for two months, then elevated to full panzer division status and sent back to the Ostfront in the autumn of 1943. Refitted in Belgium in

1944 and fought in Normandy and in the Ardennes offensive. Transferred to Hungary in 1945 and surrendered in Austria to the Americans.

2nd SS Panzer Division Das Reich. Formed as panzergrenadier division in late 1942 from 2nd SS Motorised Division which had fought in Holland, France, the Balkans and Russia. Occupation duties in France during 1942. Sent to the Ostfront in spring 1943 and designated full panzer division in the autumn. Refitted in France in 1944 and fought in Normandy and in the Ardennes offensive. Transferred to Hungary in 1945 and surrendered in Austria.

3rd SS Panzer Division Totenkopf. Formed as panzergrenadier division in late 1942 from 3rd SS Motorised Division which had fought in France and Russia. Occupation duties in France during 1942. Fought on the Ostfront 1943 to 1945. Became full panzer division during autumn 1943. Transferred to Hungary in 1945 and surrendered in Austria.

5th SS Panzer Division Wiking. Formed as a motorised infantry division in late 1940 using the SS Regiment Germania and Scandinavian, Belgian and Dutch volunteer units. Became panzergrenadier division in late 1942 and full panzer division in autumn 1943. Served on the Ostfront for its entire history. Fought in defence of Budapest and was destroyed near Vienna in April 1945.

9th SS Panzer Division Hohenstaufen. Formed as panzergrenadier division in late 1942, became panzer division in autumn of 1943. Sent to Ostfront in spring of 1944. Returned to France in time to fight at Normandy, against Operation Market Garden at Arnhem, and in the Ardennes offensive. Sent to Hungary in 1945 and surrendered in Austria.

10th SS Panzer Division Frundsberg. Formed as panzergrenadier division in late 1942, became panzer division in autumn of 1943. Sent to Ostfront in spring of 1944. Returned to France in time to fight at Normandy, against Operation Market Garden at Arnhem, and at the West Wall. Sent to the Ostfront in early 1945 and surrendered in Saxony.

12th SS Panzer Division Hitler Jugend. Formed as panzergrenadier division in 1943, mainly from Hitler Youth members. Became full panzer division during autumn 1943. Almost destroyed in Normandy fighting. Refitted and fought in Ardennes offensive. Transferred to Hungary in 1945 and surrendered in Austria.

References and Notes

PUBLISHERS in references are British unless otherwise stated. Full publication details are given with first reference to a work and in shortened form thereafter.

Introduction
[1]Shirer, William, *The Rise and Fall of the Third Reich* (NY, Simon and Schuster, 1960), p. 625.

Chapter I   The Indirect Approach
[1]Guderian, Colonel General Heinz, *Panzer Leader* (NY, Da Capo Press, 1996), p. 20.
[2]Liddell Hart, B.H., *The Other Side of the Hill* (Pan, 1999), p. 74.
[3]Macksey, Kenneth, *Guderian – Creator of the Blitzkrieg* (NY, Stein & Day, 1976), p. 16.
[4]Liddell Hart, *The Other Side of the Hill*, p. 74–5.
[5]Macksey, *Guderian*, p. 74.
[6]Guderian, *Panzer Leader*, p. 32.
[7]Ibid, p. 26.
[8]Macksey, *Guderian*, p. 87.

Chapter 2   The Expanding Torrent
[1]Liddell Hart, *The Other Side of the Hill*, p. 123.
[2]Guderian, *Panzer Leader*, p. 56.
[3]Ibid, p. 90.
[4]Ibid, p. 73.

Chapter 3   Sickle Cut through France
[1]Deighton, Len, *Blitzkrieg* (Pimlico, 1996), p. 268.
[2]Manstein, Field Marshal Erich von, *Lost Victories* (California, Presidio Press, 1994), p. 98.
[3]Guderian, *Panzer Leader*, p. 90.
[4]Ibid, p. 102.
[5]Liddell Hart, B.H., *The Rommel Papers* (New York, Da Capo Press, 1953), p. 7.
[6]Guderian, *Panzer Leader*, p. 108.

[7]Liddell Hart, *The Rommel Papers*, p. 22.
[8]Macksey, *Guderian*, p. 151.
[9]Guderian, *Panzer Leader*, p. 130.

Chapter 4   The Greatest Gamble
[1]Perrett, Bryan, *Knights of the Black Cross* (Wordsworth, 1997), p. 81.
[2]Guderian, *Panzer Leader*, p. 513.
[3]Ibid, p. 142
[4]*United States Marine Corps Gazette*, December, 1954, p. 47.
[5]Beevor, Anthony, *Stalingrad* (Penguin, 1999), p. 66.
[6]*USMC Gazette*, p. 49.
[7]Ibid, p. 49.
[8]Beevor, *Stalingrad*, p. 24.
[9]Manstein, *Lost Victories*, p. 203.
[10]*USMC Gazette*, p. 51.
[11]Macksey, *Guderian*, p. 168.
[12]Guderian, *Panzer Leader*, p. 190.
[13]Macksey, *Guderian*, p. 170.
[14]Ibid, p. 176.
[15]Deighton, Len, *Blood, Tears and Folly* (NY, Harper Collins, 1993), p. 468.
[16]Macksey, *Guderian*, p. 180.
[17]Beevor, *Stalingrad*, p. 29.
[18]Michael Veranov (ed.), *The Mammoth Book of the Third Reich at War,* (Robinson Publishing, 1997), p. 222.
[19]Guderian, *Panzer Leader*, p. 244.
[20]Macksey, *Guderian*, p. 184.
[21]Ibid, p. 184.
[22]Guderian, *Panzer Leader*, p. 246.
[23]Ibid, p. 265.
[24]Ibid, p. 265.
[25]Ibid, p. 270.
[26]Ibid, p. 297.
[27]Lucas, James, *War on the Eastern Front* (Greenhill Books, 1998), p. 148.

Chapter 5   High Water Mark on the Volga
[1]Beevor, *Stalingrad*, p. 70.
[2]Cooper, Matthew and Lucas, James, *Panzer – The Armoured Force of the Third Reich* (Macdonald and Jane's: 1976), pp. 55–6.
[3]Beevor, *Stalingrad*, p. 73.
[4]Ibid, p. 53.
[5]Manstein, *Lost Victories*, p. 314.
[6]Ibid, p. 295.
[7]Beevor, *Stalingrad*, p. 297.
[8]Tsouras, Peter G., *Fighting in Hell* (NY, Ballantine, 1995), p. 99.

[9]Mellenthin, Major General F.W. von, *Panzer Battles* (NY, Ballantine Press, 1971), p. 304.
[10]Mellenthin, *Panzer Battles,* p. 220.

Chapter 6   Sand and Steel

[1]Liddell Hart, *Rommel Papers,* p. 197.
[2]Veranov, *Mammoth Book,* p. 260.
[3]Liddell Hart, *Rommel Papers,* p. 154.
[4]Young, Desmond, *Rommel – The Desert Fox* (NY, Harper and Brothers, 1950), p. 72.
[5]Mellenthin, *Panzer Battles,* p. 66.
[6]Liddell Hart, *Rommel Papers,* p. 161.
[7]Veranov, *Mammoth Book,* p. 276.
[8]Young, *Rommel – The Desert Fox,* p. 152.
[9]Liddell Hart, *Rommel Papers,* p. 345.
[10]Young, *Rommel – The Desert Fox,* p. 153.

Chapter 7   Death Ride of the Panzers

[1]Mellenthin, *Panzer Battles*, p. 253.
[2]Guderian, *Panzer Leader*, p. 288.
[3]Ibid, p. 289.
[4]Ibid, p. 300.
[5]Liddell Hart, *The Other Side of the Hill*, p. 319.
[6]Guderian, *Panzer Leader*, p. 309.
[7]Ibid, p. 312.
[8]Sajer, Guy, *The Forgotten Soldier* (Cassell: 1999). p. 329.

Chapter 8   The Second Front

[1]Liddell Hart, *The Other Side of the Hill*, p. 354.
[2]Young, *Rommel – The Desert Fox*, p. 176.
[3]Irving, David, *Rommel: The Trail of the Fox* (Wordsworth, 1999), p. 307.
[4]Liddell Hart, *The Rommel Papers*, p. 468.
[5]Irving, *Rommel*, p. 314.
[6]Guderian, *Panzer Leader*, p. 332.
[7]In the opinion of one of his post-war interrogators.
[8]Perrett, *Knights of the Black Cross*, p. 210.
[9]Luck, *Panzer Commander*, p. 199.
[10]Perrett, *Knights of the Black Cross*, p. 211.
[11]Veranov, *Mammoth Book*, p. 514.
[12]Hugh M. Cole, *The Ardennes: Battle of the Bulge*, p. 2.
[13]Liddell Hart, *The Other Side of the Hill*, p. 446.
[14]Toland, John, *The Battle of the Bulge* (Wordsworth: 1998), p. 32.
[15]Lucas, James, *Kommando*, (Grafton Books, 1986), p. 178.
[16]Toland, *The Battle of the Bulge*, p. 265.

[17]Ibid, p. 196.
[18]Liddell Hart, *The Other Side of the Hill*, p. 464.
[19]Speer, Albert, *Inside The Third Reich* (Weidenfeld & Nicolson, 1971), p. 420.

Chapter 9   The Skies Grow Dark

[1]*USMC Gazette*, p. 64.
[2]Manstein, *Lost Victories*, p. 504.
[3]Ibid, p. 544.
[4]Ibid, p. 546.
[5]Mellenthin, *Panzer Battles*, p. 335.
[6]Ibid, p. 336.
[7]Ibid, p. 352.
[8]Hitler during a conference in late 1944, p. 106.
[9]Lucas, James, *Hitler's Enforcers* (Cassell, 2000), p. 93.

Chapter 10   Twilight of the Gods

[1]Guderian, *Panzer Leader*, p. 383.
[2]Ibid, p. 387.
[3]Ibid, p. 387.
[4]Ibid, p. 388.
[5]Ibid, p. 378.
[6]Lucas, *Hitler's Enforcers*, p. 117.
[7]Clark, *Barbarossa*, p. 427.
[8]Speer, *Inside The Third Reich*, p. 421.
[9]Guderian, *Panzer Leader*, p. 414.
[10]Ibid, p. 415.
[11]Macksey, *Guderian*, pp. 457–8.
[12]Guderian, *Panzer Leader*, p. 428.
[13]Ibid, p. 429.
[14]Mellenthin, *Panzer Battles*, p. 419.
[15]Macksey, *Guderian*, p. 241.
[16]Macksey, *Guderian*, p. 239.

Select Bibliography

Publishers are British unless otherwise stated

Arnold-Foster, Mark, *The World At War* (Fontana, 1974)

Beevor, Anthony, *Stalingrad* (Penguin, 1999)

Clark, Alan, *Barbarossa* (Papermac, 1991)

Clausewitz, Carl Von, *On War* (Wordsworth, 1997)

Cole, Hugh M., *The Ardennes: Battle of the Bulge* (Office of the Chief of Military History, Department of the Army, Washington D.C., 1965)

Cooper, Matthew and Lucas, James, *Panzer – The Armoured Force of the Third Reich* (Macdonald and Jane's, 1976)

Deighton, Len, *Blood, Tears and Folly* (NY, Harper Collins, 1993)

Deighton, Len, *Blitzkrieg* (Pimlico, 1996)

Douglas-Home, Charles, *Rommel* (Omega, 1975)

Fletcher, David, *Tanks In Camera* (Sutton Publishing, 1998)

Foley, Charles, *Commando Extraordinary – Otto Skorzeny* (Cassell, 1998)

Galland, Adolf, *The First And The Last* (Fontana, 1975)

Guderian, Colonel General Heinz, *Panzer Leader* (NY, Da Capo Press, 1996)

Guderian, Colonel General Heinz, *Achtung – Panzer!* (Cassell, 1999)

Hastings, Max, *Overlord* (Papermac, 1993)

Irving, David, *Rommel: The Trail of the Fox* (Wordsworth, 1999)

Jentz, Tom, Doyle, Hilary and Sarson, Peter, *Tiger I Heavy Tank* (Osprey Military, 1998)

Knappe, Siegfried, *Soldat* (NY, Dell, 1992)

Liddell Hart, B.H., *History of the Second World War* (Papermac, 1997)

Liddell Hart, B.H., *The Other Side of the Hill* (Pan, 1999)

Liddell Hart, B.H. (ed.), *The Rommel Papers* (NY, Da Capo Press, 1953)

Lucas, James, *Kommando* (Grafton Books, 1986)

Lucas, James, *War on the Eastern Front,* (Greenhill Books, 1998)

Lucas, James, *Hitler's Enforcers* (Cassell, 2000)

Luck, Hans Von, *Panzer Commander* (NY, Dell, 1991)

Macksey, Kenneth, *Panzer Division – The Mailed Fist* (NY, Ballantine, 1968)

Macksey, Kenneth, *Guderian – Creator Of The Blitzkrieg* (NY, Stein & Day, 1976)

Manstein, Field Marshal Erich von, *Lost Victories* (California, Presidio Press, 1994)

Mellenthin, Major General F.W. von, *Panzer Battles* (NY, Ballantine Press, 1971)

Perrett, Bryan, *Knights of the Black Cross* (Wordsworth, 1997)

Reynolds, Michael, *Steel Inferno* (NY, Dell, 1998)

Rommel, Erwin, *Infantry Attacks* (Greenhill Books, 1995)

Sajer, Guy, *The Forgotten Soldier* (Cassell, 1999)

Schmidt, Heinz Werner, *With Rommel in the Desert* (Constable, 1997)

Shirer, William, *The Rise and Fall of the Third Reich* (NY, Simon and Schuster, 1960)

Smith, Michael, *Station X* (Channel 4 Books, 2000)

Snyder, Louis L, *Encyclopedia of the Third Reich* (Wordsworth, 1998)

Speer, Albert, *Inside The Third Reich* (Weidenfeld & Nicolson, 1971)

Toland, John, *The Battle of the Bulge* (Wordsworth, 1998)

Trevor – Roper, H.R., *Hitler's War Directives 1939 – 1945* (Pan, 1966)

Tsouras, Peter G., *Fighting in Hell* (NY, Ballantine, 1995)

Veranov, Michael (ed.), *The Mammoth Book of the Third Reich at War* (Robinson Publishing, 1997)

Weinberg, Gerhard L., *Germany, Hitler and World War Two* (NY, Cambridge UP, 1995)

Wilmot, Chester, *The Struggle for Europe* (Wordsworth, 1998)

Winchester, Jim, *The World War II Tank Guide* (Silverdale Books, 2000)

Young, Desmond, *Rommel – The Desert Fox* (NY, Harper and Brothers, 1950)

Glossary

88: The famous Krupps 88 mm FLAK (Flieger Abwehr Kanone) gun which served throughout the war as both an anti-tank and anti-aircraft weapon. A variant was also mounted in tanks such as the Tiger.

Abteilung (Abt.) (plural: Abteilungen): Battalion or detachment. A battalion consisted of a number of companies and was the smallest self-contained, self-suffcient combat formation. Battalions engaged directly in combat. In theory each battalion contained 500 to 1,000 men. A **Panzer-Abteilung (Pz.Abt.)** was a tank battalion while a **schwere Panzer-Abteilung (s.Pz.Abt.)** was a heavy tank battalion containing Tigers.

Armee (plural: Armeen): Army. A formation containing one or more Korps.

Armee-Abteilung (plural: Armee-Abteilungen): Army detachment. An ad hoc formation which was smaller than an army. Often formed with scratch units in times of emergency in order to stem an enemy breakthrough.

Armeekorps: Army corps. A formation containing at least two divisions.

Aufklärung: Reconnaissance.

Ausführung (Ausf): Variant or model of a vehicle.

Axis: The military alliance between Germany, Italy and Japan.

Bagration: Code name for the Russian offensive against Army Group Centre in June 1944. Named after the famous Russian general of the Napoleonic Wars.

Balkenkreuz: The black-lined white cross on Wehrmacht vehicles.

Barbarossa: Red Beard. Code name for the invasion of Russia. Named after Holy Roman Emperor Frederick I (1123–1190).

Batterie (plural: Batterien): Battery. The artillery and anti-aircraft equivalent of a company.

Bergepanzer: Tank recovery vehicle.

Bletchley Park: The location of Britain's top secret Station X where German Enigma cipher messages were decoded.

Blitzkrieg: Lightning War. The revolutionary new method of warfare used by the Germans in the early war years, Blitzkrieg involved a swift mobile offensive by combined air and land forces and relied particularly on fighter aircraft, dive-bombers and tanks.

Brausewetter: 'Stormy Weather' – a nickname for Guderian.

Brigade (plural: Brigaden): Brigade. A formation containing two or more regiments.

Bundeswehr: The post-war Armed Forces of the Federal Republic of West Germany.

Calibre: The bore or internal diameter of a gun. The larger the calibre, the larger the projectile that can be fired from it.

Chef des Generalstabes: The Chief of General Staff. Guderian held this post during the war as did Halder and Zeitzler.

Commander-in-Chief (C-in-C): The highest ranking army officer with authority over a group of armies.

Commando Supremo: Italian High Command.

Deutsches Afrika Korps (DAK): The German forces that fought under Rommel in North Africa between 1941 and 1943.

Division (plural: Divisionen): Division. A formation containing two or more regiments. Generally contained between 10,000 and 20,000 men.

Durchbrüchwagen: Breakthrough tank such as the Tiger.

Enigma: The German cipher machine.

Ersatztruppen: Replacement troops.

Fahnrich: Officer cadet.

Fahrkarte bis zur Endstation: 'Ticket to the last station.' A phrase used by Guderian when ordering his troops to keep advancing as far as possible.

Fall Blau: Case Blue. Code name for the attack on the Caucasus in 1942.

Fall Gelb: Case Yellow. Code name for the attack on France.

Fall Rot: Case Red. Code name for the second phase of the Battle of France.

Fall Weiss: Case White. Code name for the invasion of Poland.

Feldpolizei or **Feldgendarmerie:** Field Police. The dreaded 'chain dogs'.

Festung Europa: Fortress Europe.

Flak (Flieger Abwehr Kanone): Anti-aircraft gun.

Flakpanzer: Anti-aircraft tank.

Flammpanzer: Flame-thrower tank.

Führer: Supreme leader, i.e. Hitler.

Führerbefehl: Order issued by Hitler.

Führerhauptquartier: Führer's Headquarters.

Funk (Fu): Radio.

General der Panzertruppen: General of armoured troops.

Generalinspekteur der Panzertruppen: General-Inspector of Armoured Troops, a post Guderian held from March 1943 until March 1945.

Generalstab des Heeres: Army General Staff.

General Staff: The officers responsible for overall war strategy and the planning of campaigns. General Staff officers were the intellectual elite of the German Army and were educated at the Kriegsakademie (War Academy). They wore double red stripes on their trousers.

Gestapo: Nazi secret police.

Glacis-plate: A sloping armour-plate protecting an opening.

Grenadier: Rifleman.

Gross Deutschland (GD): 'Greater Germany.' An elite Heer motorised regiment and later Panzergrenadier division.

Heer: The German Army.

Heeresgruppe (plural: Heeresgruppen): Army Group. A formation containing two or more armies. The largest German formation of the war, a Heersgruppe contained hundreds of thousands of men and operated across a wide-ranging front, e.g. Heersgruppe Nord (Army Group North) which was tasked with taking Leningrad during the invasion of Russia.

Herbstnebel: Autumn Fog. The final code name for the second Ardennes Offensive or Battle of the Bulge.

Hitlerjugend: Hitler Youth.

Jagd: Hunting. A Jagdpanzer was a 'tank hunter' or anti-tank vehicle.

Jäger: Hunter. Used in two contexts: (1) To denote an anti-tank weapon or unit, e.g. a **Panzerjäger (Pz.Jag.)** was a 'tank hunter' or tank destroyer. (2) To signify a certain type of elite light infantry, e.g. **Gebirgsjäger** (Mountain troops) or **Fallschirmjäger** (Parachute troops).

Kameraden: Comrades.

Kampfgruppe (plural: Kampfgruppen): Battle group. An ad hoc task force formed to carry out a specific operational mission or task. Usually battalion-sized, Kampfgruppen were named after their commander, e.g. Kampfgruppe Peiper.

Katyusha: Russian truck-mounted rocket artillery. Nicknamed 'Stalin Organ' by German troops. Similar to the German Nebelwerfer.

Kessel: Encirclement. 'Kessel' translates as 'Kettle' or 'Cauldron.' The military meaning comes from a German hunting term in which the game is first encircled by a large force of hunters and then driven into the centre of the circle for the kill.

Kesselschlacht (plural: Kesselschlachten): Encirclement battle. (Kessel = Kettle or Cauldron, Schlacht = battle).

Klein: Small.

Klotzen, nicht Kleckern: Loosely translates as 'Boot 'em, don't spatter 'em.' Slang phrase used by Guderian to illustrate his belief that in attack the panzers should be concentrated, not dispersed.

Kompanie (plural: Kompanien): Company. A formation containing a number of platoons.

Korps (plural: Korps): Corps. A formation containing one or more divisions.

Korps-Abteilung (plural: Korps-Abteilungen): Corps Detachment. A formation equivalent to a division and usually containing two or three burnt-out divisions of regimental strength.

Kriegsmarine: The German Navy.

Kubelwagen: 'Bucket car'. The German Army's equivalent of the American Jeep. Also known as a 'Steiner'. An amphibious version called the Schwimwagen was also produced.

L/- (kaliber/lange): Calibre/Length. The Germans expressed the length of a gun as a multiple of its calibre, e.g. in the case of the Pz III's 50 mm L/60 gun, the gun's calibre was 50 mm and the barrel length was sixty times the calibre, i.e. 3 metres.

Leaguer: A military encampment in enemy territory which is protected by armoured vehicles.

Landser: Infantry.

Leichte: Light.

Luftflotte: Air fleet.

Luftwaffe: The German Air Force.

Mittlerer: Medium.

Munitions-Panzerwagen: Tank converted into ammunition carrier.

Muzzle velocity: The speed at which a projectile leaves the barrel of a gun. The higher the muzzle velocity, the greater the range, accuracy and penetrating power of the gun.

Nebelwerfer: Multi-barrelled rocket artillery.

OB (Oberbefehlshaber): The highest field HQ which controlled all the troops in a large geographical area. Usually controlled two or more army groups. Term could also apply to the commander-in-chief of such a HQ, e.g. Rundstedt was known as OB West.

OKH (OberKommando des Heeres): Army High Command.

OKW (OberKommando der Wehrmacht): Armed Forces High Command, including Heer, Luftwaffe and Kriegsmarine.

Ostfront: The Eastern or Russian Front.

Ostketten: Extra wide tank tracks for use in Russia. Also known as Winterketten.

Pak (PanzerAbwehrKanone): Anti-tank gun.

Pakfront: A system by which several anti-tank guns were placed under a single commander who directed their fire.

Panje: The hardy small horse of the Russian peasant which the Wehrmacht adopted as a beast of burden during Barbarossa.

Panzer Abteilung z.b.V. (zur besonderen Verwendung): Panzer battalion for special use.

Panzerarmee (plural: Panzerarmeen): Panzer army. A formation containing at least two Panzerkorps.

Panzerbefehlswagen (Pz.Bef.Wg): Command tank.

Panzerfaust: 'Tank fist'. A single-shot, anti-tank grenade projector.

Panzergrenadiers: Mechanised or motorised infantry.

Panzergruppe (plural: Panzergruppen): Panzer Group. A formation made up of two or more panzer armies.

Panzerkampfwagen (PzKpfw): Battle tank.

Panzerkeil: The wedge formation in which tanks attacked.

Panzerkorps: Panzer corps. A formation containing at least two panzer divisions.

Panzer-Lehr: Panzer demonstration division.

Panzerschreck: 'Tank Terror'. Had two meanings: (1) The fear and panic experienced by inadequately equipped infantry when faced with tank attacks. The 'Panzerschreck' phenomenon decreased in the later war years as infantry became equipped with more effective anti-tank weapons. (2) The German variant of the American Bazooka anti-tank weapon. The Panzerschreck fired an 88 mm hollow charge.

Panzerspähwagen: Armoured reconnaissance vehicles.

Panzertruppen: Germany's armoured troops.

Panzerverbande: An ad hoc formation containing various armoured and ancillary units.

Panzerwaffe: Germany's armoured force.

Pionier: Combat engineer.

Raspituta: The spring thaw in Russia which turned everything to mud and enforced a halt on armoured operations.

Regiment (plural: Regimenter): Regiment. A formation containing a number of battalions.

Reich: Empire, realm, kingdom.

Reichsfuhrer SS: SS leader Heinrich Himmler.

Reichsmarshall: Honorary title created for the Luftwaffe leader, Hermann Goring.

Reichswehr: The German Armed Forces between 1920 and 1935.

Rollbahn (plural: Rollbahnen): The route of advance and supply designated for a specific panzer division.

Schild und Schwert: 'Shield and Sword'. A tactic used to destroy enemy armour through the close co-operation of panzers and Pak guns.

Schnelle Heinz: 'Hurrying Heinz'. Another of Guderian's nicknames.

Schnelltruppen: Fast or mobile troops, usually motorised.

Schurzen: Additional sheets of armour hung from a tank's sides and rear and which were designed to prematurely detonate hollow-charge projectiles.

Schützenpanzerwagen: Armoured half-tracks for carrying infantry.

Schutzenregiment: Rifle regiment.

Schwer: Heavy.

Schwerpunkt: Point of maximum effort. The point at which the panzer spearhead struck at the enemy lines in order to secure a breakthrough, usually the location at which the enemy was weakest.

Sichelschnitt: 'Sickle Cut'. Manstein's plan for the attack on France.

Soldaten: Soldiers.

Sonderkraftfahrzeug (SdKfz): Special motor vehicle. Every Wehrmacht vehicle had an SdKfz number.

SS (Schutzstaffel): Defence Squadron. The Nazi Party's para-military elite which was led by Himmler.

Stab (plural: Stäbe): Staff.

Standarte (plural: Standarten): Waffen SS regiment.

Stavka: Russian High Command.

Strategy: The overall planning and direction of a war and the various campaigns and theatres of that war.

Stuka (Sturzkampfflugzeug): Junkers JU-87 dive-bomber.

Sturmartillerie: Assault artillery – the Stug assault guns.

Sturmgeschütz (StuG): Assault gun. The Stugs were tracked, self-propelled artillery used in an anti-tank or fire support role.

Sturmhaubitze (StuH): Assault howitzer.

Tactics: Tactics are primarily concerned with individual battles and the handling of forces on those battlefields.

Totenkopf: Death's Head. The skull and crossbones emblem used by the Panzerwaffe and the Waffen SS.

Trajectory: The curve described by a projectile during its flight. Tank guns had a flat trajectory while howitzers gave plunging fire.

Unternehmen: Undertaking or operation.

VK (Versuchskonstruktion): Tank prototype.

Volksgrenadier: People's Infantry. Part of the **Volkssturm** (People's Army), the poor quality home defence militia of old men and boys raised by Germany near the end of the war.

Wacht am Rhein: Watch on the Rhine. Hitler's original code name for the second Ardennes Offensive or Battle of the Bulge.

Waffen: Weapons or armed.

Waffenamt: Army ordnance department.

Waffen SS: Armed SS. The military arm of the SS.

Waffentrager: Weapons carrier.

Wehrmacht: The German Armed Forces including Heer, Luftwaffe and Kriegsmarine. The Waffen SS was included under this term only in a tactical sense.

Wunderwaffen: Wonder Weapons. Towards the end of the war Hitler put great faith in the arrival of so-called 'Wonder Weapons' like the V2 rocket and the ME-262 jet.

Zitadelle: Citadel. Code name for the Kursk offensive.

Zug (plural: **Züge**): Platoon. A sub-division of a company.

Index